M
l
,

GLASGOW

MICHAEL FRY is an author and journalist. He has written for most British newspapers, and been a weekly columnist for *The Scotsman*, *The Herald*, *The National* and *The Sunday Times*. He is the author of a dozen books of Scottish history, including *Wild Scots*, *Edinburgh* and *The Union*.

MICHAEL FRY

GLASGOW

A History of the City

HEAD *of* ZEUS

First published in the UK in 2017 by Head of Zeus Ltd

9 7 5 3 1 2 4 6 8

A catalogue record for this book is available from
the British Library.

ISBN (HB) 9781784975821
ISBN (E) 9781784975814

Typeset by Adrian McLaughlin
Endpaper: 'Birds Eye View of Glasgow (1864) by Thomas Sulman.
Image Courtesy of University of Glasgow Library.

Printed and bound in Great Britain by
CPI Group (UK) Ltd, Croydon CR0 4YY

Head of Zeus Ltd
First Floor East
5–8 Hardwick Street
London ECIR 4RG
WWW.HEADOFZEUS.COM

CONTENTS

Preface

THERE ARE 159 histories of Glasgow listed in the catalogue of the National Library of Scotland, nearly all of them by Glaswegians. It is good that men (Glasgow being Glasgow, they are indeed nearly all men) should find just cause to praise their own city. But quite a lot of them tend towards adulation. It is, after all, as well to remember that, while most Glaswegians love their hometown, often they prefer to do so from afar, or at least from beyond its territorial limits. While a population of more than a million once lived within those confines, that figure has shrunk by a third today, and the downward trend is unlikely to be reversed even in a world of increasing urbanization. This is partly the result of deliberate decisions to shift the people of the overcrowded centre out to suburbs and New Towns. Once there, they have shown little desire to be brought back into the municipality and to share its burdens (which might be achieved by extending its boundaries, for example), though they will of course travel in to enjoy themselves. Other Glaswegians have as economic migrants moved away altogether, to different parts of Scotland or Britain, or to the rest of the world. Yet Glasgow is hard to leave behind completely, and the traveller may run into its sons and daughters, still unmistakable, anywhere from San Francisco to Sydney.

This book explores such paradoxes. It is a sort of match for my *Edinburgh: A History of the City* (2009) – different in structure, in that in *Glasgow* I take a thematic rather than chronological approach, but resting on the same view: that for Scotland the political and the cultural history are at least as important as the economic and social history. This is not the approach of the dominant school of Scottish historians, but they seem to me to give in consequence a deeply distorted view of the nation. Its economy and society have been most assimilated to the norms of the United Kingdom, while its politics and culture have remained most apart. Generally, then, Scottish history as it is still being written today remains unionist history. Here the reader will find an alternative.

For Glasgow in particular, I also take a line at variance with most of those other 159 histories. In general character they are couthy (for this genre, see chapter 10). I do not for a moment deny Glaswegians are fine folk, the salt of the earth, full of good humour and friendly fellow-feeling. But in my opinion quite enough has already been written about these admirable attributes, and in what follows I turn to other aspects of the people and their city. It is not in the end an especially cheery book. But for a place that, despite its great qualities, still has a terrible lot wrong with it, this seems to me the right approach.

It is true I set out with what Glaswegians will regard as less than perfect credentials. I have lived my adult life in Edinburgh; yet, as a freelance journalist for more than thirty years, I have found much of my work in the metropolis of the west, where I have been a frequent, at times a daily, commuter. In Glaswegian mode I occasionally lingered too long in the pub after my duties were done and arrived at Queen Street Station only to see the last train home vanishing into the tunnel. I have had good reason to be grateful for the city's hospitality, ending up with a bed for the night anywhere from an opulent mansion in the West End to the high flats at Pollokshaws (since 2009 no longer with us). Just once did I need to pay for my keep and then, since Glasgow demands style, I presented myself to the front desk of the Grand Central Hotel. Reception showed a stony face (no doubt this was not its first encounter with reprobates like me) but accepted my credit card in advance payment and sent me high up to a room which, to my delight when I opened the curtains in the morning, overlooked the Central Station's main concourse. So I could watch the world go by as I recovered from my hangover sufficiently to order lunch in the Malmaison restaurant, under the vigilant tutelage of my old friend Eligio, the maître d'hôtel.

Glasgow is Scotland's main centre for the media, but it has also smiled on my other vocation: as a historian. Thanks to the good offices of Professor T.M. Devine – then my friend, now my foe – I was appointed in 1996 to a fellowship in the centre for research in Scottish history at the University of Strathclyde. There I made the acquaintance of a rising generation of historians, a number of whom have done well and remained valued colleagues. As an oldie wiser than they were in the ways of the world, I introduced them to a few drinking dens of a character more interesting than the ones indigent graduate students were used to. In return, they taught me some things that only Glaswegians could know. There was an evening when two of us went for a pint in a pub behind the City Chambers, which turned out to be full of councillors, recognizable by their flashy pomposity. 'And they are all Protestants. This is the Protestant minority in the Labour administration of Glasgow,' observed my companion. How could he possibly tell? The clue lay in the collection boxes ranged along the bar, devoted to various blue-nosed causes: Catholics would never drink here. So little by little, over a long apprenticeship, a stranger might learn the Glaswegian codes.

Turning lastly to roads not taken, it was Glasgow that saw my final appearance as an aspirant politician – that is to say, as

Conservative candidate at Maryhill for the first election to the Scottish Parliament in 1999. I thought it prudent to put myself on the city's electoral register and did so at the address of my campaign manager, where I would often need to stay overnight. This turned out to be in the neighbouring seat of Hillhead, so I never got to vote for myself after all. But enough others did to save me my deposit – which I thought creditable enough at a time when Scots Tories were pariahs. Being at least free of any notion I might win, I again made sure to enjoy myself. I persuaded journalist colleagues to come and cover my campaign, which they did readily because the reportage would be preceded by a long lunch somewhere fashionable on the Great Western Road. The gravamen of the expert analysis of the political situation I imparted was that, while Labour would hold the seat easily, there were already signs of slippage in its supremacy. The SNP worked the big housing schemes hard: one hive of activity seemed to be Milton, at the north-eastern edge of the constituency, right on the railway line from Edinburgh, whence I could observe during my commute the playing fields, muddy and unkempt, where Kenny Dalglish and others had begun their rise to glory. In such places eager nationalists sought, and of course found, grievances that the sharp-suited apparatchiks of a complacent ruling party too casually ignored.

I even dealt with one such case myself, of a man whom perhaps the other candidates might have found too hard to handle. A wee bauchle, as Glaswegians say, he was diminutive, pugnacious and chain-smoking. His flat formed part of a crumbling block at Ruchill evidently used by the council as a dump for junkies. I found the stair littered with used needles. On the way up a couple of the tenants gazed glassy-eyed at me in my Tory pinstripes, too zonked to react in any other way. My prospective constituent had been lodged here not because he was an addict himself but because he was a perpetual pain to the city council, as a mountainous pile of correspondence attested. He was a family man with a wife and daughter, but they had moved away on account of the conditions. Now he held out grimly in the flat by himself, for if he left of his own accord he would lose his spot on the waiting list for somewhere better. Here was how the recalcitrant got treated in the lower depths of Glasgow's municipal housing system. I called on my colleague Bill Aitken, the Conservative candidate for Anniesland and soon to be an MSP, but more to the point, a councillor of long standing. He decently obliged us. Within the City Chambers he no doubt had some chips to cash, and in short order he got the wee bauchle transferred to a nice council house.

Into this book, then, there has gone quite a long experience of Glasgow, though from an outsider looking in rather than from an insider looking out. In that sense, there are many Glaswegians, or indeed friends generally over the west of Scotland, who during those thirty years have with their words and thoughts contributed to the present work, knowingly or not. I should mention first the man whose generosity in financing my research has made this whole project possible, Jim Walker of Kilmacolm and Hong Kong, a fine example of what people from the region can achieve when they go into exile. Then, in chronological order, I wish to thank those who have both put me up and put up with me in Glasgow: Kevin Done, who also left the city and rose to the dizzy heights of aviation correspondent on the *Financial Times*; Alf Young, deputy editor of *The Herald*; Jack McLean, its Urban Voltaire; Helen, Baroness Liddell of Coatdyke; John Linklater, once of Dennistoun and now teaching journalism at Robert Gordon College, Aberdeen; the Revd Stewart Lamont, minister of Kinning Park at his manse in the pyramid flats; Mungo Campbell, deputy director of the Hunterian Museum; Roger Pollen, my election manager in Maryhill; and a further journalist colleague, Katie Grant.

I have kept in touch to a greater or lesser extent with graduate students I met at the University of Strathclyde during my research fellowship: Richard Finlay, David Forsyth, Catriona MacDonald, Andrew MacKillop and John Young, who have all gone on to distinguish themselves in various ways in the field of Scottish history. At the University of Glasgow, I have enjoyed a long acquaintance with the Scottish historians Professor Ted Cowan and Professor Colin Kidd, the latter now at St Andrews, as well as with the historian of philosophy Professor Alexander Broadie, especially in the matter of his discovery of James Dundas, who in the late seventeenth century bridged a gap in the Scottish intellect between the last glimmers of medieval scholasticism and the dawn of the Enlightenment. Professor Ian Donnachie of the Open University was my sure-footed guide through the thickets of Scottish industrial history. Professor David Simpson discussed with me the tradition of political economy at the University of Glasgow. My old partner in crime in Brussels, John Cooney, was the correspondent there of the *Irish Times* while I was the correspondent of *The Scotsman*; through this bairn of Blantyre and graduate of Glasgow I came into contact with the forces for Catholic renewal that the university had nurtured in his time, centred on a profound scholar, John Durkan, and on others such as James McMillan, later a professor at the University of Edinburgh. It was a new world to me, a Protestant, and I regret that here I have not been able to make more use of what I learned then. I am grateful to Professor Tom Gallagher, retired from the University of Bradford, for a long conversation about sectarianism. Dr Sin Chai told me about the Glasgow Coma Scale. Outside academe I have taken pleasure in my encounters with Bill Mann, as when he arranged for me to speak at Glasgow's Historical Association, and when he kindly invited my composer nephew Andrew Reynolds to play on his collection of Steinways. In the same context I have been delighted to get to know the composer James MacMillan, who was generous enough to dedicate to me one of his works, 'Nemo te condemnavit', on account of my earlier studies of Highland history. Among poets, I wish to thank

Aonghas MacNeacail, for telling me about the writers' workshops of Philip Hobsbaum – whom I had canvassed during my candidacy for Maryhill, to no effect. One of the nicest compliments ever paid to me came from Bill McIlvanney, when he commended me for the lucidity of my writing.

In Scotland, history often carries a political charge. I never knew many Glaswegian Tories worth the recollection. But through Ken Munro of the European Commission, I was able to meet a generation of his contemporaries and gain insights into the circle at Glasgow University Union of John Smith and Donald Dewar from the Labour party, and of Professor Neil MacCormick who later represented the SNP in the European Parliament; none of these lived a long time but they all did great things. I had dealings with another senior politician from Glasgow, Bruce Millan, who became a European commissioner. I was actually asked for my advice by Jim Murphy when, as secretary of state for Scotland, he wanted to make a speech on wider powers for our Parliament. But I enjoy a better acquaintance with his colleague in the representation of Eastwood, Ken Macintosh, now the presiding officer at Holyrood. Like many who got to know Jimmy Reid of Upper Clyde Shipbuilders, I cherished him. Eben Wilson, the Bridgeton Piper, has been a mine of information on Glasgow's capitalists. One of them, Ivor Tiefenbrun, invited me for lunch and conversation at the premises of Linn Products.

Like everybody who needs to do research on Glasgow, I have incurred a debt beyond measure to the Mitchell Library. I want to record my thanks to the library of the university too. The resources of the Glasgow Women's Library comprehend much more than I have been able to use here. Finally, for a daughter of Bridgeton, once my agent, now my publisher, Maggie McKernan, a big hug.

MICHAEL FRY,
February 2017

INTRODUCTION
'Pretty damn active'

THE NIGHT of the Scottish referendum on September 18, 2014, saw vivid scenes in George Square, Glasgow. For some while it had been the mecca of all those in the west of Scotland, and no doubt of others from beyond, who wished and expected that by the morning their nation would have voted to become independent. In the square they had gathered in growing numbers to sing of and celebrate their aspiration. The excitement was not confined to the heart of the city. A little way off at the Stereo Club, there was for the big night a 'referendum special', courtesy of Fem Bitch Nation. The flyer for it said: 'Stereo has been pretty damn active on the political scene this year, hosting a whole range of events and discussions to encourage Glasgow's party-heavy to ensure their voice is heard.' The Glasgow School of Art, a global centre of cultural modernism, ran a club for students and others which 'has taken the referendum in its stride and will be encouraging your vote at all costs. Éclair Fifi and her troupe of supporting acts will take over the Art School on Friday, September 19.'

Éclair Fifi and her troupe also went to show how, as the campaign for the referendum had taken its twists and turns, one aspect stood out – the huge degree of public interest and participation. While generally politics had for decades been losing all verve in Britain, in Scotland the process now seemed to have been halted and reversed. In place of the accustomed central control of electoral activity through manipulation of the media and the trivialization of agendas, there had come a revival of politics in an old-fashioned sense. Whether in the Highlands or the Lowlands, politicians on the stump faced packed public meetings of ordinary folk eagerly quizzing them. Confronted with the great question of the future of their country, there were 3.6 million voters who welcomed the chance to decide.

In the final stages of the campaign, its outcome had turned much more uncertain. The No side (No to independence) led from the start, but its lead had steadily narrowed. The week before the vote, one opinion poll actually put the Yes side ahead, prompting panic in London. The prime minister, David Cameron, and the other leaders of the political parties abandoned the scheduled parliamentary business and flew north to lend what weight they could to the defence of the Union between Scotland and England. In order to entice back a crucial margin of those inclined to vote Yes, the politicians also made a Vow (the capital letter was theirs) setting out a commitment, even if they should win, to a continuing programme of constitutional reform; previously the assumption had been that, in this case, they would just forget about Scotland again. While the results of a single sensational poll were not repeated, still the referendum seemed open, or at least to have become more open, right up to the end of the campaign. At any rate there arose among the Scots gathered during the final days in George Square an excited optimism that their hopes of national independence were about to be fulfilled.

The euphoria sustained itself for three and a half hours after the polling stations closed at 10 p.m. on the night of September 18. During electoral counts one of the first things that can be ascertained is the turnout, and this time it seemed extraordinarily high at 85 per cent, the highest ever recorded in Scotland. Had it been a matter of the nationalists mobilizing a maximum of support? The reverse proved to be true: it was the unionists who had bestirred themselves to defend a cause that in 300 years had never needed such defence before. So much was at once clear when the first result came through, from the Wee County of Clackmannan. While it had long opted for Labour in British general elections, it contained a strong nationalist minority. It was the sort of constituency that needed to vote Yes now if the referendum was to be won. Yet it voted No by 54 to 46 per cent. This set a pattern for the rest of the night, and proved to be close to the eventual national outcome.

In the end just four constituencies voted Yes: West Dunbartonshire, North Lanarkshire, Dundee and Glasgow. They had certain features in common: they were not picturesque, but economically laggard, homes to an often alienated working class, looking back on a certain tradition (nowadays much weakened) of political militancy. Altogether they remained in general character about as far from Cameron's Notting Hill and Witney as could be imagined in an ostensibly United Kingdom. Of the four, Glasgow had the strongest Yes vote, of 260,079 against 226,140 – this, however, on the lowest turnout in Scotland of only 75 per cent. Four constituencies were never going to be enough: the final national count came to 2,001,926 for No against 1,617,989 for Yes.

It was Fife's declaration at 6.08 a.m. that took the No vote to over 50 per cent of the electorate. The people in George Square had triumphed in their own city yet seen their nation spurn independence. The music died and they stood about numbly, some in tears, before dispersing into the dawn. Still, too much emotion had been worked up in the previous days for that to be the end of the matter. The crowd reassembled the next evening, tired and subdued yet anxious that all their commitment should not now count for nothing. They diverted themselves by listening to speakers who rehearsed other lost causes: relief of poverty, nuclear disarmament, the housing crisis.

This time, they also met a counter-demonstration of unionists who had come to stage a party of their own in George Square, singing 'Rule Britannia', waving Union Jacks and jeering at the losers. Glasgow is a city where violence always lurks not far beneath the surface, and the situation could have turned unpleasant. But the police, some on horses, were ready for trouble. They separated the rival groups and contained them in the square, making only a dozen arrests – by Glaswegian standards a meagre tally.

The city's result was most notable for a different reason. Ever since the Union of 1707, Glaswegians had been one of its pillars. In two subsequent Jacobite revolts, nobody even suggested they might support the restoration of Scottish independence. Later the Union formed the matrix for that greatest of all Scottish enterprises, participation in the British empire, and nobody exceeded Glaswegians in zeal for it. From domination of the trade in tobacco with Virginia in the eighteenth century to supremacy in shipbuilding in the nineteenth, Glasgow profited hugely from imperial business. It made little difference even when the focus of ambition shifted in the twentieth century back to the United Kingdom as the source of support for a Scottish industrial heartland now in inexorable decline. Many solutions were suggested, but Glasgow long spurned the argument that the independence of Scotland alone could restore its place in the world. Yet on September 18, 2014, as the nation affirmed a British commitment, Glasgow rejected it. We are surely owed an explanation.

I

Trade: 'Plenty of goods'

ON MAY 29, 1576, the burgh court of Glasgow tried John Kar for hitting Katherine Hart round the mouth with a salmon. He was found guilty and fined, but no further particulars are given in the record.[1] Even in its brevity, however, it offers one or two piquant insights into the contemporary life of the place. It reveals the deep origins of Glaswegian male chauvinism, which persists to the present: in not many cities in the world do men assault women with big fish. True, the salmon would never have come to hand if the species had not been abundant in the River Clyde and its tributaries, so much so as to figure in Glasgow's coat of arms. It was a gift of nature in the days before the human race had taken to abusing it – and a valuable supplement to the Scots' meagre diet. Later, during the industrial revolution, the environmental damage along these waterways caused all the fish to vanish, except in the River Leven flowing out of Loch Lomond; today, now that things have been cleaned up, salmon swim again as far as the Falls of Clyde at Lanark. In the earlier era, when Scotland had had nothing except its natural produce to export, salted salmon was a valuable trading commodity. Glasgow did make simple manufactured goods, textiles or basic equipment for a household, but all were destined for domestic consumption in the burgh or the immediate surroundings. Nothing else got fashioned here of enough quality to attract custom from afar. Only for what might be fished, hunted or harvested in Scotland was there some demand elsewhere, so offering means to pay for the import of many necessities, together with a few luxuries.

In conforming to this basic pattern, Glasgow had little to distinguish it from other Scots burghs. We do not usually think of it today as a trading port, yet in its origins it was just that. King David I had trade foremost in mind when he granted the royal burghs their first charters in the early twelfth century. Glasgow's charter came in a second wave of burghal foundations – and not from the king, by this time William the Lion, but from its own Bishop Jocelin. In successful advocacy for William to the papal curia, Jocelin had taken the lead in arguing that the church in Scotland was not subordinate to the church in England. His reward arrived in 1175 when the king gave him a feudal grant of Glasgow and the right to hold a weekly market there.[2]

Bishop Jocelin was expected to be both a religious and a secular leader.[3] He rebuilt the church of St Kentigern or St Mungo, who had founded the see in the seventh century. But a further reconstruction in the thirteenth century left us only a column and a capital of Jocelin's edifice. On the other hand, it did give us the perfect Gothic cathedral we see today. It stood at the head of a brae rising above the Clyde, but the key to the burgh's success lay down by the banks of the river, at the lowest point, where (in about 1350) it could be bridged. If he bequeathed to later ages a legend about the 'dear green place' as an ideal setting for sanctity, much more to the point it was the best spot for a market, of equal utility for the people to its north and to its south, as for all that found in the Clyde a highway to the sea and so to the Highlands or Ireland. Markets make money, and after doing their business by the river these people could climb up to the church with an offering for the glory of God. In this way they permanently defined the curve of Glasgow's High Street. And from the Cross at the bottom, we can reasonably assume, four thoroughfares were early on formed to lead off it, lined by the burgesses' houses and tofts (plots of ground running behind). That gave the old heart of the city the shape it preserves to this day.

Glasgow continued to benefit from its strategic position. King David I had ordained a code of laws for the new urban component he had introduced into the nation, his *Leges Quatuor Burgorum*, Laws of the Four Burghs (Berwick, Edinburgh, Roxburgh and Stirling – they being the biggest in his time). These laws came to govern medieval civic life in Scotland through a Court of the Four Burghs where magistrates from each of them judged the sort of specific disputes that arose in urban communities.[4] It was the forerunner of the Convention of Royal Burghs, definitively constituted or reconstituted in 1581 and which continued in the same basic shape till 1975.[5] Its earliest records date from 1552, when it resolved to 'convene ȝairlie anis in the ȝeir to consult vpoun sic effaris and commone weil of borrowis, and for reformatioun of hurttis done thairto, as wes neidful to haif bene done'.[6] Off to this brisk start, it passed a range of legislation providing for the burghs' weights and measures to be standardized, for their customs on imports to be charged at common rates and for elections to all their councils to be held at Michaelmas. Pursuing that sort of detailed urban agenda, it saved the central authorities of the Scottish state a good deal of trouble.

By the fifteenth century there were already thirty royal burghs, spreading from their original locus in the southeast right across the Lowlands. To put it another way, business was shifting away from the areas near the border, which were constantly exposed to attack from England. As a result Lanark and Linlithgow came to replace Berwick, annexed by the English, and Roxburgh, destroyed by the English, on the Court of the Four Burghs. Yet Lanark was in fact a bad choice to represent the western side of the country. Though guarded by a big castle, it never developed into anything more than an agricultural marketplace. Glasgow had a castle too, again courtesy of its bishops, but its setting lower down a barely navigable river always made it more important for trade than Lanark. It would have been better to give the name of Glasgowshire to the county in which both burghs lay: history decreed otherwise.[7]

Privilege to the medieval mind was a matter not so much of social inequality, as it is now, more of the right granted to a particular group to govern itself under the delegated authority of the crown. Privilege amounted to a great gain for those concerned, whether or not at the expense of other groups. In practice, among the burghs, it meant the dominance of the merchants, usually organized in a guild; this was to persist into the nineteenth century. Challenges to the merchants did arise in the more thriving communities such as Glasgow, but on the whole remained under control. They arose from the natural development of the place or its business and the consequent growing complexity of the urban economy. Back in the twelfth century a burgess might himself have kept animals on his toft, slaughtered and processed them there and exchanged the products on the High Street or further afield. By the fifteenth century merchants no longer had to do any dirty work (at least with their hands). There were professional craftsmen to do it for them, ranging from fleshers (butchers) to skinners for the beasts, from cordiners (leather-workers) to websters (weavers) for animal products, from masons to wrights for buildings and byres. As in other successful trading communities, there had been a division of labour.[8]

That matched the evolution of cities all over Europe. What followed was also common to medieval society: the combining of individual craftsmen into closed corporations. When the craftsmen had first tried to follow the privileged example of the merchants, the latter resisted – and had the power to do so because they manned the magistracy of the burgh. Yet regulation for a common purpose was what they practised themselves. Before long they saw how unwashed artificers, if allowed privilege of their own, might turn into pillars of society too. That could even strengthen the burgh's collective ability to defend and promote its interests. So the balancing act needed to neutralize the rise of these social rivals did modify a little the despotism of the elite. This is a story we will follow in a later chapter.[9]

There was less of a threat to the merchants' control of external relations. In the Scottish system, each royal burgh acquired monopolistic rights over the trade of a hinterland. Though locked in this commercial embrace, town and country were conceived of as having separate interests. No merchant conducting trade could legally live outside the royalty of his burgh, that is, outside the boundaries set by the king. Nobody from beyond the royalty had any right to sell wares within it, except under strict conditions imposed by the burgh itself; even so, the unceasing efforts of the council to suppress the illicit activity of unfree tradesmen, as the interlopers were termed, show that it must have gone on anyhow. Meanwhile, the burgesses who were the beneficiaries of this regime did not compete with one another. They were a corporate body acting as one in trying to maximize profit from their trade. Their guild actually punished members who competed on the sly, for example by forestalling, or buying up goods before they had been exposed to common view at Glasgow Cross.[10]

A counterpart to the burgesses' control over the sale of local produce lay in their monopoly of foreign trade. As the blessings of commerce began to spread across the Lowlands, so contacts overseas also developed, prompted not least by the fact that the English blocked the one land frontier. After repelling their attempt at a takeover back in 1297, William Wallace, leader of the national resistance, had sent the news straight to the authorities in Bremen and Hamburg with an invitation to resume their normal traffic to Scots ports. Despite almost constant war with England, Scotland prospered enough to win a staple (a guaranteed outlet for its goods) in the Netherlands, first at Bruges, later at Middelburg and then at Veere, from 1407. The royal burghs' monopoly of this trade was obviously of most benefit to those facing the continent on the eastern side of Scotland, so was not of the same use to Glasgow. At length, however, came the age of discoveries, when Europeans voyaged for the first time to Asia and America. An opening to the oceans now promised more than any position on the narrow seas. Trade from the west of Scotland started to grow faster than trade from the east. Glasgow's business had previously been at short range, exchanging local products and re-exports of foreign commodities for food, hides and cloth. Since few traders dared to venture on the perilous passage round Cape Wrath, cargoes for northerly destinations instead had to be trundled by land across central Scotland before getting shipped from Bo'ness on the Firth of Forth.[11] Till the eighteenth century, facilities there were scarcely adequate.

While the oceans presented a much more challenging prospect than the narrow seas for a small provincial port like Glasgow, it did rise to the challenge. Some traffic across the Atlantic seems to have started up in the 1620s, bringing home tobacco – the start of a long love affair.[12] These exchanges got a boost from the English military occupation of Scotland after 1651, because then it became legal for Scots merchants to trade to the American colonies under the protection of Oliver Cromwell's regime in London. Thomas Tucker, one of its customs officers appointed to the Clyde, wrote in 1656 of Glaswegians 'who had adventured as far as the Barbados', though their expedition was apparently unsuccessful. After 1661 this trade turned illegal again, but Westminster's new Navigation Act was hard to enforce at long distance. There were already Scots emigrants in the English colonies, and one wrote from Jamaica in 1669 advising that 'if our merchants at Glasgow would join together to get a permission to trade the bringing over of servants... they might make very good returns in money or goods.' Some tried it, though cheap Scottish products proved little more attractive in America than anywhere else. George Hutcheson sailed to Boston in 1675 and reported: 'There is such plenty of goods here from London and other places in England that we can make no market here at present.' He also worried about an Indian war going on in the back country, 'worse than the rebellion in Ireland, and crueller deaths'. Still, at length he got rid of most of the cargo he had brought with him, and sailed home with a shipload of tobacco in exchange.[13]

The transatlantic traffic promised so much that Glaswegians decided to put it on a regular footing. The town council bought land downriver in 1668 and began building the quays and warehouses of what was to become Port Glasgow. After only two decades of development it saw 'great repair of strangers, seamen and others, through the increase of shipping and trade there'.[14] Meanwhile, Sir John Shaw, laird of Greenock, had been granted a burgh of barony; this did not normally carry a right to foreign trade but he decided for himself that in his case it would. He planned and constructed a harbour, to which he managed to attract such ample custom that by 1692 Port Glasgow was running at a loss, while Greenock 'has a very great trade, both foreign and inland, and particularly prejudicial to the trade of Glasgow'. Not that Glaswegians always felt bound by their own restrictive regime, and some merchants themselves used the harbour at Greenock or at smaller places along the river. By the 1680s, Glasgow's American commerce exceeded that of Edinburgh and Aberdeen together. Its merchants started to wonder if they might not be better off re-entering the English system, even at the cost of Scottish independence.[15] Otherwise their trade to the colonies would remain strictly speaking illegal, and to that extent insecure.

Mercantilism is the name given to the rigid commercial regimes that prevailed in the early modern period in Europe. They sought to make a closed circuit of the traffic between each of the colonial powers and their settlements overseas. For the individual nations this so-called system of navigation was meant to assure exports of goods and the profits from them, either in the colonies or at dedicated trading posts from which foreign competition would be excluded. The underlying assumption was that monopoly in trade offered the best means of maximizing returns from it. This was thought to be a zero-sum game, internally and especially externally: there could be no gains from trade beyond the appropriation of colonial wares and exploitation of markets for them. Neighbours were there only to be beggared.[16]

Scotland figured among the small countries that suffered from the mercantilist system, as they were meant to do. Getting round it meant defiance of the laws of the bigger countries. Yet Scotland and England were supposed to be friendly nations; or at least, they had the same monarch. While the English authorities protested at what the Glaswegian merchants were doing, the Scottish government turned a blind eye. The transatlantic trade would no doubt have grown faster without this antagonism, but it could not now be strangled.[17]

In effect the merchants were starting to test the water of free markets. Half a dozen of them were arraigned in 1695 on a charge of breaking the regulations in collusion with unfree traders of their own burgh or with strangers from elsewhere. One, John Spreul, went into print to call for at least the national restrictions to be relaxed. Scotland could wave no magic wand over its trade, he said, but might at least turn its back on an English regime set up in a spirit hostile to Scotland and likely to cause wars with rival powers. He thought Scots should instead come out as free traders, restore their traffic with Europe and penetrate intercontinental commerce. His contention that each import could be matched by a Scottish export contained some notion of comparative advantage, with open exchange among countries specializing in different products.

For example, he thought the Scots' herrings might be exchanged for Swedish iron that they would then re-export to China: 'It hath been my study and endeavour to advance and promote trade to all parts only by our own product for purchasing me what goods I wanted, as in Norway, Russia and even into the Straits [of Malacca]'. Glasgow as a whole took its new prospects seriously. The town council appointed a professor of navigation in 1681, and in 1695 set up a school of navigation with an instructor 'qualified to be useful to this burgh in voyages to Africa and America'.[18]

As things turned out, the arguments were to be settled in a different way. In 1707 Scotland entered into the Treaty of Union with England and so joined its mercantilist regime. This was a deal between the ruling classes of the two countries, and the Scotsman in the street tended to notice only the penalties it brought, in particular the new and elaborate system of restrictions and taxes placed on his country's traded goods. The benefits, apart from not being unequivocal, were not immediate either. It would take several decades for them to become clear, and meanwhile some things actually got worse. Glasgow's merchants, with few domestic products to offer on global markets, were not yet rich enough to pay for more imports to be consumed in their own region. But something they soon found they could do, in far greater security than before, was act as dealers for colonial wares, buying them in and selling them on to final customers resident outside the British system. Because this system required everything grown in the colonies to be landed in the United Kingdom before being sent anywhere else, Scotland, and Glasgow in particular, could find a niche in it as a 'warehouse economy', to employ the useful term recently coined.[19] Regardless of the ultimate wisdom of the policy, which would become the subject of relentless attacks by Glasgow's own professor, Adam Smith, it could at least free the city's merchants from the provincial limitations of their business and allow them to start accumulating capital.

Tobacco was the cargo that made the big difference. Grown in Virginia to be smoked in Europe, it offered wide opportunities for middlemen and their warehouses – in the event, for Glaswegians above all. Their requirements and risks in legal trade were different from those in illegal trade.[20] They built a quay at the Broomielaw, and improved Port Glasgow. They had to meet the cost of acquiring ocean-going vessels, an expensive commitment if the volume of trade should fall short of its potential. But when the English journalist Daniel Defoe came on a visit in 1724, he wrote: 'As the Union opened the door to the Scots into our American colonies, the Glasgow merchants presently embraced the opportunity... for they now send near fifty sail of ships every year to Virginia, and other English colonies in America.'[21]

The only form of competition the mercantilist system allowed was among British ports, as to which might win the lion's share of the colonial goods landed. Compared to Bristol, London and others, Glasgow had disadvantages as well as advantages. Virginia was the original English colony in the New World, and its population remained overwhelmingly English in character. The Scots, arriving later, needed to fit in where they could, often as factors on the estates or traders on the rivers. It was easier for them to find a niche in the hinterland, as this opened up to the cultivation of tobacco, than in the established settlements of the Tidewater region.[22] Yet even from the backwoods it was no trouble for clannish Scots to circulate intelligence about trading conditions, especially since the recipients, the mercantile elite of Glasgow, numbered only a hundred or so. And these could all the more readily exploit their sources of information because their city lay nearer to America on the Great Circle than any other part of western Europe. Its ships might cross, through northerly seas seldom plagued by privateers, two or three weeks faster than any from the English Channel, adding up to a gain of a month or six weeks on a round trip – possibly enough to allow two trips in a good season rather than just one. The benefits further multiplied in lower oncosts for transport, freight and insurance, economies of scale and the chance to minimize or spread the risks of a traffic that remained to some extent speculative.[23] Though Glaswegians by law still had to pay duties on the imports, the actual price of tobacco fell as more and more ground in Virginia and other colonies was brought under cultivation. The steady increase in oceanic traffic cut the real cost of shipping, too. And then when the merchants re-exported to European destinations, they could draw back the duty they had paid. The final price to them of their commodities was therefore low, yet capable of yielding fat profits.[24]

Meanwhile Scots carried on as they had always done with an enjoyable illegal trade. It could start by fiddling the legal traffic. By dint of targeted bribes to the tide-waiters, the lowest form of life in the customs, the shippers would arrange for their cargoes to be underweighed on arrival. They would then be overweighed as the time approached for them to be sent out again to Europe, and application could be made for the drawback. Or else, the shippers might claim part of their cargoes had been ruined by penetration of seawater into the hold of the vessel during the long voyage across the Atlantic. They would still demand a drawback for re-export of the supposedly damaged cargo.[25]

In fact, illegal tobacco became hopelessly mixed up with legal tobacco, to an extent impossible to investigate or ascertain even by the most sophisticated statistical methods of Scotland's quantitative historians. One estimate has it that, for a couple of decades after the Union, half the tobacco was smuggled in, generally through the smaller ports in the west of Scotland; but nobody can really tell. It got smuggled on too. Tobacco carried coastwise from Scotland to England became liable to a second duty, yet only a fraction of it seems ever to have been collected. The British government, tired of the shambles after two decades of mismanagement in the Scottish board of customs, abolished it in 1723. Instead it set up in Edinburgh a sub-committee of the central board in London, for good measure firing all the Scottish officers and replacing them with Englishmen.[26] A period of lower prices and stricter surveillance then apparently eliminated several weaker trading firms in Glasgow.

But in the longer term the traffic revived,[27] so much so that it would transform the economy of the west of Scotland. The early stages of the legal trade are obscure because of a loss of records, but by chance one full account of a voyage from Glasgow in 1729 has survived and shows a rate of return of 33 per cent.[28] The first available port books, for 1743–4, reveal the commerce in full swing. Legal imports of tobacco then reached 8 million pounds in weight, compared with an average of 200,000 pounds in the 1680s. No doubt Glaswegians were acquiring their addiction to the deadly weed, never lost and today helping to make them the unhealthiest population in western Europe. Yet the tobacco imported into the Clyde was not intended primarily for their consumption. In fact 90 per cent of what did get recorded went on to the far bigger markets on the continent. A surge of demand from France allowed huge deals to be clinched for delivery in bulk to its royal monopoly in tobacco. On the back of them, Glasgow sent 25 ships to French ports in 1743–4, accounting for two-thirds of the re-exports, while another quarter went to Holland and the rest mainly to Germany and Italy. By 1771 legal imports of tobacco had shot up to 47 million pounds, now representing more than half of total Scottish imports and of total British traffic in tobacco.

The merchants had a secondary source of earnings in the cargoes they sent back to Virginia in exchange for tobacco. The mercantilist system forbade colonists to manufacture the simplest necessities for themselves. To supply their lack of almost everything, 33 ships from the Clyde carried over in 1742–3 a wide range of ordinary items: candles and canvas, clothes and cloth, glass and furniture, iron-mongery and rope, shoes and saddles, sickles and spades. This was a stimulus to production in Scotland, in which the mercantile elite could invest.[29] John Gibson, the early historian of Glasgow, still lamented that in his time, the 1770s, 'manufactures, the only certain means of diffusing wealth over a whole people, were almost unknown; and commerce which, without manufactures, tends to the enriching of only a few, was carried on to a very trifling extent'.[30] He was wrong, perhaps just because the products seemed too humble to mention. But they were the start of something much bigger, as Glasgow began to deploy a capital surplus now mounting on a scale never seen before.[31] While it is true the imports of tobacco and other commodities from the Americas far exceeded in value the domestic exports of manufactures, earnings from the re-exports covered the gap.

The men running this trade, the tobacco lords, became the richest not only in Glasgow but in the whole of Scotland, the first ever to have made fortunes from international commerce. A close-knit group, they often intermarried, and kept the business in their own hands by pooling resources in formal partnerships. Retained profits allowed steady growth, even across generations. Much of the necessary capital accumulation came in inheritance, and half the traders in tobacco were sons of traders in tobacco: such was the relationship of the two William Cunninghames who resided in their classical mansion (still there) on Queen Street,[32] or the two James Glassfords shown in the family's portrait at the People's Palace, or the two George Bogles, the younger of whom went to see the emperor of China in 1774. These people merited the epithet of lords when they bought landed estates round the city and set themselves up in the sort of social status that contemporary society most respected. Their quest for it might seem to have been the reverse of dynamic and to have confirmed the existing order of things in Scottish society at large. But infusion of new blood among old lairds did release land locked up in entail and other feudal archaisms. The incomers were too canny to overlook the potential earnings from investment in an estate, especially if it had natural resources that could go into the manufacture of outward cargoes. In countless individual ways they improved their region's productive capacity, though, to be sure, as just one element in a complex of forces.[33] With the warehouse economy Glaswegians had hit on an unusual kind of commercial behaviour that was yet well suited to their own circumstances – and a shortcut to riches of the kind Scots had dreamed of. 'We may from this era date the prosperity of the city of Glasgow,'[34] says Gibson, now accurately.

When the American War of Independence broke out in 1776, it should have been a catastrophe. The trade in tobacco, having just reached a peak, was totally disrupted. Imports collapsed from 46 million pounds in 1775 to 300,000 pounds in 1777. The effects bit deeply into all Glasgow's commercial and financial services, and some merchants went to the wall. But war did offer its own opportunities for speculative gain. New markets and investments were found. The Scots returned to America after the peace of 1783 and to an extent took up where they had left off, if under a different commercial regime: imports of tobacco rose again to about 10 million pounds by 1790. The readiness to welcome the Scots back suggests the Americans had found selling them tobacco beneficial, too. Still, unprotected now from foreign competition and dogged by outstanding debts, the trade never attained its old vigour. Here as in other spheres Scots and Americans, once members of the same empire, were going their separate ways. Some rancour remained, not only over the recent past. A political commentator, John Knox, observed: 'Thus vanished, after a short possession, all the exclusive commercial privileges relative to that country [America], for which the Scots had annihilated their Parliament and their African and Indian Company [at Darien], and subjected themselves to excises, taxes, duties and commercial restrictions unknown before the year 1707.'[35]

At least there were substitutes available in this regime. They offered means to recover the income Glasgow had lost from tobacco. Britain still possessed an American empire in the West Indies, islands that together generated higher revenue than the ungrateful thirteen colonies ever had. The planters on these islands found two main commodities to offer: sugar with its by-products, molasses and rum, and then cotton. Markets in the last tended to fluctuate, and the planters liked to tie its supply to their brisk business in sugar. That type of deal gave an incentive to their customers to find uses for the cotton they received by way of it, and here the Scots excelled.[36] We will take the two categories of cargo in turn.

Between 1775 and 1812, the imports of sugar into the Clyde increased eighty times over.[37] This would scarcely have been possible unless the trade had been of long standing. In fact one of the first things Glaswegian merchants did, once they got their oceanic traffic going in the seventeenth century, was indulge their compatriots' sweet tooth. In exchange for exports of their own humble pots and pans and cheap cloth, they sought imports from the West Indies of molasses, the extract of sugarcane. This allowed a refinery to be set up in 1667, the Wester Sugar House in Candleriggs. To match it, in 1669 a second group of merchants built in Gallowgate the Easter Sugar House, 'a great stone tenement, with convenient office houses for their work, within a great court, with a pleasant garden belonging thereto'. By 1700 Glasgow housed four such factories,[38] so the new industry must have been profitable.

Unlike tobacco, mostly re-exported with little linkage to the indigenous economy, sugar forged the direct connection between oceanic commerce and domestic manufacture that would start turning a picturesque old burgh into a hive of modern industry. In fact sugar had created its first fortunes.[39] Already coming into the Clyde as early as the 1640s, the traffic in sugar received an early boost from the Cromwellian opening of the English colonies to Scots. Once this trade had started it could not really be stopped, at least not by subsequent Navigation Acts passed at Westminster.

After Scotland regained its independence at the Restoration of
1660, Glasgow's richest merchant and later lord provost, Walter
Gibson, just raised the English cross of St George on his ships to
bring sugar and other exotic products straight home, where they
could also be forwarded to Europe. When one of his captains got
caught red-handed in 1687, Gibson blithely explained to the lords
of exchequer in London that he had adopted false colours and a
false name for the vessel in question, 'such a name being necessary,
for other wayes all Scots shipps that trade to the plantations are
confiscable'.[40] One commodity for return to Virginia came from
his own smokehouse at Gourock, where he pioneered production
of the kippers known after him as Glasgow magistrates. On the
Atlantic run they were intended as food for slaves, but with his
wide horizons Gibson also chartered Dutch ships to export them as
delicacies to France before bringing back wine, brandy or salt. Yet
he always needed to keep a political eye out, and within Scotland he
made sure to stay on the right side of the royalist authorities – for
example, by also transporting to America captured Covenanters
they wanted rid of for their refusal to accept established religion.
Yet, in these troubled times, even an opportunist of his impudence
could get things wrong: having chosen the wrong side before the
Revolution of 1688 he then lost his public positions, though not
his business.[41]

But West Indian traffic was already too busy to be dependent
on the fate of a single merchant. Ready with the right political
credentials to take over stood Hugh Montgomerie of Skelmorlie,
scion of a Covenanting family who in 1689 organized the defences
of Glasgow against the Jacobites and so stood high in favour with
the new revolutionary government of Scotland. He put it to good
use by becoming a partner in the sugar factories and steadily moving
into the associated commerce, from which he made a fortune of
his own. He grew so rich as to be elected the member for Glasgow
in the last Scottish Parliament of 1702. There he generally opposed

the Union and, when the actual terms of the treaty came before the house in its last session, voted against them from the first article to the ratification. Given that a large number of his merchant brethren took the opposite line, his stance seems on the face of it odd. The clue probably lies in his West Indian connection.[42]

Much of Montgomerie's business was with Nevis, one of the Leeward Islands and a place largely run by Scots. Off the beaten track, such idyllic spots proved useful not only for the sugar that could be grown on their soil. They might also serve as entrepôts for traffic between the English and Dutch systems of navigation, intended though these were to be exclusive. Scots, who preferred to remain on good terms with both nations, made convenient middlemen. The Dutch West India Company's sphere of operations covered West Africa, so it carried cargoes of gold and ivory, later of slaves, which readily found American and European markets. Scots could penetrate the network by exchanging on Nevis the desirable goods that each system of navigation itself lacked. By 1707 some Glaswegians were apparently doing nicely out of this business. Montgomerie and his fellows saw that the Union was, apart from anything else, a major adjustment to the commercial spheres of influence in Europe, shifting Scotland irrevocably into the English sphere. That would destroy their role as middlemen and open them up to competition from south of the border that they had never faced before.[43]

In fact things did not turn out as badly as Montgomerie feared, simply because his enterprising countrymen had already been voyaging to the New World without asking anybody's permission. Exports of sugar from the West Indies would exceed the combined trade of the whole of North America for some time ahead. Nevis itself had fertile soil that lent itself to an intensive system of agriculture, and the only real problem was to find the necessary labour. Early on the supply had come from Scottish prisoners of war transported there after Cromwell defeated and captured them at the Battle of Worcester in 1651. His republic was belligerent, and soon embroiled in conflict with Spain as well. His navy set about seizing Caribbean islands: they were valuable, but how could they be secured at such long distance?[44]

One idea was to repopulate them with colonists from the British Isles. The native Carib Indians were useless for labour on plantations, while the English had as yet barely started their black African slave trade. So the first slaves were white, many of them the Scottish captives. Others from home, in a decade of economic depression, started selling themselves into voluntary servitude. This was naturally not under the same conditions that non-whites would later be forced to suffer, but in the legal form of an indenture with a term typically of seven years. After that the indentured servants could become free colonists of the island. The rule created a continuous traffic, because replacements had to be found for those liberated. An English planter recommended 'that all prudent means be used to encourage the Scots to come hither, as being very good servants'.[45] In practice, it was found that few could cope for long with the backbreaking work in the tropical heat, and perhaps not many survived to serve out their seven years. By 1700 the island had instead imported 8,000 African slaves, outnumbering the whites by five to one, and a new era in its history began. That did not displace the Scottish colony, but rather prompted it to seek fresh fields of enterprise. Scots acquired plantations on Nevis, then in typical clannish fashion ran them with managers and overseers from among their own kin, before carrying the sugar home to the Clyde on ships captained by brothers and cousins; their aim was to create a landed legacy they could leave to their sons.

From this secure base the operations could be extended far. An example came with the life's work of James Milliken and William MacDowall, after they went out from Glasgow to Nevis soon after the Union. When MacDowall returned home in 1726 he had ample funds to buy into the local sugar factories, to acquire a grand townhouse and to purchase an estate in Renfrewshire. By the 1730s, Milliken & MacDowell was the biggest merchant enterprise in the city. It disposed of enough resources to found the first bank in Glasgow, the Ship Bank, in 1750. Glaswegians seeking finance had so far needed to go to Edinburgh, and sometimes got there a dusty answer. Now Glasgow possessed a proper bank of its own, something required especially for the bills of exchange essential to capital and credit in foreign trade.[46] The expansion of this commercial empire and its ruling dynasty did not stop there. In the next generation a cousin, Alexander Houston, headed a still greater house under his own name. By this time the family's assets extended to plantations not only on Nevis but also on Grenada, St Vincent, Tobago and Jamaica.[47] Each of these had a wider community of Scots planters. But commercial empires rise and fall. Once Britain set out on its long struggle with revolutionary France, insurrections of slaves and disruption of trade caused a financial crisis in 1797 much like that of 1776, this time bringing down the house of Houston.[48]

Meanwhile in Glasgow the manufacture of sugar continued, though later it centred on Greenock, where the biggest company in the modern industry, Tate & Lyle, closed its last factory only in 1997. With local consumption so high, it also entered into the culture, even into the dialect of the west of Scotland – with the sugaries (the factories that refined the stuff), with sugarallie water, sugar biscuits, sugarbools and sugardoddles (sweeties) and a sugar-piece (bread and butter sprinkled with sugar).[49] Along with these picturesque details, even the deeper effects have today virtually vanished. History tends to remember Glasgow's trade in tobacco above all, yet the trade in sugar was hardly less important. Both produced merchants and firms of immense wealth with the financial surpluses that allowed large-scale investment in the Scottish domestic economy.[50] Both gave the local population unhealthy habits.

Yet the most durable effects of the early industrial revolution in Glasgow came from a third American commodity: cotton. This also made the greatest demands on native ingenuity. In 1707 Scotland's economic predicament had seemed so appalling because it lacked both financial clout and commercial acumen. By the end of the century such problems had been solved, so that Scots could in principle apply their resources to any type of enterprise, or reapply them if one particular sector failed in the way tobacco did in 1776. As Glaswegians turned from North America to the West Indies, they turned not only to sugar but also to cotton, and not only to trade but also to manufacture.[51]

The opportunity coincided with a technological transformation in a traditional occupation, the production of textiles. In England, output was already being streamlined with the invention of the spinning jenny and the mule. When this was linked to the steam engine perfected by James Watt, maker of instruments for the University of Glasgow, the producers freed themselves from the need to be close to a river or burn for the sake of the water power. They could then operate on a much bigger scale anywhere in the cities and towns. By 1812 the political economist Sir John Sinclair estimated that the textile industry employed more than 150,000 Scots, many still working from home but with a growing number toiling in 120 mills. The mechanization of spinning and weaving concentrated in these new complexes came, more than anything else, to symbolize the industrial revolution at this crucial stage.[52]

Such development could hardly have been foreseen in the depressed Glasgow of 1776. Scots had long made linen out of flax they grew themselves, and during the eighteenth century the import of superior strains of foreign flax greatly improved the quality of the output. There was a start to making such finer stuffs as silk, which opened the further possibility of developing blended fabrics, with two or more different kinds of fibres mixed together to create a new material. For example, linen creased easily; combining it with silk largely cured this defect, much to the delight of fashionable ladies. Cotton extended the options available. With some earlier imports of cotton from the West Indies, merchants in Glasgow had already been able to supply the weavers in Glasgow and Paisley who made fustian for men's clothing from a mixture of cotton yarn and linen yarn. In this case the American war if anything helped, for it tended to raise wages and demand at a time when cotton was in real terms becoming cheaper, flax more expensive and silk more expensive still.[53]

Profits from oceanic trade gave Glasgow funds for investment. But wealthy merchants, who took with relish to the life of a laird on the country estates they purchased, seldom wished to be more than sleeping partners in industry. Opportunities opened instead for a type new to Scotland, the entrepreneur who by his own efforts raised himself from rags to riches. Even in the later, collectivist era, the entrepreneur never quite lost his charm for the west of Scotland, and some of the earliest examples have been remembered into modern times – such as David Dale, who appeared on Scottish banknotes in 1966.[54] Dale made the most of the region's new overseas trade in cotton by tapping into domestic needs. He had started as an apprentice weaver in Paisley, became clerk to a merchant in Glasgow and then worked his way up to a position where he could launch a business – in fact several businesses – on his own account, usually relying on imports of textiles.[55] It then looked like a natural step for him to start manufacturing textiles himself, with the opening in 1786 of the cotton mill at New Lanark, in its time the world's biggest. The venture was not speculative but rather the result of hard-headed calculation: investment on this scale could for the careful Dale be justified only by the best commercial prospects. Every country in northern Europe might grow its own flax, but not every one of them could import raw cotton from colonies or send the finished blend out again. The fortune Dale made at length devolved on his son-in-law, Robert

Owen, a Welshman by birth who applied his own wealth to his social experiment at New Lanark, designed to produce a new type of human being for the industrial age.

A trading connection if anything even more successful was that of James Finlay, whose successors developed a sprawling conglomerate of businesses that only in 2004 vanished into the maw of a modern multinational. Finlay himself had in his youth tramped Scotland as a humble packman or pedlar, selling useful wares to housewives – at the time the only method of distribution outside the burghs. Later in life he made a lot of money in textile manufacture, leaving it on his death in 1790 to his son Kirkman, destined to be a leading figure not only in the commerce but also in the politics of his native city. He became the biggest producer of cotton in Scotland with mills at Catrine in Ayrshire, at Balfron in Stirlingshire and at Deanston in Perthshire.[56]

The trade in cotton brought about even wider changes in Glasgow and Scotland at large than tobacco (except in introducing the bad habit of smoking).[57] Some of these changes got under way before the War of American Independence, too: an indigenous industrial revolution was beginning, as all industrial revolutions tend to begin, with textiles. In this case the effect of international commerce went so far as to create a new element of Scottish society with its own proletarian culture. Up to now Scots had made textiles for their own households or local communities on the scale of a craft rather than an industry, with the weavers' homes as the prime workplace. It was true the weavers had been able to double their output after the flying shuttle came into general use during the 1770s. By 1795 the country had 39,000 weavers producing cotton on handlooms, mostly full time, supported by 13,000 women and girls who helped them with the fiddly tasks of dressing the loom and setting it up for work.

About the turn of the nineteenth century, handloom weaving saw in Glasgow and its region a golden age. As Scotland transformed itself into a capitalist trading nation, a new proletarian culture emerged to match the modern times. Of course, remnants of the past survived. Most royal burghs housed a weavers' incorporation; the one in Glasgow boasted a charter dating from 1528. Membership was restricted to the privileged group that had served a formal apprenticeship, often won through some link of blood or obligation with existing members. Yet the regulations grew ever harder to maintain because the weaver's job was easy to learn and the demand for his products buoyant. If he wanted to earn a living free of the controls inside the burgh, he needed only to set up his workshop outside it, in Anderston, Calton, Gorbals and other nearby communities. Part-suburb and part-village, these places were largely peopled by weavers living in characteristic cottages usually of one storey, certainly of no more than two, helped in their labour by their families. They had a slow and tedious but often still quite well-paid job that left ample time to think and talk to neighbours, friends or colleagues who might drop by. The thinking and talking might be supplemented by an evening of self-improvement. John Galt's novel, *Annals of the Parish* (1821), set in the Ayrshire of the preceding decades, depicts a typical scene at the time of the French Revolution with local weavers clubbing together to subscribe to a newspaper from which they took turns to read aloud to one another. A school of poets at Paisley, led by Robert Tannahill and Alexander Wilson, sprang from the same ranks. They were men of independent mind and their politics tended to be radical.[58] It was an enterprising, prosperous workforce, because it was a trading one: into it came imports of raw cotton, out went exports of finished goods.

Yet a brief flowering of the proletariat would before long be blighted by the large-scale capitalist enterprise that trade in textiles also fostered, with imports and exports in vastly increased volumes.[59] It followed on from a technological turning point that for the weavers of the west of Scotland meant economic and social crisis too. In 1790, William Kelly, general manager of New Lanark, had first applied steam-power to the mule, with 1,320 spindles stretching out over 150 feet at his mills by the Clyde. The new power-loom was far more productive than any individual weaver could ever be. From this point his position steadily worsened. Partly this followed on from a previous excessive influx of labour into his trade, something bound to depress wages. Partly it was owed to the ruinous failure of an ill-judged strike in Glasgow in 1812, after weavers had sought in vain to enforce the burgh's obsolete regulations on entry to their incorporation and on a minimum scale of prices. This was not the way to halt the inexorable advance of the power-loom. By 1813 the number of them at work in Scotland was 1400 and rising rapidly. They would spell doom to the independent weaver, if not finally for another couple of decades. He would suffer a lot of misery meanwhile.[60]

The larger social changes went along with the creation of complexes for the mass production of imported cotton on a scale never dreamed of in the old Scotland. Their sheer size impressed: New Lanark more than quadrupled its workforce from 400 in 1791 to 1,700 in 1820. Demand for labour often exceeded what the surrounding area could supply, especially in more remote areas where the rationale for the mill might be the availability not of workers but of water for energy. By the time steam-power became available, it was often too costly to move to a more populous place. The mills might take pauper children from local parishes, as Owen did at New Lanark, though this expedient was not in fact to be much favoured elsewhere in Scotland. Instead, migrants from the Highlands and then from Ireland filled the gap: all, yet again, momentous developments for the nation.[61]

Trade had opened Scotland to the world, and prepared the way for its industrial revolution. Like the globalisation of today, it propelled change, tearing apart cosy local communities where the people had lived for generations, forcing them into new social structures geared to the relentless demands of capitalism. Only the Scotland of the future would draw the dividends from this harrowing process of development, with greater comfort and happiness for the people than their forefathers had known.[62] Meanwhile degradation was the common lot, for the workers at the advanced stage of production as well as for those who at the other end of the chain furnished the raw materials to factories in Scotland. At the lowest point of this sequence lay the slaves who grew the tobacco, sugar and cotton that were traded across the Atlantic into the Clyde.

Before 1707 the Scots had been innocent of the slave trade, not possessing any successful colonies in the New World. After 1707 their participation in it did not take off at once, open though they were in principle to all imperial opportunities. One early opportunity arose in about 1750 with the collapse of the Royal African Company, based in London, which had pretended to a British monopoly on the shipment to America of the hapless blacks. A free-for-all now followed to take over this traffic, and among the successful interlopers was a Scottish consortium under two senior partners, Sir Alexander Grant of Dalvey, one of Jamaica's landowners with 2,000 acres, 700 slaves and property of £70,000, and Richard Oswald, hailing from Caithness by way of a commercial training in Virginia and in Glasgow, his family destined to become one of the city's wealthiest. In 1748 the company of Grant, Oswald & Co bought a disused ruined fort on Bance Island, near the present Freetown in Sierra Leone. They restored it to working order, and added a golf course for the Scots agents posted there. They set up at just the right time. With a steady rise in the consumption of sugar in Europe, the economy of plantations was being rapidly expanded in the Americas and the demand for labour with it.[63]

Circumstances favoured innovation in the slave trade, and these Scots responded. Till now, European slavers had often culled their human wares by the direct, brutal means of raiding along the African coast and simply seizing innocent blacks. Grant, Oswald & Co introduced a system that at least had the merit of being more commercial. Its employees stayed put at their well-defended fort, or at outposts up the rivers nearby, and waited for local chiefs to bring down slaves, often captives taken in war. These were then bartered for goods shipped from overseas. Leaving the traffic in indigenous hands, the Scots asked no questions about its methods. They contented themselves with providing middlemen's jobs for their relations or friends, and business for their clients. Though novices in the slave trade, they found a way of thriving without official privilege or aid against the competition of established English rivals.[64] By the 1760s, there were slaving voyages setting out direct from Scotland, from Montrose and especially Greenock, where the connection with sugar clearly counted.[65]

The slave trade was cruel and inhuman, faced a rising tide of abhorrence in its own time and is rightly reviled today. But the Scottish part in it remained undeniably modest. Its modern critics, now 'recovering' this episode in the nation's history, exonerate Scots of any great part in the trade as such, but point to the fact that they acquired property in the West Indies for the production of sugar and cotton on the backs of slaves. It was the fat earnings from such business that financed much of the development of Glasgow, including those streets – Buchanan, Glassford, Jamaica, Virginia – named after the owners of the plantations or the colonies where they owned them. They were usually absentee proprietors, preferring to spend the profits they raked in from the islands of the Caribbean Sea on their own social advancement in Scotland. At the same time, national clannishness assured jobs for the Scots lawyers, managers and overseers who went out to run the plant-ations. They worked hard not only to satisfy their employers but also to enrich themselves as fast as possible and get home again. So their existence was often a race against time, before tropical disease could claim them. Robert Burns contemplated a move to the West Indies, but given his state of health it was lucky the Kilmarnock edition of his poems (1786) came out first and persuaded him to pursue a poet's career at home. Zachary Macaulay, son of the minister of Inveraray, emigrated in 1784 as a lad of sixteen, and ever afterwards rued the memory of himself 'in a field of canes, amidst perhaps a hundred of the sable race, cursing and bawling [with] the noise of the whip resounding on their shoulders'. The experience in fact sickened him and he returned to become one of Britain's leading advocates for the abolition of the slave trade.[66]

However weak or strong the Scots' moral feelings, they had to face some facts of life. They were moving into another nation's empire, where they needed their own niches if they were to benefit from it, and by extension from the Union, at all. There was a parallel with what happened on this side of the ocean. As transatlantic trade expanded, ports along the western coasts of Great Britain specialized in different aspects of it according to their own interests and capabilities. For Bristol this meant import of sugar. For Liverpool traffic in slaves. For Glasgow it meant tobacco. Tobacco was grown by slave labour, yet Glaswegians played little part in the actual transport of slaves – not because they were morally superior, but because others had got this all tied up before them.[67]

On the other side of the Atlantic the situation was more complicated, even though the British mercantilist system did not differ materially from any other: it relied on ruthless monopolistic exploitation of exotic resources, often by means of slavery, this being reckoned (falsely) the best means of at once maintaining sovereignty and maximizing profits. In the colonial Americas, there was no more concept of free labour than there was of free trade. Monopoly, or the attempt at it, became universal, in English, French, Spanish, Portuguese, Dutch, Danish and Swedish colonies. The specialization the Scots found here was not the free port, which they had tried at Darien but failed to make work. Now the best this marginal people could do was occupy the infrastructure of the plantations: if they did not like that, they could continue to squat in poverty at home. Taking part in an economy based on slavery was the price of taking part in the intercontinental economy, the true object of Scotland's desire – and, unfortunately, available on no other terms.[68]

Of course Scots posed themselves moral questions about their dilemma. Most took their morality from the Bible, however, which nowhere condemned slavery as such. God disapproved of the enslavement of the Jews in Egypt, but because they were Jews, his chosen people, not because they were slaves; divine disapproval did not extend to the enslavement of Nubians or Canaanites. St Paul said that both slave and free were one in Jesus Christ. In this sense their differing legal status counted as nothing compared to their common blessings as believers; they did not need an earthly emancipation when they were going to get a heavenly one.[69] In a nation that read the Bible as searchingly as Scotland did, it came as no surprise that the established church had never felt the need to condemn slavery explicitly.

Scottish opposition to slavery arose rather out of secular thought, in particular out of the concern during the Enlightenment with humanity's natural rights, those not dependent on any divine sanction. Today this is often remembered as an age of reason, but it would be more accurate to call it an age of nature. After casting off the legacy of classical antiquity or of Christian doctrine, the great thinkers proceeded not by way of arid logic, but by looking to nature as the key to understanding the world about them. And this procedure could be employed by everybody from the lecturer at the university to the weaver at his loom (or even his wife): Scots were people who enlightened themselves. Enlightenments in other nations had different characteristics. They might be more academic, or more aristocratic, or more political. But in poor and stateless yet ambitious and aspiring Scotland this was how Enlightenment turned out, a broad undertaking closely connected to economic improvement. So when we recall how the merchants of Glasgow profited from commerce based on slavery, we should also remind ourselves that the professors of its university taught their sons that this, though not against the law, was an economic mistake as well as a moral offence.[70]

At the threshold of the Enlightenment stood Gershom Carmichael, who after many years teaching at the University of Glasgow became its first professor of moral philosophy in 1728. He had been a traditional sort of Scottish academic, a minister of the Kirk who always lectured in Latin, with Aristotle as his textbook. But Carmichael also introduced his students to recent developments in European thinking by pioneers of the previous century – the Dutchman Hugo Grotius and the Saxon Samuel Pufendorf, the first in the modern age to ground philosophy in nature rather than Scripture. Not that Carmichael in every way agreed with these, and slavery was one topic on which he tended to disagree with them. He argued against Pufendorf that no human can enslave another, 'for men are not among the objects over which God has allowed the human race to enjoy dominion' and against Grotius that 'consent of nations' cannot justifying depriving 'innocent citizens of their personal liberty'.[71] For Carmichael, the basic right of men and women to remain free, and not be reduced to slavery, should form part of our reverence for God's creation.[72] It was part of his liberal thinking, which also extended to ideas, such as free trade, destined to become much more important to Scotland.

Carmichael's successor in his chair in 1729 was one of his former students, the Ulsterman Francis Hutcheson. Hutcheson acknowledged his debt to Carmichael in a textbook, *Philosophiae moralis institutio compendiaria* (1747), later expanded into a *System of Moral Philosophy* (1755). Here Hutcheson spells out the individual's entitlements to life and to liberty, in particular the freedom to make personal judgements: 'These natural rights belong to all.' Modern societies live under the rule of law, and in principle 'these laws prohibit the greatest and wisest of mankind to inflict any misery on the meanest, or deprive them of any of their natural rights.' But Hutcheson's main theoretical advance lay in positing that human nature included a unique feature, a vital element of benevolence. The character of society was to be explained by, and its ethics to be derived from, not some process of reason but from the sympathy, if anything non-rational, of every human being for another, allowing us to approve of moral actions and disapprove of immoral ones. For Hutcheson it was emotion, not reason, that gives us our morality. With this he also offered a test of social institutions, as no previous school of thought had done. They could now be judged by the good they worked, or conversely by the harm they caused. This condemned slavery.[73] It also refuted Aristotle's claim that slavery simply formed part of a natural order of things where some were slaves and others free. Hutcheson retorted explicitly: 'No endowments, natural or acquired, can give a perfect right to assume power over others, without their consent. This is intended against the doctrine of Aristotle, and some others of the ancients, "that some men are naturally slaves"... The natural sense of justice and humanity abhors the thought.'[74] Hutcheson placed his hopes on liberty, though his proposals did not extend far into the practical worlds of politics or economics. But he at least deprived slavery of any moral justification.

By contrast, practical results came first for Adam Smith, from 1751 Hutcheson's successor in the chair of moral philosophy at the University of Glasgow. He accepted the ethical case against slavery but what he stressed, contrary to most contemporaries, was the economic damage it inflicted: 'The work done by slaves, though it appears to cost only their maintenance, is in the end the dearest of all.'[75] The reason was that slaves had no incentive to exert themselves, so would never behave in such a way as to maximize their utility. Slavery was then just another of the many irrational constraints on the free exercise of that natural human self-interest that conduced to the general good. It would have been a bad thing even if it had not been utterly inhumane as well, coarsening the masters and degrading the slaves.

All this fits neatly into the descriptions in Smith's book *The Wealth of Nations* (1776) of a free economy. Ever the practical man, Smith had during his time in Glasgow hobnobbed with the merchants and gathered materials for his great work. For all its reputation as a handbook of capitalism, it abounds with disparaging examples of collusion between businessmen and politicians, in what today we call rip-offs. Smith writes: 'People of the same trade seldom meet together, even for merriment and diversion, but the conversation ends in a conspiracy against the public, or in some contrivance to raise prices.'[76] He did not live into the age of the lobbyist, but he had already got the general idea. When businessmen put forward some wonderful new scheme of overwhelming benefit to the public, we should always remember that 'it comes from an order of men, whose interest is never exactly the same with that of the public, who have generally an interest to deceive and even oppress the public, and who accordingly have, upon many occasions, both deceived and oppressed it.'[77] If we ignore the special pleading of merchants, we will find that a spontaneous and unintended order arises, as voluntary exchanges among individuals produce benefits for all concerned. Smith's system of 'perfect liberty', as he liked to call it, was a turning point in the economic history of the world and, emanating from Glasgow, offered the intellectual basis on which modern capitalism was built.

Successors at the University of Glasgow continued to make clear how this new economic system had no place for slavery. Thomas Reid held the chair of moral philosophy from 1764. With him the general intellectual development of Scotland took a different turn, towards the Common Sense philosophy that formed one of the nation's chief contributions to enlightened discourse. While Reid criticized the ideas of Adam Smith and David Hume in crucial respects, he shared their abhorrence of slavery, as he explained in a letter: 'Our university has sent a petition to the House of Commons, in favour of the African slaves... the clergy of Scotland will likewise join in it. I comfort my grey hairs with the thoughts that the world is growing better, having long resolved to resist the common sentiment of old age, that it is always growing worse.'[78] One of Smith's own pupils, John Millar, professor of civil law from 1761 to 1800, held the same opinion. In his *Observations Concerning the Distinction of Ranks in Society* (1771), it was the principles of political economy, and not of religion, that guided him through the history of slavery. This had vanished from Europe at the fall of the Roman empire, and the resulting division of labour fostered economic progress. To reintroduce slavery in America with people from primitive cultures was to turn the clock back. But Millar did have, besides his empirical arguments, the familiar ethical one arising from the inalienable right to individual liberty of all human beings.[79]

A liberal outlook was not confined to the university. Even at the Merchants' House, where the slave trade found its strongest defenders, it came under vehement attack from David Dale, one of the earliest capitalists properly so called with his investment at New Lanark. In Glasgow, he organized a society for the abolition of the slave trade. At its first general meeting in 1792, it resolved that 'the traffic in the human species is founded on the grossest injustice, is attended with the utmost cruelty and barbarity to an innocent race of men and is productive of ruin and desolation of a country which the efforts of the well-directed industry of Great Britain might contribute to civilize.'[80] In the end, the professors won this debate, even if it took a bit more time: in 1807 the Parliament at Westminster abolished the slave trade in the British empire, and in 1833 slavery itself. Movements of domestic opinion had achieved their aim far in advance of those in any nation on the continent of Europe. Whatever the latest academic literature may claim, this is not overall a damning record, for Glasgow or the rest of Scotland. History shows that practical solutions to difficult problems seldom emerge from a complex reality as readily as is suggested by the posturing of the politically correct today.[81]

Liberty proved a much stronger force than slavery ever had been in driving Glasgow's development. In the modern era historic barriers to trade fell one by one, even if progress might sometimes be slowed by vested interests. Glaswegians wanted open access to all the oceans of the world, and in particular the ending of the East India Company's monopoly on traffic to the Orient. When this was abolished at the renewal of the company's charter in 1813, a ship owned by the city's MP, Kirkman Finlay, at once set out for Calcutta.[82] Finally, in 1846, the repeal of the Corn Laws ushered in the era of complete free trade for Victorian Britain.[83]

At the University of Glasgow, as at the other Scottish universities, a liberal outlook was bolstered by the fact that political economy continued to be taught as part of moral philosophy through most of the nineteenth century.[84] But by the end of it, when Edward Caird held the chair in moral philosophy for thirty years, the tradition no longer served a city at the forefront of modern commerce. William Smart, son of a textile merchant, had meant to follow his father in business but found the academic study of political economy too fascinating. In 1892 he accepted an appointment to teach it as a special subject; he was raised to the rank of professor in 1896.

The promotion came at the behest of John Caird, Edward's brother and principal of the university. Apparently worried that socialism was taking root in Glasgow, John Caird wanted Smart to counter this tendency among the city's educated youngsters. He had found the right man. Like Adam Smith more than a century before, Smart kept abreast of the advances in his discipline coming from Europe, and in particular focussed on the Austrian school of economics founded by Carl Menger. The school was in fact critical of Smith and of his mechanistic efforts to relate the value of a good to the cost of its production. Smart found instead the succinct formulation that 'value comes, not from the past of goods but from their future'[85] – that is to say, from the value that will be assigned to them by people who trade in them and use them. It was an important insight that sustained the school's continuing rejection of theories that elsewhere dominated the discipline in the twentieth century, especially econometrics and aggregate macroeconomic analysis. Since the financial crash of 2008 and the discrediting of the economics that led to it, the Austrian school has come to the fore again. In line with its approach, Smart had taken a close interest in the economics of the real world – mundane matters such as women's wages, or social issues like housing and the Poor Law, of special interest in Glasgow. By the end of his career his abilities were widely acknowledged, and he played a part, through his work on royal commissions, in laying some foundations of the welfare state. On matters of trade, he remained a champion of the *laissez-faire* approach that had served the city so well. In his time, however, protectionist sentiment was rising again, based on arguments still heard today: that foreign countries were dumping, that new industries needed nurture through tariffs, that national security should determine commercial policy. Smart refuted them all in a series of passionate public lectures in 1903.[86]

The chair Smart held at the University of Glasgow, endowed by the steelmakers A. & J. Stewart of Coatbridge, was named after Adam Smith, and for the most part its occupants have devoted themselves to the study of the great man. The one who followed Smart in 1915, W.R. Scott, was certainly a devotee and wrote a reverent study of *Adam Smith as Student and Professor* (1937). From 1945, Alec Macfie still pursued the typical academic procedure of the Scottish Enlightenment in teaching his discipline in the form of a history of economic thought. His student Andrew Skinner succeeded to the chair in 1994, but had already made his name by taking charge of a popular edition (published by Penguin) of the definitive text of *The Wealth of Nations*, republished for the book's bicentennial in 1976.[87] By this time, beyond the university, the city felt more interested in public subsidy than in free trade. But at least within those hallowed halls on Gilmorehill the memory of 'perfect liberty' burned bright.

2

Industry: 'High service, romance and adventure'

ON JANUARY 31, 1638, the town council of Glasgow granted to a partnership of merchants led by Robert Fleming the lease of a 'grait ludging and yaird at the back thairof lyand within this brughe in the Drygait'.[1] It was an old manse, where they wanted to set up a 'manufactory'. The councillors let the site out rent-free for fifteen years, and even offered to pay the cost of upkeep for the roof: they must have been really keen to strike that deal with Fleming and his friends. But it was an era of innovation in Glasgow, as in Scotland at large. Until now the burgh had had no manufacturing capacity in any modern sense, only traditional production on a small scale by the individual craftsmen who were time-served members of its incorporated trades, all intended just for the townspeople or their neighbours in the countryside around. No doubt the time had come to show a bit more ambition. The same spirit moved the whole country as it now prepared, with the National Covenant, for religious and political revolution.

The revolution envisaged by these Glaswegian merchants at their humdrum material level was to start manufacturing on a scale that might be called industrial, as already found in leading cities of

Europe. But there was more than one problem with this. For a start, nobody abroad ever looked for manufactures from distant Scotland, rather for raw materials to be processed by their own workers. The busiest traffic was with the Netherlands, source of the best of Europe's consumer goods, reaching in that nation's golden age a level of sophistication with which Scots could hardly hope to compete.[2] Perhaps, however, they might make a start at the bottom end of the market, in cheap textiles and other such products.

Alas, Scottish and cheap often came to mean Scottish and nasty. Native craftsmen wrought for local customers who had little money and just wanted goods they could afford. Before the rise of modern industry, cheap was equivalent to bad: craftsmen could seldom cut costs except by skimping on time and materials. While the goods produced might be dumped on consumers at home, foreigners complained about the inferior quality of the exports. Scots would have done better to learn from abroad, but showed little inclination for that either. When from time to time the government tried to encourage skilled artisans from Europe to come over and serve as instructors to its own people, the burgh councillors would complain. The tradesmen's incorporations sought to give the immigrants a hard time with frivolous prosecutions for breaches of the rules and the like. Often the foreigners, faced with this unaccountable hostility, just went home again – and nobody profited from all the petulance.[3]

If there were few customers abroad to buy Scottish manufactured goods, there were likewise few workers at home to make them: another of the difficulties for the venture in the Drygate would be to find people worth employing. After a protest from the burgh's freemen weavers at the threat to their business, a member of the merchants' partnership, Patrick Bell, had to promise the town council that 'thair suld be no woovis wovin of townis folkis thairin be thair servandis in hurt and prejudice of the said friemen, bot by thais onlie with the calling'. In other words, only time-served craftsmen would still be allowed to weave materials for the towns-folk, because the workers in the factory could only damage the interests of the burgh's freemen.[4] Some freemen worked on their own while others headed up a business that, at the fullest extent, employed members of their families together with journeymen and apprentices – almost little factories in themselves. The setts or constitutions of the burghs privileged them, indeed made their privilege exclusive. Nobody could practise a craft unless he joined the incorporation governing it. Inside it the craftsmen ran their own affairs and admitted new members according to their own rules, not at the behest of any law.

But a workforce for the new kind of factory in Drygate needed to come from somewhere. In the bigger Scots burghs, there had emerged, below the craftsmen, a class of skilled but unprivileged workmen with no more rights than the unskilled labourers below them. Some would have failed to gain an apprenticeship, if entering the burgh from the countryside and lacking money or local connections. Any that did gain one would still have had to curry favour with older brethren of the craft who judged their work before admitting them. Those who never made it could look forward to life as journeymen at best, not allowed to run their own businesses.[5] Or else, they might leave the royalty (the area within the original medieval bounds of the burgh) and set up in humble working suburbs such as Gorbals. There, anybody was at liberty to live, labour and offer his wares for sale, as long as he did not try to encroach on the burgh's rights. The unprivileged craftsmen outside it might expect to be obstructed at every turn by the privileged craftsmen inside it, but they could still earn a living. They also, however, exposed themselves to economic forces, good and bad, that the burghs' system of regulation had been designed to suppress. By the law, and not just because of the problems inherent in any start-up, it was not easy to introduce manufacturing to Scotland.

Manufacturing would indeed long remain in some respects an

alien concept. Most Scots, in town or country, laboured when they could or would – which, except at special seasons such as the harvest, was not always, not every day or every hour of the day. In fact the rhythms of nature or the trading cycle seldom stretched their capacities, and idleness was common. The discipline of sitting or standing in a factory for hours on end and performing the same monotonous actions in unison with fellow workers was a model of labour quite unfamiliar.[6] We may well understand, then, why the main reason the town council of Glasgow supported the merchants' manufactory was that 'ane number of the poorer sort of pople within the [burgh] may be imployit and put to wark'. If they did not do that of their own accord, there was the more radical option of forcing them to. Some councillors saw a factory as in effect a kind of poorhouse, where inmates were to maintain themselves in a material sense and to improve themselves in a moral sense: the contemporary mind did not always draw here a strict distinction. If professional independence was the pride of the freeman, then by a certain sort of convoluted logic it followed that the unfree, lacking such independence, might be put to work by the public authorities: all part of the Calvinist ethic.[7]

The Covenanter government of Scotland shared the same point of view. Parliament had passed a law allowing poorhouses to be erected by private individuals or partnerships. It was under this legislation that the merchants of Glasgow set up the textile factory in the Drygate. The town council continued to take a benign view of the venture. After the free lease for the premises it later helped the factory to obtain dyestuffs, Dutch looms and Spanish wool, besides arranging a supplier for waulking or cleansing wool. Again in 1648, as political upheaval disrupted the economy and diverted manpower, the council appointed an official 'to speir out men fitting to be employet for the manufactorie'. While the business numbered among the many ruined by the economic collapse of the 1650s, now that the facilities were in place other people could take them over: a second partnership of burgesses did so in 1652–3, followed by the weavers' incorporation in the 1660s. Some textile production in Drygate seems to have gone on till about 1685. By then it specialized in woollen goods, 'damaties, fustines and striped vermilliones, which will be a great advantage to the country and will keep in much money therein which is sent out thereof for import of the same'.[8]

But in general manufacturing expanded only slowly, sometimes helped by patronage from on high. When in 1681 James, duke of Albany, brother of King Charles II, came to Scotland as a kind of viceroy, he had in mind a programme to restore sagging loyalty to the royal House of Stewart with, among other things, economic reforms. Privy Council and Parliament approved a regime of the strictest mercantilist kind, designed to encourage local production, cut back imports and promote exports. For a time the policy even appeared to achieve some success. About sixty new enterprises were established up to the Union of 1707. While they all received protection from foreign competitors it is unclear how far they competed among themselves, something that might have developed as a motor for more dynamic progress. We can see that many grew successful enough to pay dividends as well as interest on the original capital. Yet most were short-lived and few survived the Union.[9]

Glasgow housed some of these ventures. The Greenland Fishing and Soapworks Company built or bought whaling ships and acquired premises at Greenock for boiling blubber. The whaling side of the business did not do well and was run down till, by 1695, it was abandoned altogether, but the soapworks kept going till 1785.[10] Less adventurous in conception was another woollen manufactory, founded in 1699. Yet it expanded fast till it employed 1,400 people. The city's largest enterprise at that period, it drew on resources available locally, but we do not know if its mass production of textiles produced better results than those of individual craftsmen.

Whatever the particular uncertainties, however, it seems clear that over the whole of the seventeenth century, Glasgow did achieve long-term growth, if with interruptions. By 1700 it was without doubt Scotland's second city.[11]

The next century saw much more dramatic developments. A cluster arose from the opportunities that opened up for the finishing of textiles to a higher standard, ready to be sold anywhere in Scotland or abroad. An example came in the career of George Macintosh, a Highlander who made money from a tannery before building behind a 10-foot wall at Dennistoun a chemical plant with a workforce of fellow Gaels, monoglots who could not betray his secrets. One challenge was production of the prized Adrianople or Turkey red colour in cotton, at the time an expensive import from the Balkans. In 1785, in partnership with David Dale of New Lanark, Macintosh opened at Barrowfield the first works in Britain to produce this dye, known here as Dale's Red. It was concocted by a process involving among other substances soda, salt and sheep's dung, all available in Scotland. It made a fortune for Macintosh, who sold the factory in 1805 to the merchant Henry Monteith of Carstairs. Monteith then used it to manufacture gaudy bandanas, which were quite the rage among the city's fashionistas.[12]

George Macintosh's son Charles became an even greater chemical entrepreneur in his own right. In 1807 he set up a factory at Hurlet near Paisley to process local shales for alum to be used in a wide range of cosmetic, medicinal and industrial applications. Hurlet was then the biggest chemical works in Britain – still not big enough to meet the demand, though, till he built a second one at Lennoxtown.[13] His business throve, but not enough to bring him immortality. That he won in consequence of dealings with the Glasgow Gas Company, run by bright young James Neilson, a self-made engineer. From the inaugural works at Townhead, right next to the Cathedral, gas lighting was introduced in 1818 to the rest of the city, the first place in Scotland to enjoy it. To begin with the by-products from the works, tar and ammonia, went to waste. But Macintosh thought he could find uses for them and began to buy them in from Neilson. During experiments Macintosh discovered that coal-tar naphtha would dissolve india rubber. Given this, thin sheets of rubber could be fashioned and introduced between layers of cloth to create the world's original waterproof fabric. Macintosh patented it in 1823, though the process took time to perfect. His early trials had been with wool, which made the garments stiff, heavy and uncomfortable. And if it rained in hot weather – admittedly a rare combination in Scotland – the rubber tended to melt. Still, one by one the problems were solved so that a fabric both flexible and impermeable could be provided at low cost for production of a wide range of everyday goods. By then the public had given the fabric its inventor's name (modified to mackintosh). It is still made at Cumbernauld. Macintosh's commercial career spanned six decades, and he died a wealthy man in 1843.[14]

Bleaching was the basic chemical treatment that textiles needed before undergoing more sophisticated processes. It had so far been done with organic substances. Oil and dirt in raw materials could be removed with a mild alkali, extracted from ash of wood or of seaweed – the kelp harvested in dire conditions from the western seas by pitiable Gaels. Then an acid, most often sour milk, got rid of earthy stains that prevented even dyeing. For industrial production, sulphuric acid or vitriol, or else chlorine, proved far better. By the 1820s Port Dundas, on the Forth-Clyde Canal just north of Glasgow, housed half a dozen works producing acids. But they were dangerous to those treating the textiles. Charles Tennant from Alloway in Ayrshire – Robert Burns's friend 'wabster Charlie'[15] – dealt with the risk. In 1799 he shrewdly patented a dry bleaching powder that in truth had been invented by Charles Macintosh (himself a walking chemical industry). From such a small beginning would grow the mighty St Rollox chemical works, established by Tennant in 1798 at Springburn on the northern side

of Glasgow.[16] St Rollox transformed science into money. In 1818 it
led the way in adopting the Leblanc process, using sea salt for the
manufacture of soda. A decade later it was producing 10,000 tons
of alkali a year: this sealed the doom of Highland kelp. Now the
various applications, in making soap, glass, paper, plaster and
other materials, also became much cheaper and more productive.
Once St Rollox had in its turn grown into the biggest chemical
works in the world, it advertised its status with Tennant's Stalk
or Stack, a chimney 455 feet and 6 inches tall. Built in 1841–2,
the stack towered there till 1922 when it was struck by lightning
and had to be demolished.[17] The reason for the great height was
to spread the terrible pollution from the factory downwind on
Glasgow's prevailing westerlies. The Royal Infirmary stood almost
next door, which at least meant the workers did not have to go far
for treatment of the gruesome maladies induced by the chemicals.
Here is a description of the works from 1847:

> They are, necessarily, black and dirty, and as infernal in
> appearance as we can well imagine any earthly place to be.
> The heaps of sulphur, lime, coal and refuse; the intense heat
> of the scores of furnaces in which the processes are going on;
> the smoke and thick vapours which dim the air of most of the
> buildings; the swarthy and heated appearance of the men;
> the acrid fumes of sulphur and the various acids which worry
> the eyes, and tickle the nose and choke the throat; the danger
> which every bit of broad-cloth incurs of being bleached...
> form a series of notabilia not soon to be forgotten.[18]

The factory belched forth its fumes for the rest of the century and
beyond, if at length controlled somewhat by national legislation
against pollution. Over time its technology grew outdated: in newer
plants, the more efficient Solvay process replaced the Leblanc one.
Yet in Glasgow the Tennants did not want to give up the range

of by-products they were generating, which might continue to compensate for having lost the lead in terms of process. In 1890, forty-five businesses in the city, including St Rollox, combined into the United Alkali Company under the presidency of a Tennant. It engaged in fierce competition with its English rival, Brunner, Mond & Co, till in 1926 the two were among the companies that merged to form Imperial Chemical Industries. This corporation owned St Rollox up to the demolition of the whole complex in 1964. The site was built over, first with high-rise flats and today with a Tesco supermarket.[19]

Charles Tennant had died in 1838, leaving nine children in whose hands his business at first languished. It was a grandson, also Charles, who brought about a revival on becoming a director in 1850. He possessed a range of commercial talents, being a skilled negotiator and perhaps the first capitalist to grasp how large-scale modern business also demanded flair in public relations. The star of shareholders' meetings, he found the knack of letting them feel involved while never giving much away. He kept control, in other words. He made a legend of himself in Glasgow as the central figure in a circle of businessmen who trusted his judgement and wanted nothing more than to enter into joint ventures with him.[20]

Scots engaged in constant search for fresh productive opportunities. One place they turned to in the 1870s was Spain, a nation that had earlier, and for three centuries, exploited the riches of the New World but so far proved incapable of joining the industrial revolution of the Old World. The province of Huelva, on the Atlantic coast of the southwest, had been known since remote antiquity for its mineral deposits of copper, silver and gold; the Phoenicians called it Tarshish, the Greeks and Romans Tharsis. In 1862, Tennant founded the Tharsis Company in Scotland to take over the pyrite mines of Huelva from a failed French venture, a deal coming at a knockdown price. He wanted above all to obtain for St Rollox the sulphur that was a by-product of extraction of copper from pyrites. The pyrites further contained tiny components of gold, which he also set about recovering: the Cassel Gold Extraction Company, formed at his behest in 1884, acquired the rights to a process using cyanide that raised the level of gold that could be won to 95 per cent. After these other minerals had been taken out, they left a residue of iron ore nicknamed blue billy; the generation of quantities of this prompted Tennant to establish the Steel Company of Scotland in 1872.[21]

A no less momentous development came with the formation of Nobel's Explosives, a company set up in Scotland to exploit the patents of the Swede, Alfred Nobel, inventor of modern explosives. Nobel was also an acute businessman wishing to move into the vast market of the British empire. Tennant became his partner in Glasgow. Tennant called on the services of another of the city's plutocrats, Charles Randolph, a millionaire from his manufacture of the compound marine engine and from shipbuilding in the yard he founded at Fairfield, Govan. In semi-retirement, he was keeping himself busy with plans for the improvement of navigation on the Clyde, the disposal of Glasgow's sewage, the network of oceanic shipping lines and other projects no less useful, now to include the introduction of dynamite to Britain.[22]

Nobel had first sought partners in London but failed and turned to Glasgow, home to the world's biggest cluster of chemical companies. The men running them saw the potential of dynamite at once, as Londoners could not. Negotiations for a partnership took place in 1871. The deal reflected the novelty of the risks. A joint-stock company was formed, with Nobel holding half the capital in return for transferring his rights to it. The other three directors were Glaswegians under the chairmanship of Randolph. They built a factory at Ardeer in Ayrshire, amid barren dunes to muffle any blast. This would become the British empire's biggest producer of explosives till well into the twentieth century.[23]

The chemical saga, from salt to explosives, shows what huge potential existed to diversify out of the early textile industries – and demonstrates how Scots fulfilled that potential. But this was not even half the history of their industrial revolution. The new industries needed energy and supplied it from local coalfields. Iron ore was another natural resource that might be exploited in close connection with coal, both linked in turn with engineering. Here lay a second productive cluster that made Scotland a manufacturer for the world.[24]

Scots were lucky in their abundant resources of coal, yet it was not at first obvious how important these would prove. For centuries they had been exploited for domestic use and export, but they found their main local industrial outlet in the production of salt from the evaporation of seawater in huge pans, heated by fires from underneath. The steam engine would change the whole pattern and level of demand. And apart from the use of coal as fuel, its derivatives, such as coke and liquid ammonia, became products in their own right.[25]

Coal had been dug in Scotland since the Middle Ages. At the turn of the nineteenth century it still came from mines serving just their own localities, though construction of canals had started to give them wider markets. Soon output rose to meet growing industrial and domestic consumption. By the middle of the century there were 350 collieries in Scotland, 250 of them in the west, in Lanarkshire and Ayrshire, which had replaced the older coalfield of Fife as the main sources of coal. Altogether they produced 7 million tons in 1854 before rapid expansion took output to 39 million tons by 1914. In 1800 there had been no more than 8,000 miners in Scotland. By 1870 the workforce rose to more than 40,000 and by 1914 to 150,000.[26]

The performance was not the sequel to any astounding progress in technology. Scots miners still worked as their forefathers had done, hacking by hand at the coalface in conditions never less than tough and often dangerous. The mining boom worsened these conditions: here the human degradation of the industrial revolution reached its nadir. A royal commission mounted an inquiry in 1840. Its report led to an Act of Parliament banning employment underground of women and girls, and of boys below the age of ten; up to the age of thirteen, the latter must no longer work more than twelve hours a day.[27] The average age of a miner at death was thirty-four, compared to fifty for factory hands, so to fulfil their productive potential children had to start work in the pits as early as possible, sometimes at five or six years of age. At least that now ended, but regulations on safety did not come into force till 1861, and even then were rather feeble. Life for the men in many mines would not change much before 1914.

Mining villages, lying in the shadow of the bings and winding gear, remained frightful, too. Families lived in sordid miners' rows, in homes without comfort or sanitation. They had little choice: they could afford nothing better and alternative landlords feared the miners' reputation for drunkenness and violence. Another royal commission heard in 1892 of the rows built by William Dixon & Co at Auchenraith near Blantyre, housing a population of 492 people. They consisted of forty-two single-roomed and forty-one double-roomed homes with no wash-houses or coal-cellars (coals were kept under the bed). An open sewer ran behind, with privies where users had to squat. There were but two drinking fountains.[28] No wonder the wretches confined in such places seemed to others to be almost savages. But out of segregation on the surface and shared danger underground there evolved a strong communal life, together with sturdy trades unionism. Here the first national leadership of Scottish labour appeared, with Alexander MacDonald in the 1860s and Keir Hardie in the 1880s.

At first all Scottish industries made prodigal use of the cheap coal under their feet. But as time went on, and capitalism passed through its cycles, manufacturers economized. That put mining companies under pressure too. Industrial relations in the west of Scotland were anyway appalling. Coalmasters almost ran their pits in a spirit of antagonism to the workers. It was not even as if they pushed to introduce new technology, often the cause of conflict in other sectors. On the contrary, they made little use of machinery that might have eased the men's toil. Needing a workforce with no more than basic skills, they seldom bothered about apprenticeships or ladders of promotion. Their obsession was with costs. Frequent strikes, in most of which the miners came off worse, offered the chance for the pits to take on cheap Irish immigrants and displace the prickly Scots. Robert Brown, factor to the duke of Hamilton, stated at a public inquiry: 'When the masters find that their men are attempting to impose unreasonable terms upon them they are compelled to introduce new men at their pits. These are generally Irish labourers, who in a few weeks learn to hew coals, and in time become tolerably expert colliers.' The country's biggest mining enterprise was Bairds of Gartsherrie, which owned many pits in the parishes of Old and New Monkland (Airdrie and Coatbridge). They reported to the same inquiry: 'We brought in Irish labourers, who had been working the pits as roadsmen. In three weeks we had the output of coal increased. We were obliged to protect them day and night'[29] – that is, from violence at the hands of the Scots whose jobs they had taken. By the time of a similar report in 1848 more than two-thirds of miners in Lanarkshire were estimated to be Irish, their number increasing with every successive strike.[30]

The essential requirement for Scottish success was to keep costs down. It proved easy given the nation's endowment of resources. Of special help were the many local conjunctions of raw material and fuel to work it, that is, of ironstone and coal lying close together in the ground. Transport was then seldom a huge problem in the compact industrial area of the west of Scotland, and even in the case of big capital investment the cost could often be soon recovered. For example, the 12-mile Monkland Canal brought into

Glasgow the coal dug in the Monklands, the richest mineral area of Lanarkshire. Started in 1770, not completed till 1792 and paying no dividend till 1807, the canal at length earned high profits. Others did not, to be sure, but steam-powered locomotives on iron railways would come to perform the job of bulk transportation over longer distances than the canals had never been equal to.[31]

In 1801 the metallurgist David Mushet discovered round Coatbridge richer and cheaper fields of blackband ironstone than the ones already in use. At first the find led to little saving, because the advantages of the raw material could not be exploited to the full so long as it was still smelted from inputs of cold air into the small furnaces, then common. The problem would be solved by the simple expedient of the hot blast, as patented in 1828 at Wilsontown in upper Lanarkshire by James Neilson, resourceful manager of Glasgow's gasworks. It involved blowing preheated air into the furnace, so minimizing the amount of fuel consumed in production. It let Scottish iron earn huge profits. The hot blast and blackband ironstone would, right through the Victorian era, provide the technical and geological bases for the low costs of processing in Scotland. They also meant that output remained basic. Scottish manufacturers preferred to produce pig iron, without working the metal further.[32]

The blackband ironstone of Lanarkshire generated vast amounts of cheap pig, so named from the shape of the containers into which the molten metal was run to cool. Bairds of Gartsherrie stood as the titans among ironmasters. Gartsherrie was their original farm near Coatbridge: they launched a vertiginous ascent out of the old steading through exploitation of the ore they happened to find under their fields. At their height they became the world's greatest producers of pig iron.[33] In 1828 Alexander Baird leased rights to mine ironstone at Gartsherrie and began to build blast furnaces there. He applied the hot blast technique just invented by Neilson. Baird himself further refined it, and raised his output from 60 to

250 tons of iron a week. When he retired in 1842, four of his sons formed a partnership, which expanded further to build ironworks and acquire coalfields all over the west of Scotland. By 1870, it produced a quarter of Scotland's pig iron, around 300,000 tons a year, from a workforce of 10,000 men and boys. And in that year it made profits of £3 million. Thomas Tancred, compiling an official report on conditions in the mining districts, described the Monklands in graphic terms:

> The groups of blast furnaces on all sides might be imagined to be blazing volcanoes at most of which smelting is continued Sunday and weekdays, by day and night without intermission. By day a perpetual steam arises from the whole length of the canal where it receives waste water from the blast engines on both sides of it and railroads traversed by long trains of wagons drawn by locomotive engines intersect the country in all directions.[34]

In Scotland output of all types of iron reached its apex at 2.5 million tons by 1857, but then fell as blackband ore became exhausted. Production of pig iron by itself did not follow the same pattern, as it could use imported ore. Output rose from 800,000 tons in 1854 to peak at 1.2 million tons in 1869; after severe contraction in the 1880s it was at about the same level in 1914.

Those figures at any rate showed how big an item pig iron remained in Scotland's industrial output. Cheap as it was, it still earned profits large enough to limit the ironmasters' interest in more advanced products. So Scotland had less incentive than other countries to keep itself at the technological cutting edge. Modern steel, using the Bessemer process, became available elsewhere from the 1850s. At this period the Scots ironmasters, far from integrating forwards into steel, were integrating backwards into coal, with the Bairds becoming employers of two out of three Scots miners.

If other local industrialists needed some special iron product of their own, they were well advised to make it themselves – just as the shipbuilding cousins Napier did, in the east end of Glasgow at Robert Napier's Parkhead forge and, in the west end of Glasgow, at David Napier's Lancefield forge.[35]

The age of steel came late to Scotland, but it came fast. Blackband ore was phosphoric, and the Bessemer process required ores low in phosphorus to make steel a material lighter, stronger and more versatile than other iron products.[36] The problem could be solved, though, and then Scottish steelmaking took off. By 1881 it had surpassed output in south Wales, thus far the industry's leading region. The pioneer was the Steel Company of Scotland, founded by Charles Tennant and others in 1872. They had started out meaning to use the blue billy that was a by-product from the pyrites of Huelva. For this project Tennant got in touch with the Anglo-German metallurgist William Siemens, who had a Scots wife, Anne, sister of Lewis Gordon, professor of electrical engineering at the University of Glasgow. Siemens, both eminent scientist and shrewd entrepreneur, ran experiments on possible uses of blue billy. Encouraged by the results, Tennant and friends decided to build a steelworks that Siemens was to design, applying the open hearth process he had developed, which was superior to the hot blast. In the event it proved too complex to work in this way with blue billy. But Siemens's plant at Cambuslang would succeed so well otherwise that it launched Scotland as a steelmaking nation. By 1885 there were ten firms producing almost half of British steel.[37]

One was Beardmore's, which went into steel in 1879. It operated from the Parkhead forge it had acquired from Robert Napier who, for all his imagination and resources, got into difficulty contracting for the Royal Navy. It had seemed a promising prospect when in 1861 he won the commission to build HMS *Black Prince*, one of the new class of ironclads. But he encountered such difficulties meeting the official specifications using the technology then available that he felt forced to turn for help to an English expert on naval construction, William Beardmore senior. Beardmore entered into partnership with Napier, moved to Glasgow and brought with him his son, William junior, who went on to found the public company of William Beardmore & Co in 1886. By the turn of the century his works at Dalmuir were the biggest in Scotland, an area of 25 acres specializing in the manufacture of steel forgings for the local shipbuilding industry. The company also started to make armour plate. It would diversify further into the guns that boomed for Britain in the First World War. It was by then already building aircraft too. Beardmore's and military munitions became synonymous.[38]

David Colville went into steel in 1880. He had opened his first plant in 1872 at the Dalzell ironworks in Motherwell. When the Tay Bridge collapsed in 1879, the young firm won the contract for supply of iron bars to a new bridge. Colville's son, David junior, spent some years working for the rival Steel Company of Scotland so as to master its technology. He then joined his father at Dalzell where they built five Siemens furnaces, each of 10 tons' capacity. With a steam hammer, plate mill and shearing plant also installed, they could supply both ship and boiler plates. They soon expanded into America, and the first steel plates rolled in the United States came from slabs supplied by Dalzell. They also sold steel to Germany: the ocean liner *Kaiser Wilhelm der Grosse*, which in 1898 won the Blue Riband for crossing the Atlantic Ocean in record time, had been built of plates from Dalzell. By the First World War, this was the biggest employer in Motherwell and the most productive steelworks in Scotland.[39]

The streamlined output of steel made a difference above all to the shipbuilding industry. The yards of the Clyde needed metal plates ever stronger and lighter. The steelworks of the west of Scotland answered those needs.

It was just on a small, local scale that shipbuilding had enjoyed any older tradition in Scotland. Glasgow did not figure in it because the Clyde was so narrow and shallow. Larger vessels needed to dock downstream, which was why Port Glasgow had been founded in 1668. The river upstream from Dumbarton was open just to barges. Then, as far as Bowling, the water ran so low and sluggish that locals might wade across if the tide was out. The channel would deepen itself when a series of breakwaters was built to make a faster current scour the bed, and the Clyde Navigation Trust, formed in 1809, took on management of the watercourse. By 1825 the river could carry vessels of 300 tons to the Broomielaw in the middle of Glasgow, but by 1857 vessels of 3,600 tons might manage. This meant ships could be built along the upper Clyde too, with the advantage of direct access to the city's iron-working and engineering shops. It is striking how these clustered in parts of Glasgow where cotton was spun, at Tradeston opposite the Broomielaw or Camlachie even further east; here lay a link between the textile cluster and the heavy industrial cluster of the new Scottish economy. But later, as ships grew in size, their construction had to be moved downstream again, to Govan and beyond. There the shipyards created a whole town: Clydebank did not exist in 1861 yet in 1901 was home to 30,000 people.[40]

The ships being built were by that time steamships, products of a long technological evolution in Glasgow. The steam engine devised in 1769 by James Watt, maker of scientific instruments to the university, marked a big step forward from its crude prototypes, but had still to exert its full economic impact. This was at first most visible in the steamboats that plied the Clyde: dinky little vessels built of wood, since not enough iron was as yet available in Scotland. They puffed their way among the sailing ships that remained the normal means of marine transport, consuming huge amounts of coal for the distances covered. There was a simple reason: steamships often broke down. They had been puffing since 1812 when Henry Bell's *Comet* began a service between Glasgow and Greenock. Ten years later, there were dozens going as far as Largs,

Campbeltown and Inveraray, with another on Loch Lomond. These services amounted to little more than tourist attractions: they stopped off for passengers taking a break in the hotel owned by Bell at Helensburgh. Trippers continued to go 'doon the watter' till the 1960s. Yet the charming scene proved more significant than it seemed. While just a small proportion of ships built in Britain was at that time launched on the Clyde, they included more than half the steamboats, forty-two of them between 1812 and 1820. Still, a huge array of technical problems had to be solved before they could be put to any more useful purpose.[41]

A technical challenge never failed to appeal to Victorian Scots, however. The challenge of steamships first appealed to the cousins Napier, from a family of engineers at Dumbarton. David was the great inventor and adaptor, the father of marine engineering as a distinct profession, while Robert was the man of affairs, whether in construction or in finance. David had made the boiler and produced the castings for the engines of the *Comet*. On the strength of that he decided to set up in production himself at Camlachie. In 1816 he delivered his first marine engine, and the next year began operating a steamship on his own account for the run up and down Loch Lomond. Then he turned to seagoing steamers. He built ferries for the routes from Greenock to Liverpool and from Holyhead to Dublin. For the maiden voyage on this latter passage he took along Charles Macintosh, who feared the boat would sink. He was wrong, and later Napier's widening experience enabled him to introduce a steady series of improvements to the design of hulls, condensers, paddles, screws and engines.[42]

Robert Napier's career took a different path. He interested himself in the concept of a regular service of steamships across the Atlantic Ocean. After investing in the enterprise due to become Cunard, he won contracts for steamers that over the next two decades grew larger and larger.[43] The Royal Navy arrived as his next lucrative customer. Other British and foreign shipping lines followed. By the

1850s this was big business. Napier's company became a magnet for all the brightest and best young managers and apprentices in the west of Scotland. He showed himself generous in the time, effort and encouragement he devoted to them: many went on to set up their own companies. Through them he left a human rather than a corporate legacy. Scottish capitalism remained clannish, with cousins co-operating and sons following fathers. Robert Napier, so resourceful in most ways, did not manage to perpetuate his own dynasty because he carried on too long himself, lost touch and in 1871 went out of business. Still, the Napiers were the true fathers of shipbuilding on the Clyde.

The hallmark of that industry lay in constant technical innovation. The original paddle steamers were propelled by means not best suited to Scotland's stormy waters – as their last representative on the Clyde, the *Waverley*, still shows. (In 1977 she ran on to rocks near Dunoon and in 2009 struck the pier there.) The idea of the screw propeller had already occurred to James Watt. But it fell to W.J. Macquorn Rankine, professor of civil engineering at the University of Glasgow, to perfect the technology in 1865 and render paddle steamers obsolete except for pleasure cruises. For two decades most new Scottish steamers had had screw propellers anyway, but now they became much more powerful and efficient.

The same period saw development of the compound marine engine, which recycled steam through more than one cylinder to exploit all its energy. William McNaught took out the original patent in Glasgow in 1845. In 1853, two of the Napiers' former apprentices, Charles Randolph and John Elder, began with the help of Macquorn Rankine their own experiments on compound engines of two cylinders. Their plan was to raise efficiency by reducing the friction of the moving parts, so as to increase power, cut coal consumption and improve safety. Where others had failed, Elder succeeded because, according to his professorial mentor, he 'had thoroughly studied and understood the principles of the then almost new science of thermodynamics'. Randolph's contribution came in exacting accuracy for gear-cutting and machining, with the result that these two graduates of the university of life on Clydeside were able to take out the further patent that would transform their industry. The company they founded was to revolutionize the powering of ships. Within two decades, their new engine was driving three-quarters of the British merchant marine.[44]

Scope for innovation on Clydeside had not been exhausted yet. Wooden sailing ships were being built well into Queen Victoria's reign – twice the number of steamships launched on the Clyde even in 1860. The final flourish in the history of sail came with the *Cutty Sark*, constructed at Dumbarton in 1879 and in service till 1895 – by which time an epoch in maritime history had reached its end, at least in any commercial sense. The new age of building in iron had started up more than half a century before, in 1837, when David Tod and John Macgregor, two more apprentices of Robert Napier, opened the first shipyard for that purpose at Mavisbank (where the pyramids stand by the Kingston Bridge now). Napier, in his unfailing benevolence, continued to work with them to improve the technology, still in its infancy and as yet more or less confined to the west of Scotland. Steamships did not triumph over sailing ships till they could be built on a much larger scale, which the technical advances of the 1860s at last allowed. In that decade more than 800,000 tons of iron steamships were launched on the Clyde.[45]

The arrival of steel-making in Scotland crowned the development; now, much stronger and lighter vessels could be constructed from material produced near at hand. By the end of the century, 97 per cent of ships from the Clyde were made of steel. It had been in 1879 that William Denny of Dumbarton launched the world's first ocean-going vessel with a steel hull, the *Rotomahana*, due to go on service in Australasia. A liberal employer by local criteria, Denny enlisted the practical experience and ideas of his men in a constant search for higher standards, offering them prizes for the

best productive improvements they could suggest. He introduced
competition into trials of his ships too, first with prototypes in a test
tank, then in real time for the finished products over a measured
mile. Out of these boyish enthusiasms grew his expertise, on hulls
in particular. He published many scientific papers on the subject
and on techniques of construction. His versatile range of products
extended to squat workaday vessels of shallow draught for use in
estuaries, a far cry from the sleek elegance of the *Rotomahana*.
Out of the fame he won from her he could embark on a huge
extension of his yard with a wet dock, longer berths and heavier
cranes. He was a canny commercial networker too: he forged
links of one kind and another with nineteen shipping lines, and
to fifteen of them he sold 770 ships, for more than £20 million,
between 1880 and 1913.[46]

Scotland by now had a great array of technical knowledge and
practical skills. But it also enjoyed the big advantage of theoretical
work in its universities, which by 1800 were already among the
best in the world. Glasgow took an early lead in certain scientific disciplines. William Cullen had become in 1744 a lecturer in the theory and practice of physic (actually a branch of
medicine), which let him branch out into chemistry through the
experience he gained with drugs and other curative substances.
Joseph Black succeeded him in his lectureship in 1756. Both were
typical enlightened Scots, anxious to place their subject on a more
rigorous theoretical footing, while at the same time interested in
practical applications that might be turned to industrial purposes.
The emergence of the modern science of chemistry had a more
immediate impact on everyday life than any other aspect of the
Scottish Enlightenment, and it would become still more important
in the nineteenth century.[47]

Physics also played a big role. Lord Kelvin, born William
Thomson in Belfast in 1824, came from a Scots-Irish family that
had maintained close links with the mother country. His own

father was a graduate of Glasgow, and after he and his son moved back in 1832 they regarded themselves as Scots. Young William, already showing signs of mathematical genius, was aged ten when he matriculated at the university. At seventeen he proceeded to Cambridge, where he found time to row for his college and win a sculling competition. All his life he loved water and the sea. Even in old age he kept a yacht in the bay off his home at Largs. After research in Paris, Kelvin was appointed to his chair at Glasgow in 1846. He held it till 1899, refusing all offers to move. Instead he used it as a base for revolutionizing instruction in academic science, extending its range with his own discoveries and tying it to industry and commerce.[48]

Kelvin's sharp, creative mind both defined basic physical laws and also suggested many fresh lines of research to other scientists. His work in pure theory would by itself have assured his fame. During lectures in 1851 and 1854, he expounded the laws of thermodynamics, those of equivalence and transformation or conservation of energy. The latter states that the earth retains the heat it receives from the sun, transforming it into other forms of energy. Kelvin demonstrated this with examples from all branches of physics. During his life he wrote more than 300 scientific papers.[49] Yet he believed 'the life and soul of science is its practical application', and acted on that too. He invented the submarine cable and superintended the laying of the first one across the Atlantic Ocean in 1858. In odd moments at sea he amused himself with improving the ship's compass. Realizing that the practical application of science depended on the quality of the instruments, he spent much of his life devising new ones. He invented the mirror galvanometer, which overcame the big problem so far dogging the long-distance telegraph (the longer the cable, the slower the transmission). He went into business in partnership with James White, a maker of optical instruments. The firm of Kelvin & White manufactured and marketed instruments for electrical and optical measurement, for transmission by telegraph and for aids to navigation. By the 1890s it employed 200 skilled technicians in Britain's largest and most versatile laboratory. Kelvin also took out patents connected with his submarine cables and formed another company to handle this business. In 1879 the patents earned him £5,500, more than five times his professorial salary.[50]

There was no shortage of other Glaswegians with the trained minds and scientific experience to set up and run factories making profitable use of advances in knowledge. It helped that Glasgow was the university where the national tradition of the democratic intellect kept going best. A quarter of its students in the late nineteenth century were drawn from the working class, many to study part time after they had embarked on industrial or commercial careers. On the principle of open access, they dropped in and out of courses as it suited them: of 3,000 students at Glasgow between 1871 and 1876, 36 per cent went for one session, 17 per cent for two and only 47 per cent for more than two. Otherwise they earned a living like everybody else. Kelvin held that practical training should not take place in a university: 'There is a limit to the functions of a university, which is to impart and to certify the scientific knowledge, but not to certify the practical skills of the candidates.'[51]

Right into the twentieth century, all seemed well on Clydeside. This region, for some time now the global leader in shipbuilding, was still setting records: the peak came in 1913 when it produced an amazing 23 per cent of the world's ships, with one launched for every day of the year. At its heart Glasgow claimed the title of Second City of the Empire, and in an industrial sense the claim was almost modest. With the towns round it, it made one-fifth of the steel, one-half of the horsepower of ships' engine, one-third of the railway locomotives and rolling stock, and most of the sewing machines in Britain. In no other part of the world had such a combination of forces come together to ensure jobs for the workers, fortunes for their bosses and goods for the rest of the human race. The heavy industry, shipbuilding above all, left a deep mark on the nation, apparent even today in popular myth, on the gaunt remains of the yards and in works of art, such as the vigorous etchings of Muirhead Bone. His friend, the journalist Charles Montague, put into words the world he depicted:

> There are some kinds of manual work in which men do not easily take pride – work for which there is nothing to show, or only some trivial or rubbishy thing. It is not so with the building of ships. When the riveter's heater-boy said, 'Whaer wid the *Loocitania* hae been if it hadna been for me heatin' the rivets?' he expressed a feeling that runs through the whole of a shipbuilding yard from the manager down... Each man or boy employed in building a steamer or battleship feels himself to be part-owner of something organic, mighty, august, with a kind of personal life of its own and a career of high service, romance and adventure before it. For him it comes to the birth on the day when it ceases to be an inert bulk of metal propped into position with hundreds of struts and dog-shores. At last the helpless rigid mass detaches itself quietly like an iceberg leaving the parent floe, and majestically assumes its prerogative of riding its proper element, serene, assured and dominant. For the builder of ships nothing can stale the thrill of that moment or deaden his triumphant sense of parenthood.[52]

All might have seemed well, yet in reality some things were not so rosy. Foreign competition was growing. Germany, reunified since 1871, embarked on a deliberate naval expansion that also had a spin-off in the construction of passenger liners convertible to warships if need be, and able to cross the Atlantic faster than British vessels. Japan, too, started up the shipbuilding that continues to this day from the expertise of apprentices it sent to Glasgow.[53] American construction, both naval and commercial, had long been something the British needed to keep a wary eye on. Mounting now into the ranks of the great powers, the United States founded its global fortunes on just the sort of heavy industry Scotland had pioneered. But Scotland was a small country: given their population and resources, the Germans, Japanese and Americans were perhaps bound in the end to outdo the Scots.

There were problems closer to home, not that they went unrecognized. On the contrary, a good deal of gloom pervaded Clydeside, though perhaps in Calvinist Scotland that is always so. It was disturbing how, for two or three decades now, some ships had had to be built at a loss, with yards taking their chances against fierce competition in unpredictable trading conditions.[54] Another way of dealing with such pressure was to seek business within Britain rather than from abroad, and from the public rather than private sector – in other words, to win work from the Royal Navy. In the era of an arms race with the Germans, this might have seemed sensible; but times did in the end change, if after a world war. And then it was found that the commercial acumen forged by fierce international competition had been lost, too.

Perhaps there was anyway something flawed in Scotland's way of doing business, inhibiting the long-term consolidation of the industrial lead. Bosses tended to be self-made men or the offspring of founding figures who had learned the ropes in apprenticeships. Charles Tennant the elder launched his career as apprentice to a weaver at Kilbarchan. The first skills Robert Napier acquired lay in ornamental metalwork. James Neilson started out in adult life as a gig-boy on a winding engine at Govan. Charles Randolph began as a wright in a coachworks at Stirling. David Colville the younger went as a third-hand melter to the Steel Company of Scotland once he finished his schooling at Glasgow Academy.[55]

Scots liked to keep business in the family, or at most in a

partnership of friends from the same place or generation.[56] Their every tradition and instinct spoke for working up from a diminutive scale. It had served them well in building the whole fabric of their society. The leaders of business showed in their patronage and philanthropy an intense commitment to their local communities, working there together whereas in the rest of the business of life they competed.

There was a counterpart to this in how business was carried out; in Scotland, more than in the rest of Britain, formal industrial concentration remained rare before 1914. Scots law had shaped Scotland's commercial habits, and it made every partnership a legal personality that could sue or be sued, transfer shares and, to an extent, offer limited liability. This was something for family and friends rather than for a wider, more impersonal circle of rational investors. In the running of the companies, there was little room for professional managers as long as the founders or inheritors were still around: for example, one reason so many brilliant rising men left the family firm of Robert Napier was that they knew his son James was waiting to take over after him (though James, in the event, died young).[57] On the other hand, when the proprietor had also been the manager, he grew into his commercial skills along with his business. But by the turn of the twentieth century many companies were already of such a size that most managerial functions needed delegation to a staff of subordinates who had not grown with the business and absorbed all its lessons, in the manner of the founders.[58] In neither case did management and enterprise quite come together any more.

The Glasgow of 1914 had for all its superlative industrial achievements given hostages to fortune. Its successes depended on the steady expansion of global commerce and the world's willingness to carry goods and people in Clyde-built ships. But while the Victorian era, and the early years of the twentieth century, had in general been a period of international free trade, war and slump brought back protectionism after this, even to Britain itself. That destroyed the external basis for Glasgow's prosperity. Within the city, too, secure jobs and incomes had in the old days subdued social conflict and kept recalcitrance among the workers to a minimum. Now that internal basis was destroyed as well.[59]

Yet the First World War did not at first feel like a turning point. On the contrary, demands on the traditional economy for production of coal and steel, or expertise in engineering and ship-building, had never been higher. Textiles did well, too, given the need for uniforms and sandbags, while explosives did best of all. For this classic complex of Clydeside's industries the contemporary shorthand expression was munitions, a term with wider reference than it carries today (David Lloyd George became minister of munitions, which meant much more than seeing to the supply of bullets). As fighting on the western front and elsewhere got bogged down, munitions became the intense focus of attention from the government in London as a key to victory in this conflict, which was now straining the resources of all the leading industrial countries. And the government in London felt it should be getting more out of Clydeside for the war effort. Older structures there were not geared to urgent mass production, and efforts to force the pace provoked unrest. The workforce, once so reliable and disciplined, turned militant: the Red Clyde sprang to life.[60]

But the aim at the grassroots was not so much revolution as preservation of skilled men's privileges against a drive to dilute them. This meant bringing in other workers (sometimes even women, sometimes even Americans) who would not ask for the same money or insist on the same restrictive practices. Strife spread through the social fabric; there was in 1915 a rent strike too. The social situation looked grim, yet the riot in George Square on January 31, 1919, identified by Marxists as Glasgow's missed revolutionary moment, remained just that.[61]

Still, alienation outlasted not only this crisis but also the revival afterwards of global trade during a brief boom to repair the ravages of war. Boom soon gave way to bust in a pattern then repeated several times over. The protectionism adopted in country after country put an end to all hope of restoring Victorian free trade. But no other remedy emerged. In the 1920s never less than 14 per cent of the insured workforce in Scotland was out of a job. In the 1930s, when global commerce collapsed, unemployment in the west of Scotland averaged more than 25 per cent. None of this could with any conviction be blamed on industrial agitators, favourite scapegoats though they were of politicians and business-men. The halcyon days of the nineteenth century were gone because the underlying conditions had changed.[62]

Instead, new conditions appeared, in politics and in business. The Labour Party, insignificant in Glasgow before the war, and not much better even by 1918, won a majority of the city's parliamentary seats in the general election of 1922. But it fell to businessmen to cure an ailing capitalism. There had to be industrial closures and other forms of rationalization that were bound to antagonize the workers. Corporate strategies, even when devised by solemn national councils and committees, could be ruined by central economic policies such as the return to the gold standard in 1925. While local infrastructure might be improved and the range of production diversified, that course also often meant scrapping redundant or out-of-date plants and concentrating output in more efficient units.[63]

Two businessmen dominated this scene: William, Lord Weir and Sir James Lithgow. They came out of old industrial sectors, engineering in Weir's case and shipbuilding in Lithgow's, but their ideas were new. Weir was a pragmatist, not shrinking from intervention by government where he thought private capitalism had failed. In the case of electricity, he even borrowed from the Soviet Union, with his proposals for a national grid and standardized frequencies. As far as he was concerned, the economic future lay in the hands of the British state, and the successors to his noble title have not deviated from his view.[64] Lithgow relied rather on his own personal investment and encouraged others to follow his example. In 1930 he was instrumental in setting up the National Shipbuilders Security. Financed largely out of his own ample pocket, though backed by the Bank of England, it bought up excess capacity in the shipyards and 'sterilized' them till such time as they might become viable again. Cynics noted how this gave him a stake in old rivals, Beardmore's or Fairfield, yet he ploughed the money he made back into these firms, and it seems doubtful if he ever made much personal profit. His motives lay rather in a sense of duty towards industry and employment in the west of Scotland. Co-operation was his watchword, but it only mitigated rather than negated the workings of the markets.[65]

The approach did seem to start paying off when the markets at last rallied somewhat and Clydeside's shipyards under rejuvenated management proved able to meet the demand. The launch of the *Queen Mary* in 1934 seemed a symbol of better times to come, though not until 1939 did shipbuilding output rise to the level seen before 1914. About 180,000 idle workers had by then found jobs again, while the bosses boosted capital investment. The cycle seemed to be repeating itself during the Second World War, when business boomed as convoys crossed the Atlantic to keep Britain fed and armed in the struggle against Germany; this brought tragic losses of shipping and sailors, not to speak of the bombing of Clydebank. But overall another war was good for business. Would its end mean another slump, too?[66]

Yet the Scotland of 1945 turned out to be different from the Scotland of 1918. The main difference lay in the much more powerful intervention now made by central government. During the Second World War the government established a command economy going well beyond the dimensions of the trial run in the First World War, and not just in military materiel. It also prepared the way for the welfare state and inaugurated regional aid, grasping at a new kind of centralized British polity conceived as a single unit, run by politicians and civil servants from London. Up to this point businessmen had learned to work with them, but the relationship would be recast when the Labour government after 1945 undertook an extensive programme of nationalization. It was heavy industry (though not yet shipbuilding) that got taken over by the state. And since the west of Scotland contained so much heavy industry, the measures came at the cost of a local capitalist class that lost its traditional function of leading economic change. According to the Unionist MP for Kelvingrove and former Scottish secretary, Walter Elliot, 'the transfer by statute of the control of the whole [sic] of Scottish industry to Westminster is not nationalization, it is denationalization.'[67] The old bosses did not vanish, but found something else to do. The Lithgow family, for example, was deprived of its stake in Colville's and Beardmore's and for the future concentrated its investments in other marine or even agricultural sectors. Any wider damage remained limited while the global economy entered a long boom. In Glasgow unemployment, the most salient economic indicator, stayed much lower than before the war. Even so it was higher than in the rest of Britain, while incomes lagged about 10 per cent behind the average. A region that cannot export its goods will export its people, and emigrants from the west of Scotland skimmed off about three-quarters of its natural increase in population. Basic problems had yet to be solved.

The industry left in local hands found it no easier to meet the challenges. The North British Locomotive Company went out of business in 1963, while the St Rollox chemical works was closed and razed to the ground in 1964. But the crisis in shipbuilding assumed the starkest form. By the 1960s most shipyards along the Clyde were losing money, too. They took longer to build and deliver ships than foreign rivals, no doubt because of failings in management, but above all because of delays caused by poor industrial relations. In 1965, Fairfield suffered financial collapse. A novel sort of rescue was mounted. A reorganized company, Fairfield (Glasgow) Ltd, came into being with support alike from government, private enterprise and trades unions. The price exacted by the last was higher wages – and at a level other shipbuilders had not so far seen their way to paying. As a separate venture, this did not last beyond 1968, but it provided a model for effort on a grander scale.[68]

Now under pressure to pay Fairfield's kind of wages, other shipbuilders on the Clyde found their problems worsening: only a relative newcomer, Yarrow's (here since 1906), might be sure of survival because it had won a lot of naval contracts. The rest could either sink separately or try to remain afloat together, in a general merger for further rationalization. This was the solution given official sanction in the report of a committee chaired in 1967 by Lord Geddes, a shipping magnate. It argued that to stand a chance of growing, individual shipyards should be joined together in groups. Those on the Clyde offered a convenient example: they could share resources for research and development, then produce a wider range of vessels.[69]

The report led to the formation of Upper Clyde Shipbuilders in 1968, taking over five shipyards along the river. The men in all received wages on a par with the best paid before. In exchange, UCS slimmed its workforce and sought some rationalization. But just three years into the bold experiment, it was faltering. The one good yard, Yarrow's, resumed its independence. A liquidator was appointed for the four surviving units in June 1971. The men there, led by Communist shop stewards, Jimmy Reid and Jimmy Airlie, staged a work-in. They occupied the yards and carried on with jobs in hand, being paid by the liquidator out of the remaining assets.[70] A commercial problem became political. In London there was again a Conservative government, which events showed to be even less likely than a Labour one to let shipbuilding on the Clyde sink. In the light of the region's militant history, Tories deemed it advisable to continue a policy of support for its ailing industries, till something or other turned up.

After a further reorganization, the sole survivor of UCS, Govan Shipbuilders, carried on with the support of lavish grants and loans: Weegie wit dubbed the yard Treasure Island. In 1977 another Labour government decided to nationalize the whole industry, not just in Scotland but as one big company, British Shipbuilders. In 1998, under a later Tory government and its programme of privatization, something did turn up: a Norwegian company, Kvaerner, bought the site to supply oilfields in the North Sea. As this market in its turn dipped, BAE, Britain's biggest producer of armaments, took over in 2008. Today it holds Govan to ransom, since the government in London has said it will continue to procure equipment from the yard only so long as Scotland remains part of the United Kingdom.[71] On the other hand, many shipyards in the world make their money primarily from foreign orders.

Shipbuilding, for more than a century the defining economic activity along the Clyde, today faces a more uncertain future than ever. Problems dog not just a single industry, never existing in isolation in this part of the world, but a cluster of other manufacturing activities that have tracked its rise and fall. Even after 1945, fresh initiatives were taken for the west of Scotland, in steel, cars and electronics. The question arose whether they could mutually support and reinforce each other as older counterparts had done in Victorian Glasgow.[72]

To Scots it seemed inconceivable that their economy could ever flourish without steel. But it was an industry in which great technological changes had taken place worldwide after 1945, with enormous improvements in productivity. In Scotland there still existed steel-making capacity that dated from the nineteenth century; modernization all round was needed before the industry could reap the benefits of continuous output. A response came in the construction by Colville's, now left as the biggest producer in the country, of the first integrated Scottish steel-mill at Ravenscraig in Lanarkshire between 1951 and 1957. Though bang in the middle of industrial Scotland, the location was otherwise problematic. There were no supplies of iron ore at hand; it had to come from afar and be landed at the nearest port, Hunterston in Ayrshire, then trundled overland to the works by rail. Nor, with the continued decline of heavy industry in Scotland, were there many nearby customers for the finished products, however superlative. It came as some surprise that Ravenscraig lasted as long as it did: soon threatened with closure, it was saved time and again by frantic protests. Its time was up in 1992, when the manufacture of steel on a large scale in Scotland ceased.[73]

Ravenscraig might have been saved if Scotland had had a car industry. But Scotland did not. While, in Glasgow, Albion Motors had started making cars in 1899, the company later confined itself to commercial vehicles. It missed the huge expansion of the market in cars that started with a gradual return to prosperity in the 1930s. Two more decades passed before the British manufacturer, Rootes, could be induced to set up a factory at Linwood in Renfrewshire, even then with lavish incentives. Cars need a wide range of accessories, and it was expected suppliers would now spring up round the west of Scotland. Yet Rootes, like other domestic producers, was itself already in decline, pushed faster by the expansion to Scotland. In 1967 Linwood was sold off to the Chrysler Corporation of America. This venture did not work out either, and in 1975 the British government stepped in with new money on condition of heavy redundancies at the plant. Chrysler in turn disposed of Linwood to the French company, Peugeot, which closed it down in 1981. So ended the brief history of Scottish car-making.[74]

The arrival of the American electronic corporation, IBM, at Greenock in 1953 seemed to herald a fresh phase of modernization in Scotland, promising because unrelated to the decayed Victorian inheritance. At first the factory made typewriters, printers and other commercial equipment, but in 1981 it began producing personal computers. Alas, this could not be sustained in the long run either: IBM, like its rivals, shifted simple tasks of assembly to the developing world once the workers there could be trained (and paid less). Today there are still 2,000 employees at IBM Greenock, most of them in a call centre, but the huge manufacturing halls stand empty. Other American companies had been attracted to what became known as Silicon Glen, hailed as an electronic cluster for the future. But again they concentrated on the assembly of products rather than on research and development. Without that, there could be little spin-off to home-grown enterprises. British governments seemed more interested in pulling off coups in inward investment than in setting tougher terms for the incentives offered. When the global high-tech industry hit a crisis in 2000, its Scottish subsidiaries went into a decline from which they have never recovered. One by one they followed IBM's example. The last to go was Texas Instruments, formerly National Semiconductor, which in 2016 transferred 400 jobs from Greenock to America, Germany and Japan – not even to a developing country.[75]

Glasgow was by now a post-industrial city. It continued to breed entrepreneurs – David Murray, Tom Hunter, Jim McColl – in the same way if not in the same profusion as in earlier times. They founded businesses run as well here as anywhere else. But, successful as they all were, they had no chance of restoring to the city and its region the former economic pre-eminence, not in the shape of a complex of different activities reinforcing one another. This became, like Scotland in general, a place for small and medium enterprises, interspersed with a few bigger companies (almost all in energy or finance) owned and run from elsewhere. Grandiose schemes for a reinvigorated industrial nation vanished from public discourse, because there seemed no point in even talking about it: after the defeat of so many initiatives, it was just never going to happen. At least Glasgow reconciled itself to this fate with some flair. A future as the centre of art, design, fashion and general hedonism would no doubt be more fun than the metal-bashing past, though whether it would have the same sustaining power remained to be seen. Just as uncertain was how this renewed local economy, with nothing imperial left in it, would relate to the British state. Perhaps independence was its true political expression – or so many Glaswegians seemed to think in the referendum of 2014.

3

Religion: 'Twa kingdomes'

BY NOVEMBER 28, 1638, James, marquess of Hamilton, had
had enough: a rough week as royal commissioner to the General
Assembly of the Church of Scotland, its members packed into
Glasgow Cathedral, at last came to an end. Every day the assembly
had remained in session hour after hour, pitting him against its
serried ranks of Covenanters intent on revolutionary change.
Theirs was on the surface a conservative revolution – they meant
above all to overthrow the religious innovations introduced by
King Charles I, and before him by his father King James VI, so as
to restore the pristine purity of Presbyterianism, in accord with the
National Covenant signed by crowds of Scots the previous winter.[1]

Yet the wide appeal showed that the Covenant, while first and
foremost concerned with the Kirk, was also the sign of something
deeper going on in Scotland. It arose from a desire for the nation
to be governed by its own will, if need be in defiance of a hereditary
monarchy that had turned alien since the Union of Crowns in
1603. Right through 1638, Hamilton and his king played for time
while in fact preparing to suppress the Covenanters by force. The
Covenanters responded with preparations of their own, and it
grew clear they could not be intimidated. In the end there had

been no choice but to summon to Glasgow the General Assembly they called for.[2]

Hamilton never got on top of the proceedings. At almost every turn a determined moderator, the Revd Alexander Henderson, and a resourceful lay leader, the lawyer Archibald Johnston of Wariston, foiled him.[3] It did not help that all three knew any concessions the royal commissioner made in the king's name were unlikely to be honoured by Charles I. The early sessions were largely taken up with procedural issues, the mode of election to membership of the assembly, the powers of the ministers and elders constituting it and so on. It was a bad sign for Hamilton that over these points he had to wrangle bitterly, with some of his peers already taking the Covenanters' side. He owed his own position to a surmise by his king that, as a potent figure in the society of the west of Scotland, he would succeed in overawing even people like that. In reality there was no chance.

The Covenanters had during their preparations manipulated matters to ensure the assembly would come under their control and stay under it, even if most of the ministers in attendance were probably moderate in sentiment. As something more than a clerical movement, the Covenanters could bring to Glasgow an overbearing contingent of lay elders. There were sixty-three presbyteries in Scotland; together they nominated seventeen peers, nine knights of their shires and twenty-five lairds, quite apart from forty-seven commissioners from the burghs. Also admitted were the noblemen who had signed the National Covenant, four to six gentlemen from each presbytery to accompany its commissioners, up to six lay assessors to attend each burgh commissioner – and any gentlemen not otherwise chosen might come anyway. The hangers-on had no voting rights: they were there to daunt the moderate majority of ministers.[4]

With the preliminaries of the General Assembly finally over, the fateful November 28 was to be devoted to substantive business.

Removal of bishops from the Church of Scotland stood at the top of the agenda. They had not themselves dared to turn up in Glasgow, so it fell to Hamilton to state their case to the assembly. His main argument was that the assembly had no authority to take action against them. He asked the clerk to read out a message from the king promising various reforms, but pointedly not including the end of episcopacy.

Henderson rose to reply, first stating in broad terms: 'It hath been the glory of the Reformed Churches, and we account it our glory after a special manner, to give unto kings and Christian magistrates what belongs unto their places; next to piety towards God we are obliged unto loyalty and obedience to our king. There is nothing due unto kings and princes in matter ecclesiastical which I trust by this assembly shall be denied unto our king.' But he had a sting in the tail for the royal commissioner: 'What is Caesar's and what is ours let it be given to Caesar, but let the God by whom kings reign have his own place and prerogative.'

Hamilton, a public servant of long standing as military commander, diplomat and courtier, was not easily drawn into confrontation: 'Sir, ye have spoken as a good Christian and dutiful subject... I am hopeful that you will conduct yourself with that deference you owe to your royal sovereign, all of whose commands will, I trust, be found agreeable to the commandments of God.' In any event, his own function here was 'to defend royal authority and monarchical government already established, under which I do conceive episcopacy to be comprehended... I stand to the king's prerogative as supreme judge over all causes civil and ecclesiastical.'

Henderson was not to be put off either, and he persisted: 'I now ask if this assembly find themselves competent judges of the prelates.'

Before the assembly could make any kind of reply, Hamilton interjected: 'If you proceed to the censure of their persons and offices I must remove myself.'

Henderson retorted, 'Nay, with your Grace's permission that cannot be... A thousand times I wish the contrary from the bottom of my heart, and that your Grace would favour us with your presence without obstructing the work and freedom of this assembly.'

But Hamilton told Henderson to close the proceedings at once with prayer. When the moderator still stood his ground, the royal commissioner himself declared the dissolution of the assembly in the name of the king. Nothing done there was to have authority over any subject of the realm, and if the members tried to continue their session they would be guilty of treason. Hamilton then rose from his chair and made for the door at the other end of the nave of Glasgow Cathedral. As usual, it had been kept locked during the session. Now the key was apparently not to be found. Hamilton could only fume at this final discomfiture before he got out into the open air. Whatever we may think of his position, we can feel for him when he wrote to the king saying that 'next Hell I hate this place'.[5]

Hamilton called a meeting of the Privy Council and issued a proclamation confirming and justifying his action, but the assembly continued to sit in defiance of him. Now even leading members who had so far kept their views to themselves moved into open support for the Covenanters, notably Archibald Campbell, earl of Argyll, and seven others of the king's privy councillors. Left to its own devices, the assembly got down to the real business in hand and worked hard at it: the Revd Robert Baillie, minister of Kilwinning, recalled with austere glee how it was resolved 'to have but one session in the day, to sit from 10 or 11 to 4 or 5, so we were all relieved of the expense of a dinner'.[6] The result was a list of measures defying royal authority, overturning the religious establishment and creating a constitutional crisis that in the end could be resolved only by war. On December 6, the assembly annulled the king's book of canons and his prayer book. On December 8, it abjured episcopacy. On December 10, it condemned the Five Articles of Perth, which since 1618 had been anglicizing the Kirk's forms of worship. On December 13 it individually deposed and excommunicated the incumbent bishops. On December 19 it forbade clerics to hold civil office. On December 20 it reinstituted annual general assemblies. In two weeks this Glasgow assembly had done its work, and the Covenanting revolution was well under way.

Glasgow made a fitting scene for such a momentous gathering, because in its history its religion has played a part at least as crucial as any of its secular activities and achievements. During medieval times the city had, along with St Andrews, been one of the nation's chief religious centres. In 1492 the see of Glasgow was erected into an archbishopric. Its archbishop held authority over the bishops of Argyll, Dunblane, Dunkeld and Galloway. This authority was no doubt bolstered by the fact that Glasgow had housed a university from 1451. The constant comings and goings of prelates, clerics and students kept up lively contacts with the currents of spiritual and intellectual life in Europe. But, though it was an age of change, Glasgow stayed orthodox.[7] Although by the sixteenth century Edinburgh was being acknowledged as the capital of the country, and the greater events of the Reformation of 1560 would be played out there, Glasgow's role remained important. Paradoxically, in view of the previous Catholic history, it could be said that the ultimate character of the Scottish Reformation came to be determined in Glasgow.

The reformer John Knox had spent much of his time and effort on religious battles in Edinburgh, where he was minister of St Giles. How far Knox himself wanted to institute a Presbyterian Church of Scotland on the lines others would lay down by the end of the sixteenth century is something about which reasonable men can differ. Rather, this church's actual construction had been the work of a second and Glaswegian generation of reformers, led by Andrew Melville. After Knox died in 1572 Melville, at the time teaching in the Calvinist college of Geneva, returned to Scotland

and became principal of the University of Glasgow. There had been ambiguities in certain positions taken up by Knox, a man of action rather than of ideas; Melville was a more consistent Calvinist, who bequeathed to Scotland much of what we now regard as essentially Presbyterian, especially the source of authority in the Kirk.[8]

According to Melville, this source of authority should be the church's assemblies. In place of Catholic hierarchy, spiritual jurisdiction and government were to be exercised not by the membership at large but by the narrower circles of those elected to perform specialized functions within it, in local presbyteries, in regional synods, in the national General Assembly. Nor should the sovereign have any dedicated role, unlike in England. Melville was one of the clerics who worked on the *Second Book of Discipline* (1578), drawing up a programme for Presbyterianism, not now as a reforming force but as the established religion of the country. It denounced any notion of intermediate, earthly headship of the church, either papal or princely, as 'ane title falslie usurpit be antichryst' which 'aucht not to be attributit to angell or to mane of quhat estait soevir he be, saiffing to Chryst, the heid and onlie monarche in this kirk'. Kings and civil magistrates, as members of the church, should consent to hear God's word through the voices of its ministers, and so 'reverence the majestie of the sone of God speiking be thame'.[9]

It was fitting that Melville served as moderator of the General Assembly in 1578, 1582, 1587 and 1594. But his relations with King James VI were always fraught. The two of them had a famous encounter at Falkland Palace in Fife when Melville said: 'Thair is twa Kings and twa Kingdomes in Scotland. Thair is Chryst Jesus the King, and his Kingdome the Kirk, whase subject King James the Saxt is, and of whose kingdome nocht a king, nor a lord, nor a heid, bot a member!'[10] In the end Melville so annoyed his monarch that he was sent into exile, and died in 1622 among the Calvinist community of Sedan in France.[11]

King James VI meanwhile brought back bishops to the Church of Scotland. To the archdiocese of Glasgow he appointed men he held in high regard, notably John Spottiswoode. In the next reign Spottiswoode would also be made lord chancellor of the kingdom and was to symbolize to his countrymen what seemed to them the obnoxious ideal of a nation run by conformist clerics. Under this regime, the church turned careless of the character of popular religion. Dissidents might seek out a minister also unwilling to conform or else, especially in the burghs, they might attend a privy kirk, which worshipped behind closed doors according to forms agreeable to its members. In effect they revived the proto-Protestant privy kirks that had arisen before the Reformation in a still Catholic Scotland. The available evidence does not point to any privy kirk in Glasgow; one is attested at Ayr, but whether others existed in the west of Scotland remains obscure.[12]

A privy kirk was yet quite a long way from the field conventicle, which emerged into the light of day during the 1620s as a popular form of religion. Indeed it was anything but privy, and rather relished its defiant acts of devotion in the open air. They took place especially in the west of Scotland under rebellious ministers such as the Revds Robert Blair of Ayr and John Livingstone of Stranraer.[13] They attracted big crowds in services that went on for hours or even days – a famous example came in June 1630 when Livingstone preached to 500 people in heavy drizzle at the bleak village of Shotts in Lanarkshire. Religious revival rebounded back into regular worship; it was reported during the ministry of the Revd David Dickson at Irvine in Ayrshire that 'few Sabbaths did passe without some evidently converted, and some convincing proofes of the power of God accompanying his word.'[14]

Foundations were being laid for the Presbyterians' triumph in the National Covenant of 1638, and then the Solemn League and Covenant of 1643 by which the English promised to accept a Scottish sort of church too (though they never actually did, and abandoned their commitment as soon as they could). In Scotland conventicles were now no longer necessary, but the memory of them obviously did not die because they sprang to life again after the Restoration of 1660, once more as a vehicle of resistance to the renewed royalist regime in the church, and indeed in everything else. The resistance reached a grisly climax towards the end of the reign of King Charles II. In May 1679 a gang of Covenanters murdered the Revd James Sharp, archbishop of St Andrews, on the open road in Fife.[15]

That event in the east of Scotland above all electrified the Covenanting heartland of the west. On June 1 a huge conventicle gathered on Loudoun Hill at the border of Ayrshire and Lanarkshire. John Graham of Claverhouse, earning his nickname of Bluidy Claverhouse, took charge of local operations to maintain order. He advanced towards the conventicle with an armed force, but was repulsed at the Battle of Drumclog. The Covenanters' elation did not last long, for three weeks later they faced a far more formidable expedition led by James, duke of Monmouth, to whom his natural father the king had entrusted the pacification of Scotland. He routed the rebels at the Battle of Bothwell Brig, but then ordered his prisoners to be treated leniently. Mere human mercy made no difference to a Covenanter, however. The last remnant left at liberty retreated to the hills and moors in still greater intransigence, even by Presbyterian standards. In a declaration of 1680 that Richard Cameron made at Sanquhar in Dumfriesshire, they renounced all allegiance to the crown, resolved to wage war on Charles II as an enemy of God and condemned the prospective succession of James, duke of Albany.[16]

For the mainstream of Presbyterians, meanwhile still submitting perforce to royal tyranny, the hour of liberation was at hand. The Revolution that broke out in November 1688 put them back in charge of the Church of Scotland, even though nobody in authority spoke any longer of the Covenants. The people of Glasgow found

more immediate targets: in January 1689 rioters 'rabbled' the
incumbent Episcopalian clergymen and their families from kirk
and manse. That summer, a free poll for the town council made a
local Presbyterian leader, John Anderson of Dowhill, lord provost.
The new council set about transforming Glasgow into a stronghold
of the re-established Presbyterianism. So Glasgow would remain
right through the Union and Enlightenment of the period ahead.[17]

Still, as within the burgh, persecution more widely had softened
the obduracy of the faithful who survived it. The character of the
Kirk was in fact now a compromise, not to be preserved in eternal
Covenants but at best evolving towards an evangelical piety, asking
of its members observance rather than martyrdom. All the same,
some of the older religious controversies carried over beyond
the Union. In 1712, Westminster passed two Acts of Parliament
designed to weaken Presbyterianism: the Toleration Act, which
legalized separate worship for Episcopalians, and the Patronage
Act, which gave wealthy landowning heritors the right to appoint
parochial ministers.[18] Under protest, the General Assembly sub-
mitted to these laws, and inside the British state it did not have
much choice anyhow. But those of the faithful who disapproved
started to seek redress in their own way.

In Glasgow it was in any event the town council that had acquired
the patronage of the six churches within its bounds. For these
charges it usually favoured evangelical Presbyterians, and the results
were on the whole positive: patrons, ministers and congregations
turned out much more agreeable to one another here than in the
rest of Scotland. In 1723 the Revd John MacLaurin was called to
the Ramshorn Church in the northwestern parish. A Gael from
Argyll, he overcame Glaswegian prejudice against his 'Highland
accent, which disgusted a nice ear'.[19] He gave stirring sermons that
even today read as fine examples of evangelical preaching. In his
theology he remained uncompromising: the doctrine expounded
by him and his fellows was the orthodox Calvinist one, denying

that the human race might be good by nature or that its works could bring about general salvation. And in other discourses he 'made it his business to inculcate upon the conscientious inhabitants the necessity of doing their part to bear down wickedness by giving information against offenders'.[20] He encouraged a Society for the Reformation of Manners to be set up in Glasgow, one of several in Scotland dedicated to enforcing virtue on the people. Sinners might be unregenerate, but they could still be chastised.[21]

Yet there was a more charitable side to all this, too. On MacLaurin's arrival in Glasgow, he had been at once struck by the presence of 'four or five hundred Highlanders who do not understand the English'.[22] All were poverty-stricken, some destitute – which seemed to make a mockery of one early product of the Scottish Reformation, the Poor Law of 1574. As John Knox had said, 'We are not patrons for stubborn and idle beggars who, running from place to place, make a craft of their begging... but for the widow and fatherless, the aged, impotent and lamed... that they may feel some benefit of Christ Jesus now preached to them.'[23] Little could actually be done about this amid the mayhem of the seventeenth century, but MacLaurin now tried to turn pious hope into social reality for Glasgow. In 1733 he took a lead in establishing the Town Hospital, financed by voluntary contributions of the faithful and offering some basic shelter and care, so that at least beggars could be taken off the streets.

Evangelicals still worried about the general condition of the Kirk, which even now seemed to them neither perfect nor secure. They identified its underlying malady as spiritual rather than theological or ecclesiastical, something therefore requiring spiritual remedies. MacLaurin's colleague and friend at Kilsyth, the Revd James Robe, compared an apparent loss of vitality with the vigour of an earlier era and found a 'sensible decay as to the life and power of godliness' leading to a 'dead and barren time'.[24] In 1742 he and MacLaurin, together with the Revd William MacCulloch of Cambuslang and

other ministers from round the country, organized the so-called
Cambuslang Wark (or Revival). It was to all intents and purposes
a conventicle, drawing on the courageous Covenanting history
to inspire a fresh surge of religious enthusiasm, though now
peacefully. Once again, tens of thousands of ordinary folk gathered
in a village just south of Glasgow for sermons and communion in
the open air. 'God was with both ministers and people in a more
remarkable way than ever I was witness to before,' wrote a visitor
from Edinburgh, the Revd John Erskine.[25]

MacLaurin was a complex man, combining his enthusiastic
religion with modern intellectual interests. He had enjoyed a higher
education as good as Scots could get at the time, first at Glasgow
and then at Leiden in the Netherlands. Glaswegians showed no
less admiration for this scholarly side to him: when in 1743 he put
himself forward as a candidate for the chair of theology at their
university, 'the people of the city and neighbourhood interested
themselves warmly in the fate of this election... as it was indeed
an event of no small consequence to the future education of their
clergy.' He held forth not only in the pulpit but also in print.
His essays, published in 1755 after his death, included, for example,
a 'Philosophical Inquiry into the Nature of Happiness', which stood
up well against any other work of the early Enlightenment. So he
was a respectable candidate for an academic chair, besides carrying
'the good wishes of a much larger body [than the professorial
electors], even all the rest of the town'. Yet he lost on the rector's
casting vote.[26]

Evangelicals might get their way in the town, upholding orthodoxy and revering the Covenants. But the gown, or those wearing
it, had other purposes – for example, a pioneering interest in
ethical theory as the means to a moral life in an increasingly secular
society. The university's foremost teacher of divinity from 1708,
John Simson, had breathed in the heady atmosphere of Dutch
freedom while also studying at Leiden. Holland was, like Scotland,

a Calvinist country, and Scots students should have been able to go there to complete their education without risking any taint to their orthodoxy (as indeed MacLaurin showed). Yet Holland, which tolerated its religious minorities while also remaining open to the world as a great trading nation, was not a place to trail behind in its thinking. On the contrary, it stood at the forefront of intellectual development in Europe.[27]

Once back in the rather different air of his native country, Simson carried this liberating experience with him. He was a fine teacher. He got his students to write essays and criticize the efforts of their fellows. He encouraged them to meet for prayer or discussion outside his regular classes and gave them topics to debate. He wanted them not to parrot him but to think for themselves and reach conclusions they could expound and defend. His matter matched his manner. He no longer stuck to the Calvinist belief that the whole of mankind was predestined to damnation, except for a tiny minority that God would gratuitously save regardless of any actions by them. When students asked Simson how they could be sure of their own salvation, he answered with the biblical injunction, 'Seek and ye shall find.' He wished them to become men of inquiring mind, not prigs who happened to have been born into the right church in the right nation. He believed reason to be the foundation of theology and he aimed to make orthodoxy intelligible.[28]

Simson's outlook kept him more generally in touch with the most audacious thinking of his age – for example with the deists, who believed the universe must be guided by some divine force perhaps not fully explicable in terms of Christian doctrines, and with the natural theologians, who saw God's expression of himself in nature as a complement to the divine revelation. Simson did not necessarily accept these novel positions, but he held a command of them by his students to be useful for any future defence they might need to mount of the church and its teachings. Over two decades they went on to swell the ranks of the Presbyterian clergy in the west of Scotland and the north of Ireland.[29] In Scotland they won the patronage of two of the most powerful men in the country, and especially powerful in Glasgow: John Campbell, duke of Argyll, together with his brother, Archibald Campbell, earl of Ilay. These men came from a family revered by Presbyterians: their grandfather and great-grandfather were martyrs for the Covenants under the Catholic kings of the House of Stewart. The two younger scions had long ago arrived at the view, however, that one basic principle of the Union should be an end to religious persecution – something not actually stated in the treaty, though implicit in its provision for two established churches in the United Kingdom, the Church of Scotland and the Church of England, founded though they were on different principles. With this, Argyll and Ilay wanted to see also the development of an enlightened theology less concerned with dogmas of salvation than with reason and nature.[30]

Glasgow at large still did not like this much: there were complaints to the presbytery about Simson. Though his university defended him, the complaints went up to the General Assembly in 1714. The next year it gave judgment: he had 'vented some opinions not necessary to be taught in divinity' and employed expressions 'used by adversaries in a bad and unsound sense'. He was forbidden to do so for the future, but without suffering further censure. He had, in other words, no need to change his mind. His critics thought he was getting off lightly.[31] They bided their time and ten years later mounted another offensive against him, now with a little more success. They wanted him deposed from his chair, though the assembly only suspended him: on this occasion it found his opinions 'sound and orthodox' but his teaching 'subversive'. From 1729 he was no longer allowed to instruct students, though he retained the emoluments of his chair.[32] Ilay's chief political adviser, the judge Andrew Fletcher, Lord Milton, sent him a note on the matter: 'It is the opinion of all the king's servants here [in Edinburgh] that nothing more should be done against Prof. Simson than the leaving the affair in the state it now is till another assembly, by which time some expedient may be fallen.'³³ Still, then as now, they did things differently in Glasgow. In the Kirk the case was allowed to peter out, but Simson never resumed teaching before he died in 1740.

Meanwhile, in the university if not in the presbytery, more enlightened attitudes continued to advance. The inaugural professor of moral philosophy, from 1727, was Gershom Carmichael, essentially a natural theologian, teaching a curriculum drawn from the latest ideas in Europe. His successor in 1729, and a former student of Simson's, Francis Hutcheson, took his discipline in radical new directions. Of his successor in 1752, Adam Smith, nothing more need be said here. And his successor in 1764, Thomas Reid, was the founder of the Scottish philosophical school of Common Sense, still defending a divine order in the universe but no longer tying it to Calvinist dogma. The clergy of Glasgow remained unimpressed, indeed feared the spread of this contagion into the town. It 'seems to be fast ripening for a stroak', proclaimed one preacher in 1757, citing the transformation of a once pious burgh into a place where irreligion – swearing, public drunkenness, violation of the Sabbath – had become commonplace. It seemed to him more significant than the superficial prosperity Glasgow enjoyed from the flourishing trade in tobacco (which would be the chief sin in today's politically correct terms). When Reid came down here from Aberdeen, he disliked the 'gloomy, enthusiastical cast' of the devout in his new home. A year later, he had an explanation: the Glaswegian clergy worked to keep the people 'fanatical in their religion'.³⁴

So matters carried on into the nineteenth century. The Presbyterian religious establishment continued to come under pressure, and for two reasons. The first was that the zeal of its own members, especially in the west of Scotland, fostered not only what we might call informal dissent, in the sense of mutterings about ministerial unsoundness on some point of doctrine, but also formal dissent, in the sense of the devout walking out of the Kirk to form independent congregations committed to a truer faith. Presbyterianism has never set much store by institutional solidarity, and different sects formed or reformed, seceding and coming together again, every so often. The biggest merger to date took place in 1820 when various groups of dissenters joined in the United Secession Church. It had 280 congregations, most in the west, serving by one estimate 40 per cent of the population of Glasgow. The members were mainly respectable artisans, a class marked in Scotland by puritanism, earnestness and a spirit of independence. In their own church these people wanted especially to call their own ministers so that they could hear sermons congenial to them, something the established Kirk could not guarantee because of the Patronage Act.[35]

This great and growing problem for the established Kirk was compounded by industrialization and the huge changes in the distribution of the population resulting from it. Up to the middle of the eighteenth century, half of all Scots lived north of the Highland line; by the end of the nineteenth century, half of them lived in the conurbation round Glasgow. Social upheaval on such a scale might make the Church of Scotland's particular niggles over its parochial problems seem trifling. But serious effects followed. The map of Scottish parishes changed little since the Middle Ages. There had been a few shifts in boundaries since then, but really not many. By the time of the industrial revolution a great number of tranquil, and some now emptying, parishes existed in the north or south of Scotland as cosy billets for contented ministers. By contrast there were in the central belt new stretches of urban sprawl without a church, though still allocated to booming parishes where the minister could never hope to see, let alone know, all his flock. Since Scots remained by and large god-fearing folk, the faithful in these places often had little choice but to seek an independent minister for their spiritual needs. The Kirk did build subordinate places of worship inside the most populous parishes, the so-called chapels of ease: twenty of them in Glasgow, for example.[36] But there was never enough money for all that might be needed, and under this makeshift arrangement the status of ministers in the chapels of ease remained unclear. They baptized and married and buried people, but they had no legal basis for any personal role in the systems of education and welfare that represented the true strength of the church in Scottish society; nor was it certain that they could sit in the General Assembly, and the Court of Session at length ruled, in a test case, that they could not. Then the Kirk had an even greater problem in reaching out to the industrial population. It also had a problem of hearing the voice of the industrial population inside the Kirk.

The pell-mell changes in Scottish society called for leadership of exceptional ability and energy. The Kirk might have started to find it when in 1819 it appointed the Revd Thomas Chalmers to St John's Church in Gallowgate in Glasgow, a new proletarian parish with a custom-built place of worship (demolished in 1956). It was a world away from the fishing haven of Anstruther where he had grown up, and from the bucolic Kilmany where he had found his first charge in the tranquil hinterland of Fife. In both those communities, needy parishioners were able to rely on mutual support under the minister's benevolent eye. Chalmers believed the same outlook could and should be carried over from traditional rural Scotland into its soulless industrial society. The purpose of his ministry at St John's was to demonstrate as much.[37]

For Chalmers, it all formed part of his vision of a godly commonwealth in Scotland. He wanted to solve the nation's social problems by prompting people to help one another because they believed in Jesus Christ, who blessed the poor. Modern society had grown complex, but the complexity might meet its match if Christ's commandments created a combination of personal responsibility, ties of blood, love of neighbours and a sense of local community to give the poor as much care as they needed. The crux was to get the Church of Scotland to reorganize welfare into a voluntary system, with the faithful helping the less fortunate but also teaching these to help themselves. Then the support of the state could be dispensed with (not that much was forthcoming at the time). The Kirk would again stand at the centre of Scottish life, just as before the industrial revolution. Chalmers wrote at the outset of his ministry in the East End of Glasgow:

> Out of the ruins of the present system we should see another system emerge, under which pauperism would be stifled in the infancy of its elements; and a reaching application be brought into effectual contact with the very root and principle of the disease; and another generation should not elapse, ere, by the vigorous effect of Christian education on the young, we should have to do with a race of men, who would spurn all its worthlessness and all its degradation away from them.[38]

Chalmers was a man of heroic commitment, not only here in the pastoral sphere but also, at various stages of his life, in the academic world, as a political economist, even as a mathematician – and then finally as political leader in the long struggle with the British state that led to the Disruption of the Church of Scotland. It started as a dispute over patronage, the right of lay-men to appoint ministers to particular parishes. The dispute became politicized because patronage existed by statute. To defy the statute meant to defy the British state, and in the end the only way of breaking its legislative power over the Kirk was for the Kirk in effect to disestablish itself. That happened when half the commissioners to the General Assembly of 1843 walked out and formed the Free Church of Scotland, in which Chalmers became the first moderator. At length, about 450 ministers, 40 per cent of the Kirk's clergy, signed a deed of demission giving up their charges, manses and incomes. A still-greater proportion of the laity all over Scotland would join them in their secession.[39] This was where, in the British state, strong leadership of the Kirk had led.

Then, or soon afterwards, Scotland had three main Presbyterian churches. There was the continuing Church of Scotland, the Auld Kirk, which remained established even though it now contained only a minority of the population. Next there was the new Free Church, asserting its claim to be the true Kirk that would return to establishment one of these days, though only after its own conditions had been fulfilled. While its strength lay in Glasgow and the other cities, and then in the Highlands, it set out to rival the Auld Kirk in every parish in Scotland. By 1847 it had 700 places of worship and 500 schools, together with provision for higher education. Finally, there was the United Presbyterian Church, formed in 1847 out of older dissenting sects. Its membership could best be analysed in terms not of region but of class, for it represented above all a peculiarly Scottish social group, the educated artisan. According to the religious census of 1851, 32 per cent of the churchgoing population belonged to the Church of Scotland, 32 per cent to the Free Church and 19 per cent to the United Presbyterian Church.[40]

The Free Church remained on the whole a conservative, evangelical body upholding traditional Presbyterian standards or even going beyond them: it acquired quite a taste for accusing ministers who deviated from the standards of heresy. The most famous of these miscreants was Professor William Robertson Smith, deposed from his chair in Aberdeen in 1881 for questioning whether God had directly inspired the Bible – but he had colleagues in Glasgow who shared his modern critical approach to Holy Writ. It was no doubt because the Free Church took the Scriptures so seriously that it produced theologians schooled in the progressive biblical criticism of Germany, where they often went to study themselves. They proved to be also, however, tempting targets for fundamentalists. In 1889 Alexander Bruce, professor of apologetics and exegesis at the Free Church's college in Glasgow, published *The Kingdom of God*, which disputed the idea that Christ had regarded 'men, all or any of them, as predestined to damnation'. It naturally infuriated the Calvinist diehards. The matter went up to the General Assembly, which held that the charge of heresy against Bruce was based on a misunderstanding, though by his use of language he had given some grounds for the charges against him. With that mild rebuke, he was free to continue his distinguished scholarly contributions.[41] Bruce had got support from Marcus Dods, for twenty-five years a minister in Glasgow before himself embarking on an academic career. But first he, too, needed to face a charge of heresy. Once the hardliners heard of his appointment they set about combing through his writings and found a sermon on 'Inspiration' he had delivered and published in 1877. It said: 'No careful student of Scripture can well deny that there are inaccuracies in the Gospels and elsewhere – inaccuracies such as occur in ordinary writings through imperfect information or lapse of memory, sufficient entirely to explode the myth of infallibility.'[42] To Dods the virtue of theology lay not in its immutability but in its capacity for development. And by now even his opponents were coming to accept that theologians might require at least a little latitude in their thinking. When Dods's trial for heresy took place at the General Assembly of the Free Church in 1890, the assembly voted at once to drop the charge against him.

Meanwhile the United Presbyterians evolved into a body of believers paying more heed to the Christian commitments of its members than to the quibbles of its clerics. This was at heart a church of industrious artisans bettering themselves, though some degree of internal tension might result when they did so. From their place of worship at Cambridge Street in central Glasgow, the wealthier members of the congregation, together with the minister, the Revd John Eadie, moved out and built themselves a posher kirk in the suburbs. The day it opened, a wag chalked on its door:

> This church is not built for the poor and the needy
> But for the rich and for Dr Eadie.
> The rich may come in and take their seat,
> But the poor must go to Cambridge Street.[43]

In other ways the United Presbyterians were more obviously progressive. At mid-century the three main Scottish churches, while organizationally divided, still remained at one in their conservative Calvinist theology as set out in the Westminster Confession of 1647, which depicted a human race utterly depraved by the original sin of Adam. Over time this view became harder for the average United Presbyterian to take, he often being a busy tradesman trying to do his best by his family and community on meagre earnings. If he reproved weakness, irreligion and immorality in neighbours and workmates, he could hardly accept he was in the eyes of God no better than them. The first concession to a less rigid outlook came in 1876 when the United Presbyterians eased the terms on which new ministers were required to subscribe to the Westminster Confession. Now at their ordinations they could declare they viewed it as a general statement of the faith without needing to get into the detail of which dogmas they personally accepted (the Free Church followed this move in 1879, the Auld Kirk only in 1910). Liberal theology made deeper inroads with its claim that the kingdom of God should, to whatever extent possible, be achieved on earth as well as in heaven. A United Presbyterian minister in Glasgow, the Revd Alexander Scott Matheson, wrote of this as an imperative of God's will, for 'part of that will is to grapple with social wrongs, abolish poverty and join in all lawful efforts to obtain for labour its due reward, and for the toilers a large degree of amenity in their lot.'[44] It amounted to much the same as political radicalism, or even as early socialism in Scotland; indeed Scots socialists of the day liked to compare the historical struggles of Covenanters and kings with the current struggles of labour and capital.

As for the continuing Church of Scotland, 'the best ministers and best portion of our people have gone,' lamented one of its leaders after 1843, the Revd Norman Macleod of the Barony in Glasgow.[45] For a decade or more following the Disruption, the Auld Kirk lacked direction and purpose, yet it retained an underlying strength in its ancient endowments and established status. These allowed a new generation of ministers to revive it. Macleod was one of them. On the one hand he became Queen Victoria's chaplain, and fostered her delight in Presbyterianism. On the other hand, he was a social reformer: he felt called to bring God to the poor, and vice versa. In his parish he had new schoolhouses built and a mission church to which only people in working clothes might be admitted (it was a common complaint that many felt unwelcome at regular divine service because they had no Sunday best). He challenged the rigid Scottish Sabbatarianism that shut parks and museums on the one day the workers had off. He edited a popular magazine, *Good Words,* and wrote couthy books, *Cracks about the Kirk for Kintra Folk* and *Peeps at the Far East,* a record of his tour of oriental missions. Altogether, he helped to make the Auld Kirk more open-minded and tolerant.[46]

Macleod's influence continued well beyond his own time. His successor but two at the Barony, the Revd John White, likewise embraced the social gospel and above all took it as his life's work to bring every Protestant Scot back to the established Kirk. An ominous development urged him on: not in energy or intellect, but certainly in numbers, the three main Scottish churches had ceased to grow by the turn of the twentieth century, and they keenly felt their failure among the working class. Compared to this, the controversies of the Disruption now seemed distant and dated to many Scots. If schism had alienated them, one answer was to seek reunion. In 1900 the Free and the United Presbyterian Churches came together in the United Free Church. This then embarked in 1909 on negotiations with the Auld Kirk, though at first they went slowly.[47]

White was called to the Barony in 1911, but soon went off to serve as chaplain to the Cameronians in the First World War. On his return he was among those who wanted to give Christian leadership to post-war reconstruction, and for this purpose he helped to create the standing church and nation committee of the General Assembly. Apart from everything else, it was a base from which the cause of Presbyterian unity could be advanced. On renewal of the negotiations, White became secretary on the Auld Kirk's side and emerged as the dominant figure in a long, arduous process. For its part, the United Free Church refused to accept it might be subjected to the vaunted absolute sovereignty of the Parliament at Westminster. In 1921 an Act of that Parliament conceded the point to the Church of Scotland. This was what allowed freedom from any absolute sovereignty of the British state to be inherited by the reunited Kirk, a resolution that the two sides achieved in 1929. White was elected the first moderator of its General Assembly.[48]

There was, however, a darker side to White's intense commitments. If a staunch Tory, he also represented a kind of Scottish nationalism. In the Glasgow where he had grown up, this nationalism often assumed a racial aspect. In particular it drew a distinction between Scots and Irish: in that older Glasgow, no distinction was sharper. After the twenty-six southern counties of Ireland attained effective independence with the treaty of 1922, White called on the British state to halt Irish immigration and even to deport its Irish-born residents. One of the secular tasks he foresaw for a reunited

Kirk would be to help in preserving Scotland's racial purity. He used his position as convener of the church and nation committee to have it produce a provocative report under the title *The Menace of the Irish Race to our Scottish Nationality*, which was received by the General Assembly of 1923. It accused Irish Catholics in Scotland of subverting Presbyterian values with their crime, drunkenness and general profligacy. The answer would be to end their immigration and deport those of them convicted of criminal offences or living on benefits.[49]

In support of all this, White pointed out: 'Today there is a movement throughout the world towards the rejection of non-native constituents and the crystallization of national life from native elements.'[50] Indeed there was, and at length it produced such horrifying results in other European countries as to discredit White's views for good and all among younger generations of Scots ministers. Since his death in 1960, White has come under sharper criticism in an ever more ecumenical Church of Scotland. In 1986 the General Assembly dissociated itself from the anti-papal sections of the Westminster Confession. In 2002 it expressly repudiated White's report of 1923 on *The Menace of the Irish Race*.

Without apologizing for White's views, we can at least note that they were in their way the outcome of a unique national religious history, and far from uncommon up to his time. Few contemporary Presbyterians would have seen anything wrong with them, for there were few other European countries in which the Reformation had caused Catholicism to collapse as completely as it had in Scotland. The harsh disabilities imposed on its adherents after 1560 were not finally lifted till 1793, by which time they appeared obsolete simply by dint of the fact that Catholics had almost vanished from Scotland: in all of Glasgow, there were no more than thirty-nine of them, though the city also had forty-three anti-Catholic societies. Elsewhere, the old faith lingered on only in fastnesses its persecutors could never reach – some glens of the Grampian Mountains, some peninsulas on the western seaboard, some islands in the Outer Hebrides. In the nineteenth century the population of all such places fell. The fiercest bigot could scarcely have argued that the remaining tiny pockets of native popery offered any conceivable threat to staunchly Presbyterian Scotland.[51]

Yet anti-Catholicism remained deeply embedded in popular culture.[52] One reason might have been that Victorian Scots' strongest feelings about religion were at bottom just as much about race, or what they defined as race. The only conceivable Catholic threat to their Calvinist culture came from Ireland. In the course of the nineteenth century a swelling flow of Irish immigrants washed up in Scotland, driven first by the overpopulation of an agrarian homeland lacking the resources to feed its people. The famine of the 1840s solved this aspect of the problem by starving a million of them to death, yet the flow did not flag. It was then sustained by the long Scottish industrial boom that drew across the North Channel those looking for a better life than subsistence agriculture could ever give them, and willing to take any job they could find, even the most exhausting and least rewarding.[53]

These Catholics were, since the Irish Union of 1801, citizens of the same country and in fact, with their cheap labour, performing an indispensable economic function for it. Even so, many Scots felt unable to accept them as fellow citizens. We see as much from this report of a Glasgow Fair, just one example typical of many to be found in the Scottish press during subsequent decades:

> The brawls appeared chiefly to be caused by hordes of low Irish who, so much accustomed to club law in their own unfortunate country, come over to Scotland and bring along with them all their barbarous customs and uncivilized propensities, which they practise so frequently and in such a way as threatens to ruin the youthful portion of our own intelligent and peaceable population in point of morality,

as much as they are undermining and depressing them by lowering their wages... A pitched battle took place in the Green, at which several watchmen were disabled by the crowd, amounting to some hundreds, who assaulted them with bricks and stones.[54]

That was far from the only case where ill will between Presbyterian Scots and Catholic Irishmen spilled over into violence. The Orange Order's marching season in the summer always turned out to be the worst time. That was when Gourock saw a week of anti-Catholic riots in 1851. At Airdrie in 1854, the Protestant miners went on strike till all the Catholics in the local pits were sacked; the Catholics took revenge at the races, when they set about the Orangemen in their drinking tent and killed one of them. At Dumbarton in 1855, assaults on Catholics at William Denny's shipyard prompted him to dismiss the Irish working there. At Coatbridge in 1857 Catholics disrupted an Orange parade and even exchanged gunfire with the marchers till troops came over from Glasgow to restore order. At Paisley in 1859, the police urged Orangemen on to retaliate against Catholic miners who barracked their procession. At Coatbridge in 1863, a Catholic family beat up a Protestant family whose daughter had married their son. Shotts suffered a sectarian 'general riot' in 1865. In 1872 a Catholic miner murdered a Protestant miner during disturbances at Wishaw. At Govan in 1874 another 'general riot' followed an attack by Irish nationalists on an Orange lodge. In 1875 the Catholics of Partick publicly marked the centenary of the birth of Daniel O'Connell, drawing 'a fire of jeers and disparaging comments from a crowd of hostile onlookers'; fights broke out and continued all night, till the Riot Act was read from Partick Cross. Motherwell and Coatbridge witnessed similar events in 1883, which climaxed with charges by mounted police into the sectarian mobs. On the emergence of the Old Firm, the two rival football clubs, Rangers founded for Protestants in 1872 and Celtic founded for Catholics in 1888, the occasional outbursts of sectarianism assumed a new and more durable pattern. It first showed itself at the Scottish cup final of 1909 when, after a drawn match, the crowd invaded the pitch, uprooted the goalposts, burned the nets and, outside Hampden Park, fought running battles in the streets well into the evening.[55]

Clearly, no smooth integration of Irish Catholic immigrants into Scottish society was going to take place. They themselves were partly responsible for this, in their natural desire to practise their religion and teach it to their children. In contrast there were Presbyterian Scots, not least ministers of the Kirk, who saw the very existence of Catholic churches and schools as a standing affront. The affront was reinforced in the secular sphere too, as by the fact that in industrial terms many Irishmen first arrived in the role of strike-breakers, which did nothing to endear them to the Scotsmen they put out of work. Once the immigrants' growing numbers could sustain the necessary social structures, they tended to retreat into a ghetto and not even seek assimilation, rather the reverse. For example, in other divided societies intermarriage tends to allay divisions, but most Catholics in Scotland avoided it under pressure from family and neighbours and the implacable hostility of the priest. According to one survey, for the year 1851, 80 per cent of the Irish married each other, and in 1891 the figure was still 72 per cent.[56] In their private sphere they closed ranks.

The public sphere, then, saw the difference deepened in a number of ways, sometimes again by the Catholics themselves. Scotland had repudiated episcopal hierarchy two centuries before, but in 1878 a Catholic one was restored. Rome previously designated the country as a missionary field, divided into three districts – northern, eastern and western – each overseen by a vicar apostolic. The restored hierarchy implied a single national structure with a metropolitan archdiocese. For this Glasgow seemed the obvious choice, as the second city of the British empire, a centre of trade and industry, and crucially the home of three times as many Catholics, priests and churches as Edinburgh, the national capital. Yet in the end other considerations carried greater weight. Since this was an exercise in restoration, a claim could be staked for St Andrews as having been a metropolitan diocese before 1560. Though the little grey town by the North Sea now housed only two Catholic families and no Catholic place of worship, romantic Victorian medievalism prevailed and St Andrews resumed, for pontifical purposes, its ancient status. Even so, the Edinburgh that lay within the boundaries of the same archdiocese became its effective centre. It seemed a slap in the face for rough, raucous, smoky Glasgow, though the city still got an archbishopric of its own, with no suffragans and responsible directly to Rome (it did not become metropolitan till 1947). An inaugural prelate of Irish blood might have been expected, but the first man appointed over the see was Charles Eyre, an austere Englishman of an old recusant family.[57]

This reminds us how the people who pushed through the Catholic restoration in Great Britain were often aristocrats, in Scotland specifically John Crichton-Stuart, 3rd marquess of Bute, a convert and one with the proverbial zeal. His energy initially diverted attention away from the fact that his new church in its new home was a church of the poor, and that here lay its great strength, in the slums of the east end of Glasgow or in the grimy industrial towns of Lanarkshire. As we have seen, the Protestant Churches were losing contact with the urban working class, and knew it, but this was not something Catholics needed to worry about. Whereas Presbyterian ministers often spoke with the plummy accents of the Scottish bourgeoisie (and their congregations would have been shocked to hear anything else), Catholic priests shared the lives of their flocks, not only in language but also in standard of living. They led their parishes because their parishes formed ghettoes, in the inner city or in small mining communities. If any church fulfilled the social ideal of Thomas Chalmers it was the Catholic Church, with the results he had predicted in the strength of its local cohesion. Meanwhile, many churchgoing Presbyterians fled to the suburbs still outside the boundaries of Glasgow, leaving urban monuments to their fissile Victorian history standing in architectural splendour but without congregations, a metaphor for religious redundancy that might be thought to come uncomfortably close to the truth of their condition.[58]

The secular rulers of Scotland in their turn widened the gap between Protestants and Catholics, if perhaps not intentionally. Legislation of 1872 gave the country a national system of education after long wrangles among the various Churches about how to adapt the existing provision of schools, quite generous but still patchy, to the social and economic transformations going on at every hand. From all the controversy, it was hoped, a new system would emerge that was both universal and maintained the traditional high standards. But concord did not prove possible. The government then reached the difficult decision to exclude religious instruction from the classroom, or else the new system would remain forever dogged by sectarian squabbles. Presbyterians of all shades in the end accepted the compromise, though not without misgivings. The Catholics (and the Episcopalians) refused to do so. Since they were minorities, they thought a national system run on principles different from theirs would be bound to work to their detriment.[59]

This gave rise to one of the most important markers of Scottish Catholic identity, the separate schools. In these times the community earned its living mainly by unskilled labour, which required no more than elementary education. Anyway little more could be afforded in the Catholic voluntary schools built by contributions from the poorest class of society (which besides was obliged to contribute through local rates to the national system). After a third of a century in operation, the collective effort had by 1905 equipped Glasgow with just five Catholic doctors and one Catholic lawyer.

Bookmakers and publicans, who could make money but hardly win social status in Presbyterian Scotland, were the role models the Catholic community offered its rising generations.[60]

Liberal government relented on the decision of 1872 and passed a new Education Act in 1918, taking this chance to bring the Catholic schools into the public system. Robert Munro, the Scottish Secretary who got the measure through, said they were 'generally speaking, inferior as regards building and equipment, their teachers... zealous but poorly paid, their provision of secondary schools totally inadequate and the educational outlook of the mass of their children unduly narrowing'.[61] From now on the whole of primary and secondary education was to come under the secular tutelage of local school boards that had the responsibility for providing new facilities for Catholics as the need arose; to all, however, only teachers acceptable to the church might be appointed.

This breakthrough helped to emancipate Catholics from permanent immersion in the unskilled proletariat. They began to spread across the social spectrum, with a bourgeoisie emerging especially in the teaching, legal and medical professions. Given that a political revolution was at the time sweeping the Irish homeland, the act might at its highest level be taken as sealing the peaceful assimilation of the Catholic minority in Scotland. Denominational schools as the guarantee of Catholic faith and morals have remained embedded in the Scottish educational system till the present. This parallel structure to the state's own non-denominational system was erected not without difficulty, however: it took time to build enough schools even when official grants became available, while shortages of teachers persisted. But the Catholic community had now won a stake in society that could hardly be taken away again.

The other main marker of Catholic identity was support for the Celtic football team, especially when it played against Rangers, the corresponding marker on the Protestant side, in the so-called Old Firm. George Blake's novel *The Shipbuilders* (1935) showed the two squads appearing in the guise of 'peerless and fearless warriors, saints of the Blue and the Green', as they played before crowds of working men who badly needed this relief from economic depression.[62] During the period between the wars, it was Rangers that dominated, with fourteen victories in the league championship. Celtic's heroic age came later, under the leadership of Jock Stein, manager from 1965. In 1967 Celtic triumphed against the stellar Inter Milan to become the first British club to win the European Cup. But before long deep changes in the organization of professional football, in Scotland and far beyond, raised the commercial stakes for both Glasgow's leading clubs. In international competition, any bigotry among their supporters could only do them damage, though it proved impossible to eradicate altogether. In 1989 Rangers signed their first Catholic player, Maurice Johnston – a 'revolutionary' step forward, according to a historian of sectarianism.[63] But in the longer run Celtic proved better able to deal with the intensifying pressures on big football clubs, which were brought home by Rangers' financial collapse in 2012.

Meanwhile, the formation of Scottish Catholic identity had also had deep political effects, increasingly obvious from 1918. It was then that universal manhood suffrage came in and the vote for many women too, for the first time creating a sizable Catholic electorate. Previously, among a much smaller number of voters, the faithful often accepted the authority of the priest not just in the practice of their religion but also in the regulation of their daily lives, with a residual loyalty to Ireland further narrowing their political choices. The upshot was that in the past most had supported the Liberal Party. Now they swung to the left, along with significant sections of the Protestant population. The whole city of Glasgow went that way to dramatic effect at the general election of 1922, when out of the blue the Labour Party captured ten of the fifteen parliamentary seats.

The architect of this victory was John Wheatley, MP for Shettleston, himself an Irish immigrant who, risking the displeasure of the Catholic hierarchy, had taken a lead in local agitations before and during the First World War. In national politics afterwards he was opening up a new sphere to his co-religionists, and one with broad horizons. He let them see themselves as members not only of a church but also of a social class.[64] They could then concentrate on the workplace, and not only on the parish, as a locus for collective action (the same held true of the as yet small Catholic middle class, drawn largely from the teaching profession). Labour was the obvious vehicle of expression for this outlook, though it took another decade, till 1933, for the party to win a majority on Glasgow's city council. Patrick Dollan, who built a formidable electoral machine at the municipal level, then became treasurer of the city, and in 1938 lord provost. Even opponents viewed him as a quintessential Glaswegian, so that attempts by militant Protestants to pillory his Irish background had little effect.[65] The Catholic community would prove more consistently loyal to the left than any other element of the Scottish electorate.

After the Second World War, as after the First, social change quickened. Britain set up the welfare state. This further emancipated the poorer sections of society, and so in Scotland the Catholics as well. The concept of welfare also included a general expansion of education. The raising of the school-leaving age to fifteen in 1946 kept 60,000 pupils at school who would otherwise have left, and a disproportionate number were Catholics. The burgeoning powers of the public sector helped the brighter youngsters to find jobs at local or national level, now secure in the knowledge that their religious and educational background would no longer count as a handicap (as it still might prove to be in the private sector). In the emergent Catholic middle class, parents' expectations rose. Whereas in 1921 secondary pupils had made up only 3 per cent of the total number of Catholics at school, by 1972 the proportion rose to 31 per cent. At the same date, Catholics accounted for 39 per cent of all pupils in Glasgow's secondary schools.[66] Today these schools continue to enjoy the loyalty of their own community and suffer no more than occasional sniping from the Protestant side. Most Scots seem content to follow the line their governments have always taken, that separate schooling should continue as long as the Catholic community desires it.

Getting Catholic students into university always posed a bigger problem: there were fewer than 500 of them at Glasgow by 1930, out of 4,000. After their separate schooling, many arrived scarcely knowing a Protestant, even of their own age. Now they found themselves placed in an environment they suspected of being at best indifferent and at worst hostile to both their religion and their ethnic background. The Catholic chaplaincy at Glasgow, opened in 1925, made them feel more at home, helping to organize activities in which student camaraderie could counter the enveloping coolness. But even access to higher education did not necessarily cure the community's introspection. Scottish universities, Glasgow perhaps above all, were places where students came to learn during the day and went home in the evening, rather than staying on to hone their social skills or broaden their intellectual horizons beyond the curriculum. It took developments in the outside world to change that. During a second great expansion of higher education, the number of Catholics at Glasgow trebled from 700 in 1956 to 2,000 in 1972. It was in their own circles that they started to hear of and discuss the decisions of the Second Vatican Council (1962–5), and to find these liberating.[67]

In every country, Catholic renewal was all the same something the hierarchies meant to keep under control. Pope John Paul II was the man at length elected to lead the process from Rome. In the summer of 1982 he came to Scotland, to be greeted at Bellahouston Park in Glasgow by 300,000 of the faithful: nobody had ever drawn a bigger crowd of Scots. In his homily he referred to Ninian, Mungo and Margaret, the chief saints of the nation (though not to Patrick). His advisers were keen to stress Catholicism as an authentic part of the life and traditions of Scotland, not a mere immigrant church. The visit counted as a huge success, even to Protestants. The commentator Allan Massie observed that the pope 'completed the rehabilitation of Scottish Catholicism and its reintegration into the Scottish nation'. Nothing, he went on, 'could so clearly have demonstrated the changed position of Catholicism in Scotland... than the contrast between the huge, peaceful and happy crowds... and the tiny bands of demonstrators outnumbered by the police'.[68]

The renewal was also intended to reinforce Catholics' obedience to some traditional teachings of their church now coming under question, such as its opposition to abortion and homosexuality. The man who took the lead was Thomas Winning, named archbishop of Glasgow in 1974. In the twenty-seven years he served his see, finally also as a cardinal, he succeeded in making himself to a great extent the public face of Christianity in Scotland – an incredible achievement in a country till recently so hostile to his faith. It was as much a political as a religious achievement. While Winning might have been in politics a closet nationalist, he never gave in religion the impression of setting any great store by ecumenism. Yet in his efforts to stop the new Scottish Parliament after 1999 from repealing inherited British legislation against the promotion of homosexuality in schools, he created a coalition that spread right across the country's religious communities, from the Kirk and Free Kirk to the Muslims, Sikhs, Baptists and Jews. On his death in 2001, the United Free Church praised him for speaking 'for many other denominations in Scotland and beyond', while a Muslim leader explained: 'What we loved most about your great cardinal was his sincere way of speaking up with no compromise.'[69]

Certainly the Church of Scotland was by contrast more equivocal on these modern moral questions, if only because it was also more open and tolerant. But, as things turned out, its gradual retreat from traditional standards and practices had led the way to a general weakening of Presbyterianism. This had for four centuries been a crucial marker of national identity: it used to be said that Scotland did not need a Parliament again so long as it could look to the annual General Assembly of the Kirk. There were many secular effects – on voting intentions, for example. But as the link between church and nation loosened, the way stood open for the evolution of nationalism in a secular and political form. It then appeared more attractive even to Catholics who so far, despite some residual sympathy for Irish nationalism, had had little time for Scottish nationalism. This was one of the ways in which, for a less religious country, the old communal barriers no longer seemed so solid or so stubborn. Protestants and Catholics had once had different identities. Now they could work towards a shared identity.[70] In his own way, Winning personified this: he was a prince of the Roman Church, but unmistakably a priest from Wishaw.

Yet there was one problem Winning never solved: the decline in religious observance among Scots Catholics. It had started later than among the Presbyterian majority, but by the turn of the twenty-first century the trend was clear. Few Catholics went so far as to renounce their faith, so that their proportion of the Scottish population held up – at 16 per cent or so of the total compared to 32 per cent for the Church of Scotland. But more and more of them were nominal Catholics in the sense that they stopped going to mass. Between 1994 and 2002 attendance in Scotland fell 19 per cent, to just over 200,000. The decline continued into the new century, so that today perhaps only 3 per cent of the Scottish population attend mass regularly. There has been an even steeper fall in priestly vocations. The modernist architectural masterpiece, St Peter's College at Cardross, lasted only fourteen years after its opening as a seminary in 1964 before being forced to shut down again because of a lack of vocations. Today, roughly half the Catholic parishes in the west of Scotland are threatened with closure for lack of priests. The greatest enemy of Catholicism is not now its status as a minority faith, but the secularism enveloping the whole of society.[71]

In the course of the twentieth century, the position of the Scottish Catholic community had undergone radical change. Retreat into the ghetto once helped to preserve its character through difficult times, but this was obviously not in the long run a satisfactory answer to its problems. On the contrary, the descendants of the Irish immigrants needed to break out of the ghetto if they were not to condemn themselves to being a permanent underclass. But then the razing of established working-class communities as part of an ambitious yet flawed process of urban development in turn weakened the hitherto strong identity of the Catholic community and hastened the process of assimilation into the rest of Scottish society. Its future lay in Scotland, not in ancestral Ireland; so a satisfactory way forward would need to arise out of Scottish rather than Irish conditions, which in any case had since 1900 changed beyond all recognition. From those Scottish conditions Catholics finally won a just measure of recognition and acceptance, in contrast to the Protestant ignorance and rejection of former times. This happened, however, in a Scotland fast losing interest in religion altogether, so that old prejudices and prohibitions became irrelevant.

Nobody conducted a survey of the crowds that gathered in George Square, Glasgow on the night of September 18, 2014, to see what proportion of them were Protestants or Catholics. The next day, however, there could be no doubt about the allegiance of the triumphal victors who flocked to the same space to celebrate the result of the referendum, bearing Union Jacks and other badges of unionism. Catholics had once been mainly hostile to Scottish nationalism but now, so far as we can tell, greater hostility was to be found on the opposite side of the city's religious divide. In at least one respect, then, assimilation had been completed.

4

Class: 'Staunch to Scottish traditions'

WHEN ARCHIBALD Campbell, 3rd duke of Argyll and effective ruler of Scotland for the House of Hanover, died on April 15, 1761, he was in London, or rather at his country house of Whitton, 11 miles to the west. In town he owned another mansion (on the site of the present London Palladium) where his body was then taken to lie in state for a fortnight. He received the homage of his peers and of humble compatriots in the English capital who felt grateful for his help to them over the years. He had been a great man in the United Kingdom, in the House of Lords a Scottish representative peer, a privy councillor to King George III and the holder of a host of other offices.[1]

But the duke had not wanted to leave his bones in England. On May 1, a funeral procession was formed to bear him up the long road north. Carried 'in a superb hearse richly ornamented with escutcheons', he did not reach Edinburgh till May 15. A delegation of gentlemen waited for him at the bounds of the burgh. They led the way to the Palace of Holyroodhouse, of which he had been the hereditary keeper. He again lay in state over a weekend, and on the Monday 'the funeral procession, which was very grand, passed through the city, the great bells tolling all the while'. Crowds lined the streets. The procession took an hour to pass the West Port, and that night it stopped at Falkirk.[2] The next day it continued to Glasgow. This was at last real home territory for the duke, whose ancestral lands lay a few miles beyond the city. He himself had been a student here back in the 1690s and a frequent visitor for the rest of his life, passing through as he journeyed back and forth between London and his seat at Inveraray. The lord provost, Andrew Cochrane, received his old friend and patron for the last time. Again the body lay in state. The following morning the hearse progressed through streets lined by the militia of Argyll. It arrived at Greenock, where the coffin was placed on the ducal barge, which bore it across the Firth of Clyde to the northern shore of Holy Loch, to Kilmun, the traditional resting place for the chiefs of Clan Campbell. The vault of the church of St Munn housed most of the third duke's ancestors, right back to Sir Duncan Campbell, who had died in 1453, and there Archibald too was buried.[3]

The duke had come a long way from his Highland home to flourish in the new British state. Here, after the Union of 1707, Scots learned to repress their tribal mayhem. Instead they acquired over time the habit of lining up behind a single political manager who might present a united (more or less) national front to the government in London. This maximized the chances of getting money or other favours out of it. The brothers John and Archibald Campbell, 2nd and 3rd dukes of Argyll, took over the role from the mid–1720s and fulfilled it till the latter's death. Their nephew, John Stuart, earl of Bute, tutor and confidant to King George III, was made prime minister of the entire United Kingdom in 1762 – the first (and the worst) Scot to serve in the highest office, whence he assigned control of Scottish affairs to relations and cronies. But within a year he was hounded out, and the whole of this high aristocratic system of ruling Scotland came crashing down. It lay in ruins for a decade or more till Henry Dundas picked up the pieces and built a regime that rested on the lesser landed class of country gentlemen, now prospering through economic improvement.[4]

Yet certain elements of Scottish politics remained constant. One was the relationship of the royal burghs to the national apparatus of power. Among those burghs, Edinburgh alone enjoyed some slight degree of independence, by reason of its wealth and fame; even then the capital of Scotland never balked at currying favour when it felt the need to. Lesser places always preferred to keep on the right side of the local aristocracy, and sometimes fell into more or less complete dependence on one potentate or another. During the Middle Ages, Glasgow's feudal superior had been its bishop, but the burgh needed just as much to come to terms with the nobility of the west of Scotland. The most notable were the earls of Lennox, whose title derived from the River Leven running through their territory to the west of the city. Matthew Stewart, 2nd earl, served as its lord provost about the turn of the sixteenth century. Glasgow would have counted itself all the luckier when he forged a royal connection by marrying Elizabeth, daughter of James, first Lord Hamilton, and of Princess Mary, whose father was King James II. From this couple Henry Stewart, Lord Darnley, descended; he could have used the style Master of Lennox but apparently never cared to. He became the second husband of Mary Queen of Scots and the father of King James VI.[5]

The link lasted right down right down to the time of Esmé Stewart, 8th earl of Lennox and also lord provost of Glasgow in 1580 (succeeding in both peerage and provostship his uncle Robert). Esmé had been born and raised in France. He left a wife and five children behind when, aged thirty-seven, he came to Scotland in 1579. The thirteen-year-old King James VI, after a childhood starved of affection, seems to have conceived a schoolboy crush on him. The royal swot expressed this attachment in part through intellectual discussion, persuading the pliant Esmé to convert from Catholicism to Presbyterianism. But a physical aspect was suspected. In 1582, by which time James and Esmé were exchanging kisses and cuddles in public, stern Scots forced the pair to part and the Frenchman to go home for good. The inconsolable king wrote a poem to the phoenix, his symbol of consuming loss:

And thou, o Phoenix, why was thou so moved,
Thou foule of light, by enemies of thee,
For to forget they heavenly hewes, whilkis loved
Were baith by men and fowlis that did them see?[6]

The house of Lennox then went into eclipse and, as far as Glasgow was concerned, left a void in local power for other connections to fill. The Hamiltons were one, with the blood royal flowing in their veins and, more to the point, with a great estate in Lanarkshire. Yet they tended to stand and fall with the Stewart dynasty, and at length they gave way to two rival families, the Campbells of Argyll and then the Grahams, who bore the territorial title of Montrose (though, in fact, they held most of their lands to the eastern side of Loch Lomond). A long frontier between these two clans stretched away into the Highlands, delineated on the ground through feuding. Even by 1707 the feuds were only just softening into less brutal forms of rivalry.[7]

In the new politics of the United Kingdom, James Graham, 1st duke of Montrose, initially rather got the better of the erratic John Campbell, 2nd duke of Argyll. Alas for Montrose, he was appointed secretary of state for Scotland just in time for the Jacobite rebellion of 1715, and then found his post to be a poisoned chalice. He came to grief in his private affairs too. He engaged in a constant quest for the money he needed to extend his estate, or to repay the debts he incurred through his unfailingly bad investments. Argyll was anything but a financial genius, yet never a bungler on Montrose's scale. By the later 1720s he had outdone his rival on every hand, mainly through the intelligence and cunning of his brother

Archibald, 3rd duke in waiting. In Glasgow, Montrose stayed on as chancellor of the university, but in other spheres the Campbell brothers took over.[8]

By the time of the 3rd duke's death in 1761, the royal burgh of Glasgow and the ducal house of Argyll had enjoyed close links for a third of a century. But their social distance never diminished, as we can gather from a grovelling letter to the duke from Andrew Cochrane, his friend though not his equal, and lord provost through the Jacobite rebellion of 1745:

> I hope it will be esteemed no presumption in me to assure your Grace of my faithfull and inviolable attachment to your interest and family, and of endeavouring, in my low sphere, to promote the continuance of the friendship that has long subsisted between your illustrious house and this corporation, which I hope my conduct during my Magistracy has not lessened... Thus we have the pleasure of deserving to be the object of your Grace's attention. We esteem it our great felicity that you are pleased to honour us with your patronage, and interest yourself in our concerns on all occasions. I am persuaded we will express a gratefull sense of our obligations in the most real and respectful manner. May we hope to be directed by your Grace, when it may be proper for us to apply to the ministry, and in what manner. I shall never cease to pray for your Grace's long life as a blessing to our unhappy country.[9]

After 1761, two developments upended this local order of things. The 4th duke of Argyll, John Campbell of Mamore, was already elderly by the time he succeeded to the title. A cousin of his immediate predecessors, he had no interest in continuing their political activities. He was a benevolent old soldier who, in local operations, had always spared civilian Highlanders (for instance, when he took the Jacobite heroine, Flora MacDonald, into custody in 1746).[10] He wanted to live out his last years in peace at Inveraray. And then the wealth of Glasgow's mercantile community had by now grown to such an extent that they could bid for higher social status too – which, in the conditions of the eighteenth century, meant their acquisition of landed estates in the countryside around. Soon in terms of capital at least a match for any aristocrat, and in terms of income often better off, they no longer needed to pander to the relics of feudal society. The nation was setting out on the capitalist road, and Glasgow's merchants took the first big steps. Without anything that could be called a revolution, a new class rose to power in the city.

The merchant elite of Glasgow remained small, no more than a few hundred in number depending how we define them, out of a population of 70,000 by the end of the century.[11] There were still some lesser ones happy with their humdrum traffic to the Highlands and Ireland. By contrast the greater ones brought to the burgh a whiff of the exotic, with their mahogany furniture, Turkish carpets, Madeira wine and black servants. The first to wax wealthy had prospered from the transatlantic trade, as tobacco lords exploiting the opportunities opened up by the Union.[12] This phase came to an end with the American Revolution and the severe reversal it brought to the biggest business of Glasgow's merchants. Their sons and kinsmen of the following generation found a remedy by diversifying into a wider range of commodities from afar – cotton, sugar, coffee, rice. That led on to the expansion of oriental trade in the nineteenth century. As Glasgow turned into a great industrial city, its merchants continued to flourish even in the twentieth century.

They were a close-knit group. When they stepped out they even looked the same, in the guise of the Virginia Dons, each with red cape and cloak and gold-tipped walking cane, parading on the Plainstanes at Glasgow Cross, where the common citizens, without being granted a glance or a word, made way for them. They did business with one another and they celebrated success with one another, preferring in social life to stick together in their clubs or in entertainment at home. The same held in the spiritual sphere. Most merchants were Presbyterians, among them councillors exercising the burgh's patronage of its kirks. Many showed themselves pious: for example, in their personal writings George Brown and George Bogle of Daldowie worried about their own salvation, and wondered whether their prosperity was a sign of divine favour or a mere snare and a delusion. They liked to worship at St Andrew's Church, a splendid classical building erected between 1739 and 1756 as the centrepiece of St Andrew's Square, between the Saltmarket and Glasgow Green.[13]

Merchants lived round the sides of this elegant space. Here and elsewhere, they built themselves opulent homes. Before the Union they had still stayed in tenements like everybody else, but now that would never do: what marked achievement in life was a house of one's own, preferably detached from any other. It was expensive because the proprietor needed to buy the ground as well as put up the building, and in the past only noblemen, not mere merchants, had been able to afford such extravagance. The grandest mansion of all was William Cunninghame's on Queen Street (still there as the Gallery of Modern Art), with its plaque declaring *Emergo*: quite so. Later, whole thoroughfares of individual houses would be constructed, with never a tenement in sight, but this had to be done beyond the old bounds of the burgh, on the rising ground to the west. The houses contained expensive furnishings and ornaments, not to speak of original paintings such as the collective portrait John Glassford commissioned of his family, hanging today in the People's Palace. The market for such works was so lively that Glasgow had its own school for artists, the Foulis Academy. The brothers who founded it, Andrew and Robert Foulis, were also publishers of fine editions of classical literature to grace the merchants' bookshelves. The city's refined taste caused it to employ for its public buildings the best architects of the age, Robert Adam and his brothers, responsible for the Trades Hall, the Assembly Rooms and the Royal Infirmary.[14]

In these ways Glasgow's new ruling class declared its status. It was not open to anybody. Entry went through membership of the merchant guild that had existed from early on in the burgh's history. It was primarily a local group: for native Glaswegians admission came relatively cheap and easy, while for candidates from elsewhere the entry was more difficult and expensive. We might think money and merit would have been the best qualifications for getting in, and indeed money and merit were seldom kept out for long. Yet the best qualification of all still lay in belonging to a traditional merchant family, by birth or marriage. On average, twenty-four candidates entered the guild each year, of whom ten gained the 'burgess ticket' through their fathers, six through their wives, two by purchase, three by apprenticeship and three gratis.[15]

The purpose of the merchants' guild was protection rather than competition. It restricted the range of statutory trading privilege to its members and sought to exclude others. The merchants then had no need of cut-throat competition among themselves. Small or large groups of them often entered into commercial partnerships by jointly underwriting their voyages, and the rising returns from trade encouraged this. It was good practice for the time when their mounting financial surpluses allowed them to move on into manufacturing and banking.[16]

During his years as a professor at the University of Glasgow, the father of economics, Adam Smith, got to know the merchants well; he was teaching their sons, after all. Andrew Cochrane became a particular friend of his too, and we are told that 'Dr Smith acknowledged his obligations to this gentleman's information when he was collecting materials for his *Wealth of Nations;* and the junior merchants who have flourished since his time and extended their commerce far beyond what was then dreamt of, confess with respectful remembrance that it was Andrew Cochrane who first opened and enlarged their views. Cochrane had founded a Political Economy Club, which Smith joined on his return to Glasgow in 1751. Since the club's 'express design was to inquire into the nature and principles of trade in all its branches, and to communicate knowledge and ideas on that subject to each other', it may well count as the seedbed of *The Wealth of Nations* (1776).[17]

Promotion of the mercantile interest was a political activity too. At the lowest level of the town council, the sett or constitution of the burgh guaranteed the merchants the upper hand over the other interest represented there, the tradesmen. There had been a good deal of tension between the two, tradesmen being at first excluded from any public office. The way to resolve the tension was to end the exclusion and concede to the incorporated trades at least some part in running the city. As everywhere in Scotland, however, the merchants made sure to keep on top, if sometimes by the slightest of margins. So it was here, too, after Glasgow had received the full status of royal burgh, in place of the previous episcopal superiority, from King James VI in 1611. By the sett then drawn up the merchants enjoyed a majority of just one on the council, but they would exploit it to maintain their hold on the lord provost's office.[18]

Civic officials across the rest of Scotland spent an inordinate amount of time on such petty matters as trying to get the populace to keep the Sabbath. In Glasgow, without yielding to anybody in piety, they preferred to promote trade. It was a secular activity, but not an ungodly one. The burgh counted among the few in Scotland that tended to bear out the influential thesis of the modern German sociologist, Max Weber, on the close link between the emergence of Calvinism and the rise of capitalism.[19] Calvinism was founded on a rational and logical kind of theology, which inspired calculation and efficiency in the minds of those who adhered to it. But since

God is inscrutable, the sole hints of their salvation lay in the life of virtue they felt moved by their faith to lead. One thing this in turn encouraged was good, honest, competent commercial practice. These followers of Calvinist morality, their everyday lives infused by their religious outlook, felt a need to employ all their time to the best possible advantage, whether as businessmen or as citizens. Religion especially encouraged education, which for the merchants, or rather for their sons and apprentices, taught, besides a basic academic curriculum, clear writing and expression, familiarity with bookkeeping, navigation and so on – in fact, general practical knowledge of all kinds useful in mercantile business. Then in their course of life they could make money and advance their status, which only tended to prove God had chosen them.

Yet there were drawbacks too. In a small city, nepotism followed on as one almost inevitable result of having things run by a self-selected, and rather self-righteous, inner circle. Nepotism was anyway rife in urban Scotland, and one of the main reasons why legislative reform of the burghs in the end grew irresistible. But in such a thriving community as Glasgow the nepotism might not have been quite so pernicious as in some stagnant or declining burghs elsewhere. In certain ways, it performed a useful economic function. For example, it encouraged the merchant houses to supply credit to one another in the spells – quite frequent during the eighteenth century – of monetary crisis. Even when the individual businesses just needed to maintain their cash flow, always vulnerable to fluctuations in foreign trade, they lent to one another. In later and better times, merchants still looked for credit when they engaged in capital investments outside the core of their businesses, which often required a lot of money upfront that was seldom to be recouped in the early years of operation. The merchants could never have made progress along so many paths without the credit to smooth out inevitable bumps on the way. By the end of the eighteenth century, the sums involved were growing bigger than anything Scots had ever dealt with before. It often seemed safer to keep all this within the circles of family and friends.[20]

But banks became necessary as well, though the Scottish chartered banks with their headquarters in Edinburgh proved ill-suited to Glasgow's needs. Instead its merchants set up their own, in fact three of them: the Ship Bank, the Glasgow Arms Bank and the Thistle Bank, each named after the design appearing on its notes. The original partners in these operations were every one of them members of wealthy merchant families, who as necessary brought in over time fresh partners of the same sort. The process accumulated new capital too, enough in the event to withstand even the biggest crises at home or abroad. Unlike their successors in the twenty-first century, Scottish bankers of the eighteenth century were prudent, none more so than the managing partner of the Ship Bank, 'Auld Robin' Carrick. He was author of an elaborate system of secret signs he could send from the back office to his cashier when, confronted with an anxious customer bearing bills of exchange, he needed higher authority to meet them (or not). At the death of this 'grim old bachelor', Carrick had a personal fortune of £1 million, and he went 'without leaving one plack or penny to any of the charitable institutions in the city'. But his bank was Glasgow's most successful.[21]

Moral rectitude is easier with the money to back it. Many Scots burghs turned corrupt, a fault fostered by the fact that their councils were all closed corporations representing local cliques rather than the townspeople at large. When matters reached such a pass that parliamentary commissions had to come up from London to investigate, they exposed numerous scandals; but most were petty and trivial. Glasgow's sett was no more or less permissive than others, yet here corruption seems never to have been a big problem, at least to judge from the minutes of the council or the papers of the lord provosts. All the city's great men were just too rich. They did not need to bother with paltry local fiddles when they held the trade of the Occident and the Orient in their hands.[22]

The drive of Glasgow's merchants to exploit every profitable opportunity in time matured their commercial attitudes and methods. The protectionism of the old burgh had been a defensive ploy, to protect a small and backward urban economy from more powerful competition. But the point came when Glasgow no longer needed to fear competition – on the contrary, it might match and even beat any comers. One of the great cathartic experiences in this process of self-discovery occurred during and after the American War of Independence, when the city faced all sorts of problems it had never met before.[23]

The independence of the United States might have seemed a disaster for Glasgow yet, while terminating familiar arrangements, it also created exciting opportunities. The city could now make its own deals with the new-born nation across the ocean, no longer under burdensome regulation from London. The lord provost in 1783–4, Patrick Colquhoun, understood this and tried hard to have himself appointed American consul-general as soon as the war was over: Glasgow did get the first consulate (though not occupied by him) from 1798. His colleague Robert Donald once wrote the sort of letter he might have written to any Scottish politician, but addressed it to an old acquaintance from Virginia by the name of George Washington, 'to solicit your notices of the bearer... my nephew, who I believe intends removing to your city of Washington, where under your patronage I flatter myself he may push his way in your rising states.'[24] Glaswegians were eager to keep well in with the Americans, and to a large extent they succeeded.

Glasgow was finding a promotional offensive preferable to a defensive protectionism. Its mercantile cohesion helped when in 1783 it became the first British city to found a chamber of commerce (where Colquhoun played a leading part).[25] The big difference between this and the Merchants' House was that the chamber opened itself to everybody engaged in trade and manufactures in the west of Scotland, not only in Glasgow but also in any commercial community along the Clyde. Another difference followed on – that whereas the politics of the mercantile interest had often been pettifogging, now a wider horizon appeared. One specific task the chamber set itself was to develop relations with Parliament at Westminster. For this it needed aims that went well beyond everyday trading transactions, aims better dealt with at a national than at a local level. From the political side the chamber got a warm welcome from the new prime minister, William Pitt the younger, and his Scottish right-hand man, Henry Dundas, who wanted to start putting into effect the liberal ideas of Adam Smith.[26]

One of the chamber's first moves was to lobby for fresh legislation on bankruptcy. This seemed essential now Scotland was turning from a traditional agricultural into a modern commercial society, requiring law that could deal not just with succession to castles and estates but also with more abstract aspects of corporate structure and partnership. Though the concept of 'notour bankrupt' appeared in an Act of Parliament of 1696, it could not cope with the economic progress that had since taken place. Now a gradual process of reform began. Colquhoun also wanted the chamber to identify and advance his city's wider commercial opportunities. For Scotland he invented the function of the lobbyist, and in this guise made frequent visits to London. He still did not seem to enjoy the work much, writing of 'the supineness of the landed interest' and of his disgust at grubbing politicians. But he felt proud of his achievements, especially the creation of a standing committee on trade in the House of Commons. When by 1788 it became clear his own firm would not survive the testing new conditions in Glasgow, he moved permanently to London to create a specialized agency for commercial information. In the development of this business, he tackled municipal problems there with as much vigour as he had at home. His final feat in his new abode was to create a police force

to patrol the River Thames.[27] It says much for the enterprise of
Glaswegians that, with scarcely a blink, they were able to redeploy
their capital and diversify their interests, no longer as monopolists
seeking protection but as entrepreneurs seeking profits.

A few years later there came, after a long American war, a long
French one. The Glaswegian merchants' already-great wealth
waxed fabulous through blockade-busting in Napoleonic Europe.
So far they had troubled themselves little with trade to the east,
finding so much to do to the west. It needed an exceptional
opportunity for them to break their old habits, but one arrived
in 1807, when the emperor Napoleon imposed the Continental
System, a blockade to cut off British exports to the countries he
had subjugated. The exports did not in fact grind to a halt: they
just became riskier, though higher risk also meant higher profits.
For this business Glasgow by now had the men, had the goods and
had the money too. A leading merchant house, James Finlay &
Co, set up a depot on Heligoland in the North Sea, run by Patrick
Colquhoun, and another at Gibraltar, run by the entrepreneur
(later novelist) John Galt, both under the protection of the Royal
Navy. From there, cargoes could be smuggled into nearby ports,
even those under Napoleon's military occupation. Disaffected
officers of the local customs just let everything through, and any
enemy soldiers snooping about might be bribed. Local middlemen
then often flogged Scottish textiles on to French commissaries who
bought them to be turned into uniforms for *La Grande Armée*.[28]

Much further off in Asia stretched the territories over which
the English East India Company held a monopoly of trade. As the
company's head office lay in London, ships from Scotland (or
indeed from Ireland, Wales and provincial England) were forbidden
to sail to its oriental depots. The Treaty of Union had made no
difference to the ban, even though many Scots at length found
employment in the company. Glasgow's most devout wish was
to break this monopoly.[29] A chance came, because every twenty

years the company's charter needed renewal. One renewal fell due in 1813 – which then presented the novice MP for the Glasgow Burghs, the merchant Kirkman Finlay, with a cause to champion. He got himself on to the select committee preparing the fresh legislation, and persuaded it to lift the company's monopoly. One of his own ships at once set off for Calcutta. It was a great blow struck for the emergent liberalism of the nineteenth century, yet Finlay's own liberalism proved erratic. In Glasgow he worked with the government against radical plots, and helped in setting up a network of spies to unearth them. His home suffered an attack from the mob because of his support for the protectionist Corn Laws that kept bread dear.

While Glasgow's merchants were not reactionaries, they espoused liberalism in ways wealthy men might be expected to prefer. The town council they ran was progressive by contemporary standards, presiding over a well-ordered municipality. In 1800 it obtained at Westminster a Police Act creating, for the first time in Scotland, an independent authority to maintain public order but also, in a country where the term police had wider connotations, to take charge of the environment and matters of health and safety in general. Actually the 123 policemen employed under the act spent a good deal of their time on such tasks as clearing snow or repairing smashed street-lights. The council also encouraged the first municipal utilities, the Glasgow Water Company of 1806 and the Glasgow Gaslight Company of 1817, vital to deal with the rapid expansion of the city.[30] There was need to do more amid early signs of the social degradation that accompanied the industrial revolution, but the council still had to work within the constraints of the traditional sett.

A new age at last dawned, with the Reform Act of 1832 opening up the franchise for the Parliament at Westminster and then the Burgh Police Act of 1833 doing the same at the municipal level. Scotland hailed the change of regime as a great popular liberation, yet in Glasgow it did not make that much difference. The first two MPs elected under the wider suffrage were merchants of the familiar type: James Ewing, the city's richest man and generous in his benefactions, together with James Oswald, who can still be seen today, at least as a statue, with the tallest lum hat on George Square (Ewing has to content himself with a monument in the Necropolis).[31] The political ascendancy of these plutocrats in fact remained little affected by reform. They had supported it anyway, so long as it remained 'considerate, moderate and safe, in accordance with the established order of society'.[32] But their main aim was for Glasgow to obtain its own representation at Westminster instead of, as had been the case since 1707, sharing one parliamentary seat with three smaller burghs. Most soon called themselves Liberals, if by no means all; perhaps labels mattered little when the mercantile community remained united in its opinions and outlook. Competition with Conservatives gave less trouble than rumpus with radicals, allies in reform though disillusioned by its limited results. In Glasgow as elsewhere, their agitations continued. Chartism turned out the most popular of them, even if in Scotland it never attained the same strength or fervour as in England. Its Glaswegian leader was James Moir, not a proletarian but himself a successful merchant and, in everything except his advanced opinions, a member of the city's establishment – a commissioner of police, for example. While not lacking in progressive zeal, and capable of provoking demonstrations, he was in the end a man at one with the other city fathers.[33]

Meanwhile, the progress of the industrial revolution continued to work deep changes in the economic and social structure of Glasgow. New tycoons appeared alongside the old elite, though their penetration of the political edifice would be slow. Most of the civic leaders in the late nineteenth century and even in the early twentieth century were still merchants – men like Sir Samuel Chisholm, Sir Daniel Macaulay Stevenson and Sir Thomas Dunlop.

Only the rise of the labour movement after the First World War toppled them from the civic eminence they had enjoyed ever since the days of the tobacco lords.[34]

For Glasgow, then, pressure from below on the established urban order of things had been tardy in its effects. To understand why, we might begin by looking at a particular leading section of the working class, the weavers, who faster than any others were drawn into the maelstrom of industrialization. Their trade had its origins in the Middle Ages, with the individual craftsmen who earned a livelihood from making and selling woven garments within the burgh. They were incorporated by a charter from Archbishop Gavin Dunbar as feudal superior of Glasgow in 1528. Besides its function of maintaining standards of output, the incorporation took on a charitable role 'to help and comfort of their decayit brethereine... and other godlie shows'. Its privileges within the burgh meant it was also obliged to accept the council's regulation of prices and wages, which was rigorously enforced. The incorporation at its peak contained about 400 members – a large part of the medieval population, but obviously just a tiny fraction by the time the burgh industrialized.[35]

This was why the weaving trade spread beyond the narrow medieval bounds of the royal burgh into a ring of suburbs north and south of the River Clyde. There the weavers remained unincorporated in the burghal fashion, so did not benefit from the privileges or welfare available to their brethren inside Glasgow. It was a state of affairs that might have made for hostility between the two groups (as it did in a similar situation in Edinburgh), but in Glasgow they showed greater solidarity. The risk for the weavers living inside the burgh was of being undercut in their prices by the weavers from outside. In 1605 the two groups entered into an accord which, they said, was 'for the special love, favour and kindness of the deacon and Glasgow weavers to the provost and weavers of Bridgend' (on the southern bank). What it did in practice was allow weavers from beyond the burgh to sell goods inside it on payment of a fee, so that the retail prices might be equalized. The deal proved successful, if we may judge from how it was later extended to the weavers of Calton.[36]

Otherwise, lacking privilege, the unincorporated weavers had rather to rely on self-help and co-operation. They formed friendly societies to provide for sick or disabled members. The societies might also espouse moral purposes. One stipulated that entrants must be 'under the age of forty years, above ten years, free of all known bodily diseases, a Protestant and of an honest character'. When the members convened at their meetings they could go beyond the ordinary business to discuss social and economic questions of the day. It took little more for a friendly society to become the basis for what was then called, with disapproval, a combination – in modern terms, a trades union intent on raising wages and winning other improvements in conditions.[37]

The fact that combinations formed and survived showed their members found them worthwhile, at least in local matters. They could achieve little on any greater scale, however, to counter the appearance of economic cycles as modern capitalism took shape. For Glasgow these tensions first became obvious in 1767, when a slackening of trade occurred. A group of militant weavers in the suburbs mounted a campaign of intimidation against others willing to work at the lower prices now on offer. The rebels cut webs from their errant fellows' looms and dragged them through the streets, 'showing them as a disgrace to the other workmen, whom they called out to see them; and beat them to excess'.[38] The trouble at length died down, yet worse was to follow in 1787 after another steep fall in prices. Weavers from Camlachie bent on a ritual burning of webs marched along the Gallowgate towards the city. At the boundary the magistrates stood ready to read the Riot Act, but the weavers threw stones at them. Troops were summoned; the weavers stoned them too. The soldiers opened fire, killing half a dozen protesters and wounding many more. It might look like the start of violent class conflict, but it had no sequel for three decades.

The industrial revolution now started up in earnest, with a range of technical innovations in textile manufacture especially. For Glasgow we might date the dawn of the new age to 1798, when Robert Millar brought power-looms into operation at his works in the city.[39] Even so they remained as yet too crude for the more delicate work, so specialist jobs still existed for individual weavers to carry out on their handlooms – jobs that were indeed often contracted out to them by the manufacturers. All the same, production became from now on more of a modern business than a medieval craft, affected by novel economic forces at home and abroad. In particular, foreign wars made the trade cycles more violent and disruptive. The long struggle against Napoleon brought about great inflation too. In Scotland the complex conjunction of events took the old system of commercial regulation to the point of collapse. In 1811 the weavers of Glasgow put in a request to the lord provost to convene the magistrates and fix a fresh, higher table of wages. He said he would rather see the problem sorted privately between the weavers and the manufacturers who bought their output, without worrying him or the council. The manufacturers refused to co-operate, however. Getting nowhere with the established procedures, the weavers went to the law.[40]

By June 1812 the weavers' case reached the Court of Session. It found that they did indeed possess the right they wished to exercise, of getting their wages fixed by the magistrates, and directed that this should happen. When the magistrates of Glasgow convened, they accepted the weavers' case for higher wages. But no way could be found of making the manufacturers pay, except through the wearisome and expensive process of pursuing long litigation against each of them. From then on the law ceased to help the weavers. When their patience and money ran out, 40,000 of them struck work in November. The government waited three weeks,

then arrested and charged their leaders with planning the strike –
though it was not at all clear this even constituted an offence in
Scots law. The industrial action went on till February 1813 before
it collapsed. The leaders were tried and imprisoned or, if they had
fled into England, outlawed.[41]

In court, counsel for the weavers was the Whig advocate, Francis
Jeffrey. He confronted the venerable Tory judge, Lord Boyle, with
an opinion handed down by himself some while before. Boyle
had ruled that once the magistrates had declared a price fair and
reasonable and the masters failed to comply, then the journeymen
'had the right to strike in any numbers'. His red-faced lordship tried
to claim he had been in error the last time. Scots law was developing,
he explained, not least through the institutional writers, or codifiers
of the courts' judgments; one had just given the correct view that
combination to strike was illegal. The Parliament at Westminster
anyway soon repealed the statutes on wages, in both Scotland and
England, which dated back to the sixteenth century.[42]

The whole business turned out disastrously for the weavers,
vanguard of the Scottish proletariat. They not only failed to assert
their legal rights, but lost them; they were not just beaten, but
humiliated. Their desperation even found an outlet in an attempted
armed insurrection in 1820, the so-called Radical War, in reality
a brief and inglorious episode after which three ringleaders were
executed.[43] Such sturdy, independent tradesmen had little that
was revolutionary about them, but rather represented what any
paternalist should have wished for from an educated working
class. Yet as these aristocrats of labour began to attain a social and
economic standing that might merit translation into a political
one, the authorities refused to countenance their claims and treated
them as no more than a rabble. Nor was history to vindicate their
struggle. They continued to fight in vain against falling prices for
their goods and competition from machines. In the end their craft
disappeared and the textile sector became industrialized. There was

nothing the old law, and the old outlook on life it had represented, could do to help. If it would no longer protect the weavers, or let them protect themselves, little hope could be held out to any other group. From now on it became harder and harder to maintain any legal privilege for skilled tradesmen.[44]

In a large part of the Scottish economy as it developed, unbridled capitalism mass-produced standardized goods in great enterprises. Under these conditions, the threat of strikes in the factories was the one thing that might set some limit to the power of the bosses. But a fresh crisis in the spring of 1837 showed this was not going to happen. Amid another sharp recession, the cotton spinners of Glasgow struck against a cut in wages. They had a trades union to co-ordinate their action. In the grimy suburbs north and east of the city, trouble brewed in the form of 'tumultuous assemblages'. The man charged with quelling them was the sheriff of Lanarkshire, Archibald Alison. He was an energetic conservative who gives the impression in his memoirs that he rather enjoyed confrontations. Now he rode over from his house at Possil to Oakbank, an industrial complex by the Forth-Clyde Canal, and found workers occupying a factory. They were armed just with sticks, but had beaten up twenty or thirty 'nobs', or strike-breakers. Of these Alison 'saw several... with blood upon their faces and clothes'. Glasgow's police was unable to act outside the old boundaries of the burgh, so the sheriff called up troops from their barracks in Duke Street to cow the strikers. He issued a proclamation 'warning the people of the danger they were in by joining in riotous acts and assemblages, and the determination of the magistrates to punish such acts'. With the military deployment any open defiance ceased, and at the end of three months the spinners were forced back to work on the employers' terms.[45]

But beneath the surface, skulduggery still went on. After an Irish nob was murdered in July, Alison resolved to arrest the leaders of the cotton spinners' union, who had gone underground. He enlisted the help of informers 'willing to give information if they were protected from danger'. He 'met the persons in an obscure place in Glasgow, and took their depositions', which included a tip-off 'that another individual named was to be murdered next day'. Alison found out the secret rendezvous of the spinners' leaders, the Black Boy pub in Gallowgate, and arrested the lot of them: five would be tried, convicted and transported to Australia. With that their union collapsed. The sheriff earned a reputation as scourge of the working class, but he vindicated himself with the claim that 'the stroke against the cotton-spinners' committee told with decisive violence upon all the trades who were out on strike at the time. Violence and intimidation rapidly declined in Glasgow.'[46] Not just that, but the infant Scottish trades unionism was destroyed, in effect for the rest of the century. A rigid stand by the employers with the total support of the state had crushed it.

Scottish trades unionism had its flaws, bound up with the class structure in which it emerged. Perhaps the most revealing example was to be found at Paisley, a turbulent town that still produced textiles of high quality. Its weavers wove shawls bearing the Paisley pattern borne back by brother Scots from the Orient. Here too the craftsmen were respectable and prosperous, at least while things went well, with time and taste to look up from their looms and educate themselves. The town's trades ran a library and a literary club. Weaver poets such as Robert Tannahill, Alexander Wilson and William Motherwell were urban counterparts to the ploughman poet, Robert Burns, whom they celebrated in the local Burns Club, the oldest in Scotland, founded in 1805. An observer found a 'prominent trait in the character of the Paisley weavers, and that is a pretty general taste for books. If you enter into conversation with them, you will find many of them well-informed on several subjects, particularly general history, natural history, and, of late, politics.'[47]

At Paisley as elsewhere, production had been organized in small units, often of just a single weaver and his family, using quite simple technology. It was open to anybody, with the little capital needed to set up in it, which meant the weaver might also become an employer if he did well enough to take on journeymen and apprentices. There was in practice not much difference between the artisan elite and the small employers: a formula for social mobility and, in the politics of the time, for a united front in favour of reform. But none of this could guarantee economic security. It was because mass production appeared in textile factories all over the region round them that these weavers retreated into the niche market of Paisley shawls, which might earn good money but remained vulnerable to fickle fashion. So it proved in the next recession that followed in 1841–3. The demand for shawls collapsed, and general economic conditions made it hard for the weavers to switch to another product. More than half the enterprises in Paisley went bust. A quarter of the townspeople were left dependent on poor relief. The burgh council had to declare itself insolvent.[48]

This was catastrophic for Paisley; but why, given the uninhibited capitalism of the time, could there not be faster adjustment to economic change? One commentator distinguished the independent, educated weavers from the wretched, illiterate hands in the factories:

The cotton spinning trade now established in this part of the country is highly valuable, on account of such numbers of poor children and women as are employed in its various operations, but it appears to have no tendency to improve the morals of the country. The numbers collected in large cotton mills, from families immersed in ignorance and vice, spread the contagion among such as have been more regularly educated, and profligate conduct is the natural result.[49]

Here was a disreputable underclass, different from the respectable working class that Paisley had earlier bred. Now skilled weavers, schooled, sober and decent, feared a fall into the pit of unskilled ignorance, intemperance and immorality. They just refused to be dragged under, even if they could find nothing else. In their spirit of independence, they felt superior to the pitiable creatures forced into endless hours of soul-destroying grind at power looms, often helpless women and children or hapless migrants fresh from the Highlands and Ireland. In other words, the progress of industrialization, from crafts to factories, here weakened and divided the working class.

Yet not everybody was degraded. While Paisley never again escaped the factory system, elsewhere the pride of the skilled tradesmen found fresh forms. In the shipyards along the Clyde it emerged anew from the demands made on the workers and met by them for rising standards of production in an advanced industry that would in the end conquer the world. It was not a matter, as it once had been, of the coveted legal privilege of any trade or trades. Instead, ruthless capitalism imposed the necessary discipline from on high. There was a division of labour so absolute that most employers would never dream of consulting their workers, let alone concede them a part in making decisions – not least because, as we saw above, the firms were owned and run by the founders or their sons, taking their own authority for granted. Within the workforce the older tradition of apprenticeship continued to imbue the lads just starting on the job with the inherited standards in quality of production, while also keeping out undesirable elements such as the Irish.[50]

There were some remorseless realities here, yet it was not an industrial system that provoked conflict. Over and above the degradation at the bottom of the social heap stretched a broad stratum of working-class Glaswegians who, if far from rich, accepted the conditions, made the grade and felt proud of what they achieved. The social reformer Charles Baird wrote: 'That many of the operatives in Glasgow live in comfort and are able to clothe themselves and their families, and to educate their children, is well known to all who know anything of them, and must be evident even to the passing stranger who sees their thousands pouring along the streets on the sabbath-day, apparently well fed and well clad, to their respective places of worship.'[51]

The sturdy working-class values of the weaving trade became diffused even as that particular trade headed towards extinction. Such values could enjoin political action. A weaver witness to a parliamentary inquiry boasted 'there have been more persons risen to wealth and eminence of handloom weavers than of all other trades put together in Scotland; I could name forty or fifty people who were handloom weavers who are now men of capital and character filling high situations. Two late lord provosts of Glasgow were handloom weavers in my remembrance.'[52] Robert Craig, 'an excellent specimen of an intelligent Glasgow weaver', was active in local politics. He preached co-operation among the classes and got a response: at one meeting 'after a strong appeal on the necessity of all the middling and lower ranks of society uniting to call for a thorough reform, he concluded amidst cheers and applause'.[53] Now and later, the political action that resulted was affirmative of the industrial system.

The new shipyards were still socially interesting places precisely because the bosses running them had risen out of the ranks of their workmates building the vessels. In and beyond the yards there emerged what turned out to be quite a robust alliance, stretching across the economy into politics, between an entrepreneurial elite not itself of refined or exalted origins, and a class of skilled workers sharing the same values. We might extend the alliance to include members of the liberal professions carrying out various specialist functions for the shipbuilding companies, or those from the lower middle class wearing white collars and working in the offices.

It is easy to stress the wide differences in personal incomes at the various levels of this structure.[54] But there were countervailing factors. The Scottish system of education remained the most democratic in Britain, and especially at the University of Glasgow it was easy for sons of the people to acquire, through the practical curriculum on offer there, the knowledge to assure them a rise in life. By 1910, the proportion of students from the manual working class reached 24 per cent – a number not matched again till today.[55] There was never going to be equality of incomes, but social mobility might make up for that.[56] Jock was as good as his maister.

Across that core of Glasgow's mid-Victorian society, the men espoused ideals of respectability. Even workers without much money could practise self-improvement and thrift, helped along by their religion and their literacy, while the sight of peers risen to high degree demonstrated how the common ideals might benefit them too. Social tensions still arose, though never to the extent of severing links between the bourgeoisie, which won the suffrage in 1832, and skilled workers still excluded from it. These on the whole assented to the proposition that the aristocracy's corrupt monopoly of national power was the true reason for economic distress and social injustice. This formed the basis, as we will see below, of Glasgow's popular Victorian liberalism.[57] It would indeed before long join in robbing the Tory aristocracy of power in the country. Yet it never became inclusive of tens of thousands of unskilled poor people breaking stones, toiling in factories, laying railway lines, labouring on building sites, cleaning the streets or sweeping the chimneys, driving the wagons or running the messages, or else dashing away with a smoothing iron – few of them in stable jobs and most of them therefore faced with bouts of unemployment as a fact of life.

One general consequence for Scotland might have been polarization, with sections of the nation driven apart, perhaps to the peril of the nation itself. That was what, for example, happened in neighbouring Ireland during the nineteenth century: the land-owning aristocracy, the industrial proletariat of Ulster and the population of the dirt-poor rural regions never found any common cause, but instead drifted into alienation from one another. Ireland has not been able to unite since, in the sense of class or in any other sense.[58]

Yet the Scots sustained themselves as a nation. Queen Victoria thought they had 'a quite different character' from the English.[59] She might not herself have been the one to put her finger on the difference, but she could leave that job to Alexander Sellar, Liberal MP for Partick. He painted this picture of the relations of social classes in Scotland:

While the landed aristocracy and the wealthier professional classes still keep aloof from the people, and have in a great measure adopted English tastes and habits, and Episcopalian forms of worship, and English ideas on education, the middle and lower classes have remained staunch to Scottish traditions and influences. These two classes have become in a manner blended together into one class without any very distinct line of demarcation between them. They attend the Presbyterian churches, send their children to the parochial or other schools, and to the universities, where they sit together on the same benches; they associate together afterwards, and live their own lives, influenced to an almost inappreciable extent by the vexatious restrictions and annoyances of caste which are so noticeable in the middle classes south of the Tweed.[60]

In Glasgow this Victorian social fabric lasted down to the First World War, if by that time fraying somewhat. Production, incomes and employment had all risen, though not without interruption in a Scotland with no government to guide the economy. Yet whatever else might have lacked, it was not capital, as proved by huge civic investments made in Glasgow, Paisley, Hamilton, Motherwell, Greenock and other communities of the west. They counted as models of their kind: delegations came from the rising cities of North America to study their municipal example.[61]

British state and Scottish economy stood at some distance from each other, yet it would have been difficult to find anybody who thought this a disadvantage. Even in hard times Glaswegians gave little sign of wishing for intervention from on high, but on the contrary showed every confidence they could overcome their problems by themselves and so resume their upward progress. In 1914 the city's and the region's capitalists were still experimenting, innovating and investing out of their own resources, and still enlisting the co-operation of the workers: something that could no longer be taken for granted in London, for example, the real hotbed of industrial unrest since late Victorian times. A baffled agitator, Harry McShane, wrote of the shipyards on the Clyde: 'It wasn't easy to rouse up the engineers; they were very respectable with their blue suits and bowler hats and used to come to mass meetings with their umbrellas.'[62] This may look idiosyncratic, but Glasgow's achievement was indeed a local one. The city did not get its skills and labour, much less its ideas and agendas, from anywhere else. Its values arose from the upbringing, the experience and the energies of the people who lived along the Clyde.

The achievement extended into politics. At the municipal level, with the exclusion of both the Tories and the underclass, it proved easy to run civic politics on non-partisan lines. The system relied on individuals of public spirit, successful businessmen or professionals with the time to spare. Yet they did not take a narrow, class-based view of their interests: even if unable to guarantee jobs or incomes, they did want the workers to enjoy a tolerable standard of living. At the national level, it became a Liberal consensus: that was how both bosses and workers voted. The Liberal Party had split in 1886 on William Gladstone's proposals for Irish Home Rule, but from 1906 it again dominated Scotland. In Glasgow the divisions over Ireland still went deeper than any between capitalists and socialists, so standing in the way of the development of a labour party (here the Independent Labour Party). Meanwhile a section of the Protestant workers started voting for the unionists in order to keep Irish immigrants down. In the light of some brutal realities in the workplace, socialists could look rather fey: 'Nothing is too hard for the members in their virgin enthusiasm to do. They run their little prints, they sell their stocks of pamphlets, they drop their pennies into the collecting box, they buy their ILP tea and cocoa as though they were members of an idealistic Communist society.'[63] So wrote Ramsay MacDonald, destined to become the first Labour prime minister. There was little here, least of all the commitment to temperance hinted at by the tea and cocoa, to lure the average red-blooded Scots working man.

For both capital and labour, the First World War and its aftermath changed the scene forever. There had perhaps been some chance they would be drawn closer together by the demands on industry. In particular there was one pressure on Glasgow arising from a novel source: the government in London. The drive to streamline output of munitions impinged on restrictive practices that were in any event being disrupted by the very enthusiasm of combative Glaswegians to sign up and serve their country in battle. In the shipyards and other workplaces they left behind, that raised the question of dilution, of whether their jobs should be filled by somebody other than time-served craftsmen – even by foreigners, even by women. If local management and labour could have collaborated on this, they might have found acceptable solutions elsewhere. Instead there was much tension on Red Clydeside, amid which neither side ever really got its own way – not the government either.[64] Once the war was over, the need and the chance for rapprochement dissipated, just as the opposite problem of a slump in production arose.

The time-served craftsman from the Clyde, proud of his skills and his status, had signed up with brother Scots to serve in the war, expecting to return to a familiar scene. But for those who survived the terrible losses on the western front, the sequel at home also proved tragic and wasteful, if in a different way. They found a nation bled of its Victorian vigour. There was no going back to the good old days, only the recurrence of economic crises which made Scotland comparable to those European societies that under the same stresses suffered social collapse and revolution. Industry shrank and famous companies disappeared into take-over or liquidation. Employers and workers either went elsewhere with their talents and skills or swelled the shuffling, hopeless ranks of the unemployed. Despite political agitation, no revolution followed here. Instead, for the first time since the Union, the city and the nation began to insulate itself from global progress and to seek refuge within a narrower British compass. It did not want to beat the world any more, asking rather for aid from London. The war cast a long shadow over Scotland's development altogether, and changed the way the Scots saw themselves. The grand old Victorian ideals dissolved. Scotland has never found better ones.[65]

Again, on both sides of industry, the First World War's legacy of mistrust hindered co-operation. Social divisions widened and politics, too, suddenly seemed to be all about class. The view was reinforced by fraught developments in the British public sphere from the General Strike of 1926 up to Labour's electoral landslide in 1945. This could be interpreted as at last bringing to the workers a just measure of the political power that their social and economic rise by now merited. Between the wars, Glasgow's businessmen had still tried to take the sting out of cyclical but deepening depression.[66] They sought and accepted drastic measures to keep afloat. While their exertions occasionally brought some relief, in the long run they failed to halt the economic decline. After the Second World War, nationalization left many without a role.

Others abandoned their original businesses for less demanding and unprofitable ones. Apart from a couple of heroic figures who still thought they might save the situation, there was little to keep the rest in the economy of the west of Scotland. When British enterprise underwent a rebirth later in the century, Clydeside was no longer in a position to take part. By 1992, it merely dreaded the closure of the steelworks at Ravenscraig that in effect would mark the death of Scottish heavy industry.

The fate of the Scottish economy was instead largely determined from outside, by the government in London or by international influences. Under these conditions, the practised skills of the workforce were likely to be lost, partly through emigration to more prosperous countries and partly because of the failure of the manufacturing sector to renew itself. In the latter case, the trend continued right to the end of the twentieth century, anyway becoming by that time general in Britain and other advanced industrial societies. Services in Scotland grew from 19 per cent of output in 1911 to 43 per cent by 1981, with the sector itself undergoing large internal changes: on the one hand the domestic help that had kept Victorian households running virtually disappeared, while on the other hand there was a great expansion of employment in the public sector, in schools and hospitals and so on.[67]

The results reached deep down into Scottish society. In 1921, more than one in three of employed Scots was a skilled manual worker; by 1971 this proportion had sunk to fewer than one in four. That decline accelerated round the turn of the twenty-first century. In Glasgow today, 5 per cent of the workforce are engaged in manufacturing, compared to 10 per cent over the rest of Clydeside and 8 per cent in Scotland as a whole; deindustrialization has gone further in the city than anywhere else. The rest of the workers are for the most part scattered over public and private services, with 15 per cent in health, 13 per cent in business administration and 10 per cent in retail.[68]

Scotland always housed more manual workers than England, but the change from manufacturing to services did not signify movement towards English levels of affluence. It was a counterpart in the working class to the decline of enterprise and loss of indigenous capitalism among the bourgeoisie. With commercial power being concentrated in London, Glasgow became part of a 'branch plant' economy, but one with a high rate of unemployment compared to others. Today, of the city's leading manufacturers, the Weir Group alone is locally owned. Some other big companies survive, but not as independent outfits. An example is Tennent's, with the brewery at Wellpark in the East End that it has run since 1740; its lager is the Scottish male's favourite tipple, though the cans are no longer adorned with alluring lovelies. In any event the company has been since 2009 a subsidiary of the Irish group, C&C. The prime recent example of renewal, as opposed to survival, was the Stakis Organization built up in hotels and related businesses by a Cypriot immigrant to Glasgow (who also gave the city its Greek Orthodox cathedral), but sold out to Hilton in 1999. Leisure in general remained a sector offering some evidence of successful local enterprise, as among small building contractors; in practice, leisure in this case meant pubs and betting shops. Otherwise, as the leading Liberal Democrat, Sir Vince Cable, wrote while still a young economist at the University of Glasgow: 'Local interests tend to be disproportionately composed of ex-sportsmen and friends or relations of city councillors.'[69] The public sector, in widening the range of services, did take up some slack in the labour market. The representative figure of the Scottish proletariat was no longer the skilled craftsman but the worker in the lower grades of employment by the city or the state.

None of this solved the problem of high unemployment that had dogged Glasgow since the 1920s. At the time of writing, 66 per cent of Glaswegians of working age have a job, compared with 73 per cent in Scotland as a whole. The actual rate of registered unemployment is 8 per cent compared to 6 per cent. About one household in three contains no working adult, a figure higher than anywhere else in Scotland. Unemployment is worse for men than for women, and runs at 60 per cent of the unskilled jobless. Yet a shortage of labour exists for many skilled occupations.[70]

Most of Glasgow's social problems can be traced back to unemployment and to an unbalanced occupational structure.[71] Following a deceptive boom in the decade or so after 1945, the number of jobs in the city fell, for the most part in the traditional industries and through the closure of local plants now owned elsewhere. The rate of decline was twice as fast as for Scotland as a whole. Consequences came in the shape of emigration, too. In 1945 Glasgow was one of two or three dozen cities in the world that had a population of more than a million. Today there are hundreds of such cities, some of which, as in the remoter parts of China, we have never heard of. Meanwhile the population of Glasgow had sunk by 2011 to just under 600,000, because of a deliberate policy of dispersal but also because of heavy emigration, never matched – as elsewhere in Britain – by the immigration of ethnic minorities. Most Scots emigrants were from Glasgow and the west, and more than half of them went overseas: these people and their skills were normally lost for good. Even the high birth rate in the region was outstripped by the outward movement. This was not a bad thing if it led to less overcrowded housing and to a better life both for those who left and for those who stayed. But migration was selective of the young and active, which meant that in future a weaker economic base would be trying to support a higher proportion of dependants, especially pensioners.

These features are not atypical of the British provincial cities that rose, flourished and fell with the industrial revolution, yet no other, excepting possibly Liverpool, seems to have developed anything like Glasgow's culture of class. Here it rests on a Scottish myth that might make social mobility easier. No more unlikely a personage than the historiographer royal of Scotland from 1979 to 1993, Gordon Donaldson – anything but a socialist – declared Scotland to be 'a more egalitarian country than England'.[72] True or untrue this proposition may be, but a virtue of it lies in the very fact it is hard to prove or disprove. Doubtless to the chagrin of Scotland's relentlessly determinist historians, there is no series of statistics to demonstrate the egalitarianism of the country: on the contrary, the statistics that are available – like those for mortality, educational attainment, quality of housing and so on – tend to demonstrate the opposite. They are still not enough to dispel the myth. But then, myths are seldom there to be proved or disproved. They have another function, and Scots are not alone in resorting to it: we need only think of the power of the American Dream.[73]

Myth does not describe or elucidate features of the social structure. Its purpose is to legitimate belief and action in the present, if by means of drawing on the past. For preference, it should not be mere invention but bear some resemblance to reality, or at least to certain realities. In Scotland there are enough of them, especially of a cultural kind, to be of service in the myth-making: the Presbyterian tradition, the educational system and so on. In Glasgow there has been also an economic reality stretching from the era of the time-served crafts into that of deindustrialization, of the self-made working man who forges his own fate or takes its blows coolly. Today it too has become a cultural value in a system of subjective meaning projected by Scots on the actual, the post-modern social institutions or experiences of civil society, in the hope of dealing the better with them.

This is the clue to understanding the national culture of class. Two-thirds of Scots identify themselves as working class, when objectively the true proportion must be smaller; in fact most Scots are middle class when classified according to their education, income and housing (perhaps not inside the city of Glasgow itself but certainly in Greater Glasgow).[74] There is no crude determinism at work here, none of that Marxist logic of cultural superstructure built on economic base favoured by the dominant school of Scottish historians. In reality people do not act one way or another because they occupy a particular position in society. Rather they choose for themselves the meanings, values and ideas in which to clothe the structural aspects of their society. Multiplication of statistics does not explain these choices, but cultural analysis may get us some way towards understanding them. We will pursue the matter in a later chapter.

An aspect of this culture of class is that it can generate social and political action, if not in any straightforward relationship. On the contrary, the meanings and values attaching to social class, in other words the culture of class, are often equivocal. For now we can only observe them. A good example came in George Square, Glasgow, on the night of September 18, 2014, and the celebration then of the cause of national independence as a species of proletarian culture.

5

Poverty: 'The lowest
state of misery'

ON MAY 5, 1843, the Revd Norman Macleod, minister of St
Columba's Church, Glasgow, gave evidence to a royal commission
sent north by the Parliament at Westminster with a view to
proposing amendments to the Scottish Poor Law, in force since
1574. Macleod was an expert witness on the Highlands: his church,
where he conducted the worship in Gaelic, traced its origins back
to 1770 and the efforts made then to meet the spiritual needs of
clansmen and their families who crowded into the city, driven by
conflict or clearance. Macleod was a son of the manse of Morvern
and at sixty still remained 'a remarkably handsome man, with a
broad forehead, an open countenance full of benevolence and hair
which from an early age was snowy white'.[1] A former moderator of
the General Assembly of the Church of Scotland, he had recently
been appointed a chaplain to Queen Victoria. But his flock admired
him most for his exertions to ward off famine after the failure of the
Highland harvest in 1836–7; they called him *Caraid nan Gaidheal*,
Friend of the Gaels. He diffused his benign influence through a
periodical, *Cuairtear nan Gleann,* 'Visitor to the Glens', which he
had started publishing so as to tap into the growing literacy among

Gaelic speakers. He stayed in touch with every aspect of Highland life. This was why the royal commissioners wanted to talk to him.

The commissioners especially wanted to know what happened to migrant Gaels once they got to Glasgow. Macleod had, a few years before, carried out a survey of his own:

> I employed ten individuals to visit every house in the city and suburbs. We took down the names of every individual we could find who was born in the Highlands. The statement occupies two large folio books like atlases, and shows that there were 23,000 native Highlanders whose names were arranged in columns. Then there was the number of families, the churches they attended, their condition in life and the state of each family. We found 11,000 of the lowest class of Highlanders who were not looked after by any minister appointed for that purpose. Such was the state of the Highland population in Glasgow at that time, and it is much the same now.[2]

Macleod went on to explain from his personal experience how difficult it would be for any single minister to deal with the distress behind these figures. At his church, the available resources allowed him to offer only limited relief even in the worst cases: 'It is not given in the belief that they could live upon it, it is given in the way of addition to what they might otherwise receive; and poor widows occasionally earn something by washing, cleaning out byres, sweeping rooms and places. Many of them, however, can do nothing.'[3]

Asked whether he thought these Gaels had overall improved their lot by moving to Glasgow, Macleod took leave to doubt it:

> They have free air in the Highlands, at all events, and pure water. They are found either in the highest attic here, or under ground altogether. The Highlanders who come here, and their families, are poor people, or the children of poor

people ejected from crofts. They come from a place where they have been paying £10 or £12, till they come down to wretched villages; then they are rouped out and, leaving their native place, are at length landed at the Broomielaw, where they are left without labour and work. The next time we hear of them is, that they are in the infirmary for some infectious complaints; and they are sometimes here for a year or two in the lowest state of misery – no clothes that they can go out with on the sabbath-day, and their necessities are of the most painful character, as they have not received a settlement here, and have no means of their own.[4]

The last thought gives some clue as to why this kind of privation was so hard to deal with under the existing Poor Law. To get help, people needed a settlement – that is, they had to be on the list of those eligible for relief maintained (at least in theory) by each parish. And a qualification for getting on the list was that they had to have been born in the parish. It was a rule reflecting the Scotland of 1574 rather than the Scotland of 1843. In 1574 the vast majority of Scots lived and died in or near the places where they had been born. In 1843 Scottish society was on the move, at the national and at the individual level, with a general drift from the country to the towns, and with both emigration and immigration complicating the pattern. Poor relief that depended on a stable domicile was just not going to work any more.

Poor relief had also depended on the integrity of the Church of Scotland and its competence to carry out the duties laid on it by statute. But the encounter between Macleod and the royal commissioners took place just thirteen days before the Disruption, which was to close ten years of bitter dispute with the British state in the schism of the Kirk. It became a crisis for the whole of Scottish society, of which vital structures had been shaped by Presbyterian principles for nearly three centuries – the old Poor Law included.[5]

Before the Reformation of 1560 the poor had been a charge on
the monasteries, but afterwards the monasteries no longer existed.
The reformer John Knox himself pinpointed the need for a new
system, though even in his own parish of St Giles in Edinburgh this
was easier said than done – and a tall order if he expected the canny
burgesses to pay for something of no direct benefit to themselves.
Here lay a conundrum of Calvinism: those instilled with its godly
sense of personal responsibility could take an unforgiving view of
those who did not share it. Proper objects of charity they might
be, but charity would be wasted on them if their poverty was
their own fault – better for them to get off their backsides and
fend for themselves.[6]

This was the principle behind the Poor Law of 1574. A practical effect of the Presbyterian outlook it embodied was to draw
a distinction between the legal poor and the illegal poor, or
the deserving poor and the undeserving poor. The legal poor
comprised those young and old with no relations to care for them,
then those of any age who were sick, crippled, blind or mad, that
is to say, permanently incapable of looking after themselves. They
were all entitled to help without further ado. Others might seek
support only in a crisis, during a famine or a temporary period
of unemployment. In the early days of the Poor Law's operation
they could be quite hopeful of getting it, at least from their own
parishes, if it was a matter of their just needing a little extra to
tide them over. That often proved acceptable at this stage in
the evolution of the system – which would, however, turn less
generous in the eighteenth century and less generous still in the
nineteenth century.[7]

Help might be offered out of the legal assessments, or local rates,
that could be imposed in each parish for support of the poor. They
were not, however, obligatory. Under the act of 1574 the provost
and bailies of each burgh became responsible for its operation.
Municipal and parochial boundaries often coincided, which meant

the authority of the magistrates reinforced that of the kirk sessions in poor relief as in all else. The worthy citizens sitting in these seats of petty power often preferred to avoid local taxes, and to keep the provision of relief reliant on collections from congregations, on charitable bequests or on other forms of giving. The overall level of resources therefore remained limited. For a couple of centuries it seems to have more or less sufficed, at least in normal conditions. In Sir John Sinclair's *Old Statistical Account*, compiled in the 1790s out of reports from ministers, there was little complaint about any shortfalls of relief for the legal poor.[8]

The illegal poor were all the rest without work. Often they turned into vagrants on the move and so not amenable to regulation, many probably just looking for a job away from home, if perhaps sometimes covertly living from theft. In any event, Scots law here made no distinction, and none of them was entitled to help. In modern times we have encouraged people to seek a job in some other place if they cannot find one where they are. The older Scotland frowned on this, and so put up a barrier to its own faster economic development. In short, national policy towards poverty showed a mix of relief for the legal poor and something often approaching persecution of the illegal poor till these should one way or another cease to fall foul of the law, preferably by finding a job in their own parish.[9]

In practice, statutory relief even for the legal poor was an ideal only built up slowly, by trial and error. The provosts and bailies had been given the power to raise a tax or assessment on their burghs because, while the system remained parsimonious, it did carry some costs. They needed to give their consent to any tax, and they were seldom in a rush. Glasgow raised its first assessment only in 1638, half a century after the pioneers among the other royal burghs.[10] It then applied the law strictly. For instance, the town council barely tolerated the destitute Highland boys, many uprooted by civil war, who soon flocked in asking to be fed. In the winter of 1649–50, as famine threatened, the council relented far enough to let them be looked after 'till the cold season pass'. Yet they were all shipped out down the River Clyde in February, when the weather could not have warmed up that much.[11] Through the seventeenth century the Poor Law continued to operate at this rudimentary level, often interrupted by the troubles of the time.

With the Union of 1707, problems of poverty took on fresh forms. The burghs expanded, in Glasgow's case so far that it had to be divided into six different parishes. It became harder for any minister to know everybody under his charge or to distinguish between good and bad claims for relief. And urban churchgoing failed to rise in line with population, so that the relative size of collections fell too. The trends would continue for another century till most burghs needed to impose legal assessments. And in the new capitalist economy that finally emerged, the distress was unlike anything known before, a matter not of personal character among the poor but of macroeconomics and the cyclical deficiency of demand. Though hampered by past practice, the burghs of Scotland had to find novel means of relief.[12]

Glasgow took the lead. It was a city of entrepreneurs also open to social experiment, to an extent not obvious in the more conservative professional class of Edinburgh. Nor was Glasgow ruled, like Edinburgh, by a corruptible, heavily indebted town council indifferent to the problems its bad management caused for poor relief, among other matters. For example, Glasgow made medical provision for the poor by dividing the city into districts and assigning a surgeon to each, while in Edinburgh it was possible for paupers to get treatment only if surgeons offered it of their own free will. Glasgow was altogether the more charitable kind of place. Still, it looked first after its own and made no attempt to enter into arrangements beyond its bounds with the nearby parishes of the Barony, Gorbals and Govan, where there were people in just as much need as any inside the city.[13]

Poor relief was at this stage the responsibility of four groups in Glasgow: the general kirk session with ministers and elders from each of its six churches, the town council, the incorporated trades and the Merchants' House (the latter two giving help only to their members, or the families of their members). In 1731, amid public complaints about a rise in destitution and begging, the four groups decided to start working together and pool their resources for the poor. They delegated their powers to a board of management chaired by the lord provost and operating according to a new set of rules.[14]

The main consequence came in the erection in 1733 of the Town's Hospital, the first poorhouse in Scotland. Sited at a pleasant spot by the Clyde it had the purpose of housing, clothing and feeding those citizens of the burgh unable to look after themselves, all within a single public institution.[15] This indoor relief, as it became known, was supposed to be given in return for work, which would keep such people off the streets in daytime. But any hope the poorhouse might be viable as a productive unit soon proved vain, so there was in reality no chance it might pay for itself. Things could hardly have been otherwise when most inmates were the impotent old, the orphaned young or the disabled. The managers of the poorhouse probably thought to follow the principles of 1574, or at most only adapt them to some inescapable facts of urban life, unemployment and homelessness. Bold as the experiment was, it did not in fact prove to be a permanent answer to these problems.[16]

By 1774 the Town's Hospital was full. Something had to be done for the people who could find no room there. The answer was outdoor relief delivered in kind, that is to say, as a monthly allowance of oatmeal financed from an assessment on the citizens; paupers who preferred cash instead needed to apply to one of the kirk sessions.[17] Outdoor relief, or support to applicants living in their own homes, would remain necessary and offered the advantage of being cheaper. There was still a stipulation that the allowances should never be enough to provide the sole means of subsistence. Those taking them had to sign a disposition giving the poorhouse a claim, if they died, on the value of their possessions up to the amount of relief granted – just as those entering the poorhouse had to turn over all their goods to it. No Glaswegian was going to get something for nothing.[18]

Scotland so far remained innocent of the modern trade cycles, throwing thousands out of work at once, which were now to become the main cause of unemployment and which overwhelmed the existing arrangements to deal with it. The parsimony of the Poor Law tended actually to intensify pressure for people to move out from the countryside into the towns, as if there were not enough forces working to that end anyway. In the burghs the ministers of the kirks, like their rural brethren, again bore the burden of distributing such resources as the statute provided. They often did so in an uncoordinated and inconsistent fashion, there being no central authority to impose any other system. They could still never legally hand over money to non-natives of the parish, so not to the economic migrants. And especially they were supposed to leave all the able-bodied unemployed to their own devices. For these, in the circumstances, the hopeful move to the town might turn out to have been not such a good idea, given the difficulties of ever making their way back.[19]

Across the west of Scotland, the problems often had their worst impact in smaller communities tending to rely on a single type of production. When recession struck the specialized weaving trade of Paisley in 1820, the workers decided they needed something more than desperate, temporary measures to deal with the recurring bouts of instability they were facing these days. Over 800 of them – much more than a pauper residue – sought to establish their entitlement to poor relief by going to law. They made a claim to the parish and, when it was refused, to the sheriff of Renfrewshire, who granted it. The parish appealed to the Court of Session. The court decided for the parish, confirming that even in the new industrial economy there could in Scotland be no such thing as general legal entitlement to relief on grounds of unemployment. Each parish would therefore remain free to give what help to the jobless it wanted – and if it gave nothing, that must be the end of the matter. Change in society did not mean change in the Poor Law, then: so long as each parish held authority over its own relief, there could be no uniform national regulation and no liberalizing reform at that level.[20]

At least the citizens of Glasgow did not remain indifferent to the growing poverty on their streets. If Presbyterian prudence and civic scruple kept down the money passing through the channels of public relief, that still left scope for private charities. The amount collected in the poor rate reached a peak amid the economic crisis near the end of the Napoleonic War, and from 1815 was actually falling as an even deeper depression followed the peace.[21] Relief was now spread more and more thinly over the rising numbers out of work, till it amounted to little better than a pittance. By the ethos of the system, this should have been a chance and a spur for jobless Glaswegians to show they could fend for themselves. Still, when some looked as if they were failing the test, their richer neighbours did not as a matter of fact leave them in the lurch, but concentrated their help in the private charities; the money so dispensed ran at seven times the amounts doled out from the poor rate.[22]

In such conditions, it is easier to understand than some modern scholars have allowed, why from 1819 the Revd Thomas Chalmers tried his experiment in the East End of Glasgow of running a system of welfare on an entirely voluntary basis.[23] This indeed broke with the established practice in assessed parishes, yet it fitted in well with the recent resort to private charity as the citizens resisted taxation. It could even be seen as a bold and imaginative move by Chalmers to take under the wing of the Church of Scotland – and by the same token to make use of its structure and organization

– the charitable impulses still to be found in the population at large. It might then restore a social role the Kirk was in danger of losing. So, far from constricting aid to the needy, this might have seemed the best way of increasing it. Certainly that was what Chalmers wanted from his ministry at St John's Church in the Gallowgate, and to a fair extent he got it.[24]

Chalmers moved there during an economic crisis that prompted questioning all over Britain as to how to deal with the resulting distress. The English already believed their own Poor Law cost them too much, though it, too, offered nothing to those it defined as the undeserving poor. Chalmers never thought much of the English: 'In all parts of England the shameless and abandoned profligacy of the lower orders is most deplorable.'[25] As for Scotland, he had no wish to penalize actual incapacity, to cut off destitute people unable to look after themselves. Still, those destitute people able to look after themselves must do so – and that, he judged, would be most of them. One of his first moves at St John's was to appoint deacons to visit parishioners claiming relief and see whether they merited it. There was no simple benchmark, but the deacons would suggest to their charges how they might start fending for themselves, if necessary with help from family, friends or neighbours. Not till other possibilities of support were exhausted would aid from the parish be confirmed and continued. The implied overall reduction in relief was not itself the object of this exercise, however, which lay rather in the reformation of individuals who, through self-help, would lessen their own degree of dependency. At the same time the rich were called on for greater charity. From both sides, a more moral and independent community might be created. The available money could then be turned to better uses than a dole, notably to building new churches and schools for the spreading industrial districts.[26]

The charismatic Chalmers blended high hopes with good intentions, and at St John's his scheme seemed to work well enough:

while the population of the parish rose during his ministry, the quantum of pauperism dropped. But dispute over his achievement, or otherwise, continues down to the present. Historians brought up in the Scottish socialism of the late twentieth century have taken the sniffiest possible attitude to Chalmers' exertions as being at bottom motivated by dogmatic callousness;[27] little of the revisionism of English historiography on the Poor Law has so far crossed the border.[28] It is a valid critique that not every parish would or could find a Chalmers. Still, in his own time he was much admired for his depth of commitment to his work and his decision to go and live among the poor (as few modern academics would care to do). Even in the Scotland of the twenty-first century we may yet develop a more open attitude to the idea that poverty will be best treated by engagement of local communities and fellow human beings, rather than by impersonal handouts from the bureaucracy of a state washing its hands of further consequence.[29]

In 1823 Chalmers left his ministry at St John's for academic life at St Andrews. Though he believed his experiment had been a success, it did not long survive his departure. In Scotland and the rest of Britain, there was to be no cure for poverty while economic development remained so erratic and unstable. For the time being the Tories remained in power in London, and it was the Whigs that from opposition pressed for reform, including a new Poor Law. After they took office in 1832, they dealt first with the English system, which they considered far too lax. The government appointed a royal commission, and two years later brought in fresh legislation. Its great novelty was the workhouse, where people unable to support themselves could live and labour – if in surroundings made so unpleasant that they would not want to stay unless they had no choice.[30]

It was a harsher regime than in Scotland, but the Whig government still regarded the Scots Poor Law as rather exemplary and saw no pressing need to amend it. That changed with the recurrent economic crisis of these years: steady, sustained growth would not resume before the middle of the century. Meanwhile migrants to the towns had to cope as best they could. If they got a first foot on the urban ladder it was often in a job where they did not earn enough to feed, house and clothe themselves, let alone a family. Many sank below the level of subsistence. The west of Scotland suffered worse than most regions. Already in 1837 soup kitchens were feeding 20,000 of Glasgow's poor, one in ten of the population.[31] The burden on the city turned still worse when its boundaries were extended in 1846 to take in the ring of grimy suburbs on the edge of the old burgh. The death rate in urban Scotland actually rose during this decade, with terrible epidemics of cholera or other infectious diseases. Mortality in Glasgow, in a population weakened by the effects of poverty, was the highest of all.

Fierce public debate followed. On one side of it stood William Pulteney Alison, professor of physiology at the University of Edinburgh. He showed in his professional life deep sympathy for the poor, and recognized 'the utter inadequacy of private benevolence'.[32] In 1840 he published a pamphlet, *Observations on the Management of the Poor in Scotland*, attacking the lack of provision: 'The upper ranks in Scotland do much less (and what they do they do less systematically and therefore less effectively) for the relief of poverty and of sufferings resulting from it than those of any other country in Europe which is really well regulated, and much less than experience shows to be necessary.'[33] Alison demonstrated how Scotland in fact just cast many of the unemployed adrift, the economic migrants above all. It was cruel to them and it let the rich escape their proper responsibilities. Clearly, Alison's views stood in contrast to those of Chalmers, and the subsequent argument between the two was as much about social philosophy as about practical measures.

It moved on from the abstract to the concrete when in 1840 both men accepted an invitation to present their views to the public in

Glasgow. Their debate filled Blackfriars Church, just off the High Street. In his opening speech Chalmers went back to the days, two decades before, of his ministry in the East End. People had criticized it, yet they could not deny the results: poverty and crime were reduced by the example set at St John's. If those results had still not turned out quite convincing, that was because the town council of Glasgow never co-operated in extending the system. Turning to his adversary, Chalmers addressed their opposing views. Alison believed the urban environment had to be improved before individuals could improve themselves. Chalmers believed the reverse. For him the first step was the Christian awakening of personal morality, after which better social conditions would 'necessarily follow'. The spirit retained its saving power even in the most degraded surroundings, and the preaching of the Word with the practice of charity could break the cycle of despair. Firm in that belief, Chalmers offered to return from his comfortable academic chair to the hard graft of the parochial ministry and conduct another experiment like the one at St John's, provided this time the corporation co-operated with him. Money? There was no shortage of money, Chalmers thundered. Why, every year the working class of Glasgow spent more than a million on drink. Here was money that, with religious and moral instruction, they would want to use for self-help and communal benevolence. In his response Alison made the mistake, still made by Scottish academics today, of trying to persuade his audience with a barrage of statistics. He proved no match for the practised eloquence of one of the best preachers of the time, by turns poignant and witty. Still, this was an argument not to be won by a single confrontation.[34] For the rest of the nineteenth century the history of Scottish poor relief became in many ways an inconclusive battle between Chalmers's principle of voluntary effort and Alison's call for statutory action.

These Scottish arguments continued to be influenced from south of the border too. A lawyer in London, Edwin Chadwick, had acted

as secretary to the English royal commission of 1834, but soon came
to doubt if its proposals could by themselves win the battle against
poverty – there was a need to address deeper issues than how much
relief to pay to whom. He started on a new report, to be published
in 1842 under the title of *The Sanitary Condition of the Labouring
Population*. This time it covered Scotland as well as England, and
may have been the first document to bring to wider attention
the appalling conditions in Glasgow. It showed, for example, that the
population of the parish of Blackfriars had grown by 40 per cent
since 1831 but the number of dwellings not at all. The delegation that
came with Chadwick, to peer down the dingy wynds and closes at
pinched, verminous Glaswegians, felt shocked by the overcrowding
in the old burgh. Along the High Street the back-courts had not
even the open, stinking drains common in other Scottish towns:
rubbish and excrement just got heaped up in huge middens till
some private contractor thought them worth carting away. One of
the investigators, J.C. Symons, waxed eloquent over these horrors:
'I have seen human degradation in some of its worst phases, both in
England and abroad, but I can advisedly say, that I did not believe,
until I visited the wynds of Glasgow, that so large an amount of
filth, crime, misery and disease existed on one spot in any civilized
country.' Chadwick's team were no strangers to life in the slums: all
British cities housed their share of squalor, contagion, starvation,
wretchedness and overcrowding. Yet, in his words, 'the condition
of the population in Glasgow was the worst of any we had seen in
any part of Great Britain.'[35]

Chadwick was not saying anything unknown to Glaswegians.
The chief constable, David Miller, himself observed that in 'the
very centre of the city there is an accumulated mass of squalid
wretchedness which is probably unequalled in any town of the
British dominions'.[36] Charles Baird, a reforming lawyer, showed
the visitors round, perhaps to this scene, which he had recorded
after calling on three women in their tenement:

They were all actually in a state of nudity, not having clothes sufficient to cover their nakedness. Before I could speak to them they were obliged to cover themselves in something like old torn bed coverlets. The house was completely destitute of beds or other furniture – positively nothing. The inmates were starving, having no food whatever in the house, and it appears they had shut themselves up for the purpose of dying; their modesty having prevented them from making their circumstances known.'[37]

Baird further noted that no amount of personal prudence might save people from penury because of 'the sudden convulsions and fluctuations of trade, the high price of provisions... and above all their liability to diseases'.[38] He put it all down to drink: 'In London, the proportion of public houses to other houses is as 1 to 56; in Glasgow it is as 1 to 10; every tenth house in Glasgow is a spirit shop; I should say, as far as my statistical researches have gone, that the proportion of whisky drunk in Glasgow is twice or thrice as much as in any similar population upon the face of the globe.'[39]

Alison was also with Chadwick in Glasgow. Both knew poverty and disease went hand in hand. Alison, the medical man, believed poverty caused disease. It created an environment through which germs could spread: cure poverty and disease would be cured too. Chadwick believed disease caused poverty. The first concern should therefore be with sanitation, so as to get rid of the filth and stench in which the cycle of deprivation started up. Of course both were in their own ways right, and in any event they did not disagree about the need for some sanitary policy. By now they were knocking at an open door of public opinion. Alison might attack bourgeois indifference, yet nobody snug in a big house could ignore how epidemics spread outwards from the teeming tenements. While Chadwick's ideas at length limited the extent of the contagions, they did not ward off other pitiless companions of poverty, the harrowing infant mortality or the mysterious consumption (tuberculosis had yet to be identified as an infectious disease).[40]

Meanwhile, the Conservatives regained power at Westminster in 1841. An acute crisis arose almost immediately at Paisley when its textile industry collapsed. None of the thousands of weavers thrown out of work had any clear entitlement to relief. Victorian politicians always felt wary of intervening in a local economy, but in this case were alarmed at the scale of the problem. A delegation from the stricken town, led by its treasurer, David Murray, and by one of its ministers, the Revd Robert Burns, went down to lobby in London. They may have felt surprised and gratified to be invited to No. 10 Downing Street to meet three of the most powerful men in Britain: the prime minister, Sir Robert Peel, his colonial secretary, Lord Stanley (as earl of Derby, a later prime minister himself), and the home secretary, Sir James Graham, who by reason of his residence in Cumberland knew something about conditions on the other side of the border.[41]

It turned out to be in its way a classic confrontation of Scotland and England. Peel was an ice-cold character with, according to Benjamin Disraeli, a smile like a silver plate on a coffin. Stanley represented the aristocrat in politics, who thought a chap might jog along on £40,000 a year. Graham was another austere administrator, but did most of the talking. He, according to Murray, 'threw off a great deal of official reserve and was not only quite prepared to listen to our statement but start the question of our pound notes, and too great banking facilities, as the cause of our distress, by promoting and encouraging over-trading'. With one gratuitous jibe at the Scots, he changed the subject to deliver another: 'He said that people in the large towns of Scotland drank too much whisky.'[42] This was to wave red rags across the table at Scots moral and earnest, though anything but deferential or reticent. The zealous Burns worked himself up into a fury, denouncing the

Corn Laws, which he argued were the main cause of distress – but which this Tory government, so far anyway, had committed itself to keeping. Peel decided it was time to bring matters to a close. He said that, while his government could do nothing itself, it would support any charitable appeal. The Scots, ushered out the big black door of No. 10, were being brushed off.

Or so it seemed. Yet Peel did not forget the scene or the passion it had provoked. He asked the provost of Paisley and sheriff of Renfrewshire to send in regular reports on how the crisis was unfolding. On the strength of these, he dispatched north in the spring of 1842 a senior civil servant, Edward Twisleton, assistant commissioner for the Poor Law in England. Twisleton arrived at Paisley on March 7. The next day he met the relief committee and disclosed he had a large sum in his keeping subscribed by Queen Victoria in person and by the marquess of Abercorn (each of whom gave £500), then by members of the government – Peel, Stanley and Graham again – who each gave £225, but as private individuals. Paisley could have this money provided its able-bodied male applicants for relief were made to work under supervision at least ten hours a day, and provided relief got changed from cash to kind – that is to say, to foodstuffs from stores the committee itself would need to run. Twisleton stressed that, while great personages of the British state were intervening in Paisley, the state itself would not intervene. The prime minister and home secretary had laid down how the relief should be administered (in fact, according to the English Poor Law) but they were not committing the government as such to any action or to any aid.[43]

The men struggling to save Paisley little liked the tidings from Twisleton, but what could they do? He at least promised not to let the people starve. His conditions were accepted. He became dictator of the town, distributing supplies through the stores to the unemployed who in return had to work for them. Graham saw this as a short-term expedient, however, and recalled Twisleton once the worst was over. He feared it might be noticed elsewhere if his commissioner stayed too long on the spot, what with the government proclaiming the virtues of non-intervention. Twisleton left at the end of June 1842. Graham expressed 'satisfaction with the prudence which marked his conduct of a very difficult and painful duty'.[44]

On the political level it was by now clearly no longer possible to pretend nothing needed to be done about the poor in Scotland, even before the Disruption crippled the Kirk in 1843. Peel had already set up the royal commission on the old Poor Law under Robert Dundas, Viscount Melville, who reported within a year so that an amending Act of Parliament could be passed in 1845. It would remain in force till 1948. Compared to the earlier counterpart in England, Melville answered to a much more cautious brief, 'to consider in what way the present law may be made to work most efficiently, without making any very material changes'.[45]

Still, changes there had to be, and the choice lay between those of Chalmers and those of Alison, with the English programme of Chadwick in the background. The benign Melville tried to see the best on all sides. He said 'it was very desirable... if possible, to let the country feel that they must make adequate provision for those who are legally entitled to it, but also to take the country along with us, by allowing them to do it in their own way, provided they do it effectively.'[46] What he meant by the first point was appointment of a national Board of Supervision to oversee the workings of the fresh legislation and to make sure, by setting national norms of good practice, that all the poor got some basic subsistence. What he meant by the second point was preservation of the parish as the unit through which the aid would be channelled. The Act of 1845 that followed his report was intended to rest on these principles.

But the Disruption of the Kirk had already cut across the deliberations. It meant parishes being duplicated through ecclesiastical schism – so which should administer the amended

Poor Law, and could they all do so anyway? The answer was to create what amounted to a new species of secular parish for behoof of the poor. Each would have a parochial board – in the end 866 of them – elected every year by ratepayers under a complex franchise that favoured owners of property and excluded the poor themselves.[47] There was obviously a step up in the scale of the system and nobody could really know how, or if, it would work. One official in charge of it, Henry Hunter, a disciple of Chalmers, described a scene he witnessed:

> In Glasgow, the advent of the Act caused a great upheaval. Poor people of all kinds thought they were now provided for life. One thousand to thirteen hundred individuals besieged the office each day of the week, demanding relief, hundreds of them waiting till midnight before their cases could be examined. The sight of such a multitude was deplorable, consisting as it did of all kinds of characters – the aged, the infirm, the drunkard and the idler, children in arms and at the feet, all mixed up in one motley multitude. Pauperism in the city increased at the rate of 10,000 a year, and this at a time when employment was good, provisions cheap and the general health quite ordinary. This lapse from the principle of independence and self-reliance was greatly augmented by a rush of people from Ireland, who thought the new poor rate had turned Glasgow into an Eldorado.[48]

They would soon find out if it could work. The first thing a new system needed was money to pay the poor their subsistence. On this point, the act left the method of finding resources to the parochial boards. But a flow of detailed regulation from the central Board of Supervision began to force them to abandon their initial preference for voluntary contributions. In 1845 a quarter of the parochial boards raised a poor rate, yet by 1894 the proportion had gone up to 95 per cent. Collection of the money was not always straightforward: in Glasgow in 1867, one in three ratepayers, over 20,000 individuals in all, failed to pay the rate and so forfeited their parliamentary franchise (this being the penalty).[49]

Then the parochial boards had to decide who would get relief and who would not. These could be thorny questions, for the poor people of Scotland turned out to be a litigious lot. Possessing a right of appeal, they made full use of it: in half a century of operation after 1845, the Board of Supervision dealt with 20,000 cases. During the first decade the main point at issue was whether the existing ban on relief for the able-bodied unemployed would hold. William Lindsay, a cotton-spinner out of work and starving, a widower also with four children under the age of ten, brought a test case. He 'had nothing to give them [and] had applied, on these grounds, to the inspector of the parish of Gorbals, in which he had his settlement, for relief, but was distinctly refused'. An appeal went to the sheriff of Lanarkshire, Archibald Alison, the Tory scourge of trades unions but in the matter of the poor more lenient; he was the brother, after all, of William Pulteney Alison. Sheriff Alison again turned Lindsay himself down, yet ordered the parochial board to pay relief for the children, they being destitute by reason of their father's destitution and able to do nothing for their own support. Here was a big potential breach in the existing law. The parochial board appealed to the Court of Session. The importance of the case was recognized, and it went before the full bench of thirteen judges. In February 1849 they held by a majority 'that an able-bodied man, who is out of employment, and destitute of the means of subsistence, has no legal right to demand parochial relief for relief to his children in pupillarity'. So that was that: the new Scots Poor Law would remain just as mean as the old one.[50]

If the position on outdoor relief stayed unchanged, there was at least the possibility of extending indoor relief, that is, of building poorhouses. We can distinguish this from the English concept of workhouses. In England the inmates of these places lived under a punitive regime forcing them (as the name suggests) to work for their keep, at picking oakum and the like, the aim being to bring home to the able-bodied unemployed their moral failing. But since in Scotland such people enjoyed no entitlement to relief anyway, the concept was irrelevant.[51] Here the poor would not be tyrannized, though they would not be cosseted either.

Glasgow used the opportunity of the new act to close down and demolish the old Town's Hospital. The inmates were moved to a complex on the northern side of the city that had since 1809 served as its lunatic asylum (the lunatics now got shifted out of town altogether, to Gartnavel). This was a big establishment of 1,500 beds erected on the model of the panopticon, which allowed all inmates to be observed by a watchman without their being able to tell whether or not they were being watched. Of course it would be physically impossible for the watchman to observe everybody at once, but the fact they could not know when they were being watched meant they all had to act as though they were. In this way their behaviour came under constant control.[52]

Otherwise, the internal regime was not so much severe as squalid. Inspectors would later be 'constantly shocked at the use of the water-closets as sculleries and pantries'. One arm of the panopticon had only two washtubs for 290 inmates – which meant that on their bathing days it took twelve hours for them all to take their turn. And then, 'for the daily ablutions of both sexes of this class [ordinary inmates] there is no provision under shelter. In summer and winter they must go to taps and basins in the open air in the back yard.'[53] At least in Scotland the poor could answer back. The governor of the poorhouse tried a scheme of employing a select group of inmates to carry out the menial task of manufacturing firelighters: 'When a few days' trial had perfected the details, the governor intimated to his gang of forty that in future a full day's work must be performed; ten men instantly gave

notice of their intention to quit the house and removed themselves from the roll.'[54] But these must have been exceptions: as a
rule, Scottish poorhouses still sheltered primarily the sick, insane
and disabled. In 1850, 21 establishments existed with room for
6,000 people. By 1900 there were 65 of them with room for 16,000
people.[55] Even then, numbers being higher than ever before, the
proportion of paupers relieved by this means amounted to one in
seven,[56] compared to one in three on indoor relief in England.[57]
Scots in need preferred to stay away from the poorhouse and rely
on outdoor relief: of those 16,000 places available by 1906, just half
were taken up.[58]

How, then, did the poor manage otherwise? If on outdoor relief,
they could also benefit from the numerous charities that were a
mark of the Victorian social conscience – many set up to deal
with particular problems, from deafness to desertion by a spouse.
On principle they helped rich and poor alike, but the poor stood to
gain most from them. Glasgow offered perhaps the widest range of
charities among all the Scottish towns and cities, from orphanages
and refuges to hospitals for the treatment of venereal disease. They
tended to be led by big businessmen, often themselves generous
donors, who were used to running things and could attract
subscriptions from their fellows.[59] They met one aspiration of the
Scottish bourgeoisie, for communal leadership that also smoothed
social relations and defused political tensions, not least through
co-operation with a skilled working class itself committed to
self-help and voluntary initiative. It was part of the wider social
order in Scotland, where respect between worker and employer
together with shared pride in the success of an industrial society
raised everybody's sights – and made things possible that would
otherwise have been improbable.

This social order posited besides that workers in need did not
have to be just passive recipients of aid from on high, but could
also take an active part in mutual aid. To help people through the

common problems of everyday life, from losing a job to sickness to funerals, there were contributory friendly societies, over 200 of them in Glasgow.[60] Savings banks offered another safe haven for small funds. Founded in 1836, the Glasgow Savings Bank grew to be the biggest in the country. A more general counterweight to unbridled capitalism lay in the Scottish Co-operative Wholesale Society; despite the national name, it always had its main sphere of operations in Glasgow. It was formed in 1868 for the purpose of purchasing or manufacturing goods to be retailed by a chain of local co-ops, which fostered thrift through the payment of dividends to their members.

More generally in ordinary life, informal types of support within the working class helped people to make ends meet. Family and friends lent money to one another, took in washing and cared for children, boarded lodgers and kept an eye on the stair. In the neighbourhood, supplies might be bought on tick and problems of cash flow could be met at the pawnshop or via moneylenders. It was better than the poorhouse anyway. If the statutory system of relief seemed miserly, incapable in itself of meeting all the needs of the poor, that did not signify that the needs were never met, rather that they were met by other means.[61] Altogether, we cannot confine our definition of poverty to those in receipt of poor relief.

The twentieth century would open in Glasgow with these Scottish traditions of welfare still robust. Like other industrial communities of its time, it contained extremes of wealth and poverty. Anything else was unlikely to have been the case in a European city exceeded in size only by London, Paris and Berlin. In any event its local rival, an Edinburgh only half the size, displayed a similar range of problems, more limited in scale but not in severity.[62]

The obvious sign of Glaswegians' poverty was the state of their housing. More people lived in tenements here than in any other British conurbation. Compared to cities of the plain like London or Birmingham, Glasgow occupied a constricted site between the river and the hills, so that it would have been hard to find another kind of dwelling able to accommodate the supply of labour on the scale needed by local industry. The city spread out as far as it could, but was also constantly rebuilt within the space available. All the same, it was now no closer to abolishing slums than it had been in 1866, when Glasgow's first Improvement Act saw sweeping powers granted to the council by the Parliament at Westminster. The council had at once set about putting them into vigorous operation. At the outset, 15,000 condemned dwellings had been scheduled for demolition but, when the scheme reached completion, another 20,000 were somehow there.[63] This was perhaps the best index of poverty.

It was a general problem over the west of Scotland, bound up with building traditions put under strain, like so much else, by the industrial revolution. A particular difficulty lay in the fact that a poor population much on the move was almost bound to face shortages of housing. On the clearance of insanitary buildings, their tenants might not have anywhere else to go, as one inspector found: 'To eject the people from these houses in a summary manner would cause great hardship and a domestic revolution, for they could not get houses anywhere else in Kirkintilloch. But if the best of the indifferent houses are to be tolerated for a few years, then wooden flooring should be substituted for the earth floors, and the windows or some of the panes made that they could be opened to admit fresh air.' In 1901, an inspection in Port Glasgow of an area of 43 acres revealed that 'out of 438 dwelling houses only 55 have more than two apartments and the third apartment, where there is one, is generally a mere closet. It is estimated that fully three-quarters of the inhabitants of the area are well-to-do working people in regular employment and earning good wages.' Yet 'I have no hesitation in affirming that the area is insanitary – insanitary to a degree that could hardly have been imagined as possible nowadays, in a British town.'[64] Another inspector at Hamilton in 1908 drew 'special attention to the backyard in Burnside Lane...

'The yard is unpaved and was in a dirty condition when I visited. There was also a WC on the ground floor where the lock had been forced, and the apartment was in a state of indescribable filth – in fact littered with faeces.' A third inspector in the town in 1914 came to 207 Quarry Street: 'This is the dirtiest house of the series. The mother of the house, on learning the purpose of my visit, said "There's a lot to be dune here to mak the hoose richt." I agreed.'[65]

As some of these examples show, bad housing was not solely due to poverty. In a prosperous region, demand for homes – and for better homes too – grew steadily, yet the building industry remained vulnerable to the cyclical capitalist economy. Even during good times the Scottish system of feudal tenure, in which the purchaser of land had to pay an annual fee to the original landowner, pushed up the price of developing it. Building standards were also stricter in Scotland, due to the conditions set down in the feu charters, which could make it more expensive to exploit equivalent sites in Glasgow than in London. The compensation for this handicap came in building as densely as possible, before offsetting the higher costs of construction by passing them on to the tenants in the form of steep rents. The tenants then themselves often added to the overcrowding by subdivision of the tenements.[66] That was why the normal dwelling for the Scots working class grew so cramped. The tenements came to follow a standard pattern: four storeys, with two flats each on a landing up a common stair. The problem lay in the fact that many flats were tiny: half the population lived in one or two rooms and at a density of more than two people to a room. In 1911, the notorious 'single ends' accounted for two-thirds of Glasgow's housing stock.[67] Sanitary standards were low, too: flats shared a toilet, or even a sink. Some local customs did not help – for instance, the practice of keeping dead bodies in the home for three days before burial.

Little in the way of systematic housing reform had been attempted before the First World War, but the social strains it caused

at home proved to be a turning point. In 1914, 90 per cent of
Glasgow's housing stock remained in private hands. It was the
economic and political turbulence of wartime that forced the first
interventions by central government, initially with the limits put
on rents in response to strikes by the tenants. Afterwards, an era
of legislation opened. The Housing Act of 1919 authorized local
councils to start providing homes for the people. As if to symbolize
a new order in Glasgow, schemes appeared on the fringes of the
built-up area with designs and materials quite unlike anything else
in the city. The poor had known only crowded streets of tenements
with shops and pubs on the ground floor, and often lived their lives
on the pavements because the flats were so small. Now, in place of
Scotland's usual urban chaos and din, there would be the space
and peace as introduced in England since the turn of the century
by the model of garden suburbs. Building fashions were to change,
but Glasgow had set itself on a path from which it proved hard to
turn aside. At the peak in the 1970s the corporation owned 67 per
cent of the city's housing stock – yet this still included some of the
worst in Europe, much of it of recent construction. Even today,
after a range of forces has been at work to reduce that proportion,
Glasgow possesses a much higher share of social housing than any
other city in Britain.[68]

At the outset, the trend seemed benign enough. In Glasgow,
too, the new housing was kept at a low density, diffused over wide
tracts of land at Mosspark or Knightswood. Buildings tended to
be of two novel types, the first still tenemented but on only two or
three storeys, the second in the form of the 'flatted villa', a detached
or semi-detached house with a home on each floor. This would
have its own front door, perhaps a small garden and in any case
improved domestic amenities – hot and cold running water, inside
toilets. The first schemes were built to high specifications, but
soon quality suffered because of the cost. By the 1930s they were
coming on the cheap: Blackhill was a notorious example, along

with others crammed on inferior land near railways or gasworks and acceptable only to the poorest people. While these estates and their modest comforts might transform life as it had been lived before 1914, they also introduced a new kind of poverty. They lay in satellite neighbourhoods far away from jobs, services and social life, offering little by way of common facilities to bind together their atomized communities. Anything less like the old Glasgow would be hard to imagine. Yet planners and civic officials viewed the breach in urban tradition with equanimity, if not satisfaction. This was what made it a new age: complaints from the tenants who actually had to live on the schemes went largely unheeded. In fact, an immense store of new problems was being hoarded up.[69]

Housing innovation still remained at quite an early stage when the Second World War supervened. The loss of six years' civilian building, together with some destruction by air-raids, had a worse effect on congested Glasgow than on most cities. Besides, for a period after the war, exports took priority over housing. Homeless Glaswegians, if they were not to squat in empty property, needed to be given temporary shelter in prefabricated houses, mass produced in former aircraft factories. The city council, in the toils with its slums for the better part of a century, now came under challenge over its evident failure to find decisive solutions to this prime aspect of poverty. Social expectations ran high given the sacrifices of wartime. After 1945, central government felt impatient to step in.[70]

In the first direct intervention, the Scottish Office published the Clyde Valley Regional Plan, proposing to decant population from the middle of Glasgow to the periphery or beyond. That would take the proud city council down a peg or two. An aspect of Glaswegians' pride was that they numbered a million (one of only a couple of dozen such concentrations of people in the world at that time). Of these, the poorest 700,000 lived on 1,800 acres in the middle of the urban area at a density of 400 people per acre:

'One seventh of Scotland's population is thus compressed into three square miles of central Glasgow.'[71] A further instalment of reform came with the Town and Country Planning Act (1946), which among other things allowed a ring of land round big cities to be defined as green belt, where no development could take place. In Glasgow's case it included much of the periphery acquired in successive extensions of the boundaries (the latest in 1938). The rehousing of thousands of families would therefore need to be carried out still further away, as overspill in so far undeveloped places.

Here was the origin of the New Towns, most built in the west of Scotland: East Kilbride (1947), Glenrothes (1948), Cumbernauld (1956), Livingston (1962), Irvine (1966). Plans for a sixth New Town at Stonehouse in Lanarkshire then got abandoned as the policy went out of fashion. Today it is even condemned for 'skimming the cream' of the city's population and rehousing the best citizens in a new environment that could never have been created in the old urban core. In other words, the skilled workforce and their young families moved right out of town (along with the industrial investment that would guarantee them a living), to leave behind the oldest, the poorest or the otherwise least employable people, who then effectively dwelt in ghettoes, or at best in cheaper housing schemes without amenities. Yet overall the policy did achieve its object of permanently reducing the population inside the municipal boundaries by about one-third.[72] In the twenty-first century, scores of the world's cities have populations of a million or more. Glasgow is no longer one of them.

The city council was not to be deflated quite so easily, however. Within its boundaries, it set about its own radical remoulding of the urban landscape.[73] The plans shifted industries and communities to virgin sites, usually well beyond the centre. There was then a wider effect on the townscape, where a mixture of uses had always been evident. Now social functions were separated. New industrial estates were laid out on specially designated land, as at Hillington or Queenslie, while workers for them were concentrated in tower blocks not necessarily near at hand. Most then depended on public transport, but it no longer always went where they wanted to go. For example, on the Subway – which opened in 1896 and followed the pattern of population at that time – there are several stations where hardly anybody gets on or off these days. Planners focussed rather on roads, though in 1966 Glasgow had only one car to eleven people (compared with one to four in Surrey). Yet the plans for urban motorways were among the most ambitious in Britain. They cut right through and blighted residential quarters on the northern and western sides of the inner city, which by this process became fresh havens for the poor. The ring of motorways that would have allowed through traffic to bypass Glasgow altogether was not completed till 2011.

Just as salient was the rapid and intensive building of tower blocks, some again in big new schemes making use of greenfield sites on the periphery: Easterhouse, with 11,000 dwellings, Pollok with 9,000, Castlemilk with 8,500, Drumchapel with 7,500. Meanwhile, historic quarters within the city got flattened to make room for more of the blocks. The population of Anderston, for instance, plummeted from 32,000 in 1951 to 9,000 in 1971. Most spectacularly the policy affected Gorbals, one of the oldest, poorest yet liveliest proletarian districts, home before and right through the industrial revolution to the most deprived workers, to many criminals and ruffians, latterly to a community of Jewish refugees. Colourful the ensemble might have been, but without doubt the place was also a slum, so the 1960s saw it demolished and rebuilt to designs by the modernist architect, Edinburgh's Basil Spence. Visually uncompromising, his blocks of flats turned within a couple of decades into new slums because of inattention to such tedious details as ventilation, so that internal walls and ceilings crumbled in damp and mould. Nor was all well outside the blocks, for the novelty of the housing style again could not counter the wider communal problems of deindustrialization and lack of access to jobs and services. The model neighbourhoods themselves became a huge civic problem. Today several have been knocked down in their turn.[74]

There seems to have been little misgiving among Labour councillors that they were acquiring too high a proportion of the housing stock, and with it the duty of its allocation and administration. On the contrary, the corporation evidently believed the only way to plan and administer the city was by this very device of owning a high proportion of its social capital. The impairment of the private sector and the decimation of owner-occupancy opened up the prospect of an urban population composed almost entirely of poor municipal tenants. In Scotland it became axiomatic that public housing should be a powerful tool for the redistribution of income towards the lower end of the scale. By 1981 the public rented sector dominated Scottish housing with 55 per cent of the total stock (against 26 per cent in England). In the west of Scotland the figure was even higher: over 80 per cent in Clydebank, Monklands and Motherwell. By the same token, relatively few Scots owned their own homes: only 35 per cent of Scottish households compared to 58 per cent in England and Wales in 1981. Nobody seems to have conceived that this policy might spawn new social problems of its own.[75]

In due course the policy did at least attain a crude surplus of housing, in that the units theoretically available more than matched the number of people needing homes; some of the bleaker blocks were never fully occupied. But the policy took no account of social change, as a more mobile population with decaying familial structures emerged. Even without that, the lack of facilities in the post-war schemes would have been bad enough. There were, of course, other causes for complaint, such as the lack of local jobs, the high cost of transport, inadequate maintenance and the monotony of the architecture. These legitimate grounds for criticism may explain in part, at least, the growth in crime and vandalism in these areas, though clearly other factors were at work too. The fact that the authorities were apparently powerless to combat the trend added to the anger and bitterness felt by many law-abiding citizens in these places. Still, for others, the move into the schemes initially meant a huge improvement in their living conditions and their experiences as citizens of Glasgow. No longer could they be evicted unannounced, nor did the rents increase without notice. By the time the city council braced itself for a fresh housing policy, the times had changed but so had the people. Regardless of the bad living conditions or outside disdain for them, the sink estates had become home to many poor Glaswegians. This had an effect when a further effort at restructuring the deprived areas followed in the 1980s.[76]

The Labour Party, ruling almost everywhere in the west of Scotland, had developed a positive hostility to private building – from time to time reinforced by developments at the national level, as during the British premiership of Margaret Thatcher. In 1984 Jim MacLean, Glasgow's housing convener, declared an actual ban: 'Any sites identified for housebuilding will no longer be given to private developers. The ground will be kept in our land bank for public building.' This bank had at the time enough land for 12,000 houses, but curbs on public spending meant the council lacked the cash for new development. Inflation in the United Kingdom was still to be conquered, yet Labour's policy deprived poor Glaswegians of their best defence against it. Professor Donald MacKay, chairman of the development agency, Scottish Enterprise, said it 'may come a close second to the Berlin Wall as the most formidable obstacle to geographical mobility yet devised by man'.[77]

In what happened next, it is useful to distinguish between the wider west of Scotland and the city of Glasgow itself. A Housing Act of 1980 let tenants buy council houses on favourable terms, which were further improved from 1986.[78] In East Kilbride, sales reached half the New Town's housing stock by 1991. Similarly, in Cumbernauld and Kilsyth, sales went above 40 per cent. Even in Motherwell, where the local authority's sales remained lowest, they approached 14 per cent. The Conservative government in London reckoned this to be one answer to poverty: it gave the former tenants capital, which they might use to change their socio-economic status (though few appear in fact to have done this). Meanwhile inside Glasgow, and partly in reaction to the previous excesses there, a different course was followed as popular agencies for urban development sprang up. Local residents mobilized themselves in the alternative model of the housing association, managed by and for themselves in a more measured and sensitive manner than the local authority had shown, with central government looking benignly on. Glasgow has today transferred most of its stock to about 100 associations, with the added advantage of paying off its own previous housing debt of £1 billion. Time will tell if the new order can end the alienation of many Glaswegians from their environment.

Meanwhile, islands of Victorian tenements still stand. They are no longer the abodes of poverty (that designation belongs rather to the later housing schemes), not when they have been converted for living in the twenty-first century. Those surviving the corporation's earlier craze for demolition appear desirable today: with modern plumbing installed, they are perfect for a more mobile population. In Glasgow they were often of sound construction in attractive red or honey-coloured sandstone (attractive, at least, till covered in soot), they seldom rose higher than the street in front was wide and they contained bigger rooms than those in council flats. The aim had once been to get rid of them, yet now their uses for urban living have been rediscovered. All they need is to be cleaned up.[79]

The Victorians believed bad people caused bad housing, whereas nowadays we tend to put things the other way round. What can be said of Glasgow is that the dire state of its housing and the worst problems of its poor do seem to go together. Even taking account of this, there is still the 'Glasgow effect', defined by the fact that in other cities of Britain and Europe populations equally deprived do not sicken and die at the same rate as Glaswegians.[80] For example, today the social profiles of Liverpool, Manchester and Glasgow are almost identical, yet premature deaths in the last city reach a level over 30 per cent higher than in the first two cities, and all deaths a level about 15 per cent higher, across practically the entire social spectrum.[81] They die from the big killers: cancer, heart attacks and strokes. They also die from the maladies of despair: drugs, alcohol and suicide.

It is true that for the 1.2 million people of Greater Glasgow there has been a slow improvement in life expectancy, but it still adds up to less than seventy-two years at birth for men (nearly seven years below the British average of seventy-eight years) and seventy-eight years at birth for women (over four years below the British average of eighty-two). Even right at the top of the heap, the wealthiest 10 per cent of Glasgow's population have a lower expectancy than the same group elsewhere. At the bottom, things get really bad: according to a report by the World Health Organization in 2008, the life expectancy at birth for men in the ward of Calton in central Glasgow was fifty-four years, compared to eighty-two years in leafy Lenzie, a suburb 8 miles away. It appears unlikely, on the historical data available, that Glasgow has during the past few decades become relatively much poorer than Liverpool and Manchester, yet the gap in mortality has widened: to take a salient example, deaths in Glasgow related to alcohol rose fourfold between 1991 and 2002. In other words, the 'Glasgow effect' may be of recent origin.

What could the reason be? In the worst parts of the city, Glasgow's people were subject to many stresses that conspired against making their lives long and happy. Even the skilled elite of the old working class would have been exposed to industrial diseases of which the causes had yet to be discovered. Many other jobs were dirty or dangerous. At length the damage extended from the physical to the psychological level, as proletarian existence lost its former purpose. With the dismantling of the industrial base in the 1970s, there are now some families with four generations that have never been in work. Much of Glasgow's population also seems impervious to medical advice. Its diet, once meagre yet quite wholesome, is today filled out with a surfeit of all the bad things: saturated fats seasoned with alcohol and tobacco, causing hardened arteries and heart attacks, lung cancer and cirrhosis of the liver. In the final decades of the twentieth century the most pitiable Glaswegians took refuge in addictive illegal drugs, which set off a fresh cycle of disease, degradation and criminality. Much of the violence in the city became connected with drugs. The various ways in which Glaswegians render themselves comatose has provided the rest of the world with a convenient comparative means of measurement, the 'Glasgow coma scale', gauging an unconscious patient's response to external stimuli.[82] But the connection of trauma and poverty has proved even more pervasive.[83]

In one way the 'Glasgow effect' is an extension of personal affliction into the social sphere, with stress and alienation exceeding what might be expected from objective conditions of poverty.[84] In the words from 2004 of Scotland's chief medical officer, Harry Burns, we are dealing here with 'a psycho-social problem that will not be fixed by targeting conventional risk behaviours'. The ultimate answer lies in repairing a fragmented society where many feel they have no control of their lives: 'We must not concentrate on deficits but on assets, skills and capacities. We must build social capital so individuals can offer each other friendship and mutual support.' Good health depends in part, then, on whether people feel threatened or supported by their environments. The poor are least likely to feel this.[85] We can reasonably posit that poverty, along with the anger and alienation entailed by it, causes political demotivation too, something also long obvious in Glasgow. The referendum of 2014 did not correct this aspect of the city's condition, but the level of electoral participation showed it had given the people more hope than anything else they have experienced in recent times.

6

Womanhood:
'Varied harmony'

ON MAY 27, 1849, Catherine Cranston was born at 39 George Square, Glasgow. The building lay on the western side of a space still largely preserving the original classical layout and architecture of 1781, before commercial or municipal development had worked the changes we see today. Those changes were already beginning, however – no. 39 housed the Edinburgh and Glasgow Hotel, named after the recently opened railway between the two cities and standing ready for travellers right next to the exit from Queen Street Station. Almost from the start the line had been a huge success, carrying a million passengers a year and generating brisk trade for any other businesses that could cash in. The beneficiaries would in the long run include even baby Kate because the hotel was the property of her father, George Cranston, who had started out in life as a baker before identifying here in the middle of his hometown his great opportunity. The family prospered but continued to reside on the premises till they moved to a home of their own in Sauchiehall Street, which Kate would only leave on her marriage in 1892. The lucky man then was John Cochrane, owner of an engineering works and later provost of Barrhead, where the couple lived in some style. In those days marriage usually marked the end of a working woman's career, yet Kate had at this point hardly started on hers.[1]

The Cranstons did not belong to the old mercantile aristocracy of Glasgow, nor yet to the new industrial elite, but in their own sphere they showed the same resourceful spirit. Kate's brother Stuart was to earn his living as a dealer in tea. From this he moved on to invent the concept of the tearoom, destined to be a central feature of the city's social life in its golden era up to the First World War. He opened his first one in 1871 at 2 Queen Street, where he charged twopence a cup, 'bread and cakes extra'.[2] The idea caught on, and by 1896 he had five tearooms round the centre of the city. At this point he turned the business into a limited company, and in due course opened three more. He became a successful entrepreneur, in other words, though without sharing the ritzy tastes and flamboyant habits characteristic of the type in Glasgow. In fact he was what the contemporary city called a faddist: he lived on fruit, nuts or seeds, and never touched a drop of alcohol. After he died in 1921, his company continued till 1955.

Stuart's commercial capabilities probably did most to drive the family's fortunes, but Kate is the one remembered for its success. In 1878 she set up her own Crown Tearooms on the ground floor of a temperance hotel in Argyle Street.[3] The range of products she offered was wider than her brother's, and in fact she described herself as a restaurateur. She impressed the discerning with her distinctive décor, which struck an unmistakably feminine note. This was a novelty for Glasgow, a city always dominated by its males, as much among the middle as the working class. The businessmen's club and the proletarian pub might have been worlds apart in their function and appearance, but with their consumption of alcohol and tobacco, with the topics that came under discussion and the language in which it might be couched, they were at one in deterring women. Booze did not fuel everything in this masculine world. Since the seventeenth century there had also been coffeehouses, patronized by Glasgow's oceanic traders. But the coffeehouse, too, was monopolized by men, while women always entertained at home. According to the novelist Neil Munro, 'Miss Cranston, clever, far-seeing, artistic to her fingertips, and of a high, adventurous spirit, was the first to discern in Glasgow that her sex was positively yearning for some kind of afternoon distraction that had not yet been invented.'[4]

The tearooms invented it. Male customers were not excluded from them, but the female customers set the tone – as did the female employees, for Kate was a perfectionist and disciplinarian keenly concerned with training her staff, while tempering her strictness with a sharp sense of humour. Above all, however, the tearooms offered a venue where the woman customers could be *entre soi* and live out, for an hour or two, a vision of modern urban chic. Full equality of the sexes in Glasgow has perhaps even today not yet been achieved, but Kate demonstrated that from her time on there was always going to be progress towards it. To the end of her life her eccentric, old-fashioned style of dress, with mid-Victorian flounces and frills and fancy hats, showed her readiness to flout convention and suit herself; of course, they advertised her business as well. Described by the architect Edwin Lutyens as 'a dark, busy, fat, wee body with black sparky luminous eyes',[5] she was cheerful and generous, if sometimes also cantankerous and bossy. Above all, she proved to Glaswegians how a female might successfully run a business.

In 1897, Kate opened another tearoom in Buchanan Street that caused a still bigger stir. It owed its striking interior to two of the city's avant-garde young artists, gifted but as yet little known, George Walton and Charles Rennie Mackintosh, with the latter's wife, Margaret Macdonald, as decorator. This was also the heyday of the Glasgow School of painting, and the tearooms turned into an aesthetic adjunct of it. The journalist William Power wrote: 'Together the designers produced something which was at once

severely simple and strikingly original, a varied harmony which
was based on the square and the straight line, with black and
white, grey and brown, as the leading shades, relieved by small
sections of rose and emerald green, and by fresh flowers chosen by
Miss Cranston herself.' [6] Three times a week she sent a donkey cart
driven by a boy in green livery to deliver the flowers from her own
garden at Barrhead with precise instructions for their display.

Kate continued to push out the boundaries of her business. She
later employed Walton and Mackintosh to redevelop the whole
building on her original premises in Argyle Street, and then used
Mackintosh again at a further site in Ingram Street. According
to Neil Munro, 'Kate Cranstonish' was a favourite term of the
city's glitterati, used to refer to 'domestic novelties in buildings
and decorations not otherwise easy to define'.[7] The culmination
came in Mackintosh's dazzling Willow Tearooms on Sauchiehall
Street, opened in 1903 and today the sole working survivor of
her empire. An eye-catching bow window on the first floor, with
mullions and decorative leaded windows, indicated the position
inside of the 'salon de luxe'. Here, for both exterior and interior,
Mackintosh was given a free hand. He designed the structure itself
and then furniture, cutlery, even menu cards: 'Chicken & Ham
Rissole & Sauce 9d, Fried Turkey Egg 6d, Small Cold Roast Lamb
10d...'[8] The stream of commissions Kate offered him right up to
1917 carried this often struggling architect through hard times. For
her sustained patronage of Glasgow's avant-garde designers Kate,
as the critic Nikolaus Pevsner said, 'deserves the art historian's
unstinted gratitude'.[9]

The death of Kate's husband in 1917 shattered her. They were a
devoted couple, and Cochrane had been a strong support in her
business. She disposed of the tearooms, never again wore anything
but black and took up residence once more in George Square, this
time in the North British Station (nowadays Copthorne) Hotel
looking across to where she had been born. In her last years she

became vague and alarming, and died of 'senile decay' in 1934. She left most of her large estate to charity.[10]

Today the Willow Tearoom in Sauchiehall Street is in business again. The counterpart in Buchanan Street has since 1997 seen a second coming in the shape of a 'sympathetic restoration'. The interiors for the one in Ingram Street, latterly in the ownership of the city council but neglected and finally dismantled by it, have meanwhile been partially reconstructed for display, with the ladies' luncheon room forming the centrepiece of an exhibition about Mackintosh held in 1996. His hometown, which often ignored and disheartened him while he was alive, has at last come to acknowledge his modernist genius. But it could never have blossomed without private patronage, and Kate Cranston was the most loyal of his patrons.[11]

Mackintosh, a working-class lad from Townhead, was typical of the Glaswegian male in his tendency to depression relieved by heavy drinking and smoking, which would bring him to an early grave at the age of sixty. It was of course highly unusual for a man of his background to devote his life to art, and just as unusual to have such a part played in it by women – not only Kate Cranston but also his wife Margaret Macdonald and her sister Frances, with the latter's husband Herbert McNair. Margaret could have enjoyed a career of her own, but she preferred to work together with the others. As soon as she graduated from college in 1894 her watercolours and designs began to attract attention because of her penchant for stretching and distorting the human form. By the time of her *Mysterious Garden* (1911), she had developed an unmistakable personal manner, typified by aloof female figures with bodies either elongated and emaciated or else hidden by diaphanous garments like flowers in full bloom. Yet she also made a name for herself in the wholly different medium of metalworking, notably to produce a chaste beaten panel, *The Annunciation* (1896).[12]

The sisters had met Mackintosh while studying with him at Glasgow School of Art, and McNair came into the circle as a colleague from the architectural practice, Honeyman & Keppie, where both men worked. The couples formed an artistic ensemble dubbed the Spook School, with reference to their use of mystifying symbolist motifs in various genres. Even before their marriages, they all collaborated in painting complex watercolours or designing posters and ornaments. They drew on European models to create an interplay of architecture, decoration and painting. They also revived the Celtic imagery that left a lasting effect in Scotland and elsewhere. Scottish creative activity had never been so eclectic, and the equality of the sexes within it never so complete. In the end it was practically impossible, and hardly useful, to separate out the respective roles in the joint oeuvre.[13]

In the two couples' development and success the common matrix of the Glasgow School of Art played a big part. Originally founded in 1845, it was itself undergoing a transformation away from the kind of conservative college typical of Victorian Scotland. From 1885 Francis Newbery and his wife Jessie ran it. They widened its horizons and overhauled its syllabus. Students could now look for a different experience from the endless copying of Old Masters which was a typical means of instruction elsewhere (and had been here before).[14]

Francis Newbery's educational philosophy stressed the importance of a thorough technical training for students, in order to immerse them in a range of traditions, but also sought to develop their artistic individuality. He clearly succeeded in the case of young Mackintosh, after he took him in hand and, among other things, sent him on a travelling scholarship to study the art and architecture of Italy, something that would otherwise have been quite beyond his means. The rest of the students, too, benefited from their principal's promotion of their work among Glasgow's prosperous bourgeoisie and his cultivation of connections far beyond. Over time he was able to make prestigious international appointments to his staff and generally refashion the school on the European lines of an *Académie des Beaux-Arts* or *Kunsthochschule*. Meanwhile Jessie Newbery opened the doors to women, with a generous policy on admissions and a reformed curriculum. For herself, coming of a family of textile manufacturers in Paisley, she felt keen to promote embroidery as a form of art. In the school she created a new department for it and established the place of needlework in artistic design. She was the reputed inventor of the 'Glasgow rose' – actually rather more like a cabbage, yet striking in its aesthetics and demanding on the creator. There are fine examples in Margaret Macdonald's 'Willowwood' panels for the tearooms, where further copies would have been available for sale. Jessie said: 'I liked the opposition of straight lines to curved, of horizontal to vertical. I specially aim at beautifully shaped spaces and try to make them as important as the patterns.' She and her husband altogether pushed out the school's frontiers to embrace a range of novel genres: metalwork, glasswork, pottery, woodcarving and so on.[15]

All this took place amid a general cultural flowering in the wealthy city. The Glasgow Boys had already emerged as pioneers of a revolt against the older Scottish artistic establishment and its academic sort of production, which kept a palsied grip on national institutions, exhibitions and education for young painters in Edinburgh especially.[16] The Glasgow Girls were the group that Francis and Jessie Newbery called into being to complement the Glasgow Boys. The Girls followed the same sort of professional path, though hindered by greater difficulty in gaining the recognition that was their due. In aesthetic terms, they went beyond painting to embrace a range of other genres, so that art and craft came to stand on an equal footing.

The role of the Glasgow School of Art was to provide the framework for women to train and practise; in the three decades

before the First World War, the proportion of female students rose
from a quarter to nearly a half. And they were often able to study
under women teachers, another novelty. Among these figured Jessie
King, who had made her own name as an illustrator of children's
books and then created a department of bookbinding, focussed
on design. Nell Brown and Annie French founded a department
of ceramic decoration, also to be joined by Helen Walton, sister of
George Walton, Mackintosh's collaborator on the tearooms.
Dorothy Smyth, who started up a department of commercial art,
introduced varied techniques to it: sgraffito, gesso panels, illumin-
ation on vellum and woodblock printing on textiles. Her abilities
and the results she achieved for her students were such that she
would have become head of the school in 1933 had she not died
in between being appointed and taking up the post. De Courcy
Dewar concentrated on design in the department of metalwork; her
own work included jewellery, plaques, caskets, buttons, sconces,
surrounds for clocks and mirrors.[17] Outside, she was involved with
the cause of women's suffrage, for which she produced bookplates,
programmes and calendars. It was no coincidence that the school
became a hotbed of the local suffragette movement, with the
students making banners to carry on demonstrations.

Innovation continued well beyond the period of intense
creativity about the turn of the twentieth century. The First World
War took some of the women from the school to the western front
to serve as nurses, and of these Norah Gray transformed its horrors
into art in portraits of wounded soldiers. Afterwards, as Glasgow
sought to get back to normal, the school's graduates seized the
opportunities this opened up at home and abroad. Eleanor
Moore, following her physician husband to Shanghai, turned from
Scottish to Chinese portraiture. Margaret Brown deployed her
figurative talents as advertising manager for Arnott's department
store and in satirical pamphlets for her nationalist husband. Louise
Annand, beside her own work as an illustrator, at length won the

job of running the educational service in Glasgow's museums. The further range of genres in which the women artists worked was remarkable. Agnes Parker became a wood engraver, notably for the illustrations in an edition of the medieval work, *The Fables of Esope* (1931), while May Wilson and Eliza Bell continued the tradition of ceramic artistry into the 1940s and 1950s, hand-painting *objets d'art* in floral patterns. Three pioneering sculptresses emerged from the school: Ivy Proudfoot, with her best-known work *The Loving Birds* now in the McLean Gallery at Greenock; Hannah Frank, a Jewish girl from Gorbals who excelled herself in her gaunt *Woman with Bird*; and Helen Biggar, whose statuesque figures connected with her career as wardrobe mistress and costume designer for the Ballet Rambert. The most celebrated graduate of the school in mid-century was Joan Eardley. Her painting covered a wide range of subjects, with one prime element being her depictions of the tumbledown tenements and ragged children of Glasgow's slums.[18]

Yet the Glasgow Girls remain today relatively little known, and most have won wider attention only in collective exhibitions. It was a slow process. In 1961 the Kelvingrove Art Gallery held a show of Scottish painting featuring the Glasgow Boys in abundance but including not one picture by a woman. Even in those pre-feminist days, and even in this macho city, the omission was glaring, especially as several of the Glasgow Girls remained alive and working. Yet it took another thirty years for more public recognition to come in the exhibition 'Glasgow Girls: Women in Art and Design 1880–1920', held in 1990. Besides that, an exhibition on Charles Rennie Mackintosh, travelling from Glasgow to New York, Chicago and Los Angeles in 1996–7, brought out the role in his life and work of his wife Margaret; it is now on permanent display at their reconstructed house in the Hunterian Art Gallery.[19]

All these achievements made a disparate ensemble: how, then, can we generalize about Glasgow Style? It arose from synthesis, of bourgeois enterprise and artisan respectability, of ostentatious sophistication and delicate naturalism. To other influences we must add a sense of this being an industrial community with aesthetic requirements of its own. Glasgow felt proud of the engineering feats it paraded before the world at international exhibitions in 1888 and 1901, then at a Scottish national exhibition in 1911. The concept of craft here included skill and precision – rather different from the folksy, chintzy manner cultivated by the leader of the Arts and Crafts movement in England, William Morris. Glasgow's wealth arose above all from metallurgy, and Glasgow Style was pervaded by the possibilities of bending, puncturing, welding and moulding matter by art as well as by science. With its wealth now a century old, the city had the leisure and education for generous patronage. Yet, unlike the middle class of Edinburgh dominated by the learned professions, the equivalent Glaswegians were even yet a precarious and volatile bunch respecting lucre, not lineage or land. Economic base determined cultural superstructure, and wealth needed to be shown off.[20] But this enabled women of an artistic bent to break through into a realm of freedom their sex had never known in the city before.[21]

We have dwelt here on women's achievements in art in Victorian Glasgow. One reason for this is that it remained hard for them to make a personal mark in much else. Till this period, they would have needed noble rank to appear as more than mere names in the city's annals. In the pre-modern era, there had been here as in other Scots burghs some aristocratic presence, with landed families often intervening in civic affairs. The most powerful in Lanarkshire were the Hamiltons, and amid the upheavals from the Restoration of 1660 to the Union of 1707 the Duchess Anne proved to be their mainstay. By any standards a great lady, she had been born at the Palace of Whitehall in London, where her mother served as lady-in-waiting to Queen Henrietta Maria, wife of King Charles I. Anne's father, the first duke of Hamilton, was executed in 1649, just six weeks after his sovereign.[22] As duchess in her own right, she married William Douglas, a handsome younger son of the marquess of Douglas. She was by contrast plain, with a big nose and mouth and receding chin, but her husband told her, 'when I see the ways of others and thinks on you, I cannot but acknowledg myself most happie in so verteus a parson.'[23] The couple were to enjoy an affectionate working partnership of forty years. While the duke represented the family in public life till his death in 1694, the duchess gave birth to their thirteen children and ran the estates.

The successor to the title proved unworthy. In fact James, 4th duke of Hamilton, had always been a disappointment to his parents. Even so, this wastrel counted among Scotland's great men and as such became the leader of the parliamentary opposition to the Union of 1707. He was quite unsuited for the role, constantly compromised himself and let his side down when most needed. After 1707 he spent all his time in London, to die in a duel in 1712.[24] His mother still survived at Hamilton Palace and now she sat silent in her room for weeks, overwhelmed at how her heir had wasted his life. She also knew that, for the family's sake, everything once again had to depend on her. At the age of eighty she set about paying off her dead son's debts and bringing up his children, since their mother took little interest in them. And she continued with the energetic improvement of her estates. On the lands in Lanarkshire she rebuilt the school and the almshouse at Hamilton, set up a woollen mill and opened coalmines, while providing bursaries for needy students; Strathaven too received a church, school and waulking mill. On the Isle of Arran she constructed the harbour of Lamlash and provided a ferry, while appointing a preacher, doctor and schoolmaster. She gave Bo'ness in West Lothian a charter of regality, endowing it with certain burghal privileges. Under her patronage it became a thriving port, an outlet for cargoes from Glasgow to the North Sea. She still had her hands full of the business of the estate when she died in 1716.[25]

One duchess could not by herself liberate her sex, but a process was being set in train. Towards the end of the eighteenth century Elizabeth Mure of Caldwell, of a leading landed family in Renfrewshire, looked back on all the changes affecting gentlewomen in the era of progress she had lived through. At the outset, their existence weighed on them: 'Domestic affairs and amusing her husband was the business of a good wife... No attention was given to what we call accomplishments.' As daughters grew up, 'they were allowed to run about and amuse themselves in the way they choiced even to the age of women, at which time they were generally sent to Edinburgh for a winter or two, to learn to dress themselves and to dance and see a little of the world.' Then, after marriage, it was back to rural idiocy: 'If they read any it was either books of devotion or long romances, and sometimes both. They never ate a full meal at table; this was thought very undelicate, but they took care to have something before dinner, that they might behave with propriety in company.'[26]

More refined manners did at length spread round the country. As Elizabeth Mure noted, it was at the tea tables that the women 'pulled to pieces the manners of those that differed from them; everything was a matter of conversation; religion, morals, love, friendship, good manners, dress'. It is interesting that she connects this in a social sense with the easing of Presbyterian rigour that heralded the Enlightenment. About 1730, she reckons, 'those terrors began to wear off and religion appeared in a more amiable light. We were bid draw our knowledge of God from his works, the chief of which is the soul of a good man; then judge if we have cause to fear. The Christian religion was taught as the purest rule of morals; the belief of a particular providence and of a future state as a supporting every situation.' After that, 'the old minister was ridiculed who preached up hell and damnation; the mind was to be influenced by gentle and generous motives alone.'[27]

When the Enlightenment did arrive, it still tended to handle the distaff side gingerly. Adam Smith, professor of moral philosophy at the University of Glasgow, never said a word on women in either of his major works, *The Theory of Moral Sentiments* (1759) or *The Wealth of Nations* (1776). The first to venture on the subject of the sexes was John Millar, professor of civil law and a pupil of Smith's, in his *Observations Concerning the Distinctions of Ranks in Society* (1771). He devoted an entire section of this book to 'The Rank and Condition of Women in the Different Ages'. Here his treatment of sexuality and love showed the Enlightenment moving beyond bloodless abstraction. On the contrary, it often rested social ideas in terms of human emotions. For Millar, sex lay at the source, since 'sensual pleasures may be connected in many cases with the exercise of social dispositions'. In later essays he sought to explore this intricate relationship of civil society and domestic affection. Sexual passion, once sublimated in the love of a married couple, cemented the family and gave a basis for morality to the whole community, so that it 'laid the foundation of political society'. This was a cause of culture, too, for development of taste and appreciation of beauty marked it out, not least in the 'delicacy of sentiment' revealed in modern conventions of politeness.[28]

Women, Millar argued, had had to wait for the emergence of commercial civilization to 'become neither the slaves, nor the idols of the other sex, but the friends and companions, in the modern and domesticated family'. This was an institution united by 'esteem and affection' even as it remained divided by labour. The later stages of material development, especially the acquisition of immovable property, had brought greater inequality to society yet also a higher status for certain female beneficiaries of the process. The resulting leisure and tranquillity for this lucky minority then started to evoke from men 'a great respect and veneration for the female sex'. The effect on European manners had been lasting.[29]

Little of this was yet to be seen in Glasgow itself, however. From the eighteenth even into the twentieth century, it did help a little that for the learned professions – the church and the schools, medicine and the law – home and place of work often remained the same, with a wife on hand to lighten a masterly husband's social and professional encounters. As for commerce, in a thriving burgh some sort of equality of the sexes existed in those businesses, especially of tradesmen, that drew on the efforts of an extended family, the wives and children along with the journeymen and apprentices, to form a single unit of production. Inside it there could then be a division of labour: while the burgess and boss directed the operations, his spouse might attend to the detail and see to the welfare of the young folk. But with the progress in the city of the industrial revolution, entailing the much greater size and capitalization of business, came a split between home and work. Women got squeezed out of economic activity, even of subordinate roles in their husbands' enterprises.[30] Management of business in Glasgow became for the next two centuries a masculine prerogative.

Even at the end of the Victorian era this loss for the bourgeois woman had been only partially redressed. If she wanted more freedom, the first requirement was to liberate herself as best she could from her biological role.[31] In Glasgow and elsewhere in Scotland, by the 1870s it became common for wives of professional husbands to concentrate their childbearing in the early years of marriage and not to have any more babies beyond their early thirties. By 1900 the average number of children in families of this class fell to fewer than five. Soon a fair number contented themselves with two, setting the trend for the rest of the twentieth century. As a result even married women started to discover that, beyond a certain time of life, they became free to make some choices of their own.[32]

For that, however, these ladies had also better have some money, and money in Glasgow's bourgeois households was the business of the man. Even if a woman owned property, she still lay under severe constraints in Scots law. At her marriage, her movable property passed under her husband's control, a provision that did not come to an end till 1881. She might own heritable estate but could do nothing with it unless her husband consented, till this part of the law was in its turn changed in 1920.[33]

The law of marriage had been handed down from feudal Scotland, but under the pressures of commercial society it began to bend.[34] In Glasgow the high bourgeoisie, before it married off its daughters, took to drawing up contracts or trusts so as to protect the property it was contributing towards a new branch of the family – for instance, to stop resources being squandered by a spendthrift husband. The particular agreements might give the bride some say over the property she brought with her into the union, or even over the property acquired by the couple after-wards. An agreement could, for example, stipulate that the interest on her own investments was to be paid direct to her, without going through her husband. Such provisions in practice gave her a degree of financial independence. And later, if she survived long enough, widowhood would more or less liberate her, because the law of marriage then ceased to apply. Some widows were among the wealthiest people in Glasgow, and even among the lower middle class they could often do more than eke out a bare exist-ence, providing not only for themselves but also for a household of dependants.

Women who were rentiers in their own right might as a rule rely on three sources of income: bank deposits, urban property and family trusts. Many formed part of the army of small savers handing their funds over to a lawyer who could use them, through the various vehicles of investment that capitalist Scotland invented, to finance anything from railroads across the Rocky Mountains to sheep stations in the outback of Australia. The modern form of investment trust first appeared in 1873, and half a century later

Glasgow contained a dozen of them.[35] Bank deposits had the virtues of liquidity and accessibility for the depositrix, for her family and for any businesses the family owned. Independent women, especially spinster sisters, were important sources of capital for these businesses, especially in times of crisis. Urban property offered another safe investment. If it was commercial property, it could be leased to entrepreneurs in the family on favourable terms and so generate a return for them all. A woman with these types of income often used it not just for herself but also for the family's general benefit. She could support its own enterprises or invest in others. She could hold property, employ lawyers and accountants or administer large estates.[36] A final advantage was that at her death the sources of the income – the trusts or jointures yielding her annuities – reverted to the family.[37]

But the world of work began to beckon bourgeois women in Glasgow, too. Though some of them were early widows, more of them never married. The plight of spinsters as members of the bourgeoisie had often seemed wretched.[38] While young women of a lower class could find jobs, for those of the middle class there were few culturally acceptable routes to employment. These hapless creatures often seemed to themselves and others redundant, with no personal or professional purpose in life. If they could chance on a niche of their own it was usually in education and dressmaking, in both of which the wages could be pitiful. Yet work might be a necessity if they wished to avoid burdening fathers not always able to support a troupe of adult daughters, whatever the prevailing social mores might expect.

In late Victorian Scotland, however, wider opportunities began to appear. The Education Act (1872) provided for universal elementary schooling, and one immediate effect was to improve the previous patchy provision for girls. For boys in Scotland it had been reasonably easy to get a good start in life – certainly easier than for boys in other countries. Yet for girls it always proved harder, partly through lack of special facilities for them in the days before mixed education, partly because at all social levels there were families thinking it unnecessary or undesirable for girls to be taught anything much. By contrast, equality of the sexes was implicit in the legislation of 1872. The boards running the national system at the local level made their schools mixed. In the parallel development of the independent sector many new girls' schools would be built, normally staffed by women teachers. In Glasgow they included a girls' section of Hutcheson's Grammar School in 1876, Westbourne School in 1877 (now merged with Glasgow Academy), Park School in 1880, the High School for Girls in 1894, Laurel Bank School in 1903 (now merged with Hutcheson's). By the end of the century teaching became the commonest occupation for women.[39] Altogether, private education provided employment at several levels, from governesses living in with wealthy families to those, effectively businesswomen, who ran their own boarding schools.

Nursing offered another occupation for women favoured by the times, in particular by rapid advances in medical science and provision for public health. In Glasgow, the Royal Infirmary was founded in 1794, followed by a wide range of general and specialist hospitals. This did not in itself prove to be a sufficient condition for greater female employment – which at first, indeed, retreated. Scotland's midwives had always been women, mainly old crones who also served as bearers of ancient lore. With midwifery turning into the science of obstetrics, men elbowed them aside. The University of Glasgow's chair of midwifery was founded in 1815, and always (right till 2007) held by a man. But while a male medical profession might carry on without women doctors, it could do little without women nurses. For girls enclosed in claustrophobic Victorian households, especially if they grew up into spinsters with time to fill, a nursing career could be an escape. They would be required to live in a nurses' home under an imperious matron, as a condition for their fathers' or brothers' consent. They were not paid much more than the domestic servants they formerly had at their beck and call, and their low level of wages provided a sort of subsidy for the system. Yet they could find reward in their dedication and their contribution to public health.[40]

Commerce in its more modern forms began to open up to women as well. In the old days, perishable goods had been sold in markets on the streets of Glasgow, and raucous female stallholders earned their living this way. Textiles and hardware were displayed to the public in warehouses, and in general shops existed only for more specialized lines, often imports. That changed as prospering citizens demanded a wider range of consumer goods. Often the women led the demand, with a desire to satisfy ever more sophisticated tastes; they would often also prefer to be served by their own sex. As a result, Glasgow's shopping streets contained many businesses run by women, usually for apparel of various kinds: dressmakers, furriers, hosiers, milliners, seamstresses, staymakers, specialists in babies' clothes. When married couples set up homes there was further lucrative female business for furnishers, upholsterers, dealers in fine china or in Victorian whatnots – also, targeting the prudish, the frills to conceal suggestive table legs. Evidence from commercial directories suggests much of the city's retail commerce serviced the domestic sphere, with women selling to women.[41]

Another change for the better was that intelligent, efficient, well-spoken women could fill new jobs in commercial offices, at the typewriter or switchboard. Those who in later generations might have become academics, accountants or lawyers went into the offices because that was where the best work available to them could be found at the time. The trend started towards the end of the Victorian period and by 1911 Scotland had 30,000 women so employed, the forerunners of many more in the new century.[42] On a small scale, women even began to penetrate the heavy industries and, for example, find jobs in shipbuilding firms – at least in the back offices, where they might be called on to design the cabins and furnishings on the great passenger liners. The step from there to female enterprise in any stricter sense remained a big one. Kate Cranston proved to be unique in the public standing she won, but the international exhibitions held in Glasgow in 1888, 1901 and 1911 featured sections on 'women's industries', showing the wide range of goods they were making. Altogether quite large numbers of spinsters and widows found work, even ran small businesses and otherwise engaged directly in the market.

Those who instead stayed at home directed the household from day to day on behalf of their husbands, which meant also managing a staff of servants. This produced a relationship between employer and employee different from that in the commercial world outside. A right-thinking mistress liked to take girls from the working class generally in hand. In Glasgow she usually found them from agencies recruiting in the Highlands and in Ireland, and she assumed it was for her to instil in them habits of industry, thrift and churchgoing, reinforced by daily prayers and readings from the Bible. They would then be not only introduced to their proper sphere but also instructed in the skills necessary for the comfort of their future husbands and families.[43] They might learn respect for authority too. Once they left their own homes, their fathers' authority passed to the masters of the employing households, or to their deputies, the wives. When the girls married, the authority then shifted to their husbands. Maids would meanwhile be serving their betters while keeping their place, not to say bearing witness in wider society to the value of respectable manners and morals. It could be seen as a logical progression in an ideal Victorian social order.

At the upper level of society women had usually just to put up with any discontent they felt, channelling it into self-improvement, good works or at most a mild interest in winning the vote. Otherwise the consequences might be unpredictable, as illustrated by the notorious case in 1857 of Madeleine Smith, daughter of a high bourgeois family with a stately residence in Blythswood Square. She managed to have an affair with a hapless young French gardener, but then to get rid of him when her parents found her a suitable Glaswegian husband. The means she chose was arsenic, or so the charge against her ran when she came to trial. It was found not proven, yet Madeleine had to leave Glasgow for London, where she found life more to her taste in the artistic circle of the aesthete, William Morris, and the Fabian Society.[44]

Women lower down the social scale faced different problems. One important result of the industrial revolution was to make many more of them economically active, but this brought its own difficulties. Not only were a lot of new jobs created but a lot of old jobs were also destroyed, amid rising social friction, including friction between the sexes. The huge textile factories rising up round Glasgow represented the city's economic progress; here women could perform the required mechanical operations just as well as men. But men had been the spinners and weavers of the past. Those who saw their jobs now vanishing felt they should have the first claim on fresh forms of livelihood. They might form trades unions to protect themselves, a course of action that in the west of Scotland almost always failed. Or else they might turn to violence and intimidation. In 1824 a parliamentary inquiry heard of the case of Messrs James Dunlop & Sons, a partnership that had built a cotton mill at Calton and installed spinning machines:

They employed women alone, as not being parties to the combination [trade union], and thus more easily managed, and less insubordinate than male spinners. These they paid at the same rate of wages, as were paid at other works to men. But they were waylaid and attacked, in going to, and returning from their work; the houses in which they resided, were broken open in the night. The women themselves were cruelly beaten and abused; and the mother of one of them killed.

In the end the company felt forced to sack all their female spinners and employ only male ones, 'most probably the very men who had attempted their ruin'.[45]

Even so, in the early stages of the industrial revolution relatively few men had jobs in factories because relatively few wanted one. These jobs demanded submission to a discipline of a kind new and unfamiliar to the average Scotsman. Especially in the west of Scotland, they arose from expensive investment in mills with complex machinery that operated ceaselessly. The workforce had to conform to its mechanical requirements, labouring in unison and under discipline at soul-destroying tasks. Only the most desperate men were likely to tolerate them. Evidently the cotton spinners at Calton came into that category, as did other male workers in Glasgow right up to the recession of 1841, probably the worst of the century. Once it was over, a steady improvement in living conditions followed. Now Glaswegians could look for jobs in which they might take pride, rather than just seeking a subsistence at whatever cost.[46]

But young girls, sent out to work by their families, could not even count on the limited choices open to young men. It had been at an earlier time the norm for those not yet married to remain under the parental roof, earning their unpaid keep with whatever menial tasks needed to be done round the house. The new jobs in factories lay within the capacities of women, or indeed of children, because they seldom required much physical strength. These fresh pools of workers could also be paid less than men. And since women and children were the dependants in a Scottish family, used to doing what their elders and betters told them, they were the more amenable to harsh discipline in the workplace. A parliamentary inquiry found that two in five women workers had yet to reach their eighteenth birthday and the largest single cohort was of girls aged thirteen to fourteen.[47] A manager from Glasgow asserted from his experience that 'women do not generally work much in factories once they get married;' not more than one in twelve of the employees was aged over thirty-one.[48]

Families grew big because wages rose and parents were not afraid to have children when they knew they could contribute early on to the family's income. As long as the husband remained in good health, the wife was likely to enjoy a tolerable standard of living – though the same woman might later face irksome years as the carer for an old man, and ultimately as a widow, to whom a clutch of teenage children could be a precious support. By the end of the nineteenth century, a quarter of Glaswegian households had women as their heads, after losing their men for one reason or another, and it fell to them to provide for the offspring or other dependants. These hard-working housewives often took on further burdens to eke out their income. The clothing trade offered outwork, for example, and most of it went to women. They could carry it on at home, but it was still sweated labour.[49]

Marriage did not always bring the drudgery to an end, however. With much male employment seasonal or otherwise unstable too, the economics of the working-class household might demand that women carry on their toil as long as they could or, if they had to stop for childbirth, resume as soon as practicable afterwards. Now, instead of families of craftsmen all pitching in together at home as in the old days, wives never saw their husbands on weekdays between dawn and dusk. Children, so far from being brought up in the stable frame of the extended family and its internal disciplines, were put to work in a factory at the age of ten or eleven (if not before) and seldom saw the light of day. Bourgeois observers noted the loosening of familial ties among all those employed in this system, and attributed many moral evils to it. Sheriff Archibald Alison of Glasgow believed three-quarters of the girls lost their virginity before they reached twenty years of age.[50]

Yet the woman emerged as the real strength of the working-class family in Glasgow, on hand to hold things together while the man went off with his mates to the pub or got into fights at the football. By that same proletarian tradition he would have handed his wages over to his wife after deducting his own pocket money for smokes and drinks. She then needed to deal, usually on her own, with shopkeepers, pawnbrokers and moneylenders. She had to pay the rent, as well as feed and clothe herself and her family while struggling against the odds to keep house and children clean. It was also for her to come to terms with the landlord and his factor, and to haggle over rent and arrears: 'A clean rent book was more than a source of pride, it was a badge of approval, a buffer against control and a possible passport to better housing or employment.'[51] At least in the stairheid parliaments she had moments to spare and enjoy as she exchanged gossip, opinion and advice with her neighbours.

Within all these tight constraints on their status and activities, women might still fail and fall outside the accepted structures of Victorian society. By one misfortune or another, or by a series of them, they could lose husband or home or job or all three. And then, in the worst circumstances, they might face the grimmest prospect imaginable, of eking out an existence by selling themselves for sex.[52]

Glasgow had in the past been a god-fearing, strictly regulated, orthodox Presbyterian burgh. Prostitution on any scale arose as a consequence of the industrial revolution, or rather of its social strains. By 1815 it was found necessary to open a Magdalene Asylum, with the purpose of rescuing fallen women.[53] The asylum remained relentlessly active for the rest of the century in the city beyond its walls, too. The managers led a campaign to get the Glasgow Fair moved from its traditional site on the Green. It had for centuries been held there in the middle fortnight of July, formerly for the sale of livestock or hire of servants, now for amusement, with circus, concerts, plays – and prostitutes. One summer the asylum's aptly named Repressive Committee sent a delegation that found the site to be 'a prolific source of evil' and 'just one huge brothel'. The agitation against all this grew so clamant that in 1871 the corporation shifted the Fair further out to Camlachie.[54]

The old core of the city turned into a den of vice once respectable citizens fled to salubrious suburbs to escape the deepening urban decay. The University of Glasgow followed in 1870 and left its beautiful buildings, dating from the seventeenth century, to be knocked down and replaced by a goods yard. The principal, the Revd Thomas Barclay, gave as the main reason the problems of instructing the city's youth amid its worst slums. In particular, holding classes in the evening had become disagreeable or even dangerous when students needed to run the gauntlet of pestering prostitutes who hung round the gate of the college. Youngsters from outside Glasgow often stayed in this part of town too, and might find themselves living on the same stair as fallen women.[55]

Glasgow's prostitution in its turn became the object of virtuous bourgeois investigations, by men preferring to remain anonymous. One took the pen-name of Shadow. He was an evangelical Christian who never shrank from pushing his way into the stews, to witness what was happening, to distribute tracts, to bring to light the shenanigans beneath the surface of a great commercial city and to call for public action to put things to rights. He sought to move his readers with the plight of pathetic women and children caught up in it all as helpless victims. Yet he could be brutally frank about things that shocked him:

> The smell, as we enter, is suffocating, made still more so by two scavengers carting away the filth from a receptacle within a couple of yards of the door. The room cannot be more than eight feet by ten, exclusive of two recesses for beds. In each of these are three unfortunate women, and on the floor are two others, with a man, apparently a protector – making nine persons in all sleeping in the apartment.

The window shutters and door being closed, nothing but a small contracted chimney is left for ventilation.[56]

It is not too clear why anybody would want to have sex in such surroundings, but Shadow assured his readers there was plenty going on. He reckoned there were 1,800 prostitutes in Glasgow who also provided a living for 1,350 'bullies or fancy men' and for 450 'mistresses'. They were to be sought out in 450 brothels receiving an estimated 80 visits a week each, to yield a total of 36,000 acts of coition a year. Each one would cost the customer a shilling, but while he was at it his pockets and wallet would be routinely rifled of something like the same sum, after he had already spent double that on drink in order to conquer his inhibitions. The total annual turnover of Glasgow's sex industry amounted to more than £500,000 (£48 million in today's money). Its practitioners were also its victims: each year 300 prostitutes died.[57]

Another investigator presented his findings in the manner of an official report, as *The Moral Statistics of Glasgow in 1863*. He reckoned the prostitutes in the city to number 2,500, a figure higher than Shadow's because 'sly harlots' were included, working part time from lodgings or hired rooms and probably with an ordinary job too. They again supplemented their incomes by stealing from their customers: 'It is well known that scarcely one theft out of a hundred is reported to the police, the plundered victims being afraid to expose their folly.' Still the recorded rate of female crime in Glasgow was exceptionally high. In 1861 there had been 4,000 arrests of women for being disorderly, 8,000 for being drunk and disorderly, and 10,000 for 'prowling'. The worst result, this observer thought, lay in the corruption of the young. The 350 prostitutes who, by his reckoning, died every year were replaced by a supply of innocent girls lured from the country to be seduced and then put to work in the brothels.[58]

As for the boys, 'how often in Glasgow... have we observed

as many as four, or six mere lads, from 14 to 17 years of age, surrounding a prostitute and drinking in with loud laughter, and the kindled itching gusto of disastrously awakened lust, the frightfully obscene remarks which flowed so naturally from her putrid lips.' The solutions lay in policing and in evangelization, though the author of the *Moral Statistics* conceded that practising Christians might also succumb to the whores' wiles. But somehow Scots had to learn to control their sexual urges – even or especially the adolescents, who should take warning at a diagnosis from the Glasgow Royal Asylum: 'We have been so thoroughly impressed with the conviction that masturbation is a more fruitful source of insanity than is generally supposed, that we resolved to investigate accurately the male cases admitted. We have assigned in nineteen cases masturbation as a cause of insanity... one-sixth of all the male admissions are cases of insanity the physical cause of which is masturbation.'[59]

The progress of industrial society was not by itself going to produce equality of the sexes. In most nations, that needed political action by women themselves. In Scotland the campaign for the suffrage started up in earnest after Britain's second bout of electoral reform in 1867–8, which gave the vote to much of the urban male working class. Women could also qualify for the first time, as ratepayers – that is to say, if they were heads of property-owning households. But this vote they could use only in local polls for town councils, school boards and so on. Those without the vote might still stand for such bodies, on condition they were married. All the same, most women who took up any political activity were single, middle class, well off, in their convictions liberal and otherwise involved in the philanthropy of the Victorian city, seeing that they regarded paid work as neither necessary nor acceptable. Membership of a women's suffrage society offered another public-spirited way of spending free time. These societies appeared in Scotland in 1867, in Edinburgh and Aberdeen. For no obvious

A shiny new engine from the North British Locomotive Works is sent on its way from Broomielaw to some imperial destination, about 1910.

These smart lads at Fairfield's yard in Govan were an industrial elite in the making – but, before the year 1915 was out, conscription would have claimed many for the western front.

Quite unusually for Scotland the basic structure of Glasgow's cathedral survived the Reformation intact, and is here depicted by John Slezer in 1690 – the year it returned from episcopalian to presbyterian worship.

Pre-industrial technologies long persisted, being often a matter of pride to the individual craftsmen – here commemorated in stained glass windows at Maryhill burgh halls.

An image by Thomas Annan, the pioneering photographer, of a close off the High Street of Glasgow, complete with barefoot bairns and a privy midden (right), where human waste was dumped.

A barefoot boy by the ashbin of his tenement at 59 Crown Street, Gorbals, about 1910.

Early attempts at improvement got rid of dark closes and stairs, and opened up
the flats to light and air – fine if the weather was good.

In her pomp, Catherine Cranston of the Willow Tea Rooms,
pioneer of female emancipation in Glasgow.

At the opposite end of the social and economic scale for Glaswegian
women, Wee Maggie, the Calton weaver.

No expense was spared for the flamboyant interior of the City
Chambers, opened by Queen Victoria in 1888.

Kelvingrove art gallery and museum, opened for the great exhibition
of 1901, retains its wide appeal for Glaswegians.

It is easy to see why the livery of Glasgow corporation trams was dubbed 'champagne and chartreuse'.

The Labour pioneer, Keir Hardie, managed at the same time to look proletarian and natty.

The day that proletarian revolution came under the Red Flag to George Square, Glasgow – but was never planted firmly.

The uncompromising rhythmic abstraction of Zaha Hadid's Riverside Museum gives Glasgow one of the finest examples of contemporary architecture.

reason Glasgow lagged behind, till in 1872 an open-air meeting to support women's suffrage took place on the Green. The crowd was said to number about 1,000, 'chiefly working men of the most intelligent type'.[60]

The campaign for the suffrage should be seen as part of women's general assertion of their rights, something always more likely among the middle and upper classes. Victorian society assigned them subordinate places and roles that not all were prepared to accept: hence, in particular, their demand for access to the universities and the professions. An association was formed to get women into the University of Glasgow in 1877.[61] The imposing new edifice on Gilmorehill at last threw open its doors to them in 1892, and two years later four female graduates, the first in Scotland, took degrees in medicine. Other disciplines followed – arts in 1895, science in 1898, education in 1904, divinity in 1912, law in 1919. In 1921, Sister Bernardine of Notre Dame College, a zoologist, became the first woman and only the second graduate to be awarded a PhD by the university. In 1892, a mere 6 per cent of the students were women. By 1908 the proportion had grown to about a quarter, and seldom afterwards fell below that level. Most graduates went into secondary teaching and medicine.[62]

A number of these women also joined in the campaign for the suffrage, which before the turn of the twentieth century was never a vehement affair, rather one of sedate public meetings and reasoned petitions to Parliament. One or two Glaswegians figured among the militants in England, notably Flora Drummond, nicknamed the General because she led marches wearing a military uniform and mounted on a horse. She had been radicalized by a personal problem: that she possessed all the qualifications for her chosen career as a postmistress except height: at 5 feet 2 inches, she was judged too short. She decided that this was just an excuse, and that it amounted to discrimination on grounds of sex rather than of size. She played on both in her confrontations with politicians.[63]

Militant action within Scotland did not appear till just before the First World War, when male politicians' foot-dragging exhausted the patience of some suffragettes. They hated Herbert Asquith, MP for East Fife and prime minister from 1908, because of his 'Cat and Mouse Act' under which their imprisoned sisters on hunger strike were released if their condition grew critical but hauled back once they revived. They physically attacked him twice, first in August 1913 while he was on holiday at Lossiemouth, golfing with his daughter. Then, in November, he went to unveil a statue at Bannockburn of his later predecessor at No. 10, Sir Henry Campbell-Bannerman, who had been the scion of a mercantile dynasty in Glasgow. On the way a woman crouched down in the road to halt the prime minister's car, and as it stopped four others rushed up and lashed at him with dog-whips. Only police in a car behind could save him.[64]

By 1914 the violent protests reached the city of Glasgow itself. A riot ensued when the police tried to arrest the leader of the militant suffragettes, Emmeline Pankhurst, at a public meeting. Others meanwhile set light to pillar-boxes, to unoccupied mansions, to a clubhouse at Ayr, to a laboratory at St Andrews and to the railway station at Leuchars. They hoped the insurers required to pay for the damage would bring pressure to bear on the government to grant the vote to women. But the same year the outbreak of the First World War halted the public disorder. Calls to patriotic duty touched the suffragettes too, prompting them to offer their services in nursing wounded soldiers and other good works. In Glasgow, however, there was a circle of women, Mary Barbour, Helen Crawford and Agnes Dollan, who continued their political activity. Among other social protests, they helped to organize the rent strikes as privations on the home front worsened.[65]

The franchise as a focus for protest was anyway about to be removed. In recognition of women's contribution to the war effort, the Parliament at Westminster passed an act early in 1918 giving the vote to female property-holders over the age of thirty. In 1928, all women aged twenty-one or older were enfranchised on a par with men.[66] Previous protesters moved into conventional politics. Helen Crawford became a leading figure in the Independent Labour Party and attended the second congress of the Third International in Moscow in 1920, where she met Lenin. When the ILP rejected affiliation to the Third International, she joined the Communist Party of Great Britain and sat on its executive committee. Others contented themselves with a local role. Mary Barbour was elected to the corporation of Glasgow in 1920, and later set up a clinic for family planning. Agnes Dollan followed her on to the council in 1921; she was the wife of Patrick Dollan, Labour's organizer in the city and a future lord provost.

For the women of Glasgow it was otherwise hardly a new dawn. While five of them got elected to the council in 1920, the City Chambers remained for the time being under the control of the surviving mercantile elite, whose Victorian view of females, in life let alone in office, had changed little. By the 1930s a new local caucus of Labour councillors emerged, yet showed little interest in any further stages of emancipation: no woman was chosen as lord provost till Jean Roberts in 1970.[67]

On the parliamentary level, matters had moved along at a less glacial pace, with the first female MP, Agnes Hardie, elected in 1937 at a by-election in the constituency of Springburn. She was the sister-in-law of Keir Hardie, whose brother George she succeeded in the seat on his death; Glaswegian socialism early on developed nepotistic habits. At Westminster she became the champion of shop assistants, whose trades union she had earlier organized. Even Labour's landslide at the general election of 1945 brought only two more women from Glasgow into Parliament, Margaret Herbison and Jean Mann – and they needed to go out into the sticks to find their seats, in North Lanarkshire and Coatbridge respectively. Britain's first Catholic woman MP was Alice Cullen, who won

Gorbals for Labour at another by-election in 1948, going on to serve the constituency till her death in 1969. As a 'champion of the slum dweller'[68] she enjoyed public respect, but she still offered no exemplar to the city's male chauvinist Labour Party. The torch of political feminism passed into quite other hands, notably those of Winnie Ewing, a Glaswegian lawyer who won a sensational victory for the SNP in the by-election at Hamilton in 1967. She was the start of a line of spirited female nationalists, continuing with Margo MacDonald, victor of the by-election at Govan in 1973, and Nicola Sturgeon, first minister of Scotland, representing the same seat (with changed boundaries) since 2007.

All that can be said for Labour's stick-in-the-mud attitude was that it reflected social reality in Glasgow. Middle-class women might be denied chances to get on in life, but the position of working-class women was often far worse. Violence against them remained quite common. When in 1927 Will Fyffe recorded 'I Belong to Glasgow', a song that at once became a civic anthem, it contained a verse nobody seemed to find exceptionable at the time:

> There's no harm in taking a drappie,
> It ends all your trouble and strife,
> It gives you the feeling that when you land home,
> Well, you don't care a hang for the wife.

Quite likely this was a euphemism for knocking her about. The local custom did not pass away with the old Glasgow: even today, the police report that the incidence of domestic violence more than doubles after football matches between Rangers and Celtic.[69]

But even abused married women can be in a better position than single women, whether pensioners or single parents. Among the latter the poverty of Glasgow is worst of all. Four out of ten families with children in the city have only a single parent – the highest rate for any local authority in Scotland, equivalent to more than

26,000 households. Many receive no income except for benefits. Fewer than half the single parents in Glasgow are in paid work, part time for the great majority of them. They have earnings on average only one-third of those in households headed by a couple. Single mothers also tend to suffer worse health, and are much more likely to be the victims of violence. Outside the home, many in this plight resort to prostitution. They are to be found on the grid of streets between Anderston Cross and Blythswood Square, hanging about on the corners, bare-legged even on freezing nights, with skirts temptingly short but faces gaunt and haggard, their bodies bent against the wind, waiting for the next client. In the Victorian era, women were forced by poverty or alcoholism to sell their bodies. Little has changed, except that the thirst for drink has been replaced by a craving for drugs. Rape and violence are common threats to these pathetic creatures, as are robbery and refusal to pay. In recent times, a number of the girls have been the victims of gruesome murders.[70] Yet the authorities in Glasgow have refused to recognize the sex trade to the extent of accommodating it in licensed saunas, as has happened in other cities. Here the prostitutes are safe from violence and can be kept free of disease. Since the oldest profession is unlikely ever to be stamped out, regulation of it seems the next best thing. Yet in Glasgow, of all places, some persistent streak of puritanism insists it can somehow be suppressed.

It might be hard to conclude the twentieth century was one of great progress for Glaswegian women. Progress has all the same taken place, often in unexpected ways, despite the pressures on the social structure of a city in economic decline. War, for example, was an instrument of the progress. In 1911 fewer than 6,000 women filled industrial occupations on Clydeside, yet by 1918 more than 31,000 women worked on munitions alone. It was the result of the dilution of labour in Glasgow's skilled trades for the sake of the war effort, in other words of bringing in workers who had not served their time as apprentices and gained the privilege of a

job for life. The overriding need as the struggle against Germany
ground on was to increase the production of armaments, and for
this the unskilled, including women, had to be brought in, if at
lower rates of pay. Towards the end of the war one in three working
women was in her job as a substitute for a male who had gone off
to fight.[71]

The struggle against Hitler demanded even more national effort
than the struggle against the Kaiser had done, and after 1939 there
was little of the earlier resistance to dilution in the industrial
workplace. To put it another way, many more women found a job
making munitions. The greatest concentration in Glasgow could
be found in the Rolls Royce factory at Hillington, where 10,000 of
them helped to produce engines for the Spitfire aircraft. These and
their male colleagues were all, by Clydeside's standards, unskilled
workers, yet the management wanted to pay the women less than
the men. It took a strike in 1943 supported by both sexes to force a
change of mind. From then on there was equal pay for equal work
at Rolls Royce, and over time in other factories too.[72] The needs
of post-war reconstruction kept many women on in employment
after 1945. The creation of the welfare state and the prosperity of the
1950s further improved their social and economic standing. Better
education, housing and health made it easier for those bringing up
families to hold down a job at the same time.

By 1970 most females in employment were married, and were no
longer frowned on or pitied as they once had been. Contraception
limited the size of their families, while labour-saving domestic
appliances made housework less of a slog in grimy Glasgow.
Women could now look beyond the home for some satisfaction
in their working lives. Their needs were better answered in an
economic structure moving away from heavy industry manned
by males towards light manufacturing and services. Amid this
modernization of Scotland, it might be the men who went on the
dole while the women found the new jobs.[73]

A majority of the Scottish workforce was female by the turn of the twenty-first century – though still not employed on the same terms as males, with jobs often part time and pay usually lower. A division of labour would have started at school. Bright boys chose science or practical subjects taught by male teachers, while bright girls chose the arts or courses with a social or commercial content taught by female teachers. These girls would usually go on into sectors of employment – shops, hotels, finance, education, social work, health service – where they earned wages about 75 per cent lower than those of men. At the higher levels of business and the professions, where female emancipation had in some cases only just begun, men still far outnumbered women. An investigation in 2012 found that no more than seven of Scotland's top thirty listed companies had a woman as chief executive,[74] though the number of non-executive directors was rising. In Glasgow enterprises including Aggreko, the specialist in temporary power; Devro, the world's leader in sausage skins; and Scottish Television, the broadcaster, had recently put women on their boards. In the top thirty companies there were altogether 242 female directors.

Yet times were also changing. Information technology trans-formed many of the transactions of everyday life – including what, for example, had for decades been a primarily female attribute, skill in typing. In Glasgow's late Victorian offices, male managers had directed female typists. But now secretarial functions were defeminized because typing opened the way to the internet, an essential tool in the entire range of modern work, indeed in modern life generally. Whenever away from the office the manager was likely to type in his messages himself, while his secretary might turn into the 'personal assistant' ready to take responsibility for some necessary decisions during his absence. All this only reflected the blurring of social functions and sexual roles in society at large, so that earlier confident assumptions about masculinity and femininity turned vaguer. Admittedly, however, this was likely to take place more slowly in Scotland, and in Glasgow especially, than elsewhere.[75]

The best we can say is that unfathomable changes were going in the relations of the sexes in Scotland, with men as well as women needing to adapt. Women's lives no longer depended on wages earned by men, and sometimes the roles had been reversed. Glasgow used to house many big families, but now both sexes could join in planning their families and making sure to provide for the children they did have. It might be part of the planning that the wife was left scope to work, the stigma that once attached to this having gone for good. On the contrary, there needed now by law to be equal opportunities for education and training. At the turn of the twentieth century it had been thought that political emancipation was the key to this. In the event, greater political representation for women turned out to be almost the final step in the equalizing process. The inaugural election to the new Scottish Parliament in 1999 saw forty-nine women win seats, making up 37 per cent of MSPs, the third highest figure for any national legislature in the world. By the time Nicola Sturgeon came to form her first cabinet in 2014 she was able to achieve, in the new jargon of the twenty-first century, gender balance.

7

Patricians:
'Model municipality'

ON OCTOBER 8, 1856, the lord provost of Glasgow, Andrew Orr, had a pleasant public duty to perform at the inauguration of the new deacon convener of the trades, James Wilson. As part of the ceremony, amid the classical elegance of Robert Adam's Trades Hall in Glassford Street, Orr gave a speech on behalf of the town council welcoming Wilson to his duties. It was tactful for the lord provost to gloss over the fact that these duties amounted to a good deal less than in former times. After the municipal reform of 1833, the original duopoly of merchants and tradesmen in the government of the royal burgh had ended, with their authority passing instead to a general body of voters. The process left for Trades Hall only a residue of charitable functions: helping orphans to get an education, promoting best practice in apprenticeships and generally succouring the needy round the city. Orr, not therefore having much by way of practical business to dwell on, made his speech more inspiring with a vision of things to come, as foreseen by him and his colleagues on the council. It turned into a classic statement of what Victorian Glasgow was all about.

There is nothing Glaswegians love so much as praise of their own city, but Orr went further with the ideal he held out of a 'model municipality'. It was already being realized in some essentials: 'We now have all the powers and privileges, with a larger population and a great amount of territory, than is embraced in the municipal bounds in any other city in Great Britain.' Life here had grown so alluring that lesser places clamoured to share in it:

> We are envied, not only by other cities, but by our immediate neighbours. We have a large and efficient police force to keep peace within our boundaries, but still all our citizens are not satisfied to remain within our circle. They are building villas beyond our limits, and inviting our police protection to follow them there. At Govan, Maryhill and Partick, and other places, they are looking to us to extend to them police protection, and to incorporate them; and I believe that nothing would be more beneficial than to amalgamate the four parishes in and around Glasgow into one great municipality; and thus including, as it would, parochial, municipal, statute labour and police matters in one system, Glasgow would be pointed to as a perfect model of a great city governing itself... Here we have 400,000 citizens following every industrial and other pursuits, accumulating wealth, properly using their political privileges, and governing themselves so as not to require a single officer of the imperial government to care for or look after them. I ask, is this not one of the most beautiful examples of self-government which it is possible to conceive?[1]

National sentiment was starting to stir again in Scotland, but Orr's patriotism seems to have been local. In some ways Glasgow had by now little in common with the rest of the country, its old-fashioned cities, small burghs or emptying hills and glens. Links with America, Europe and Asia were closer than those with London, or even with Edinburgh.[2] At any rate, the last of the limitations imposed on the city by its own history fell away, and it was thinking bigger than ever before. The 400,000 citizens that Orr mentioned came about halfway between the 77,000 recorded in the census of 1801 and the almost 700,000 in the census of 1901. Though the visible path of the growth is distorted by extensions of the urban boundaries, the figure would pass a million during the First World War.[3] Everything else in the city during its great century took place against this background of the relentless pressure of population.

Orr was typical of the city's elite at the halfway point. Its members stood at the forefront of commercial society as defined a century before by Adam Smith, father of economics and professor at the University of Glasgow. In his time, merchant dynasties had ruled the local roost, but to maintain their position they needed to be on the alert to economic and political developments worldwide. Originally they were the tobacco lords. In the nineteenth century, the West Indian 'sugar aristocracy' became the first to take over, according to a social observer, Archibald Alison, sheriff of Lanarkshire. Soon they faced competition from a novel nobility of manufacturers, the cotton magnates. Hot on their heels followed the calico printers, then finally the ironmasters and coalmasters. What carried each successive group forward was the wealth it won, exceeding in every generation that of the last. Social climbing, even so, took longer than economic lift-off. Alison thought the newer clusters of the burgh's elite sat uneasily with the older ones, as people who 'were scarcely ever to be seen in their circles, and obviously when they were, belonged to an inferior grade in society'.[4]

As for the council itself, in governing Glasgow it would come to stand on two principles – strict economy in finance and the welfare of the people. The wealthy businessmen elected to run the city felt proud of the profitable inventiveness and efficiency with which they did so. But they grew reluctant to entrust the promotion of welfare to the mechanics of classical political economy. With the vision and ambition to create an ideal industrial society, they sought to bring the energy of the capitalists and the morals of the citizens into harmony rather through strict regulation. It gave social control to the bourgeoisie, but also offered much to the workers. These could be kept tranquil at a time when labour was rising as a political force elsewhere. The policies reinforced assent to a system where clashes of capital and labour got deliberately defused. Though candidates of different persuasions sought and won seats on the council, they did so not as members of a party but as individuals; it is misleading to look at them through the prism of a political system, such as ours today, where party counts for almost everything. Even if differences on particular matters were clear and publicly acknowledged, the councillors might act in a non-partisan manner to play down their divisions.[5]

A new public spirit was being born in Glasgow, collectivist and interventionist. It looked alien to the libertarian radicalism of most Scots, and it found its local critics too. One of them would call the city's corporation 'the oppressor of the West', using the Parliament at Westminster merely as a 'means of registering its decrees'.[6] But another noted in awe that 'our municipality is a microcosm of our state... our imitation of imperial housekeeping is very faithful.'[7] Its principles might well have derived from the special situation of a stateless nation, where the sovereign authority resident in another country was asked only to provide the statutory instruments for local institutions to pursue the general welfare in the freedom they chose for themselves. Scottish political histories tend for this period to focus on the parliamentary level, which has indeed its own interest. But for the ordinary citizen the municipal level, here as elsewhere operating in relative autonomy, was of far greater practical importance. Glasgow became a sort of city-state, and in these pages we will treat it like that.

The municipal analogy with the greater imperial entity has a particular ring of truth in one respect: the development of a bureaucracy. Classical political economists were sceptical of bureaucrats,[8] yet that did not deter Glaswegians. Indeed their urban bureaucracy soon outgrew the national bureaucracy, which still got by with the mere relics of the old Scottish state – the office of lord advocate and a couple of aides sitting in a room at Parliament House in Edinburgh. Even before 1833 Glasgow disposed of somewhat more; the town clerk, a diehard Tory by the name of James Reddie, in post from 1804 to 1852, kept hold of a staff of his own as he manipulated the law to make himself irremovable by the reformers. In the burgeoning burgh a broader bureaucracy in any case just grew.

John Carrick had come as a boy to Glasgow to be apprenticed to an architect, and in 1844 he was appointed superintendent of streets, at that time with an office in the jail at Saltmarket and a single assistant to help him. As he started the job, urban redevelopment on a large scale was already being contemplated. By 1862 he received the novel designation of city architect. The intervening period had seen a series of horrible epidemics, especially of cholera, which seem to have stimulated his environmental activism. He devoted 'hours upon hours to a complete survey of the localities in which fever was reported, to interviewing the proprietors and factors on the spot, and to carrying out as far as seemed possible the structural alterations which were of the most immediate importance'.[9] This was the start of his life's work.

Later, in 1872, the city council hired its first full-time medical officer of health, having so far made do with a part-timer. James Russell came with experience of the Royal Infirmary, of the poorhouse and of the specialist hospitals for fevers (infectious diseases). He had learned that preventive medicine in an industrial community depended on the improvement of living conditions; the town council needed to take action in this 'semi-asphyxiated city' where everybody had a cough. His heart was tender: 'Of all the children who die in Glasgow before they complete their fifth year, 32 per cent die in houses of one apartment; and not 2 per cent in houses of five apartments and upwards. There they die, and their little bodies are laid on a table or on the dresser, so as to be somewhat out of the way of their brothers and sisters, who play and sleep and eat in their ghastly company.'[10] But his actions would be tough, as we will see below, and not least on the poorest class of people.

Then, in 1873, the council poached James Marwick, since 1859 town clerk of Edinburgh, for the same post in Glasgow. This dominating figure steered municipal policy for the next three decades. He was the highest paid civic official in Britain, with an authoritative style of leadership to match. For him, his remuneration imposed duties of loyalty, impartiality and incorruptibility, and he expected the same of his subordinates. The first thing he did was overhaul the municipal administrative structure, requiring his officials to devote their energies solely to public service; previously they had been moonlighting young lawyers. Marwick would otherwise lobby intensively for Glasgow's legal boundaries to be extended in line with the physical growth of the city, which could only suffer if its bourgeoisie moved out (it has proved a perennial problem). He took as a personal mission the achievement of a Greater Glasgow, pressing the project on adjacent local authorities and on central government in London. Altogether, his enhanced control and cohesion were evident from the sheer size of the civic workforce, which would reach 10,000 by the end of the century. These employees became more than just functionaries: they embodied an ideal of good government aiming to reshape the moral character of the people.[11]

The history of the lord provost's office ran in parallel to this bureaucratic one. In 1833 it had still been largely honorary; by the end of the century it was much more clearly political. Municipal reform threw the town council open in the sense that many more citizens gained the right to elect their councillors and, through the councillors, their lord provost. These voters still made up only a fraction of the city's total population, however, and in practice the reform at first made less difference than might have been expected. The old merchant oligarchy carried on in its leading role for a good while yet. Still, times were changing. When the senior bailie, William Gilmour, addressed the inaugural meeting of the reformed town council, he said: 'We cannot certainly for a moment lose sight of the importance of our office, and the responsibility attached to it, and we may rest assured that the world will not. Every eye will be directed towards the working of the liberal system.'[12]

The last lord provost before 1833 had been James Ewing, thanks to his plantations on Jamaica the richest man in Glasgow, and just elected one of its Liberal MPs to boot. But his own liberalism, like that of others in the ruling circle, tended to be erratic: while he was in commercial policy a free trader, in domestic affairs he remained rather minimally progressive.[13] His successor was Robert Grahame, a veteran reformer though also a director of the mighty chemical works of St Rollox. Then came William Mills, the first Glaswegian to use steamships for seaborne trade with runs to Liverpool and London. Later there was James Campbell, textile merchant, himself a Tory but father of the future Liberal prime minister, Henry Campbell-Bannerman. Campbell's successor, James Lumsden the elder, stood a little lower in commercial status: he made his own pile from stationery, a typical new consumer product for an age where businesses and bourgeois households took greater care than before in writing letters, setting down their thoughts over the glossy sheen of his headed sheets of customized notepaper. Lumsden also provided a precedent for Orr, who was in the same line of business. He shrewdly diversified to produce a wide range of ephemera: picture-books, song-sheets, business cards, greeting cards, posters, pamphlets, circulars, invoices, tickets. In due course his company went upmarket too, publishing expensive volumes with gilt leather bindings, such as the *History of the Cathedral and See of Glasgow* (1897), the sort of book every prospering citizen might want to show off on his shelves.

It was as a leader of the city's enterprising bourgeoisie, then, that Orr set out his vision of a 'model municipality'. He occupied the lord provost's chair from 1854 to 1857 and retired from it with a knighthood. Before his elevation he had been an active councillor for a dozen years, during which he notched up several achievements. One was to help give the sooty city the green parks that brightened its black visage. The 136 acres of Glasgow Green, there since the beginning, by now stood surrounded with smoking chimneys, while those citizens of the central area who could afford it moved out to salubrious suburbs. For their benefit, the 85 acres of Kelvingrove Park to the west had already been created before Orr presided over the council's acquisition of the 150 acres that would become Queen's Park on the south side, named after Mary Queen of Scots who had lost her final battle at Langside nearby. The most renowned landscape gardener of the day, Sir Joseph Paxton, was employed to lay it out. Scotland's first football club, also called Queen's Park, started up in 1867 and used it for their games till Hampden Park was built for them in 1909.[14]

Just as Orr became lord provost in 1854, he lost his closest friend on the council, Archibald McLellan, who had made his fortune building horse-drawn carriages for fellow plutocrats but remained above all 'a most ardent lover of the arts'. He left, besides his money, 500 paintings and sculptures he had acquired during his lifetime. Orr took it on himself to realize McLellan's dying wish – that these works should be formed into a public collection for the benefit of Glaswegians: 'Edinburgh, London and almost every other city of importance on the Continent... hold their galleries of art as one of the glories of their towns, and a never-ending source of delight and gratification to their people. To deny this would be going in the face of the enlightened men of Europe. Why should we, one of the first commercial cities of modern times, be behind in this great work of civilization?'[15] Its merchants had long been artistic patrons but McLellan was the first true connoisseur, setting an example for succeeding generations. His own main interest lay in the Dutch and Flemish paintings of the Golden Age, but he also bought important Italian Old Masters and a range of French works. His bequest was big enough to finance a home for his collection too, the McLellan Galleries, which also became the main space for other exhibitions in the city till the Kelvingrove Art Gallery arose at the end of the century. The site in Sauchiehall Street contained besides the Glasgow Institute of the Fine Arts, eventually to become the Glasgow College of Art and to be rehoused in its own revolutionary new building by Charles Rennie Mackintosh.[16]

A still greater civic memorial of Orr's term of office was the legislation to bring to Glasgow pure water from Loch Katrine, far away across the hills to the north. The supply in the city, still drawn from wells in view of the hopeless pollution of the River Clyde, had grown grossly inadequate, if not a danger to the citizens. In 1806 the Glasgow Water Works Company was founded as a private enterprise, yet a feeling arose that such a basic human need should not be consigned to the market. The reformed town council started to think on this, but not till 1852 did it approve the scheme for bringing the supply from Loch Katrine that would be completed by 1859. It was a magnificent feat of Victorian engineering. Sir Walter Scott had hymned the beauties of the scenic loch, but now a dam at one end artificially raised its level by about 6 feet so that at its new extent it was 11 miles long. Then the force of gravity alone sent the water flowing downhill towards Glasgow, under enough pressure to reach the city without pumping along all its 26 miles of aqueduct and 13 miles of tunnel. The system delivered 50 million gallons a day. Queen Victoria herself came to open it.[17]

Orr, like many wealthy investors of the time, put his own money into the network of railways steadily covering Scotland and still in good part there today. He was most interested in the Glasgow and South Western Railway that served a triangular region in between Glasgow, Stranraer and Carlisle. It was formed in 1850 through the merger of earlier railways already covering much of Ayrshire, from which the branch to Stranraer and Portpatrick then got built to link with the ferries to Ireland. The company initially made its profits carrying coal out of the local mines. Later it provided a convenient network for commuters into Glasgow, where it built the terminus of St Enoch Station. To create outward traffic as well, it had the first man-made golf course designed at Turnberry on the Firth of Clyde, with the luxurious hotel overlooking it. The southern side of the triangle running westwards from Dumfries across sparsely populated country, though featuring romantically in John Buchan's *Thirty-Nine Steps* (1915), did not survive the closures of the later twentieth century. But at its peak in 1921 the company had over 1,000 miles of line.[18]

All that was just what a single member of Glasgow's ruling caste could achieve in its great days. A whole series of them would bestow their blessings on the city during the second half of the nineteenth century. In 1886 the publisher James MacLehose brought out a tribute to them, *One Hundred Glasgow Men*. In the preface he said this:

> Glasgow has in times past been singularly fortunate in having its municipal affairs attended to by leading citizens, men who having by energy, ability, and high character succeeded in achieving wealth and credit, felt themselves constrained to devote an important part of their time and energy to the service of the city. Sir Andrew Orr and the successive lord provosts under whom he served were men of this class, and their memory deserves and receives all honour. The extension of the city, and the larger powers which are being from time to time devolved on the town council, make it of the highest importance that civic affairs should be directed by men of proved business experience, of enlarged views, and of recognized social position. There never was a time when this

was more necessary than the present, and if the duty which every good citizen owes to the community be not recognized by those who are most able to serve the city, the result can only be detrimental.[19]

The civic duty expounded here started to take on its new and formidable dimensions in the decade after Orr had made his speech on the future of Glasgow. Following him as lord provost in 1863 came John Blackie, head of the publishing house founded by his father; its success arose above all from printing annotated editions of the Bible – big business in Scotland. The younger Blackie lamented the social degradation the industrial revolution had brought about – typified by the fact that 'the immense masses of population have no resource but a spirit shop at every 50 yards'.[20] Ultimately such human weakness was what the 'model municipality' would cure.

To start off with, in 1866, the Parliament at Westminster passed at the behest of the city council a new Police Act for Glasgow. It was a species of private legislation familiar to MPs. Scots burghs had often obtained Police Acts, more than forty of them since the middle of the eighteenth century. The term 'police' was during this period of wider application in Scotland than in England (or in the United Kingdom of the present day). Adam Smith had defined it in his *Lectures in Jurisprudence*, delivered in 1762–3, 'as the second general division of jurisprudence... which properly signified the policy of civil government, but now means the regulation of inferior parts of government, viz: cleanliness, security, and cheapness of plenty'.[21] The main aim of Glasgow's Police Act of 1866 was to modernize the standards of the built environment. The boundaries of the city had been extended two decades before to take in new suburbs. Now the bourgeois west with its spacious terraces and parks stood in stark contrast to the proletarian east with its grimy tenements and workshops. The contrast persists even now, though

mixed up with later developments. But that is not for want of the
Victorian city fathers' efforts to efface it. Between the two ends
of the spreading urban sprawl the area round the old High Street
contained its worst slums, and any renewal had to start by clearing
them. As lord provost, Blackie did all he could to help Carrick,
whose comprehensive survey of the old burgh led in 1865 to
plans for the redevelopment of 88 acres of slums. What remained
now was for the town council to acquire the powers, notably of
compulsory purchase, to carry out these plans.

Meanwhile, Blackie and Carrick took a trip to Paris to view the
vast transformations carried out since 1853 by Baron Haussmann,
prefect of the Seine, on the authority of Emperor Napoleon III.[22]
This project delivered a range of practical developments while
making Paris the grandest and most architecturally harmonious of
all European capitals. The crowded and unhealthy medieval quarters
were cleared and replaced by avenues, parks or squares. Broad
boulevards brought light into the darkest quarters. Handsome
buildings sprang from the ruins of the slums. To make the master
plan as comprehensive as possible, surrounding suburbs were
annexed to give a compact and manageable shape to the city above
the ground. The plan bestowed equal attention on the city below the
ground, with the construction of sewers, fountains and aqueducts
to bring running water into the interiors of every building and into
the gutters of every street. It all worked for the ordinary Parisians
who were now provided, often for the first time, with modern
housing, sanitation and communications. But the boulevards would
also allow for the same Parisians to be ridden down by regiments
of cavalry if they threatened yet another revolution. The spacious
framework of the city, fit for an imperial regime, afterwards served as
a noble capital for the renewed republic that the people established
when they did stage another revolution after all.

Blackie and Carrick wanted to carry some of these lessons
(presumably not the political ones) home to Glasgow. They said

on their return: 'We have now for the first and last time the opportunity of gaining by a well-considered effort, or losing forever by the neglect of a few great principles, the gratitude and fond regard of generations to come.'[23] They saw themselves as planners on a heroic scale, bringing the light of reason to the creation of an ideal city reborn from first principles out of the annihilation of the antique past.

Of course, the lessons from France had to be adapted to local conditions. The drumlins of the Clyde Valley, dropped by retreating glaciers at the end of the last Ice Age, stood in the way of any Parisian kind of vista. Great Western Road, laid out in the 1870s, is about the nearest Glasgow gets to, say, the grandeur of the prospect from the Place de la Concorde to the Arc de Triomphe. Blackie and Carrick had rather to resort to another rationalist type of structure, the logical grid of right-angled junctions that they carried westwards from the bounds of the old burgh. The grids would be filled with tenements arranged in hollow, rectangular blocks, reminiscent of the Parisian *hôtels particuliers* and their airy, internal quadrangles. Of the latter the Glaswegian equivalents were the back greens (to be preserved by a ban on backlands, the buildings that in the old burgh had lined the closes behind the frontage to the street). In this Scottish city, vista would depend rather on topography, on sudden glimpses of river or hills as the ground and the roadways rose or fell.[24]

On June 11, 1866, the corporation obtained from the Parliament at Westminster the Glasgow Improvement Act. It went much further than the Police Act, being concerned not just with details of construction but with the development of the whole city. It proved in fact to be the prelude to the first great programme of urban regeneration in the British Isles. It set up an improvement trust to raze the oldest, meanest and foulest parts of the burgh. In the central area, thirty-nine new streets were then to be formed and twelve old ones reconstructed, incidentally entailing the conversion to roadway of 65,000 square yards of ground formerly covered by tenements and closes.[25] Improvement was carried out with a vengeance: no other British city had ever before done what Glasgow now did in a few years. Demolition went on so fast that by 1874 the homes of 15,000 people had been knocked down.[26] The Glasgow of Adam Smith and James Watt vanished.

Instead there arose a modern city, its past invisible apart from a few relics consciously preserved. It eschewed any make-believe in the Scots vernacular style, such as that found in the rebuilding, modest by comparison, of contemporary Edinburgh. From 1867, the capital's programme of urban regeneration started up as a more introspective and piecemeal affair, demolishing old buildings only after their dilapidation outweighed their historical or architectural interest.[27] By contrast, Glasgow looked outwards and forwards, turning its back on a past of antique squalor to seek in its axial planning a dignified regularity.

Once the Improvement Act was in place, the city fathers' direct responsibility stopped: it was now to be a matter between the improvement trust and private enterprise. Individuals or corporations would be invited to feu out plots of land and build on them under the trust's regulations. For example, every new non-public edifice was to be limited to a height equal with the width of the street in front. Since the width often extended to 50 feet, this led to the stretches of spacious streets we know today, originally all on four storeys to the front, with each house knitted to the next by the uniformity of its cornice. As a further touch, Carrick often insisted on the new buildings being faced in dressed and polished ashlar.[28]

The result was imposing streetscapes, stopped short of monotony by the subtleties of their architecture and by the varied terrain on which they had been raised. They would reach their apogee in the terraces of the Great Western Road beyond the River Kelvin, employing a Roman classicism that blended beauty and utility.

Like a Roman, Carrick tempered his clear and level-headed prag-
matism with a love of beautiful design. His robust functional
buildings came lightened with grace and poise. The blend of the
aesthetic and the practical was on a lesser scale than Haussmann's,
yet still an extraordinary achievement. Nor did its harmony turn
out quite as gracious as the Parisian kind, though it still defined
the city of Glasgow till after the Second World War.[29]

As for the money, Glasgow had to fend for itself: finance for
the huge enterprise would come entirely from its own resources.
The Improvement Act authorized a tax of sixpence in the pound
of rateable value on occupiers of property within the city. Some
citizens objected to coughing up even for such an exalted public
purpose, though nobody seemed to expect there would be enough
of these rebels to eject Blackie from his seat on the council at that
year's municipal election. Yet this was what indeed happened to
him in his own central ward, by a majority of just two. Fulfilment
of his project passed into other hands.[30]

It devolved instead on the new lord provost, James Lumsden
the younger, whose father had served in the same office from 1843
to 1846. They headed their family's engraving and publishing firm,
founded in 1783. By then it was best known for its editions of
children's books, printed in short runs of high quality and sold
at sixpence a copy, a price far beyond the means of the ordinary
family. To increase turnover, the same books would be released
under multiple covers (which turns them into collectors' items
today). This became a standard practice of the Victorian book
trade, and made the Lumsdens millionaires. James the younger's
term of office proved to be momentous, marked above all by the
shift of the university from the High Street to Gilmorehill. Edward,
prince of Wales, and his wife, Princess Alexandra of Denmark,
came to lay the foundation stone of the new college, and afterwards
Lumsden received a knighthood. In 1870 he succeeded Orr as
chairman of the Glasgow and South Western Railway Company.

Once Lumsden retired from his own family firm in 1876, he spent most of his commercial energies as director, then chairman, of the Clydesdale Bank. Meanwhile the city's improvement went on.[31]

Blackie and Lumsden embodied two approaches to the great urban project: progressive idealism as against hard-headed economy. The first aimed to create a moral, god-fearing city, the second to secure in any event a watertight balance sheet. The ethical energy in Glasgow arose above all from the Presbyterianism reinvigorated by the Disruption and the establishment of the Free Church of Scotland in 1843. There was a side-effect on the earlier dissenting sects of the eighteenth century: to protect their position, they came together into the United Presbyterian Church in 1847. Both the new churches were modernizing forces, dominated on the one hand by an emergent middle class and on the other by a respectable working class that alike saw capitalist enterprise and social philanthropy as complementary.[32] Blackie was a member of the Free Church, but he worked closely with two United Presbyterians – Carrick and then Victorian Glasgow's leading architect, Alexander 'Greek' Thomson, who built and decorated Blackie's own house for him at 7 Great Western Terrace. They were all zealous champions of urban reform on high principles, to which in their own spheres they sought to give physical shape. The finest of it came in Thomson's three great Glaswegian churches (of which only one, at St Vincent Street, survives intact) exemplifying the vitality, wealth and confidence of this new elite.

But the fiery philanthropic evangelism behind Glasgow's improvement was to be tempered by a steady sense of commercial calculation, first in Lumsden himself. In 1866 the abrupt transition from Blackie's regime showed the difference between the enthusiasm of an altruist and the caution of a businessman. Lumsden's officials jettisoned Blackie's scattier schemes, with heavy hints that his grandiose goals had toppled over into perilous profligacy. The obvious outward sign of this financial tension in the municipal background was that, while the clearance of slums went on apace, the rebuilding took much longer.[33]

As the improvement trust now knocked down the centre of the city, it did nothing to rehouse ejected tenants. On the contrary, by its operations it drastically reduced the stock of cheaper housing, so that the poor had if anything to go yet further down-market to find a new home. Next to the cleared areas, any sound accommodation soon filled and became overcrowded with displaced slum-dwellers. In a bit of a rush, some private speculative housing did spring up to fill the gaps, but a quarter of the flats still consisted of a single room. In 1861, one in three families had lived in such places: it took half a century for the ratio to be reduced to one in five. Over time, it is true, bigger flats of two or even three rooms were built. But of the latter, during the same half-century, the proportion in the whole housing stock rose only from 13 per cent to 19 per cent. Since demand continued to exceed supply, the neediest families subdivided these larger properties once again into single units and just replicated the old overcrowding. In addition to the lack of privacy came inadequate facilities for personal cleanliness and domestic waste, with the squalid provision of communal toilets on the stair, washing houses out the back and middens besides: all nearly unbearable in the heat of summer or cold of winter.[34] By the early twentieth century, novel domestic facilities – hot water, electric lighting, ventilation and inside toilets – did start to be put in.[35] Yet for the most part, as contemporary observers pointed out, the improvement trust had only replaced old slums with new ones. Glaswegians asked themselves why, after the deployment of such stupendous efforts and resources, the overall result was not better.

A basic test was the health of the population. Scots perhaps suffer a genetic weakness, or at least have too many harmful habits, making them rather unhealthy people – something as true in the nineteenth century as in the twenty-first.[36] In 1901 Scottish babies were expected at birth to live a mere forty years (compared with forty-five for boys and forty-nine for girls in England, figures about the same as in France and Germany); the equivalents today are seventy-four for boys and seventy-nine for girls in Scotland, seventy-five for boys and eighty for girls in England. Yet, then and now, bad health went together with excellent medical provision in Scotland. Poverty cancelled out the advantages of high professional standards in health and of ready access to them.

In Glasgow the Royal Infirmary, where treatment was free, had opened in 1794. The vast growth of the conurbation over the next century prompted an equivalent increase in facilities for treating the industrial population. Some hospitals were built under the Poor Law, for the East End in Duke Street, for the south side in Eglinton Street, for the north of the city at Stobhill and for the west at Oakbank, with buildings often crowded and sordid however hard anybody tried. A far better performance came from voluntary institutions, of which the biggest was the Victoria Infirmary founded in 1890. The university had established a lying-in hospital in 1834 and then the Western Infirmary, erected to accompany the move to Gilmorehill in 1874. There were specialist hospitals for fevers at Ruchill and at Belvidere (this used for isolation of the victims of an outbreak of the plague in 1900 that killed sixteen people). Women had special facilities at Redlands (also staffed by women) and the Royal Samaritan Hospital. There was an eye hospital from 1824, a dental hospital from 1879, a cancer hospital from 1890, an ear, nose and throat hospital from 1905. The poor might be specifically targeted: an ophthalmic institution opened in 1868 'for the treatment of diseases and injuries of the eye in the cases of the afflicted poor' while a central dispensary was there from 1889 'to give gratuitous advice to the sick poor'. As the boundaries of the city expanded, the corporation of Glasgow became the owner of hospitals, such as Knightswood, belonging to local authorities it absorbed.[37] Most of the finance for all these was from private donations, first raised among the prosperous middle class but then also among the workers, who organized schemes within their places of employment to meet members' medical needs. Meanwhile the administration of the infirmaries benefited from the complimentary (and complementary) expertise of businessmen and professionals on the boards of management.

One of them was Lumsden's close friend and eventual successor as lord provost, James Watson. A wealthy stockbroker, he served for twenty-two years from 1844 as the inaugural chairman of Glasgow's stock exchange – so he had money enough for good works. He helped to found three model lodging houses for male migrant workers not yet able to set up a household of their own (and wanting to keep away from the poorhouse). For adults seeking to enhance their technical skills, he patronized the Mechanics' Institution. Committed above all to clearing the slums, he had been involved with Blackie in the Philanthropic Company, set up in 1861 to acquire property for clearance and so ease the process of redeveloping it. He served on the improvement trust from the beginning.[38] The great innovation under Watson was that in 1872 the city council appointed James Russell as its first full-time medical officer of health. He set about his duties with vigour. He employed an inspectorate with powers to have the streets, closes and middens cleansed, the houses disinfected and the numbers living in them controlled. Every flat would be measured up to determine how many people it could legally accommodate, with 300 cubic feet allowed for each individual. A metal disc, or ticket, was affixed to the door stating this number, removal of which was an offence. It was now a 'ticketed house'.

But almost from the start, the rules became so widely flouted as to make them unworkable. The corporation carried out 40,000 inspections a year, with its agents hammering on the doors in the small hours to catch out the unwary, and illegal, sleeping inside: 'Each pair of sanitary inspectors is expected to make one hundred visits per night on all four nights of the week. They have a complete list of all the ticketed houses in the area. These houses they usually visit after midnight, continuing their systematic inspection generally from midnight to four o'clock in the morning.'[39] In one case, eleven adults were found to be occupying 880 feet of cubic space (eight more than allowed). As the inspectors poked about, they discovered that a further seven had escaped and climbed out on an adjacent roof.[40] None of this deterred the tenants of ticketed houses from supplementing their meagre incomes by renting out space to sleep on their floors. With a persistent shortage of accommodation in the city, they never lacked for takers. In 1896, there were 25,000 ticketed houses, mostly flats of a single room, meant to hold 85,000 people. The inspectors found nearly 4,000 cases of overcrowding – a figure that rose by 1904 to 15,000. Russell himself feared the corporation might be taking on more than it could manage: 'The public of Glasgow already trust too much to authorities and officials for the solution of their social difficulties – more, I think, than any other community.'[41] But Archibald Chalmers, who succeeded as medical officer of health in 1900, remained unrepentant – and candid about the corporation's right of entry:

No one who knows anything of the habits of the people affected by them – the unskilled labourer and the class lower still, our criminal classes – can have any doubt of this necessity nor as to their efficacy and usefulness. If you relaxed your repressive efforts, the old state of affairs would return in a few weeks. We must not be restrained by any squeamishness about ticketing new property and giving it a bad name, if we find that overcrowding has been transferred with the old tenants of your demolished property. If a landlord finds that such a process deteriorates the value of his property, then he must prevent the overcrowding, otherwise ticketed it must be.[42]

Resources remained under pressure in a Victorian economy much more unstable than that of today, with effects on everything from the budgets of the corporation itself down to the finances of both rich and poor, who might be threatened with bankruptcy on the one hand, destitution on the other. Misfortune could strike out of the blue: the most notorious example came with the failure of the City of Glasgow Bank in 1878. Set up to serve small savers, it nevertheless made a bad habit of paying lavish dividends. The accounts for its final year showed deposits of £8 million, while a dividend of 12 per cent was declared – a trifle bold when a little bit of deficit on actual banking operations had appeared the year before. This was the tip of an iceberg. In October 1878 the directors all of a sudden announced the closure of the bank. For a while they had behind the scenes been trying desperately to support a house of cards. It now emerged that they were in fact sitting on net liabilities of more than £6 million, with a lot of toxic loans to Australian mines, Argentine ranches and American railways. In order to cover all this up on a rigged balance sheet, they reported fictitious holdings of gold. To financial insiders an inkling of the fraud had leaked, so that the directors felt forced to spend more of the money they did not have to prop up the price of their own shares by secret purchases. The twenty-first century would have found here nothing to teach the nineteenth. A crash was inevitable – and then 254 of 1,200 shareholders faced ruin, being as yet unprotected by limited liability,[43] while scores of Glaswegian businesses went under. The directors of the bank were arrested, tried and jailed.[44] In the city at large, a virtual halt to private construction followed. Meanwhile, 30,000 ordinary Glaswegians found themselves dependent on public charity.

To make things worse, recovery from the crash of 1878 proved to be so slow that Carrick advised the improvement trust to postpone further works. Originally it had drawn up a rolling programme for the demolition of houses and displacement of tenants. This at first went well, with the cleared land regularly sold at prices well above the estimated value. Now things came to a standstill, and the condition of the trust's remaining old houses worsened till there was no choice but to knock them down anyway. It found itself burdened with large tracts of empty, unsaleable land.[45] Not till 1894 could all the areas scheduled for demolition be cleared and rebuilt, at which point the trust's remaining property and powers were to pass back to the council.

The lord provost during the crisis of 1878 was William Collins, head of the publishing house founded by his father of the same name. William senior had started life as a weaver at Pollokshaws. A self-educated and deeply religious man, he founded a chain of Sunday schools in Glasgow and became an elder of the Tron Kirk in 1814. He was one of those who called to it the Revd Thomas Chalmers, the great preacher who became the deepest influence on his life, not least in teaching him that religion and capitalism went together. In 1819 Collins closed his school and went into publishing. The book that launched his business was Chalmers's *The Christian and Civic Economy of Large Towns*. In 1829, Collins founded Britain's first temperance society.[46]

Collins junior inherited much from his father: driving ambition, a thriving business, membership of the Free Church, commitment to total abstinence, support for good causes. In commerce, every-thing he touched seemed to turn to gold. In 1861 he moved into the fine new premises at Herriot Hill, later Cathedral Street, that his successors continued to occupy for more than a century. In 1862 he was appointed queen's printer for Scotland. His firm anticipated our modern age of advertising jingles, another reason for its success:

Satan trembles when he sees
Bibles sold as cheap as these.[47]

Collins was elected to the town council in 1868, and in 1877 he became lord provost. As his first big job, he organized a fund for relief of those left penniless through the collapse of the City of Glasgow Bank. He was knighted in 1881, by which time his company had nearly 2,000 employees working 28 presses and producing 2 million books a year, apart from the first of the many millions more personal diaries that they churned out (and still do to the present day). His life, like his father's, was one of hard work, driving ambition, strict economy, generous philanthropy and exemplary care for his workers. He declared: 'Property has its duties as well as its right.'[48] In applying this principle to the work of the town council, he insisted on the close scrutiny of its expenditure and above all on the promotion of temperance among Glaswegians: they called him Water Willie. But this was not enough to solve their problems.

Limits to the possible had appeared if the heavy expenditure of the reforming corporation was to be covered by revenue raised from the existing population of ratepayers. With the steady growth of the built-up area, one way forward would be an extension of the boundaries to keep pace as the richer Glaswegians moved out to new suburbs. The first such measure had been taken in 1846, but that did not stop lord provost Orr proposing a second one a few years later. Marwick would make it a reality. While the improvement trust was creating a finer city, he saw that the suburbs still remained more desirable. The continual building upheaval in the centre in fact underlined the superior amenity of the districts beyond. In the earliest of those catchy slogans the corporation still likes to deploy, Marwick chose 'Greater Glasgow' as his watchwords. The small peripheral burghs lining the boundaries were bound to resist calls for amalgamation from the predatory city. In the unstable 1880s the opposition died away, however, as Marwick banged on about the value of collective strength and financial security. An official commission recommended Glasgow's expansion, and legislation followed in 1891. The municipal area more than doubled in size to incorporate bourgeois suburbs north and south of the Clyde. Higher spending on fresh urban projects, financed by the extra revenue from the city's enhanced wealth, then followed.[49]

Marwick found a firm ally in John Ure, the lord provost who succeeded Collins in 1880. He was a flour merchant, deacon of the incorporation of bakers and a member of the town council since 1856. His great achievement so far had come in reorganizing the disposal of the city's sewage. Now he raised his own and the citizens' sights. Since the demolition in 1812 of the old Tolbooth (except for its steeple), municipal offices had been scattered round the town, a state of affairs that grew ever more unsatisfactory as their functions multiplied. There could be no more fitting crown to Glasgow's civic pride than the magnificent City Chambers proposed for a site on George Square that had been chosen and purchased by Carrick. Ure laid the foundation stone in 1883: it would, he said, inspire 'a feeling of assured permanency and stability in our system of local government'.[50]

There had been an architectural competition for the project, won by a young man from Paisley, William Young. His brief was to give the council a palace that would reflect the city's status. No expense was spared. Like the rest of George Square at that time, the building followed the classical tradition, though the stranger might be fooled by its flamboyance. The showy grandeur of the interior included pillars of granite, staircases of Carrara marble, ceilings decorated in gold leaf and public rooms richly inlaid with wood from all over the world. The exterior sculpture, by James Ewing, culminated in a Jubilee Pediment, with Queen Victoria enthroned in triumph, surrounded by emblematic figures of Scotland, England, Ireland and Wales, alongside the colonies. She came to Glasgow in person to open the place: so the industry and wealth of the Second City of the empire was set in stone.[51]

Perhaps this sumptuous symbol also reassured Glaswegians and visitors alike that the financial troubles were a thing of the past. The next phase of development had indeed already started to transform the local economy, in the shape of the long shipbuilding boom that, with interruptions, was to give Glasgow its halcyon days of global supremacy in this sector and last till the First World War. The boom drew in some of the old mercantile elite, including John Muir, of the family now running the house of James Finlay & Co. Muir went into partnership with an English shipping magnate, Charles Cayzer, to set up the Clan Line, based in Glasgow, for the run to India. They did not get on well, but Muir, 'the greatest bully in the trade, and the worst tempered man in Scotland', met his match in Cayzer, 'who scoffs at his tantrums, and who rebuffs his interference with language which is... frequent and painful and free'.[52] Muir turned to public affairs. A member of the town council from 1886, he became lord provost three years later. In 1891 he presided over the passage of the Act of Parliament for extension of the municipal boundaries. He had the Kelvin and Dalmarnock Bridges built, rehoused the Mitchell Library in its present amplitude and acquired for the city the St Andrew's Halls. He and his wife hosted glittering receptions in the City Chambers.

The corporation's ambitions extended to public utilities and services as well. This was not a democratic process: it did not meet any obvious demand from the people of Glasgow, who on the contrary had to have municipal regulation enforced on them with rigour and zeal. Nor did richer citizens always approve, seeing in public activism a threat to private property. But the corporation kept three purposes of its own in mind. The first indeed arose from the paternalist argument that it would just be better for the municipal authority to act in the interests of all. The second was to promote urban innovation, especially if it involved new technologies likely to stretch the resources of private investment. The third was a plain search for profit.[53]

Muir himself played a personal part in a couple of the most ambitious schemes of municipal trading, to supply the city with its own gas and electricity. The first had its origins back in 1817, when James Neilson set up the Glasgow Gas Light Company at Townhead. It stood just west of the cathedral and produced 'inflammable air', with other extracts from coal such as coke and ammonia. These could be sold on as feedstock for chemical plants and dyeworks; the huge complex of St Rollox stood next door. The gasworks shifted to Tradeston in 1835, and the corporation took it over in 1869. From then on its output was known as town gas (a term still useful to distinguish it from natural gas, like that coming today from under the North Sea). It was stored in enormous gas-holders to be distributed round the city. Muir extended the gasworks, and at the same time prepared to introduce electric street-lighting, with the help of Glasgow's most eminent scientist, his friend Lord Kelvin. It was a controversial project because numbers of private entrepreneurs stood ready to cash in on this new source of power. The corporation of Glasgow was equally determined to keep control of it. It wanted to protect the gasworks in which it had invested so much, and that meant regulating electricity to stop its competition becoming too fierce. The council obtained an Act of Parliament in 1890. It bought ground in Waterloo Street and erected a generating station there. Early in 1893, James Bell, Muir's successor as lord provost, had the privilege of switching on the street-lighting in a public ceremony. Soon afterwards a general supply for private lighting became available from Glasgow Cross to Park Circus.[54]

Bell was a capitalist with interests in steamships, railways and banking, but he had a warm heart: he gave 10,000 of the poor a dinner to mark the marriage in 1893 of the duke of York (later King George V). His own main municipal initiative came in the corporation's takeover of the tramways. From 1873 a private company had run horse-drawn trams, leasing the tracks from the council. Under the enabling legislation the council might assume ownership after twenty-one years. Bell decided this would be the way to bring together the far-flung parts of his newly extended municipality. The system was not just to be acquired but also rapidly modernized. By 1901 the council had fully electrified it. Better wages, shorter hours and various perks benefited the crews. The original 92 employees rose to 9,000 as the number of tramcars increased from 220 to 600, nearly all built in municipal workshops. The length of track doubled to 130 miles, while the number of passengers carried annually also doubled to reach 177 million. It kept on soaring, for travel was a bargain: all but the longest journeys cost no more than a penny. The public enjoyed a comfortable, frequent, cheap service – and though the speed of the trams was restricted to 8 miles an hour, one came along every few minutes even on outlying routes. The junction of Jamaica Street and Renfield Street was said to be the busiest in the world, with 500 tramcars an hour passing by during 20 hours out of the 24. And every year the operations earned a financial surplus. The second city felt proud of its municipal enterprise, efficiency and profit.[55] The system lasted till 1962, when on the evening of September 4 a memorable and, to most observers, moving procession of tramcars old and new made their last journey through the streets. The buses that replaced them did continue the old livery of orange and green – or 'champagne and chartreuse' as some wags said. But somehow it was never the same.[56]

It was also during Bell's term of office that Glasgow acquired its own underground railway, usually called the Subway. Work began in 1891 and the service started up in December 1896. That made it the third oldest system in the world after the London Underground (1863) and the Budapest Metro (May 1896). In Britain, it remains the only one to operate completely beneath the surface. It is also among the few railways in the world with a gauge of 4 feet or 1.2 metres (against the standard gauge of 4 feet 8 inches or

1.4 metres). At first driven by cables, the Subway was later electrified in its turn. But there would be no extension of the network: the twin circular tracks today follow the same route as at the outset, with some of the original stations actually closed. At the price of frequent refurbishment the system is still in use, though now it runs in part through areas of the city almost emptied of human habitation, so with few passengers to attract.[57]

The next outstanding lord provost of Glasgow, Samuel Chisholm, was a grocer by trade (if finally on a grand scale), an evangelical by religion, a radical in politics – though a social step down from the august lord provosts of the past, many of whose families had gone bust in 1878. They would not have been surprised that he lacked social graces. His pompous moralizing infuriated his opponents. They mocked him as an overbearing and humourless faddist from the absurd extremes of do-gooding liberalism, an impression his confident and abrasive style did nothing to allay. He was striking in appearance, too, with a flowing silver beard that added to the patriarchal image. He relished public debate and made a formidable presence on the platform, especially when tub-thumping about temperance. In the general election of 1895 he tried to get into Parliament, standing for Camlachie. But a Labour candidate intervened to split his vote, and the sitting Liberal Unionist held the seat. From then on Chisholm stuck to municipal politics. He was elected lord provost in 1899, this time with the help of votes from both Liberal and Labour.[58]

So far, the improvement of Glasgow had been a patrician enterprise, carried on by venerable city fathers in an enlightened spirit shared with other worthy citizens. It now branched out into new channels. One still had a high purpose, to bring culture to toiling Glaswegians. This was the idea behind the opening in 1898 of the People's Palace and the Winter Gardens (for exotic plants to be cultivated under glass). The ground floor of the palace provided reading and recreation rooms, with a museum above that and a picture gallery on top. The complex stood at Glasgow Green, next to the poorest part of the city, and the aim was to give the locals a hopeful glimpse of the wider world. The former Liberal prime minister, Lord Rosebery, came to inaugurate this addition to the city's attractions, which he praised as 'a palace of pleasure and imagination around which the people may place their affections and which may give them a home on which their memory may rest'. It would be 'open to the people for ever and ever'.[59]

In a positive and public sense, exhibitionism became part of the Second City's culture. Altogether, it would hold four great exhibitions of science, art and industry. The first took place at Kelvingrove Park in 1888, with the aim of drawing international attention to local achievements in all these fields, as well as of raising money for a new museum, art gallery and school of art. It succeeded in these aims so that, under Chisholm, a second exhibition could be held in 1901 (later ones came in 1911 and 1938). His marked the opening of the Kelvingrove Art Gallery, in a striking building by James Miller. Countries with close ties to Glasgow came to exhibit; among these Russia made the biggest show with four pavilions paid for by Tsar Nicholas II, one featuring a typical village on the steppes. Further pavilions – all lost, alas – were the work of Charles Rennie Mackintosh. Other attractions included a rollercoaster, a water chute, an Indian theatre and sculptures made of soap.[60]

This was the Second City enjoying itself, but Chisholm also promoted projects that moved onto more commercial and contested territory. From 1901, the city owned a telephone network. The telephone was a Scottish invention, the achievement of Alexander Graham Bell (though only after he had moved to America). Besides being an inventor he was a businessman, who at once set out to exploit his brainchild with the Bell Telephone Company. In 1877 he had returned to Glasgow to give a demonstration of how music played in one room could be heard in another over a telephone line. That especially impressed members of the corporation's fire committee, who at once saw how, with phones placed at strategic points, they might give the alarm far faster than via any other device. The city, alive to the possibilities, opened a small exchange in 1879. This suffered the handicap that every single call needed to go through an operator; there was no direct dialling. In 1883 a Glaswegian, David Sinclair, invented an automatic switching device that allowed the first exchange, with six lines, to be opened at Coatbridge. Within a couple of years Glasgow had 1,300 subscribers. It was the prelude to a wide local network, with fifty trunk lines serving towns across the central belt, and then extended to London. But the municipal ownership was always controversial. In 1908 the system was taken over by a National Telephone Company, much to Chisholm's disgust.[61]

Still, the main task for Chisholm during his term of office had been a return to public housing as the first priority for the council, now that the experience since 1866 showed how much there was still to be done. He caught a mood in the city of disillusion with the improvement trust, which was indeed rather running out of steam. He had got himself appointed its convener in 1892. He faced a situation where the private building trade was always slow to provide for the masses. But, since the recovery from the city's financial crisis, a Glasgow Workmen's Dwellings Company had been formed to build homes for rent. Its preferred market lay among respectable working people, the 'industrious poor' as opposed to the 'dirty, destructive, depraved' of the ticketed houses. The company meant to educate its tenants in the advantages of social improvement, so installed in each tenement a resident caretaker 'to supervise the people generally and press steadily upon the habits of filth and disorder'. Would-be tenants were tested as to character and income, and nobody needed to apply who did not have a month's rent already saved up.[62]

That still left the question, social and commercial at once, as to where the feckless, the vicious and the criminal would go. If the corporation could deal with them, even private landlords and builders might accept this form of municipal socialism. Because, in an entirely private market since 1866, rehousing had only haltingly followed demolition, so the corporation might legitimately argue it needed to step in. Chisholm went further and argued it should build model dwellings in place of the cleared slums – again, all to be paid for by local taxation and so in danger of antagonizing bourgeois ratepayers or landlords. Yet nobody seemed to favour a free market in housing: itself remarkable in Victorian Scotland. Or at least the authorities planning and supervising redevelopment looked to no such solution, not even if supplemented by philanthropy or public regulation. In other words, there seemed in principle little reason why the corporation should not build dwellings along with everything else, as an extension of its general range of public services. On this argument Chisholm initiated the biggest advance in policy to be made by the corporation of Glasgow in the imminent twentieth century.[63]

The long-term effects on the city's housing were discussed above, but the immediate political battle proved interesting and significant in itself. From the Parliament at Westminster, Chisholm obtained in 1897 another Improvement Act. As an experiment, the council had already erected two blocks of tenements on the eastern side of Saltmarket. The new legislation would allow it to add 1,200 flats round the town with the express purpose of housing the 'poorest classes'. By 1914 there were 2,000 more such council flats. They looked nothing like modern tower blocks but came in the style of the rest of the city – tenements of four storeys with shops on the ground floor. Yet in the event, the tenants were again the respectable working classes: clerks, policemen, craftsmen, shopkeepers and others with regular wages that would allow them to pay the rents.[64] Every landlord in Glasgow, private and public, preferred this type of tenant.[65] Now, with the corporation's intervention, fears as well as hopes arose: critics prophesied that it would create homes for an army of employees who, when casting their votes in municipal elections, would use them to support candidates favouring cheap, subsidized rents; then those occupying public housing could live at the expense of all the other citizens. William Smart, professor of political economy at the university, thought that while in the abstract 'cheap rents are as desirable as cheap food', housing supplied by the corporation added up to 'nothing more nor less than the municipality offering a bounty to come and dwell in Glasgow'.[66]

While the scene was set for future housing action, it remained the least satisfactory part of Glasgow's social experiment. Old property continued to decay, and as soon as the worst slums got cleared the next worst appeared in their turn intolerable. The city was no closer to abolishing slums in 1902 than in 1866. Originally, 15,000 had been scheduled for demolition, and this target was in fact reached after the third of a century envisaged for the completion of the initial scheme. Meanwhile, however, a further 20,000 older tenements had reached the end of their useful lives, to be condemned in their turn.[67]

This was not the only reason why the opposition grew to Chisholm and his whole programme. A Liberal Unionist, Robert Crawford, claimed that 'municipal government as it is realized in Glasgow is pure socialism'.[68] The city must know it ultimately relied on capitalism together with the rights of private property, yet here was a lord provost bent on skewing the market so as to suppress competition, apparently for nothing more than his own civic empire-building. The spat spread beyond Glasgow itself. During 1902 *The Times* of London, never a friend to Scotland, ran a series of critical articles about municipal socialism, after briefings by Chisholm's personal enemies. The paper suggested that in Glasgow an over-ambitious authoritarianism threatened to create 'a communistic society'.[69] Pressure was mounted to hold a parliamentary inquiry, which did indeed eventually come about.[70]

While the outcome proved inconclusive, it revealed there were people, not just in Glasgow but also elsewhere in Britain, out to get Chisholm.

One key to this was that Chisholm linked slums, poverty and vandalism with the availability of alcohol. Naturally, then, he won bitter enemies among brewers, distillers and publicans. When he brought in new licensing regulations to cut opening hours and ban service by barmaids, the trade viewed this as the start of prohibition by stealth. Once Chisholm announced his intention to seek a second term as lord provost, contrary to the convention in the council, it was the last straw. All his foes, political and commercial, ganged up to campaign against him in his ward of Woodside, and they found ammunition enough. After a bad-tempered campaign, reminiscent of that against Blackie in 1866, Chisholm in his turn was thrown out.[71]

A general electoral reaction against the old regime in the council followed. The Tories, (supported by the Liberal Unionists) took control for the first time since 1833. It was a presage of things to come, rather than a decisive change in itself, and by 1911 Glasgow again had a Liberal lord provost, Daniel Macaulay Stevenson. A son of the city from a politically radical background, he had himself grown rich from his shipbroking business. The contrasting features in his personal history played against each other during his term of office.[72]

Stevenson had early in his career involved himself in the Glasgow Workmen's Dwellings Company. This was for him not altogether a simple philanthropic initiative but had rather the ulterior motive of teaching the city council, by example, the advantages of embarking on its own public housing programme. Municipal socialism was already practised in various fields, but Stevenson wanted a wider extension of what he preferred to call 'civic co-operation'. He was not an old-fashioned radical, and others of his favoured causes already smacked of the liberalism of a new century.[73]

Unlike his evangelical colleagues on the city council, Stevenson took no great interest in religion. He shocked them with his continental views on relaxing the social restrictions of the Scottish Sabbath. But he persevered, and in 1898 secured the opening on Sundays of municipal museums and art galleries, so that the workers could get to them on their one free day. The corporation already owned the Mitchell Library, the grandeur of which might, however, overawe the schoolchild, the housewife or the working man. Stevenson established a system of free public libraries with branches all over the city (at the present time thirty-three of them) on money promised by the philanthropist Andrew Carnegie. The libraries were mostly built in areas of dense tenements, where they stood out in their monumental baroque style (most of them to designs by James Rhind); they created local landmarks rather than just depositories of books. The biggest was at Woodside, in Stevenson's own ward.[74] Years later in 1913, while serving as lord provost, he boasted of the success of his initiative, pointing out that every year there were 7 million borrowings.

Stevenson's business often took him abroad. He was an internationalist convinced that free trade among the nations would lead to universal peace and prosperity. In his quest to improve civic services he often looked to foreign examples. His millionaire brother-in-law, Robert Heidmann, was a senator of Hamburg, and the German system of local government seemed to him particularly admirable.[75] Stevenson came to be regarded as a global expert on this aspect of public affairs, but it did not help him that the First World War broke out in the final weeks of his term of office. Now he was suspected of pro-German sympathies, even though he took a full part in the immediate efforts to recruit troops for the western front.

The First World War marked the end of the patrician age in Glasgow, though the old elite lingered on for more than a decade after the armistice in 1918. The lord provost during the war itself was

Thomas Dunlop, candidate of the newly united Scottish Unionist and Conservative Party. Inside the corporation it was unofficially represented by a group calling themselves the Moderates, later the Progressives, formed in 1913 in reaction to already unmistakable signs of a swing to the left among Glaswegian voters. Its moderation (perhaps not its progressiveness) was to be defined by its resistance to the municipal policies of the rising Labour movement, especially on housing.[76]

Glasgow and the rest of the Scottish Victorian cities had high hopes for their future, even though they could not precisely foresee it. One thing they wanted was to shape it for themselves: they had always refused to rely on the British government, but rather made their own way along the expensive path of private legislation. At Westminster and elsewhere, the reason they gave was that they could then attend to specific regional needs – which in truth did even within Scotland's small compass vary widely, making the value of national legislation questionable and its fulfilment arguably impracticable. Still, beneath that rationalization we might perceive a familiar, indeed historic, Scottish aversion to letting central authority mix in and dictate local affairs.[77]

A wealthy urban patriciate recruited from a narrow social and religious range, had ruled Glasgow. Besides its political power, it also dominated the social and cultural life of the city. It shaped the urban fabric with an austere decorum to reflect its ambitions and aspirations. But by the first decade of the twentieth century, the pool of talent supplying this elite was growing detached from the life of the city, because many of its members moved their own homes beyond the boundaries to more spacious suburbs. The process of detachment was hastened by the reconfiguration of Glasgow's politics after the war. Reform of the franchise in 1918 allowed the lower middle class and the working class into the political arena and made the whole city more democratic. There was, however, a price to pay.

8

Plebeians:
'Feelings of discord'

ON APRIL 27, 1888, a parliamentary by-election took place in Mid Lanarkshire. The constituency ran down the left bank of the River Clyde from Dalserf to Rutherglen, leaving out the royal burgh of Hamilton. It contained some pretty spots by the river and at Calderglen, but for the rest it was a bleak stretch of country dotted by mining villages and other industrial settlements. Since the creation of the seat under the Third Reform Act of 1885, its Liberal MP had been Stephen Mason, a Glaswegian merchant. But three years later he resigned in somewhat mysterious circumstances and rushed off to Australia, where he was a heavy investor in agricultural mortgages. Financial conditions in the colonies remained notoriously unstable, and the entire Australian banking system, along with much else, would crash in 1890. As the debris was being cleared, it came to light that Mason's business had liabilities of £500,000 and assets of £3,000.[1] This perhaps explained his hurried exit from public life in Scotland, but the revelation did not affect him personally: he was already dead.

If all the capitalist skulduggery had been known among the voters of Mid Lanarkshire in 1888 it might conceivably have made a difference to the result of the by-election, which saw the appearance of the first Labour candidate in British political history, Keir Hardie. He stood because neither of the two big parties, the Liberals or the Unionists, could find a good local man, or so they said. In fact both selected English barristers without Scottish connections or ambitions, wanting merely a cushy billet at Westminster. In the constituency the pair got a lukewarm reception, and locals wondered why Mid Lanarkshire could not do better. The miners of Larkhall, who knew Hardie from his earlier efforts to organize trades unionism in the pits, urged him to put his name forward. With the wider franchise, industrial action might now be translated into political action, specifically into parliamentary representation of the workers by the workers. It was at the time a novel concept, but Hardie threw caution to the winds and accepted nomination. His campaign turned out to be a mess, however. At his public meetings he showed a provocative truculence that did not go down well, attacking the clergy and the royal family while getting drawn into angry exchanges with hecklers. In the event, even most of the miners in the constituency remained loyal to the Liberals. On polling day Hardie won only 617 votes, 8 per cent of the total.[2]

Hardie had been born an illegitimate child in conditions of great poverty. His start in adult life, from the age of eleven, consisted of ten years working down the pits. Yet even as a youngster he showed a lively interest in the wider world. He went to night school to learn to read and write, and practised shorthand by scribbling the outlines on a blackened slate with the wire used to adjust the wick of his lamp. He came to love the poetry of Robert Burns, though he also tackled more challenging texts – Thomas Carlyle's *Sartor Resartus* and John Ruskin's *Unto This Last*, both fierce critiques of modern commercial values.[3] Hardie seems to have had little contact with religion till in 1877 he joined the Morisonians, an evangelical sect founded by the Revd James Morison of Kilmarnock.[4] It rejected the Calvinist doctrine of predestination, holding instead that heaven was open to all who repented and believed. In that sense it showed a democratic outlook, and it had a ready appeal for working people, especially in the west of Scotland, put off by the bourgeois character of conventional churches. Hardie was typical: self-taught, self-helping, afire with zeal to redeem humanity after his own conversion, though at this stage looking to personal salvation rather than to social reform. But later he would always say he first learned his socialism from the New Testament.[5]

In 1878 Hardie became agent in the district of Hamilton for the Lanarkshire Miners' Union, founded by Alexander MacDonald, a pioneer of the Scottish labour movement. MacDonald was a moderate leader who recognized the weakness of the workers' position in the Victorian economy and so advised them to avoid disputes. In evidence to a parliamentary committee he said they 'should endeavour to meet their employers as far as they can'. Seeing no way past the capitalist organization of society, he thought winning political friends was the best means of getting legislation in his members' interests.[6] He at first took a shine to Hardie, but they soon quarrelled. Round Hamilton the miners' wages were being cut and Hardie, contrary to his mentor's advice, led them out on strike; in fact the stoppages continued, on and off, for a year. One became known as the 'tattie strike' because it took place during the potato harvest, and the miners lived from howking tatties for local farmers. But the strikes all failed, and Hardie had to leave the area. He carried with him the reputation of a fierce fighter for his members but also of a rash rabble-rouser as he moved, newly married, to Ayrshire.

Now Hardie needed to eke out a living for a family as well. He opened a small grocer's shop at Cumnock and also sold insurance. But more and more he lived off freelance journalism. Though self-taught, he proved to be a natural. From 1882 he contributed as a regular columnist to the *Ardrossan and Saltcoats Herald* under the pen-name of Trapper, recalling his boyhood job of tending the trap-doors that ventilated a mine. His columns were often autobiographical, but through them he developed his political and social outlook in an evolutionary rather than revolutionary direction. Once, in his rather purple prose, Hardie looked forward to a future 'when the war hatchet will be buried for ever, and when Capital and Labour shall meet together under a roof tree, to smoke the pipe of peace, and as the smoke slowly ascends it shall carry with it into oblivion all the feelings of discord that ever existed between those twin brothers whose best interests are inseparable'.[7] Ardrossan was a coaling port, so Hardie could expect of his readers some interest in the politics of the mines. He often wrote on this subject, setting his hopes for better conditions in the pits on the Liberal Party, especially the more radical party that emerged after William Gladstone split it over Irish Home Rule in 1886. These years also saw growing militancy in the trades unions. Though it was a constitutional cause that led Gladstone to the left, the shift offered a chance for Scottish workers to assert their economic interests and make some political progress towards a democracy of self-respecting, self-improving citizens.

Hardie returned to the labour movement in August 1886 when he took the job of secretary to a new Ayrshire Miners' Union, set up in parallel with unions in Lanarkshire, Fife and elsewhere. The manifesto he drafted struck a more radical note than before: 'Those who own land and capital are the masters of those who toil. Thus Capital, which ought to be the servant of Labour and which is created by Labour, has become the master of its creator.' The answer was to restore the original, natural order of things.[8] The Scottish miners' unions soon joined in a federation with a nominal membership of 25,000. Their main aim was an eight-hour day, with restriction of output – the 'wee darg' – to counter downward pressure on wages. But the federation collapsed within a year. Even so, it left Hardie with the warm regard of the miners that eventually led to his candidacy in Mid Lanarkshire.

After that chastening episode the obvious way forward was to found a Labour party, seeing as how a single Labour candidate had got nowhere. A start might be made if the rag-taggle from the political fringes that had supported Hardie in Mid Lanarkshire could be persuaded to come together under one umbrella. They ranged from the Highland Land League, concerned first and foremost with crofters' rights, to a Labour Electoral Association in London to the First Socialist International. These and others sent delegates, twenty-seven in all, to the meeting in Glasgow in May 1888 that set up the Scottish Labour Party. Its formal inauguration came in July with, as president, Robert Cunninghame Graham, MP for North-West Lanarkshire, as vice-presidents Gavin Clark, MP for Caithness and John Murdoch, leader of the Highland Land League, and as secretary Keir Hardie.[9] The policies it adopted were not especially socialist, rather a selection from the radical causes of the time: home rule for Scotland, local option in the prohibition of alcohol, and above all land reform, even nationalization of the land.

The Scottish Labour Party did not enjoy a long or successful run either. Just the routines of electoral organization taxed it beyond its limits, and members seemed more intent on squabbling among themselves than on fighting their political foes. Efforts to persuade the Liberal Party to adopt working-class candidates again foundered on the reluctance of the local associations. Before long Hardie decided he was never going to get anywhere in Scotland. In 1890 he put himself forward for the constituency of West Ham South in London. From his point of view it was a sensible move. The Scottish Labour Party would manage to nominate only three candidates for the general election of 1892, none with the slightest hope of victory. But, in West Ham South, Hardie did succeed in drawing together a wide range of support, including the Liberals of a working-class seat. He beat the incumbent Tory.[10] His arrival at Westminster was also his political farewell to Scotland. While he kept a home at Cumnock, he would never again come forward as a candidate north of the border. His career from now on was to be a British one. In his first important gambit, he summoned a national conference of the political and industrial sides of the labour movement to a conference at Bradford in 1893. It set up the Independent Labour Party (ILP), to which the Scottish Labour Party affiliated before dissolving itself; no native socialist body then remained in Scotland.[11]

All the same, the ILP had an eventful Scottish history in front of it. While it got off to a slow start, time was on its side. The Liberal Party, dominant in Scottish politics for half a century – and itself never all that united – had now entered on a process of slow fragmentation. The ILP was just one among a range of new forces emerging as cause and consequence, to compete and overlap with one another because Scottish liberalism had always been so broad. Most of these groups proved to be variably radical, depending on the single issues of the moment. One such issue after 1885 was the representation of labour, and it remained an open question as to whether this would be achieved inside or outside the Liberal Party. The very existence of the ILP might imply the latter, yet it did not close off the former.[12]

The ILP took a position on a wide range of other matters, which in a decentralized party might differ as between Scotland and England. At its Scottish end the positions tended to be high-minded, even sentimental, often shot through with Christianity; Hardie had himself given the cue here. While the ILP wanted to follow an evolutionary rather than a revolutionary path, it was too idealistic to take easily to the opportunism needed to build a party for the masses. It found little time for theoretical debate or industrial disputes, preferring to concentrate on practical good works, mainly in local government. It did have cultural pretensions, since in Scotland higher education was not restricted to a narrow social elite: here a few sons of the proletariat succeeded in reaching university, and through them the party could gain some access to the workers and a better appreciation of their needs. Its relationship was edgy with what passed for the main body of Marxist intellectuals in Britain, assembled in the Social Democratic Federation, which managed to establish the odd Scottish branch.[13]

Altogether the ILP built up a reasonable strength in Scotland, with about forty branches soon after its foundation, most round Glasgow and in practice autonomous of the leadership in London. Such was the modest, earnest shape of mainstream Scottish socialism into the first decades of the twentieth century.[14] Since the ILP showed no great interest in success at the hustings, it had little. At its first test in the general election of 1895, all seven of its Scottish candidates were heavily defeated (while for good measure Hardie lost his seat in London).

A big reason for the ILP's slow start was its uncertain relationship with the trades unions. These, having their hands full of industrial disputes they seldom won, found as yet little time for political ideology. In England they were growing in strength but in Scotland they had remained weak ever since the crushing of their prototypes in the social conflicts half a century earlier. The traditions of the crafts on Clydeside if anything militated against trades unionism, and only about a quarter of the men in the shipyards organized themselves in this way; for the rest, apprenticeship followed by formal admission to the closed shop offered them means enough to defend their interests, in a system that also met with approval and co-operation from the employers. A good example came in William Denny's big shipyard at Dumbarton, where the boss excluded Catholics from the workforce because that was what his Protestant employees wanted: no thought of proletarian solidarity here. And if the solidarity was to be religious, then it would probably push the workers to the political right. Here lay the source of the strong working-class Liberal Unionist vote in Glasgow after the schism in the parent party of 1886.[15]

Trades unions were found rather in industries with a record of open antagonism between capitalists and workers – a situation relatively unusual on Clydeside itself, but familiar in the surrounding coalfields. There, however, the persistent attempts at actual organization had met with only passing success. Most strikes failed, as Hardie knew from his own experience. That did not stop the workers trying: in 1894 the Scottish Miners' Federation, revived under Robert Smillie, led a four-month strike of 70,000 men. Unions in Scotland were evidently capable of cobbling together at least a little money and organization, which made it useful for the ILP to cultivate relations with them.[16]

Something still lacking was national organization. Trades unions in Scotland were local, so they could only co-operate at a local level, and as a rule did so through the trades councils in the industrial centres. These were composed of representatives of every union in the one town or district and they pursued a range of common interests, occasionally including co-ordinated industrial action. Glasgow had had such a council since 1858,[17] set up with the help of the ubiquitous Alexander MacDonald. By 1864 most unions in the city affiliated to it. It then hosted one of the first conventions of similar bodies from across Britain, conceived as a preliminary move towards the formation of the Trades Union Congress (TUC). The council in Glasgow also expanded its membership beyond the bounds of the city, especially to the miners in Lanarkshire. It helped to set up unions for workers – sailors, carters, dockers – who had so far had none. It gained something of a reputation for industrial militancy, though political interventions still proved at this stage more difficult. It did support Hardie's candidature in Mid Lanarkshire, but then declined to affiliate to his Scottish Labour Party, mainly because it had in mind to establish a Labour party of its own based on an alliance of trades councils.[18] In Glasgow itself, it ran candidates alongside those of the Scottish Labour Party at the general election of 1892.[19]

Trades councils became the liveliest form of proletarian organization – in the event a bit too lively for the TUC, which in 1895 banned affiliations from them. At this move the Scottish activists felt so angry that two years later they broke away to form their own Scottish Trades Union Congress, which did allow such affiliations. The result could be seen at the STUC's first national meeting in 1897, when it bared its political teeth to call for the nationalization of the land, the mines and the railways. With 40,000 members at the outset, it was strong enough to maintain its separate existence. All the same, unions in Scotland generally remained smaller, weaker and poorer than those in England, with parochial attitudes that did nothing to foster a sense of working-class solidarity. 'The Scottish nature does not lend itself to combination,' Beatrice Webb bleakly noted after a visit to Glasgow in 1897.[20]

A third development of the labour movement in the final decades of the century came with the expansion of co-operatives. The Scottish Co-operative Wholesale Society had been formed in 1868 to buy or make goods for sale in local stores and bypass petty bourgeois shopkeepers. At the opposite end of the supply chain, the society set up a complex of factories at Shieldhall in Glasgow to produce a wide range of foods, furniture, clothing and hardware. Where possible, it sourced its own raw materials too, eventually acquiring grain mills and timber merchants in Canada as well as a tea plantation in Ceylon. The society also extended into service industries, including hotels, transport and banking. Its undertaking business, arranging members' funerals, proved especially popular.[21]

Even in this heyday of Scottish capitalism, its operations did not go unquestioned, then, least of all in a Glasgow where the city council itself ran services that elsewhere would have been left to the free market. Seldom were the councillors in any sense hard-line political partisans. They might have personal attachments to one party or another, with loose, though identifiable, groupings of Liberals and

Conservatives, even the odd radical, and after the schism of 1886 the Liberal Unionists too. In any event they collectively adopted an open and pragmatic attitude to policy (though tending to be authoritarian in its execution). Against this background, it was easy for the ILP, the unions and the co-operative societies to formulate a common programme at the municipal election of 1894, allocate the candidacies among themselves and bear expenses jointly. They were rewarded with the election of their first councillors. By the end of the decade the leftist alliance was achieving further success, holding ten of the council's seventy-five seats.[22]

Given the encouraging omens, Hardie was authorized to approach the STUC with a view to extending from a local to a national level the co-operation between the political and the industrial sides of the labour movement. After he had personally outlined his ideas to the annual congress of 1899, it passed at the prompting of the socialist delegates a resolution in favour of united working-class action at the next general election. A further conference of the two sides, together with the Social Democratic Federation and a few co-operative societies, was summoned to Glasgow in January 1900. This established the Scottish Workers' Representation Committee.[23] It might be regarded as the first example in Britain of a Labour party on the broad modern lines – except it proved to be a false dawn, simply because the forces of the left remained so feeble in Scotland. While Scots were ready to act in advance of their English comrades, they could scarcely compete once these got their act together. It was with the Labour Representation Committee formed in England a little later that the future lay.

The further experience of the Scottish committee spoke for itself. It had a poor electoral record right through the nine years of its existence. At the general election of 1900 it presented just one candidate. By-elections were more promising, and the best chance came in North-East Lanarkshire in 1901, when the chairman, Robert

Smillie, was chosen to stand. Being against the Boer War and for Irish Home Rule, he got much initial support from radical liberals. There was talk of adopting him as the official Liberal candidate, but again the local association would have nothing to do with a working man. Smillie went ahead by himself and suffered heavy defeat. The Scottish committee also fought the general election of 1906 independently. It contested five mining constituencies, coming last in all. The Labour Representation Committee insisted on standing in four other seats, despite the weakness in them of trades unions or any alternative basis for a campaign. It won two: one in Glasgow, one in Dundee.[24]

Away from the electoral arena, however, these were not barren years for the ILP in the west of Scotland. It attracted an active younger generation with fresh ideas. One was Jimmy Maxton, a schoolteacher in Glasgow elected chairman of the Scottish region in 1912. Another was Tom Johnston, a journalist from Kirkintilloch and founder of *Forward*, the ILP's newspaper; with his polemical books, *Our Scots Noble Families* (1909) and *History of the Working Classes in Scotland* (1920), he set out to reinterpret Scottish history. A third, John Wheatley, a councillor for Shettleston, was remarkable in being both a Catholic and a socialist at a time when his church would have no truck with the left. In 1906 he founded a Catholic Socialist Society that in 1908 affiliated to the ILP. As these men rose within its ranks they pushed it in more of a socialist direction, though they could not yet build bridges to the mass of the working class.[25]

Given the detachment of the ILP from industrial conflict and the feebleness of the unions at the grassroots, some scope for militant agitators opened up. Only the Social Democratic Federation had so far at all represented Marxism in Scotland, and that punily. James Connolly, after sojourns in Ireland and America, came home in 1902 imbued with the most extreme doctrines of the left, those of syndicalism or industrial unionism. He forced a split in the federation and led off the fundamentalists into a Socialist Labour Party. Its entirely Scottish membership was reflected in a Calvinistic insistence on purity of Marxist dogma. Meanwhile, in 1911, the rest of the federation joined with other groups to form the British Socialist Party, which was to become the nucleus of the Communist Party after the First World War. It had a good many members in and round Glasgow, the most prominent being John Maclean, teacher, writer, orator and, in the longer term, myth-maker. Qualified as a schoolteacher, he took, as his main contribution to the coming red revolution, to offering instruction in Marxism to working-class activists. From 1912 he gave classes at rooms in Bath Street, which from 1916 were supported by the trades unions in a Scottish Labour College. At its inaugural meeting, 471 delegates from 271 unions came along – but Maclean was by this time in jail.[26]

Such agitation as took place among Scottish workers up to 1914 needs to be placed in perspective.[27] The trades unions did not care for confrontation because they were bound to suffer huge handicaps in any contest with the extremely hostile employers. The workforce was hard to organize. At the top end, the labour aristocrats – the skilled craftsmen – might scorn joining a union. At the bottom end were the shiftless and despised, often Irish, labourers, living in slums, godless and violent, squandering their meagre wages on drink, an affront to the Scottish values that the labour movement also shared. Scotland had no strong national unions but only local ones, often impermanent, loosely joined in fragile federations. Trades councils remained more effective, but with the result that strikes tended to cover a number of occupational groups in one district, rather than to develop into disputes involving all the workers in a given trade. Besides, industrial harmony generally prevailed. In a reversal of the later roles, Glasgow actually looked down on London as a hotbed of unrest.[28]

After 1914 the position of Scottish socialism was transformed.[29] Red Clydeside remains even today a central experience for the nation's left. It has been the subject of endless interpretation and reinterpretation, rendering the contemporary reality somewhat opaque. In any event, it was a good deal more complex than modern myths allow.

On the one hand, the official trades unions were anxious to avoid domestic collisions and would not, for fear of antagonizing the government in London, back the wave of strikes that convulsed Clydeside as the production of munitions got into gear. The ILP's position was similar. The main thrust of agitation against the war came instead from militants who organized themselves in the Clyde Workers' Committee. But here too motives remained mixed. Some leaders of the committee, Willie Gallacher the most prominent, were members of the extremist parties. Others, such as David Kirkwood, were simply shop stewards trying to do the best by the men they represented. They joined forces as the authorities forced the industrial pace, especially by means of dilution – the introduction of unskilled workers into the closed shops of the skilled workers. In December 1915, the minister of munitions, David Lloyd George, visited Glasgow to plead for this course to a mass meeting. He was shouted down. Even so, a compromise would be reached early in 1916. It mixed concession with repression: agreement to let the unions control the details of dilution was balanced by the arrest and deportation of the leading agitators.

The unrest still did not come to a halt. Trades unions grew and new ones were formed for the unskilled workforce. Most remained local and highly responsive to members' grievances. If necessary they could support one another through the trades council of Glasgow.[30] Further dispute arose, for example, when the government sought to persuade the shop stewards of a need to extend conscription to some skilled workers so far exempt. Discontent spread beyond the industrial scene, too. Protests over wages and prices, poor housing and rapacious landlords were to be found commonly in Britain, but often in more acute form in and round Glasgow. It is a moot point whether the Russian Revolution had any impact on Scotland during the last dreadful winter of the war, as all over Europe politicians began to despair of restoring peace or of calling forth much more sacrifice from their peoples.

The industrial front remained disturbed beyond the armistice till the great confrontation early in 1919, with the climax of the forty-hour strike and the riot in George Square on January 31. This the police just about kept under control, though there were soldiers and tanks waiting in case things went wrong. Three ringleaders – Willie Gallacher, David Kirkwood and Manny Shinwell – were afterwards jailed, but the magistrates let off the others arrested in the square. That marked the end of such revolutionary hopes as any of them had entertained. Gallacher conceded that few of his comrades were actually seeking revolution, but said they might have brought one about if only they had marched on Maryhill Barracks and fraternized with the troops stationed there, following the recent example of St Petersburg.[31]

Instead the agitators busied themselves with the formation of a communist party, though they disagreed on what kind. Maclean advocated a purely Scottish one, with the argument that Clydeside was nearer to the necessary upheaval than any other part of Britain. Gallacher, who had just visited Moscow and fallen under Lenin's spell, returned with orders to found a British party and seek its affiliation to Labour. Maclean refused to join it and tried in vain to set up his own outfit, socialist and nationalist at once, on the model of Sinn Féin. Thereafter he faded into obscurity, and died in 1923. Meanwhile, in 1920, the Communist Party of Great Britain had been formed out of the British Socialist Party, the Socialist Labour Party, the left wing of the ILP and a number of shop stewards. It enjoyed relative strength in Scotland because the founding groups were better organized and bigger than in England. Even so, they remained a tiny minority, usually setting their hopes on infiltration of the Labour Party. It would have none of this, and expelled them all in 1925.[32]

A debate continues down to the present day on the left about whether Red Clydeside really offered a revolutionary opportunity for the working class. The idea once gained some traction among socialist historians, but nowadays is taken less seriously. The protests in industrial Glasgow, if vigorous, had after all never aspired to the transformation of capitalist society. They were about the war, and then not so much about the war itself as about the behaviour of those running it. This had consequences for the wages and social conditions of workers in the west of Scotland that provoked opposition first from individual agitators and then in the form of political campaigns, primarily by the ILP. Embroiled in the detail of industrial dispute, few of the agitators dared to condemn the struggle against Germany as such. For that cause Glaswegians were making huge sacrifices, and it would have taken a brave man to tell them the sacrifices were in vain. Nor, with the one obvious exception of Maclean, did the leaders develop a class analysis of the war, let alone think to threaten the power and authority of the British state.[33]

Once all this trouble blew over it grew clear that, among the factions on the left, the ILP had come out the strongest.[34] Its Scottish membership tripled between 1914 and 1918, and it gained wide sympathy among a working class in Glasgow thoroughly fed up with the government. Taking seriously the regular practice of local and parliamentary politics (rather than rehearsing an uprising), the party equipped itself for the challenges of peacetime. It was Glasgow that became the centre of a more popular and more socialist ILP.

A political breakthrough for the left did not come till later. The general election of 1918 took place straight after the armistice, before the soldiers were all home, before registrations could be completed under the new universal male franchise (with votes for women of a certain age too), and before political life returned to anything like normal. The most salient result was the collapse of the Liberal Party that had dominated Glasgow since 1832 – hardly predictable in 1914, but possible after the demands of war had torn apart the Victorian two-party system. The distribution of the governing coalition's 'coupon' by David Lloyd George, now prime minister, and by his Unionist partner, Andrew Bonar Law (who sat for Glasgow Central), bore harshly on the independent Liberals. They held not a single one of the city's fifteen constituencies, of which ten went to the Unionists, three to Coalition Liberals, and one each to Coalition Labour and Labour. It was the last that now found its great opportunity.[35]

Hardie, who had died in 1915, always said a breakthrough for Labour would never come without the close co-operation of the trades unions. The relationship of the political and industrial sides of the movement was finally formalized in the constitution that the party gave itself in 1918. It rested on a kind of federalism, offering a role also to the constituency parties and to the socialist societies. At the same time, it set up a central leadership that in the long run was to exert increasingly tight control. As a whole, the constitution suited English more than Scottish conditions.[36]

Labour in Scotland after all still consisted of little more than the ILP, with which no other affiliate could compete. It had never managed to get especially close to the trades unions, and grew uncomfortable in a unified structure dominated by them. It perceived the spread of constituency parties as another threat, even though in Scotland they did not develop fast and many long remained nothing but glorified trades councils. While Labour advanced at the ballot box, its Scottish membership by 1927 stood only at 11,000, out of a British total of 300,000. Instead, it was the ILP's branches that fulfilled the role of 'keeping the Labour interest alive'. Arthur Woodburn, a future secretary of State for Scotland, wrote: 'The ILP was small and intimate. The Labour

Party by its size could not have this advantage.'[37] Even so, with Labour's adoption of a socialist constitution, the ILP tended to lose its sense of purpose as an intellectual vanguard. It found no new one: carping over the details of policy often seemed the one way to maintain its identity.

Meanwhile, however, the ILP triumphed in Glasgow at the general election of 1922, capturing ten seats and, in Scotland at large, contributing eighteen of Labour's twenty-nine MPs. The wonder of the achievement moved them and their following to an almost religious fervour. Before the victors left Glasgow they held a service of dedication at which their speeches on the promise of socialism were interspersed with the congregation's singing of Covenanter hymns. Hundreds came to give the MPs an emotional send-off at St Enoch Station. Kirkwood, now MP for Dumbarton Burghs, looked exultantly round and proclaimed: 'When we come back all this will belong to the people!'[38]

With hindsight, others took a more sober view. Shinwell wrote that 'the Scottish contingent was, in fact, composed of a typical cross-section of an industrial country representing, not so much the political attitudes of the electors, but their disillusion with the policies of Westminster, especially as regards housing and unemployment.'[39] Yet on Clydeside these factors proved decisive. Here housing problems remained worse than anywhere else in Britain. The old economic security of the craftsmen's elite was evaporating as well. A further important local factor came in the conversion of Catholics to Labour, after the bloody struggle for the independence of Ireland had destroyed their previous allegiance to liberalism. Two of them, John Wheatley, the dominant figure in Glasgow's ILP, and Patrick Dollan, his electoral organizer, were the architects of its victory at the polls. Altogether the developments of these years allowed socialists to break through from being isolated sectaries to becoming leaders of a mass movement. They showed themselves harder, more combative, more intellectual than the

English Labour leaders, who were mainly trades unionists, often dullards and not always socialists.

The ILP had an immediate effect at Westminster as well, in swinging the election of Labour's leader in favour of Ramsay MacDonald, at that time regarded as the candidate of the left.[40] This induced the false impression he would feel himself in its debt and join with it in committing Labour to a precise and immediate programme of socialism. On the contrary, he was trying to give the party an aura of respectability, which could hardly be supplied by the Clydesiders. Within a few months his relations with them cooled drastically, as their truculence and rowdiness in Parliament aroused his deep displeasure. Wheatley was all the same invited to join MacDonald's cabinet when Labour took office for the first time in 1924. This did not placate his friends. They distinguished themselves in these precarious months of power by absolute refusal to admit practical politics might be allowed to modify ideology.

Under the Conservative government that followed from the end of 1924, the Clydesiders saw a chance to bring Labour back to what they regarded as its true path. Wheatley's answer to the dissipation of doctrine lay in restoring the role of the ILP as an internal powerhouse of socialist ideas. Now retired to the back benches, he worked out, mainly in pamphlets, an alternative economic strategy of higher public spending, nationalization, controls on trade and a minimum wage. He brought his plans together in the document 'Socialism in Our Time', published in 1926. Maxton was meanwhile elected chairman of the ILP. He sought to prepare it for a more messianic conception of its future. He wanted it to be not just a socialist think-tank but the spearhead of a neo-Marxist mass movement. Yet his strategy was misconceived. The wider Labour Party and the country at large showed little interest in socialism on his terms. Disruption in its name seemed folly when Labour had progressed so far through moderation and won the workers more power than ever before.[41]

Others in the ILP also now doubted the wisdom of turning further left. Shinwell and Johnston had been led rather in the opposite direction by the realities of ministerial office. The demands of running the party's machine did the same for Dollan, who in Glasgow was actually stronger than Maxton. Still they could not outwit him, failing in an effort to depose him from the chairmanship in 1929. Under these pressures there was no chance of his rallying the whole ILP to his ideals, support for which was more or less confined to a small band of humdrum Glaswegian backbenchers. They moved rapidly towards a clean break with Ramsay MacDonald when he returned to office in 1929. Their behaviour in the Commons hampered, even endangered a government anyway in a minority, with caution forced on it by a need for Liberal support. Some hope remained that Wheatley might act as anchor to his wayward, impetuous chairman. But he was not readmitted to the cabinet and died in 1930. Maxton, with little to lose and nothing to restrain him, was free to transform the quarrels into a struggle for power against Labour's leadership. There could be little doubt of the outcome.[42]

Even the crisis over the formation of the National Government failed to repair the widening breach. During the general election of 1931 the ILP ranged itself with Labour in a campaign against cuts in benefits, the issue that had caused the rupture between Ramsay Macdonald and his former comrades. But to all intents and purposes it stood as a separate party. Maxton and three others were returned. Since Labour's rules no longer allowed formal opposition to a selected candidate, the question arose for the ILP of disaffiliation from the party.[43] A special conference was called to consider it in July 1932. Maxton had reached the conclusion that no other course was possible. In the absence of an obvious compromise, three-fifths of the delegates voted to quit. So ended an alliance that had lasted since the foundation of the Labour Party, and in Scotland was largely responsible for setting it on its feet.

All the same, the main body of the ILP parted without remorse. On the contrary, such emotional force had built up behind the secession that, in a mood of suicidal wildness, the special conference proceeded to sever every link with Labour. Dual membership of the ILP and other parties was forbidden, so that nobody could fudge the choice. But that ensured the disintegration rather than the independence of the ILP. It plainly miscalculated the reaction among the rank and file, many of whom had spent years in the service of the movement. It also meant losing the ILP's share of the political levy from the trades unions, cutting its one tangible link with them and promising a bleak financial future.[44]

Most members of the ILP could not accept all this. The Scots were especially unhappy and defected in droves. They formed a Scottish Socialist Party under Dollan, which remained affiliated and later merged itself with the constituency parties (so giving Labour the proper local organization it had so far lacked). Scots membership of the ILP dropped drastically from 16,000 in 1932 to only 4,000 in 1935.[45] Held together by the oratory of Maxton, it hung on to a handful of parliamentary seats right through the Second World War, and even through the Labour landslide at the general election of 1945. But after his death in 1946 the end was not long in coming, and the remaining MPs rejoined Labour's parliamentary group at Westminster.

Labour now faced just the Tories as enemies to reckon with. At the parliamentary level Glasgow's politics remained competitive enough right up to the general election of 1959, though not exciting in any other sense. Labour MPs, having done their stint and learned on the job as town councillors or officials of trades unions, showed no vision wider than the local one – the only serious policies they ever had concerned essentially municipal questions such as housing. But it was clearly the right formula for the party's growing political dominance in the city, with an eventual monopoly of the parliamentary seats, till the collapse and annihilation of 2015.[46]

Before establishing that dominance, however, Labour had at the municipal level had a tougher time for longer. Voters went to the polls every year, but only one-third of the councillors came up for re-election each time. A revolution on the scale of the one in 1922 in parliamentary representation was therefore impossible. For the time being the right-wing Moderates continued to control the city council, though with their position gradually weakening. They had problems finding candidates to contest Labour's safer seats. If these could not be won, contests remained important just to keep the left on the defensive and to blood young Unionists for later political careers. Once upon a time the hopefuls would have been happy to pay their own expenses, but among the city's stricken middle class that was no longer always true.[47]

More generally, even if the Moderates were saving Glasgow from socialism, they could not halt the inexorable decline of the Second City. Recurrent economic recession put the council in an ever more desperate position, as social expenditure soared while the tax base shrank. It scarcely helped that the two big parties in the City Chambers, Moderate and Labour, shared the general belief that housing was the first priority. The differences lay in the view taken of the need for private housing and of the level of rents in the public sector: the Moderates would have made more land available for the first and have charged more for the second, closer to the economic cost of the provision. With, in the event, little or no private housing being built in the city, the point became academic.[48]

The big issue for the urban middle class was the rates. The Moderates had cut them from the high wartime levels, but a decade later they were creeping up again. By the 1930s the same dilemma operated at the local as at the national level, with the slump both raising unemployment and reducing the money available for public services: there was no easy solution. Obvious targets for savings lay in the programmes of public housing, which some argued were merely creating hotbeds of socialism. And then the corporation's own workforce had perhaps grown too big, especially seeing that it was likely to vote Labour as a guarantee of jobs and pay. But the Moderate regime had not so far stinted on these heads of expenditure either. It was true most of its councillors sat for safe middle-class wards, and had plenty to gain from calling for cuts, in outlays and in the rates alike. On the other hand they sat alongside colleagues representing working-class constituencies who needed to be more careful about what they said.[49]

What finally dealt the death-blow to Moderate municipal government was the Scottish Protestant League, a small splinter group that had originally sprung up out of popular antagonism to the subsidies for Catholic schools available under the Education Act of 1920. Now the scope for sectarian grievance grew, as skilled craftsmen persuaded themselves they were being undercut by cheap labour in the competition for jobs. The league called for Irishmen to be deported, without appeal if they were on welfare. Its founder and leader, Alexander Ratcliffe, gained a seat on the city council in 1931 together with one other candidate. In 1932 the league stood in eleven wards and took a further seat. In 1933 it stood in twenty-three wards and won more than 70,000 votes, 23 per cent of the total. While it never succeeded in achieving any of its aims in policy, it did succeed in destroying for good the Moderates' control of the city council: they lost a net thirteen seats in this municipal election. With its historic task fulfilled, the league promptly faded away. Labour took over Glasgow.[50]

At first Labour still depended for a majority on the ILP. The two parties did not always see eye to eye, preferring to pursue their own feuds instead. A paradoxical result was that the priorities of the Labour council after 1945 differed little from the priorities of the ILP before 1939, and may indeed have been reinforced by defectors from the latter party as it dwindled. For example, David Gibson, convener of the housing committee, had followed this path and, after failed parliamentary candidacies, found his fulfilment on the corporation. He wanted to build council housing as fast as possible, and he was the man who at length hit on the tower block as the means of delivering it.[51]

In the long run the legacy of all the internal rebellion, and of the efforts to defeat it, was to make Labour in Scotland, and especially in Glasgow, more uniform in outlook and more authoritarian in conduct than it otherwise would have been. The total dominance of Labour in the city is illustrated by the fact that, right up to 2017, only two out of twenty-eight lord provosts did not belong to it. Latterly, even the councillors of all other parties could be counted in single figures. Glasgow resembled a one-party state, and it pursued policies to match.[52]

It was reasonable enough for the council to set housing as the overwhelming priority after 1945, on a view that those who most needed help should be helped first. But that meant the better off had to find new homes for sale in the dormitory suburbs outside the city. From now on almost all additions to the housing stock inside the city were municipally built and let. At the peak, of 300,000 houses within the boundaries, 180,000 or 60 per cent were council houses, while in Bearsden and Milngavie or Eastwood, suburban districts just beyond, 80 per cent of houses were privately owned. With youthful and economically active families being in effect forced out, the problems of urban renewal and environmental improvement had to be tackled at ever increasing cost by a declining population of older and poorer families. The members of the middle class can be accused of abdicating their responsibilities when they moved from the city, but it would not have helped that local political life largely excluded them. All the same, it was a course that Labour consciously took.[53]

This exclusive model for local government, as opposed to others that might have served, shaped Scottish Labour as a whole right the way through the period of its hegemony till 2015. Before 1914 the representatives of the middle class, especially of the high middle

class who ran things, had seen the corporation of Glasgow as something like a joint-stock company. After 1933, Labour conceived of it
as a social service, above all for public housing at low rents and for
the municipal employment of teachers, firemen, policemen, tram-
drivers and so on. At the level of the manual worker, too, there
was a direct labour force supplying tradesmen and navvies for the
various building projects without resort to private contractors.[54]
But that was as good as it got. A new ruling elite contained men
who lived by politics but without being schooled in the traditions
of civic probity that had been the ideal of the old mercantile
class – which, from its deathbed, felt shocked as a city once
praised for being a model municipality became steadily mired in
bribery and corruption.

Alternative models could be neutralized through assimilation.
It proved easy enough in the case of the trades unions, by allocating
them seats on the council from which to defend their members'
interests; the railwaymen in particular took advantage. On the
capitalist side, small businesses would find it beneficial to befriend
their local representative, too. Over time bigger companies learned
to deploy more lavish resources to win support from councillors
for whatever project they might have in mind. In the end perhaps
even members of the opposition in the City Chambers (at least
till 1979) might take their place in an all-embracing structure for
running Glasgow on lines that suited the ruling party because it
could control them. It boycotted only the SNP, once this became
a serious electoral competitor. Labour felt offended by the image
it had cultivated for itself from the start: radical, popular and
Scottish (especially since in Glasgow most nationalists leaned to
the left too).[55]

Yet this still did not become, as in parts of England, a Labour
party of the toiling masses; the membership in Scotland was
always proportionately much smaller than south of the border. The
situation turned into something like that in Eastern Europe before

1989, when the boundaries of party and state had grown steadily blurred by the power of an orthodox cadre; the same happened here in Glasgow, except at a local rather than national level. Above all, the ensemble provided an apparatus by which the resources of the public sector could be allocated to the range of clienteles. The best procedure was found to lie in the dispensation of the available largesse through an inner circle of councillors. For this the party did not need a big membership; on the contrary, anecdotal evidence suggests it preferred a small one and so kept out unreliable types such as academics. What the new Labour elite could do was call up its troops whenever necessary. Jimmy Allison, later to be the party's national organizer, remembered that when he came from Paisley to Glasgow in 1971,

> false memberships were rife... in Glasgow, Lanarkshire, Dunbartonshire and Renfrewshire. I recall one selection for a regional seat in Shettleston where the average branch attendance was normally around 8 to 10 people but when I arrived at the hall I thought I had turned up at a bingo session by mistake. There were about 300 present, and although David Marshall, the constituency party secretary [and later MP for the same constituency], had a list of names which corresponded to those present, there was no way we could tell if those present were genuine members.[56]

A further aspect of all this was nepotism: the tendency among the occupants of the petty seats of power to rely on the people closest to them – their families and friends – and in return to see these got what they wanted for themselves. Labour dynasties arose, oddly in a party that finds the hereditary principle so objectionable in other spheres. The Carmichaels offered a prime example. George Carmichael, a founder member of the ILP, had a son James who became the last man to win a parliamentary seat for the party when he held on to Bridgeton in the by-election after Maxton's death in 1946. This Carmichael soon went over to the official Labour Party and remained the MP till he retired in 1961. The clan was quickly back at Westminster when his son Neil became the next year MP for Woodside, then Kelvingrove, where he stayed till 1983. His brother-in-law, Hugh Brown, was meanwhile MP for Provan from 1964 to 1987, and his wife Kay a queen of the quangocracy.[57]

Councillors are more numerous than parliamentarians and, as heirs to a tradition of protest, often found themselves caught between the devil of political management and the deep blue sea of their constituents' needs. There were councillors who, like the city's social workers, teachers, housing managers, police officers and so on, struggled against fatigue and disillusion to maintain their idealism. But chronic economic crisis in Glasgow and the west of Scotland generally determined that every human transaction – a sale of goods, a request for a liquor licence, an application for a council house, the renting of a market pitch or the tendering for a municipal contract – was to some degree affected by the prevailing clientelism. In other words, it was coloured by class, religion or ethnicity – or to put it more brutally, sectarianism. The consequent structure of political command and control prompted activists to regard bribes and rewards as legitimate tools for the exercise of power and the reinforcement of loyalty from the client groups. There was often a bargain: the briber might get a new council house, and the councillor some expenses to spread among other members of his faction so that they might live by politics. The system cemented the political class at its centre and the social constituencies on its periphery.[58]

There were also councillors who just saw politics as the road to a better personal way of life than mere work. Glaswegians grew used to strange stories about local politicians and their exotic junkets. The deepest corruption in the west of Scotland was not a matter of minor perks or even criminality, rather of a lack of active democracy in supposedly democratic institutions. With a single party in power for so long, individuals in crucial positions could make themselves irremovable. As a witness of this sorry scene said, 'Someone who has been a convener of a powerful committee for more than five years has their own fiefdom. Other party members are loath to vote against him for fear of losing their seat at the table.'[59] Massive Labour majorities in the council meant, then, a lack of debate on crucial issues, a jealous sharing among cronies of the fruits of office and the incessant feuding of cliques behind the scenes.

Public dissent was suppressed so far that most actual policy became excluded from the political process. This meant proposals could not be discussed or improved by debate. Glasgow's media were largely neutered. And it would, of course, have been out of the question for any bunch of bourgeois do-gooders to monitor or criticize, let alone seek to counter, the realization of the civic ideals Labour had set itself. Yet the average councillor inevitably found it hard to balance a daily burden of casework in minor but often complex matters of housing and planning with any longer or wider view. That had to be left to the city's bureaucracy, which remained powerful long after the departure of the patricians who had first called it into being, and formed the link between the old regime and the new. With philanthropy in much shorter supply than in Victorian times, and voluntary action no longer much of an alternative to municipal uniformity, intellectual and practical innovation could only come from professional administrators and planners.[60]

Many of these professionals were incomers to Glasgow and to Scotland, attracted by the challenge of remaking the nation's biggest city. For example, the two men who took on the redevelopment of Gorbals came from Edinburgh, Robert Matthew and Basil Spence. Matthew was the inaugural professor of architecture at the capital's university, who joined in vandalizing nearby George Square to create an 'academic precinct'. Spence already had under his belt the big commercial commission for Glasgow Airport at Abbotsinch, where he created a terminal that perhaps served as a model for some of his domestic buildings. With these and others, a novel official bourgeoisie arose which, in line with sociological theory, forwarded its own functions and interests. It was geared to advising politicians and executing policy, but with ideas generated in its own ranks rather than by any remotely democratic process. An interest group wanting something done was better advised to go to the professional or bureaucrat concerned than to the councillor representing the people it might affect. This was also why, if a policy began to err – for instance, as the high-rise blocks revealed their shortcomings, at least to the tenants – those affected found it so hard at the political level to get their needs taken seriously and to bring about any change of plan. The whole system had a bias against democratic innovation. As one of the few thinking councillors, a Liberal Democrat, said: 'Any elected politician has to convince a highly sceptical group of managers that his ideas are realistic. Overwhelmingly, they are happy with the current system, and can think of many reasons for not bringing in new ideas.'[61] In the end there was stalemate: grand design gave way to routine municipal management of an apathetic population.

Scottish economic policy had been based on the hope that this improved infrastructure, together with regional aid from London, would create the conditions to attract to Clydeside the new industry needed for diversification and long-term recovery. The alternative approach of 'picking winners' had proved too prone to political pressure and wishful thinking, but facilities available to everybody could be endorsed by all political parties. Alas, they still failed to bring the desired results in Glasgow. Politicians and planners learned from experience that the economy largely goes its own way, whatever they may say or do about it. Industrial incentives and capital spending are not in themselves enough to create a productive labour force and innovative or efficient management.[62]

Even less could such measures maintain communal coherence. The city council thought to minimize disruptive behaviour in the population through its control of a high proportion of the housing stock. It might then segregate honest and industrious tenants from idle and rowdy ones; for these, a scheme like Blackhill became notorious as a dump. A search began for specific programmes of action, especially as social work started to develop into a profession from about 1950, to arrest the disintegration of family and neighbourhood.[63]

Yet often for the law-abiding tenant the most disturbing feature of life in the new Glasgow was that social order appeared to be breaking down. The poverty, squalor and degradation of this great industrial city could indeed lead to a harsh, indifferent attitude to life and self-preservation. There had been recurrent moral panics since the 1880s when the first gangs appeared, usually sectarian and linked with football. In their fights they were by 1914 already using swords, hatchets, machetes and lead-weighted clubs rather than mere fists. The police responded in kind, and had some success before the outbreak of the First World War offered alternative means of sating this new Glaswegian bloodlust. After 1918 recurrent depression on Clydeside helped to rekindle the violence and give the city a fearsome reputation far beyond its own bounds: this was the era of the 'Glasgow Smile', the scar on the face of the victim slashed by a razor. The notorious novel, *No Mean City* (1935), by H. Kingsley Long and Alexander McArthur, depicts the world of the tenements in Gorbals; the anti-hero's family of eleven shares a room and kitchen, and in the opening scene he rises from his cavity bed to piss in the sink. The gangs might have fought mainly among themselves, but their involvement in theft, racketeering, gambling and intimidation represented a far wider threat to public safety. The situation grew so bad that an Englishman, Percy Sillitoe, was drafted in as chief constable. This self-styled 'hammer of the gangs' set out to suppress organized criminality. He smartened up his own rather demoralized force, compulsorily retiring all its friendly local bobbies with thirty years' service and introducing the 'Sillitoe tartan', the black and white diced pattern on his men's cap-bands, modelled on the Glengarry bonnets of the Scottish regiments. He also equipped them with the latest technology. He used intercoms to connect police cars with police stations – previously they would first have had to find a police box. He set up a network of informers, including barmen in the pubs where the thugs drank. He made some progress – though perhaps the outbreak of the Second World War again had a more powerful effect in giving members of gangs more ample opportunities for killing, and overseas too. Sillitoe went on to become head of MI5.[64]

But that all still lay in Glasgow's dark ages. An idealistic expectation of the welfare state from 1945 was a greater degree of social harmony, as the standard of living rose and the problems of hardship faded away. Yet in the new housing schemes the old habits of the slums reappeared. Gangs sprang up again – this time perhaps in more dangerous form, younger and more feral. In the 1930s the members of a gang had often been quite mature: it gave them an identity and focus for their energies in the absence of any economic security. Now there was mere anomie, with the communal controls of the tenements lifted amid the isolation of the high-rise blocks. Once young lads had a start in a life of delinquency it was easy to move on to more serious offences. Glasgow became one of the most violent cities in Europe. The situation grew still worse with the spread of illegal drugs in the 1980s. It led to the organization of crime on a larger scale, since long chains of supply had to be forged from the exotic producers right down to the dealers on the streets, and sometimes this was done under the cover of activities that on the surface might appear legal. Wars in the East End involved rival gangs selling drugs and stolen goods from ice cream vans, roving retail outlets with alluring carillons; the failings of Strathclyde Police in the face of this impudence earned it the epithet of 'serious chimes squad'. There was the alternative of private security companies, but the trade in drugs penetrated them too. While here it was a matter of private enterprise, the socialist paradise had evidently not provided the antidote.[65]

It was time for progressive Glasgow to try something different. The city's ideal image of itself as an industrial, proletarian community in its economy, politics and culture, all moved by the stirring myths of Red Clydeside, was being reduced to a hard-drinking, gang-ridden, materially deprived reality. An alternative appeared with the approach of the twenty-first century. It was of a post-industrial city, even a pioneer of neo-liberal experimentation, or at the very least a tourist destination and locus for a fresh surge of Glasgow Style, not now in the aesthetic achievement of Charles Rennie Mackintosh and the Glasgow Boys but in modern consumerism: retail, fashion, nightlife, conspicuous consumption generally. It was in the city itself that John Struthers and his agency produced the icons and slogans of the advertising campaign that he dubbed 'Glasgow's Miles Better'. The attempt to rebrand the place proved in many ways successful. To its own citizens and to strangers, it highlighted Glasgow's cultural riches, its mild (if wet) climate, its environment with more parkland per head of population than any comparable place in Europe, and above all its suitability for enterprise.[66]

Glasgow won accolades, such as the title of European City of Culture, and mounted international events like the Garden Festival. The derelict frontage along the banks of the River Clyde was transformed, while in the hinterland on both sides the older housing schemes got replaced, if still with rather anonymous buildings, or were at least given a facelift. Some older tenements had their sides decorated with huge murals. Despite the corporation's puritanical attitudes to the licensing laws, many new pubs and clubs opened in the centre of the city, though not the sauna/brothels found elsewhere in Scotland. Glasgow's eloquence was constantly deployed in talking the place up.[67]

There were things that did not change, however. If the general standard of living improved, Glasgow's economic position relative to other cities in Scotland remained much the same: it was too far away from the North Sea for the oil industry to make a difference, and financial services on the whole preferred Edinburgh as their base. Despite the buildings adorned in bright colours and set amid skilful landscaping, the city could still look bleak under its leaden skies to visitors unfamiliar with it; the motorway circling the centre did not help. Even to Glaswegians, much of the big talk might sound like little more than that.[68]

The Labour Party remained in overwhelming, undisputed power and some of its local leaders started to appear as media personalities (though sometimes for the wrong reasons). From the novel commercial possibilities rich pickings might be available for the city, for the developers and for the councillors themselves. A member of the minuscule opposition in the City Chambers wrote this: 'The Labour group could see no further than property development. They routinely ignored the objections of hundreds of local residents, and were intent on building flats on every square inch of Glasgow. Nothing was safe from the gaze of our planning department; even parks and green belt were considered no more than development opportunities.'[69]

It was all in tune with the times, but the ruling party's image in Glasgow soon tarnished after New Labour took over in London in 1997. So long as Tony Blair and Peter Mandelson gave full rein to their fascination with wealth and power, their followers in the west of Scotland saw no reason to abandon their own time-honoured, and relatively modest, practices. There was, however, a steady divergence of outlook. While Scottish Labour retained its allegiance to what it defined as socialism, Blair and Mandelson saw nothing much wrong with capitalism, or at least nothing they might not be able to handle. The gap was for the time being papered over because, with the re-establishment of the Scottish Parliament in 1999, both sides could take refuge in constantly proclaiming the virtues of the Union.[70]

But a series of cases demonstrated how strong the undercurrent of corruption in the west of Scotland's Labour Party still ran. In Monklands, the local authority immediately to the southeast of the city, there was a battle over allegations that a Catholic mafia in Coatbridge held control of the council by means of jobs for the boys and discrimination against Protestant Airdrie. The issue had figured in a parliamentary by-election in 1994, though it did not stop Labour holding on then. Inside Glasgow, a redistribution of seats before the general election of 1997 entailed a cut in the city's representation at Westminster and fierce battles among the sitting MPs to keep their jobs. Mohammed Sarwar, MP for Govan, narrowly defeated Mike Watson, MP for Central, in an internal contest for the new Central seat, but saw the normal Labour majority slashed at the actual polls. A couple of weeks later a newspaper plastered its front page with a story accusing him of electoral malpractice; he was cleared but his political ambitions had been blighted, and he at length went back to his native Pakistan. One of Paisley's two MPs, Gordon McMaster, committed suicide three months after the election. He and his colleague, Irene Adams, elected in simultaneous by-elections in 1990, had meanwhile made local enemies with their tireless campaigns against drugs. Their neighbour, Tommy Graham, MP for Renfrewshire West, was recruiting members in Paisley in order to see himself through the redistribution. His party suspended him over allegations of spreading malicious rumours about McMaster's sexuality. Paisley had already become a byword for intimidation and corruption in its criminal class; the habits seemed to be catching.[71]

The shenanigans were not confined to the parliamentary representation. Glasgow's city council remained dominated by cliques that often appeared indifferent to the public impact of decisions they pushed through. From 1972 to 2003 every single lord provost they elected was a Catholic. When the honour fell on Alex Mosson in 1999, it did so despite revelations in the press of his criminal record – admittedly a long time ago – involving convictions for assault and housebreaking, habits brought on by his alcoholism. The real power lay with the leader of the council, Stephen Purcell, but in 2009 he was forced to resign after admitting the stress of the job had made him in his turn resort to drink and drugs. To the old guard on the council it seemed the kind of behaviour only to be expected from a flashy youngster who had destroyed their influence and replaced them with a coterie of sharp-suited, modernizing activists cast in his personal mould. Senior members of his own party felt only too happy to whisper innuendos about his private life.[72]

In the City Chambers, scarcely a trace remained by this time of the spirit of Red Clydeside. Instead Glasgow's socialist elite was remarketing the place as a franchised retail centre for global brands, with a bit of authentic gritty realism thrown into the sales pitch. The urban sprawl beyond the City Chambers could be largely left to speculators and hustlers. The practical result might be seen along the banks of the Clyde, soon lined with yuppies' flats of no architectural distinction: not that this made them any different to the office blocks and hotels lying back from the river. As the eye progressed to the outer suburbs, it could observe where the new narrative had banished the city's social deprivation, with its tell-tale signs of decaying tenements and grim housing schemes, shabby shopping centres and pubs built out of breeze-block with wire grilles over the windows, and half their customers smoking on the pavement in front. It became hard for Glaswegians to vent their frustrations in a workers' city that its Labour rulers pretended was something else. While the voters had long been apparently biddable, at last they turned on their political masters. In the general election of 2015, Labour lost every parliamentary seat in Glasgow to the SNP.[73]

9

Image: 'Great white hope'

THE OPENING ceremony for the new Glasgow School of Art took place on December 15, 1909. Presiding over it was Sir James Fleming, who for a quarter of a century had been chairman of the board of governors. Once a student at the school, he afterwards rose to be the city's main manufacturer of crockery. He made a fortune that allowed him to patronize a wide range of charities – a typical curriculum vitae for someone of the Glaswegian commercial elite. Another dignitary present was Sir John Stirling Maxwell, a scion of the older landed class, an even more eminent public figure with even wider artistic interests, including the superb collection of Spanish paintings he kept at his residence of Pollok House. Sir John moved a vote of thanks to the architect of the school, Charles Rennie Mackintosh, saying he 'had the real faculty of being able to adapt a building for the purpose for which it was really intended', the present example being 'a conspicuous success of that kind'.[1] Mackintosh expressed his thanks and on behalf of his firm, Honeyman & Keppie, presented Fleming with a jewelled silver casket containing a decorative signed scroll – probably of his own design, for it was in the style of the Viennese Secession, the avant-garde artistic movement

that counted him as one of its own, though it was otherwise little
known in Glasgow.

The celebrations went on for three nights, centred around
packed performances of a masque, *The Growth of Art*, put on by the
director of the school, Francis Newbery. Glaswegians love to party,
so we can assume they made these revels something to remember.
Nobody seems to have paid any attention in London, but the
events would have been noted among the circles of Mackintosh's
friends and admirers in Paris or Vienna, in Brussels or Turin. There
was a review in New York's modernist journal, *International Studio*:

> The architect… a former pupil, has impressed his strong
> individuality on the building. At the same time the evidences
> of care and thoughtfulness in adapting the various parts to
> their special purposes are many and striking. The system of
> lighting has been carefully considered, and a novel kind of
> window introduced. The studios are large and well planned,
> and every possible facility is provided for careful study. A
> special feature of the celebrations was the exhibition of work
> by eminent artists who studied formerly at the school, or who
> have been identified with its work.[2]

Glasgow was by now a city of European rank, in fact the continent's
fourth biggest in terms of population, and could play its own part
in international cultural developments.[3] Along with Barcelona,
Hamburg, Paris, Prague, Riga or Vienna, it had become a
powerhouse of Art Nouveau – the reaction against the academic art
of the previous age, inspired instead by natural forms and structures.
Glasgow's own input, the Glasgow Style, also arose from synthesis,
of bourgeois enterprise and artisan respectability, of ostentatious
sophistication and delicate naturalism. To other influences we must
add a sense of this being an industrial community with aesthetic
requirements of its own.

The city felt proud of the engineering feats it paraded before the world at international exhibitions in 1888 and 1901, then at a Scottish national exhibition in 1911. The concept of craft here meant skill and precision, different from the rival Edinburgh's blend of vernacular and manual. Both stood in contrast to England, where the leader of the Arts and Crafts movement, William Morris, called the Forth Bridge 'the supremest specimen of all ugliness'[4] – not a sentiment comprehensible in Scotland. Glasgow's wealth arose from metallurgy in its various applications, and Glasgow Style was pervaded by the possibilities of bending, puncturing, welding and moulding matter through art as well as science. The city fathers, with their fabulous riches now a century old, had the leisure and the level of cultivation to offer generous patronage. Yet, unlike the middle class of Edinburgh, which was dominated by the learned professions, the equivalent Glaswegians were even yet a precarious and volatile bunch who respected lucre, not lineage or land. Economic base determined cultural superstructure, and wealth needed to be shown off.[5]

For Mackintosh, the prime practitioner of Glasgow Style, the challenge was to clothe 'in grace and beauty the new forms and conditions that modern developments of life – social, commercial and religious – insist upon'.[6] At the School of Art he, a man of humble origin, one of a dozen children of a policeman at Townhead, had been able to cultivate his aesthetic sensibilities. Newbery took the student under his wing and sent him on a travelling scholarship to study the art and architecture of Italy. That connected Mackintosh to a classical tradition of European and of Scottish creativity that he was to transform in his own ways.

There had up till now been two main styles of architecture in Scotland. One was the Scottish vernacular, or baronial: picturesque yet at bottom utilitarian, inherited from the builders of medieval castles, but also to be found in other public buildings of olden times – tolbooths, townhouses, trades halls and the like. Glasgow had contained plenty of this kind of architecture before it was swept away by the civic improvements of the nineteenth century. Even then it began to be replaced by modern imitations, put up in Saltmarket and High Street, as the centre of the city was rebuilt.[7]

The classical tradition took over. It had arrived in Scotland rather late by European standards. Not before the end of the seventeenth century did it put in an appearance thanks to William Bruce, the first Scot to make architecture his profession. His finest achievements were the restored Palace of Holyroodhouse in Edinburgh and the magnificent residence he erected for himself on the other side of the Firth of Forth, Kinross House by the shore of Loch Leven. Bruce spent his whole creative career in the east of Scotland, so far as we know. But at one stage, during his work on Hopetoun House in West Lothian from 1699 to 1703, he may have employed as a young apprentice William Adam, son of a family of stonemasons at Kirkcaldy. Adam grew up to be the second of Scotland's great classical architects, responsible for buildings in every region, country houses such as the House of Dun in Angus and Duff House in Banffshire, or public buildings such as Robert Gordon's Hospital in Aberdeen and the Royal Infirmary in Edinburgh (of which mere fragments remain). He worked his way west, too, to build the duke of Hamilton's hunting lodge of Chatelherault and the old parish church in the nearby burgh of Hamilton, even penetrating the Highlands with his plans to reconstruct Inveraray for the dukes of Argyll. Then he designed, within the modern boundaries of Glasgow, Pollok House for the Maxwells (though it is unclear how much of the original is preserved in the present mansion). He turned up at last inside the city itself, where in 1744 he erected the New Library for the university – which vanished, alas, with the rest of its beautiful buildings when the entire complex was demolished in 1870.[8]

It could, then, have been some personal connection with Glasgow's commercial elite that brought two big commissions for the most renowned of Adam's three sons, Robert: the Royal Infirmary and a new Trades Hall, both built 1791–4. The Infirmary lasted a century, to be replaced by the present complex on the same site, but the Trades Hall survives to this day. It may not be Robert's greatest work but it is full of his characteristic motifs. It follows the Palladian formula imported into Scotland from the aristocratic mansions on the *terra firma* of the Republic of Venice, with a rusticated ground floor under a *piano nobile* and then an attic storey on top of that. It features several kinds of Adam's favoured 'movement' in the lines of the parapet, the deep-set Venetian windows and the projecting raised portico, with a central window flanked by pairs of Ionic columns. Here as elsewhere, he makes free play with the various classical elements rather than following any particular model from antiquity.[9]

After this accomplished start, classicism became the dominant style in Glasgow. Most other British cities preferred Victorian Gothic, and even Edinburgh has more of that than its western rival does. Glaswegian churches are something of an exception, following the ecclesiastical fad that started with ritualism in England and in Scotland produced an archaizing desire to link Presbyterianism, hitherto scornful of passing fashion, with medieval antecedents. But this trend did not pick up till later in the century, and earlier examples are rare: the Catholic Chapel (now Cathedral, 1814–7) of St Andrew by James Gillespie Graham and the Ramshorn Kirk (1824–6) by Thomas Rickman. Instead Glaswegians of all denominations worshipped in classical churches – at St Jude's Episcopal (1838–9), Elgin Place Congregational (1855–6), Trinity Duke Street United Presbyterian (1858), St George's-in-the-Fields (viz. Woodside) built by the Church of Scotland in 1885–6. Later, a more Italianate local version of the original classicism developed, much as in Italy itself, because Glaswegians also liked to lighten the Latin austerity: it is to this we owe the John Street United Presbyterian Church (1858–60), but above all the magnificent

culmination of the City Chambers. The most imposing example
of all, Kelvin Hall, is no longer with us because it burned down
in 1927. Yet on the whole for such a show-off city, Glaswegian
classicism remained chaste.[10]

Glaswegian classicism had suffered, however, one real violation.
In 1868, Edward, prince of Wales, and his wife Princess Alexandra
of Denmark came to the city to lay the foundation stone for its
new university.[11] This was to stand on Gilmorehill, a drumlin
or small hill among several others dotting the landscape to the
west. Each assumed the shape of a shallow cone, and on this
particular drumlin a thousand labourers had been employed for
a year removing earth to flatten the top ready for the university's
buildings. As soon as the prince had performed his own duty, the
builders would be able to make a start.

The city marked the royal visit with a holiday, and conferred
its freedom on the prince and princess. They then drove west
cheered by huge crowds. About 20,000 people had gathered on
Gilmorehill itself, a multitude 'so great as to be, to a certain extent,
beyond control'. Stands erected for the occasion sagged under the
weight of spectators crowding on to them; those who had paid for
seats found many already taken by 'boys, servants, workmen about
the place and so on'. Still, the actual ceremony went off without a
hitch. The lord provost, James Lumsden, gave a lunch for the royal
couple. They left straight afterwards, though not without handing
over 100 guineas as a contribution to the construction; later
Queen Victoria would send £500. That evening the corporation of
Glasgow held a civic banquet where the guest of honour was the
principal of the university, the Revd Thomas Barclay, a Shetlander
by birth whose long beard made him look, so his students said, like
the reformer John Knox.[12]

It would still be a couple of years before the first classes could
be held amid the wide open spaces of Gilmorehill. Meanwhile
the university needed to carry on regardless at its cramped original

site on the High Street. The buildings here, two centuries old, were exquisite examples of native Scottish architecture that had developed, under the influence of the Auld Alliance, out of French styles adapted to a cold climate. But by now this quarter of the city, once picturesque and charming, was a slum. Rich people had abandoned it for salubrious residences on the surrounding drumlins, leaving the poor behind them. The general council of the university minuted that it was 'one of the last places in the city which one would now propose for professors to reside in, or for students to frequent'. The site posed a moral and an economic hazard, because 'owing to the progress of the city westwards, the present buildings are no longer conveniently situated for those classes of society in Glasgow which are most interested in the university'. The move to Gilmorehill would 'bring university education more generally within the reach of those citizens who are in the best condition and circumstances to avail themselves of it'.[13]

In 1870 the new building on Gilmorehill at last opened. Even so, it was not quite ready and would need another two years before it was finally completed. No matter, the moment had come for the move from the High Street. On April 29 that year's session closed and the students met in the common hall of the college to take their leave. On July 29, the senate convened there for the last time. It would next day hand over possession to a railway company intent on clearing the site for a goods yard. The entire library was shifted to its new home without the loss of a single book. The removal men took more interest in the silver – a fine, antique collection built up over centuries, since it was the custom for graduates to donate a piece to their *alma mater*. Somehow, along the three miles from the High Street to Gilmorehill, this collection vanished except for one loving cup, two tassies and three candlesticks.[14]

It was by contemporary standards a gigantic edifice waiting out on Gilmorehill to be filled with the academic paraphernalia. Its length of 540 feet, with tower and spire 100 feet high, made it the

largest public structure erected in Britain since the completion of
the new Houses of Parliament at Westminster ten years earlier.
Like them it was built in Gothic style, putting a certain stamp
on the urban environs. Even today it dominates all views of the
western side of Glasgow. We have got used to it now, but at the
time many thought it an unhappy addition to the architecture of
Scotland's biggest city.[15]

Vehement protests had arisen against the destruction of the
college in the High Street. The reason for this act of vandalism was
supposed to have been that in strict financial terms it would be
difficult to do anything else. The university had not enough money
to restore the original fabric, and the one way it could realize funds
was to sell up and build on a new site. Still, the official excuse did
not account for the course matters then took. The university had
appointed a building committee that came to be dominated by
Allen Thomson, professor of anatomy. He was a skilled chairman,
but he also wished to make his number in academic circles in
London (where he would soon move). In architectural terms
he cultivated a special interest in the Gothic revival – itself all
the rage in London, as we still see in the Houses of Parliament,
Foreign Office and other novelties of the period. The architect of
the Foreign Office was George Gilbert Scott. Thomson wanted
him for the University of Glasgow too. Before any decision on
a new design there was supposed to be a competition. Thomson
sidestepped the prescribed procedure and offered the commission
straight to Scott. The architect would later explain his work in these
terms: 'I adopted a style which I may call my own invention...
It is simply a thirteenth-century or fourteenth-century secular
style with the addition of certain Scottish features peculiar in that
country to the sixteenth century, though in reality derived from
the French style of the thirteenth and fourteenth century.'[16]

In Glasgow and elsewhere there were those who still thought
the style alien and phoney. Scotland possessed Gothic buildings

of its own, genuine ones dating from the Middle Ages. But nothing of note had been built in this style after Parliament House in Edinburgh during the 1630s. Architectural innovation went on, with the native tradition developing into the baronial style that would be given a modern impetus by, above all, Queen Victoria's rebuilding of Balmoral. Meanwhile, prestigious new construction tended to reflect the impress on the national culture of its philosophical concerns with individual and civic virtue, in the classical style recalling the country's intellectual debt to the ancient world. This could be seen in the cities and right round the country, in great structures and in humble ones.[17]

The same was true of churches – for even Scottish religion had turned rational, at its higher levels anyway. By the Presbyterian way of thinking there could be nothing to associate religion especially with the Gothic style, as in the minds of the English architectural gurus of the age, John Ruskin, Augustus Pugin and George Gilbert Scott himself. They held the Gothic style to be uniquely Christian, indeed Catholic: Scott was born a Catholic, Pugin converted and Ruskin was tempted. Scots did not share this outlook. They had since the Reformation built kirks in various styles, the main requirement being the adaptation of the historic types of structure to Presbyterian worship, focussed on pulpit rather than altar. In the west of Scotland examples existed from the sixteenth century in the Old West Kirk at Greenock, from the seventeenth century at Fenwick, from the eighteenth century at Killin.[18] By the turn of the nineteenth century Scots were putting up places of worship that followed the forms of Greek Revival too. For Glasgow, this would continue longer than elsewhere with the work of Alexander 'Greek' Thomson in the form of the three churches he built for his own United Presbyterian sect, in St Vincent Street, Caledonia Road and Queen's Park. Only the first remains intact; the second is a ruin and a German bomb destroyed the third in 1943.

Academic requirements are different from religious ones, but it comes as no surprise that Thomson felt incensed at what arose on Gilmorehill. He took it as an insult to the city's own architects that an ancient Scottish university had turned its back on enlightened Scotland to ape the medievalism of Oxford and Cambridge. He unburdened himself to the Glasgow Architectural Society in a lecture 'On the Unsuitableness of Gothic Architecture to Modern Circumstances'. In particular he dismissed the idea of the Gothic style being uniquely Christian: 'This might have some weight in the Romish Church, but to Protestants of any sort, and more particularly Presbyterians, and still more particularly Presbyterian dissenters, the argument seems very absurd, for what has the philosophic Christianity of the Reformation to do with the sensuous ritual of the middle ages? The architecture, which was a consistent part of the latter, is diametrically opposed to the former.'[19] Lest he be suspected of Glaswegian parochialism, he went on to draw some comparisons with recent developments in the classical capital: 'Donaldson's Hospital in Edinburgh, of which great things were expected, fails to excite even a passing remark; while the High School, the fragments of the National Monument, Dugald Stewart's Monument, the Surgeons' Hall, and the Institution on the Mound, continue to illuminate their respective localities with the light of truth and beauty, giving to our northern metropolis an air of refinement which no other city in the kingdom possesses.' Thomson dismissed Scott's claim that he had employed a native style in Glasgow's new university: 'For all that remains of Scottish architecture in the new design, it might as well have been left out altogether.'[20] On the contrary, Scotland's architectural tradition had been betrayed, in predictable consequence of denying any local practitioner the chance to design one of the most important public buildings likely to be put up in Glasgow during the nineteenth century. Even if classicism was to be spurned – absurdly – as not learned and academic enough, it should have been possible to build something in the alternative Scottish Baronial style.

Though the University of Glasgow lacked cultural confidence in its architectural choices, this could not be said of the Victorian city as a whole. Greek Thomson's work was central to it.[21] In a Britain now given over in its building practice to Gothic gargoyles or bombastic battlements, he protected Glasgow from tasteless excess. His was not a classicism preserved in aspic, still less as slavish imitation: he embellished the basic style with elements alien to it in any purist sense, though always harmoniously blended into it. He realized that a genre now two millennia old, and represented everywhere from Philadelphia to Bombay, could lend itself to infinite variation. All he had to do was make sure that in Glasgow it reflected the character and tradition of the city.

For this boomtown Thomson designed every type of building, decorated by an encyclopaedic diversity of classical and pre-classical motifs. He laid out whole suburbs at Langside and Regent's Park, where he himself lived. He created grand terraces along the Great Western Road and gave them majestic interiors. He planned a huge tenement in Eglinton Street and lesser ones elsewhere. He built individual dwellings in the form of suburban villas, the Knowe at Pollokshields or Holmwood House at Cathcart, today run by the National Trust for Scotland as a memorial to the man and his work. This work reached its climax in his three United Presbyterian churches. They adapted a classical idiom to demanding sites, sloped or otherwise irregular. Out of the challenges there emerged not just Greek Revival but, more to the point, controlled compositions balancing diverse geometric masses. It was an achievement novel and modern, unlike anything else built in this era. The huge elongated dome at Queen's Park offered the most striking feature of all; its loss is a great tragedy. And while creating these extraordinary structures, Thomson felt happy to furnish an industrial city with the workaday edifices also necessary to it: offices and warehouses such as the Grosvenor Building, Grecian Buildings, Egyptian Halls and Buck's Head.[22]

Thomson was not a lonely genius, but exerted a deep effect
on his city. He showed it how to channel its wealth into modern
architecture monumental in its Graecism yet lightened by exotic
elements – Egyptian, Romanesque, Persian, Indian. The mixing
of genres was what made him Romantic as well as classical. In
other hands the transition might have faltered and dissolved
into a jumble of alien, eccentric and unreadable features. But he
could accomplish with aplomb the abstracting shift from classical
theme to Romantic variation. And his whole oeuvre showed there
might be historical inspiration even in the task of building for an
industrial society – by erecting not mock temples and mausolea,
and not only churches either, but also bourgeois villas, proletarian
tenements and commercial premises.[23]

With so much of Victorian Glasgow gone,[24] it is hard to see
now how Thomson shaped the city in its heyday – including the
influence he still exerted after his death in 1876. It is seen at its
best round Queen's Park, where the partner in his practice, Robert
Turnbull, carried on working for a further quarter of a century.[25]
Though Glasgow underwent protean change, there remained a civic
coherence, vigorous elegance and spontaneous order in its evolution,
often swanky with swagger, even bombast. It all added up to more
than the inchoate mass of similar industrial conurbations. The
journal, British Architect, wrote of Thomson in 1888: 'The strong
influence of his work is apparent in nearly all Glasgow architecture,
giving to it – the city – a character unique among the large cities
of this country.'[26] While he was trained in Glasgow and seldom
left it, he saw himself as a European rather than Scottish architect.
He was homebred but outward-looking, just as he was classical
but Romantic. Inventive and theatrical, steeped in cosmopolitan
history and inspired by evangelical religion, he brought exotic allure
and cultural distinction to Victorian Glasgow's wet, grimy streets.[27]

Glasgow was now a big city yet it still, like the other Scottish cities,
in some respects retained the character of a small town. Thomson

would not have got as far as he did without cordial contacts among the urban establishment, in particular with the Blackie family whose eminence was as much political as commercial. We have already noted that Thomson built and decorated lord provost John Blackie's own house at 7 Great Western Terrace. He also designed the firm's printing works in Stanhope Street (demolished in 1967). In return Blackie published a number of Thomson's plans in his compendium of *Villa and Cottage Architecture* (1867), intended as a handbook for all those about to transform British landscapes with sprawling suburbs. Blackie's son Robert, who acted as art director for the firm, together with his successor Talwin Morris, figured among the first in Glasgow to recognize the developing genius of Charles Rennie Mackintosh, and to use his designs in their production. It was for another of the clan, Walter Blackie, that Mackintosh built his most striking example of domestic architecture, Hill House at Helensburgh.[28]

While a student, Mackintosh won the travelling scholarship Thomson endowed in his will. After his return from Italy the young man exhibited his own watercolours in a student show. Its judge was the portraitist, James Guthrie; when told some drawings were by an architect, he turned to Newbery and said, 'This man ought to be an artist' [that is, a painter].[29] Mackintosh would carry on painting right through his life and at the end return to it as his main preoccupation. He and his wife Margaret, with their in-laws, Herbert and Frances McNair, formed a clique known as The Four or, in jest, the Spook School, with reference to their use (in various genres) of mystifying symbolist motifs. A case in point was the posters Mackintosh drew for the *Scottish Musical Review*, quite shocking to the taste of the time. The magazine *The Studio* leaped to their defence but had to admit 'Mr Mackintosh's posters may be somewhat trying to the average person'.[30] Since it was hard to make a living as an artist, he went from the architectural classroom to join the practitioners, Honeyman & Keppie. He had also learned, like many young Glaswegians, to drink and smoke too much. That did not stop him working: on the contrary, he would stay up all night at his firm's offices refining his plans, emptying a bottle of whisky as he did so.

Mackintosh could not be called a classical architect, though he had the inherent discipline of classicism. His early work showed some sympathy for it, but he soon turned away to follow the seductive lines, the exotic forms and sinuous elegance of Art Nouveau. Little that was visible then remained of any aesthetic influence Thomson might have exerted on him. Leaving the classical rules behind him, Mackintosh carved out a new sphere for himself. This explains why, though architecture is the most public of all the arts, in Mackintosh's hands Glasgow Style often achieved its most authentic expressions in the private sphere. He left a fine example with the interior of his own house in Southpark Avenue at Hillhead, which he recast after moving there in 1906. Demolished in 1963 by the university, it was reconstructed within the Hunterian Art Gallery.[31] We need to look outside the city for houses Mackintosh built entire. He found at Kilmacolm in Renfrewshire a patron, the merchant William Davidson, who in 1900 gave him his first chance to create both interior and exterior of a complete building, Windyhill. He and Margaret designed the furniture, fireplaces, panelling, glass, lighting, decoration, even the storage, where they brought their designers' skills to bear on built-in cupboards. Then in 1902 the publisher Walter Blackie commissioned from Mackintosh a new home overlooking Helensburgh down the River Clyde. On the outside, Hill House was modernized Scottish Baronial, with harled bartizan and steep gable, reminding us how Mackintosh admired this national style so different from his own – he had for it, he said, an 'instinctive affection'.[32] Yet on the inside all was Art Nouveau enhanced by *Japonisme*. Attention to detail even extended to prescribing the colour of cut flowers the Blackies might place on a table in the living room, so as not to clash with the décor.

Just as dazzlingly domestic were the tea rooms Mackintosh created for another generous patron, Catherine Cranston. They became a Glaswegian institution, spots in a male chauvinist city for women to get away from husbands or fathers. The Glasgow Art Club, for which Mackintosh signed off the drawings, offered a sort of equivalent to the more aesthetic type (rather rare) of Glaswegian male. For the real men of the city's hard school of journalism, he designed the old office of the *Herald* in Mitchell Street with its dramatic water-tower, now a centre for design and architecture. He also projected the printing works of the *Daily Record*, almost hidden off Hope Street between Renfield Lane and St Vincent Lane.[33]

Mackintosh got a different opportunity with his commission for a church at Queen's Cross – a small site by the junction of Garscube Road and Maryhill Road in a proletarian quarter. There appeared nothing much avant-garde about the building from the outside. The congregation was of the Free Church, and wanted a plain place of worship. It consented to a dominating window that was Gothic in inspiration, but this allowed Mackintosh the chance to work in a big floral motif. He could then do more of what he wanted with the pulpit, galleries and communion table, in discreet supplement to Presbyterian sobriety. The church with its distinctive massing more than holds its own in a row of tenements, confronted as it is today with modern tat. In the elements there is profusion but no confusion: the faithful reflection of the interior in the exterior is one thing that makes Mackintosh an heir of Greek Thomson.[34]

The rest of Mackintosh's personal legacy lay in educational buildings. He designed two schools, one the Martyrs' School at Townhead (in the street where he grew up), the other at Scotland Street in Govan. Local school boards had simple and obvious requirements for classrooms, a hall and so on, and the marvel is to see how he worked with them to flood the buildings with light, then to decorate them in Art Nouveau on doorways, ironwork and woodwork. Both need to be imagined in their original environment

of close-packed tenements, all vanished today to leave the Martyrs'
School on its own with an adjacent church and backdrop of New
Brutalism – though at Scotland Street this isolation perhaps even
enhances the view of the school's glittering towers from the nearby
motorway. The third example was Mackintosh's masterpiece,
Glasgow School of Art on Garnethill. His firm won the contest
to design it in 1897. It was built in two stages, the first in fluid
Art Nouveau, the second in 1907– 9 in purer geometric forms,
heralding the European Secession movement. The design is eclectic
in a second and typical sense, for the straightforward, rational shape
of the whole forms the setting for an infinity of internal adornment
in timber, stone, iron, tiles, glass – at its finest in the library, with its
air of a medieval scriptorium for all its unmistakable modernism.[35]

Now that Mackintosh has grown famous and his style familiar,
it becomes possible to identify further works in which he seems to
have taken a hand even though the collective practice of his firm
kept his contribution anonymous. His output at any rate always
differed in appearance from that of the senior partner he reported
to, John Keppie, who favoured the more ornamental 'beaux-arts'
style.[36] For example, to Mackintosh are now ascribed, on account
of their asymmetry, the medical hall at Queen Margaret College
and the Ruchill Free Church Halls. Mackintosh besides left designs
never realized in his own time, from which some modern buildings
have been derived – the 'Artist's Cottage and Studio' at Farr in
Inverness-shire and the 'House for an Art Lover' in Bellahouston
Park, Glasgow.

In 1913 Mackintosh quit Honeyman & Keppie to set up his own
architectural practice. But this perfectionist insisted on controlling
every project down to the tiniest detail, and found it hard to obtain
work. In 1915 he and Margaret left Glasgow for Suffolk in England,
where he was arrested as a German spy because local yokels could
not place his thick accent.[37] Still prosperity eluded the couple, till
in 1923 they abandoned architecture and moved to France to devote

themselves to painting. They stayed two years before Mackintosh's worsening health forced a return to London. In 1928 he died at the age of sixty from cancer of the throat. He had had his hours of triumph, but the difference between his career and those of Robert Adam a century before, or of Alexander 'Greek' Thomson in an older generation, was that his genius won little recognition in his own nation in his own time. Yet he put Scotland at the forefront of the architectural avant-garde. It was an extraordinary achievement in a nation with no state and so no official patronage of the most public of arts: not that his work would have appealed much to the average politician or civil servant.

So much grew clear as, with the transition from patrician to plebeian urban government in Glasgow, public regulation took over from private enterprise as the main determinant of its architectural style or styles. It is true that, in the centre of the city, the period up to 1939 saw a new generation of monumental commercial buildings modelled on the neo-classicism of the United States (another country where the tradition had continued to flourish and develop).[38] But the suburbs grew apace, not least because of the explosion in council housing. After 1945, the huge peripheral schemes started going up. Pollok, Easterhouse, Castlemilk and Drumchapel grew from a plan for independent satellite townships with a mixture of housing and amenities arranged in neighbourhoods on the pattern of the contemporary New Towns, to which they were intended as an alternative. But the city never had enough money to finish the job. People who moved out from the centre felt lost amid the low-density, semi-rural housing. In the amorphous schemes the schools and the churches (in pairs for Protestant and Catholic) were often the sole buildings that identified individual neighbourhoods. Since other facilities did not materialize, the monotonous tenement blocks seemed desolate. Nor did things improve when the city's high-rise blocks, more than 100 of them at one time or another, added vertical to horizontal isolation.

Then from 1979 housing policy shifted once more in favour of the private sector. In the centre of the city dozens of redundant warehouses were turned into apartments. Otherwise there was no improvement on the housing scene. Scattered round Glasgow, estates now stand of small houses of a sort to be found in any town and village in Britain, built meanly in brick rather than in the red sandstone of local tradition. Interspersed are blocks of flats clearly not belonging to the public sector – like those visible from Kingston Bridge – but still in a different way unsightly. None has any feeling for siting or for Glasgow's particular character.[39]

The city was so well furnished with public buildings from the nineteenth century that few new ones proved necessary for the twentieth century. One was the Sheriff Court (1986), designed by Keppie, Henderson & Partners, a descendant of Mackintosh's old firm. Here they pallidly recalled his legacy in internal chequered screens supposed to have been inspired by him, though over-borne by a 'dumb monumentalism' achieved at 'vast cost'.[40] Then there was the extensive gallery in Pollok Park built to house the Burrell Collection (1983), the eclectic assemblage of 8,000 objects bequeathed to the city by Sir William Burrell in 1944, on condition of their being given a home of their own. The 'low and rather wandering building largely of glass, stainless steel and smooth pink stone from Dumfriesshire' is by Barry Gasson.[41] Finally the Royal Concert Hall (1987), closing the upper end of Buchanan Street, represents the work of Leslie Martin, who long before had designed the Royal Festival Hall in London (1951). It seems obvious the two are from the same hand.[42]

Though by the turn of the twenty-first century Glasgow had fresh cultural aspirations, architecturally they needed to be fulfilled from outside Scotland. This was true, in particular, of three striking buildings that arose along the now-deserted banks of the Clyde below the centre of the city. One was the Armadillo, or Clyde Auditorium, designed by Norman Foster in his characteristic materials of steel and glass. An undistinguished Scottish Exhibition and Conference Centre already stood by the site, and the auditorium, with 3,000 seats, was intended to increase its capacity. It opened in 1997, at once acquiring its nickname. Comparisons have been made with the Sydney Opera House – though we are assured this was not the architect's inspiration, which came rather from the abstract concept of an interlocking series of ship's hulls, in reference to the local maritime heritage.[43]

On the opposite bank lay Pacific Quay, which as dockland had been left high and dry by the onset of containerization. The media were attracted to this accessible site, above all BBC Scotland, which had been occupying a jumble of buildings in the West End since before the Second World War. At the quay it engaged the English architect, David Chipperfield, to build a brand-new headquarters. His exterior, a steel cube, did not win universal admiration, but his interior was stunning. Resembling a Tuscan hill-town or an Assyrian ziggurat, it might have dwarfed spectators with its implied corporate power, yet it also beckoned them into the creative spaces of its various open plans (in sharp contrast to the warrens of most broadcasting buildings). The bad news came in 2004 when the BBC, chanting the mantra 'on time and on budget', booted Chipperfield off the project halfway through, and to finish the job hired Keppie Design (a further generation of Mackintosh's firm). Glasgow has treated too many architects, famous or not, in a cavalier fashion. Here was an egregious example, but Chipperfield took it with admirable composure.[44]

Back on the northern bank, the Riverside Museum arose in 2011. The architect, Zaha Hadid, had won her international reputation by liberating her art in expressive, sweeping, fluid forms that offer multiple points of perspective and evoke in a fragmented geometry the chaos and flux of modern life. The museum is a good example, contrasting the line of the roof with its jagged range of peaks and troughs (like a distant view of the Highlands from the same spot) with the space beneath in the form of a Z-shaped tube, one end invisible from the other. It is purpose-built for the city's collection of transport, previously housed at Kelvin Hall. It stands on the site of a former shipyard next to the confluence with the River Kelvin, so that a Victorian clipper can also be exhibited on the water alongside. But its layout can disconcert visitors who also complain that many of the vehicles on display are mounted on platforms at too great a height to be inspected; car buffs recall how in Kelvin Hall the exhibits were set out at ground level, allowing visitors to look inside and admire the polished antique dashboards or gleaming gear-levers. While the museum adds distinction to Glasgow, it is achieved by connecting to international developments in architecture rather than by rekindling a local creative spirit. There is value in doing so, but in the end Glaswegians would be better finding once again for themselves a place at the forefront of architectural modernity.[45]

It was through Glasgow's overseas links that the second great genre of the visual arts, painting, had started to flourish here during the Enlightenment, in that the merchant elite became the main source of the necessary patronage. Edinburgh, it would be fair to say, remained the capital of the nation in the arts as in other things. But there the three great painters who formed the core of the Scottish classical school, Alexander Nasmyth, Henry Raeburn and David Wilkie, found no successors of equal quality. Instead, after the foundation of the Royal Scottish Academy in 1826, the local artistic scene tended to get bogged down in the sort of institutional squabbles typical of the place. While its painters bickered among themselves about whose pictures should be accepted for exhibition and how high they should be hung, artists from other parts of the country had little chance of a look in. Those in Glasgow grew so exasperated at being ignored that they agreed among themselves to spurn the Royal Academy. These were the Glasgow Boys. Their city would not possess a purpose-built public gallery of its own till

Kelvingrove was erected in 1897–1901. Meanwhile the McLellan
Galleries in Sauchiehall Street, put up by a rich merchant to house
his own collection of paintings and bought by the corporation of
Glasgow in 1856, had to serve.[46]

The Glasgow Boys forged ahead, painting in styles different from
the academic production Edinburgh had sunk into. If they hardly
added up to a distinct school by themselves, they did operate as
a group in the sense of influencing and supporting one another.
They were all friends and took working holidays together. They
would fan out from Glasgow, to the Borders or indeed to the east
of Scotland, where they seemed to find a greater wealth of scenes
they wanted to paint. With them, formal portraits, ideal landscapes
and historical scenes gave way to realism and naturalism, not
limited by any requirement of decorum or dignity in the subjects.
The Boys captured many facets of Scotland never painted before.
It helped that they worked in the open air: the people they painted
were real people in real places, not models in galleries. And the
Boys opened themselves to the rest of the world. They embraced
change and they created modern art in Scotland.[47]

Many of their paintings have become as familiar as the works
of the preceding classical period. James Guthrie's large, sombre
canvas of a *Funeral Service in the Highlands* sets a scene that would
have been foreign to Lowlanders at the time and is no longer to
be witnessed at all today, while his *Hind's Daughter* captures, in
a little girl at the menial task of harvesting cabbages, a kind of
self-confident dignity. W.Y. Macgregor's best-known work is his
Vegetable Stall, but his townscapes repay attention: they make Crail
or Melrose or Oban or Stirling look as if they were somewhere in *la
France profonde*. E.A. Walton (brother of the George Henry Walton
who worked with Mackintosh) does the same for Helensburgh,
David Coventry for Highland fishing villages. In contrast, *The
Druids Bringing Home the Mistletoe*, by George Henry and E.A.
Hornel, carries the viewer far away in time, as is emphasized by

a canvas gorgeous with polychrome and gold; later they would carry him far away in space too, when they went to the Far East and fostered the minor Scottish school of *Japonisme*, something to which Arthur Melville later contributed. Of all the Glasgow Boys, John Lavery comes closest to the French impressionists: the mood of *The Tennis Party* is summed up by an elegant young man in plus-fours leaning on a fence and smoking his pipe, while sunlight dapples the lawn. Can this be Newlands? But Lavery did not dally in Glasgow. He was commissioned to portray Queen Victoria when she came to visit the international exhibition of 1888. This launched his career as a painter to high society, and he moved to London soon afterwards.[48]

It is surprising that the potential pictorial drama of industrial Clydeside appeared to leave all these painters cold. If they were the Glasgow Boys, where might we find their images of Glasgow? It was a matter of their city allowing and impelling them to be what they were, rather than giving them subject matter to paint. For a start, only Glaswegian wealth made their work possible. One or two had a merchant or a shipbuilder for a father, and so the means and confidence to pursue their artistic careers. For the rest, the local opulence created a market for paintings, and a discerning one. Captains of industry could invest their fortunes in them, as they did in the international market for art just when it began to develop. The shipping magnate Sir William Burrell became the most memorable example after donating to the city of Glasgow his vast collection, including works by Cézanne, Degas and Rodin, now housed in the gallery named after him. Against such competition the Glasgow Boys were put on their mettle, but they rewarded the patronage that came their way.[49]

For striking images of industry on Clydeside we need to look to a later generation, one which at last found in this aspect of Glasgow not just drama and interest but even a kind of beauty. In the years before the First World War, the vigorous etchings of Muirhead

Bone conveyed the awesome complexity of it all, and the dwarfing of the individual in the vast productive hive that yet furnished matter for common achievement and pride. Bone, like Mackintosh, studied at Glasgow School of Art and served an apprenticeship in an architectural office, but in his case his draughtsmanship became more or less the same as his etching. Much more than any Glasgow Boy he was the chronicler of the city. In him the austerity of black and white proved good not just for recording architecture but also for capturing the mood of a community defined by its labour.[50]

Yet it was colour, rather than black and white, that in the same period started to distinguish the nation's painting above all. A new generation of artists rejected the Victorian cultural legacy – the nostalgic sentimentality of the kailyard in writers like J.M. Barrie and its visual counterpart in the paintings of 'cabbage patch and cottar' by Guthrie and Hornel. In contrast, they wanted their native art to engage with a wider world, especially with the concerns of international modernism. The group that came to be known as the Scottish Colourists would often have been found in Paris during the years before 1914 – they were young men still defining themselves as painters and perfecting their technique in the city where all the world's aspiring artists came for example and inspiration. Here art was ceasing to be earthbound, as it threw off the shackles of classicism or indeed of realism and naturalism to engage with the new subjects and forms of expression.[51]

Painters went on to explore and extend the inherent qualities of discrete elements in their art. This is what the Scots did with colour, and so made a promising start to the nation's painting of the twentieth century. Perhaps it was coming from such a cold, gloomy country that prompted them to concentrate on that, to subvert the classical use of tone and texture in portrait and landscape, then to react into a blaze of brightness.[52]

The Colourists count as a national school, yet two of them, John Duncan Fergusson and Leslie Hunter, had close links with Glasgow and the west of Scotland. Fergusson was the most public face and voice of the group: 'Everyone in Scotland should refuse to have anything to do with black or dirty and dingy colours, and insist on clean colours in everything. I remember when I was young any colour was considered a sign of vulgarity. Greys and blacks were the only colours for people of taste and refinement... Well! let's forget it, and insist on things in Scotland being of colour that makes for and associates itself with light, hopefulness, health and happiness.'[53] His wife Margaret pioneered modern dance in Scotland, and his exuberant canvas of *Les Eus* is a testimony to them both. Hunter had done the shrewd thing for a youngster in Paris by getting to know Alice Toklas and Gertrude Stein – though then they shocked him by introducing him to the painting of Matisse.[54] Considering what Matisse was achieving at the time with his *Portrait de Madame Matisse* or his *Nu Bleu, souvenir de Biskra,* let alone what Picasso was achieving in his Blue Period and his Rose Period, the Scottish Colourists indeed remained a trifle tame.[55] If they could be confident and vibrant in the use of strong colour, it was still a rather timid range of subjects they chose compared to their French and other continental counterparts – insular landscapes, domestic interiors, fashionable models. And they never ventured into the seamy side of life, as the Parisian impressionists had once been happy to do: no can-can, no absinthe here.

But once home again, the Colourists showed that what they had learned in the paradisal, pre-war Paris might be adapted to a distinctive Scottish idiom. Indeed they transformed the national pictorial traditions. Each in his own style, they redefined the qualities of light and colour in one medium and another. In Scotland, alas, this was by no means a recipe for instant popularity and success. They could not count on much of a sympathetic public to encourage them and buy their paintings, so it was hard for them to earn a living. All the same we can appreciate, a century later, how they renewed the art of their country and made a contribution to the continued autonomy of its figurative achievement.[56] They saw themselves as modern European painters, yet their example of dedication and independence helped the succeeding generations in Scotland to find a way forward in a new world of art without signposts, where it was possible to journey in almost any direction.[57]

The steady material development of the Victorian era fell victim after the First World War to recurrent depression. But it brought a cultural reaction in the shape of the Scottish Renaissance, founded on a feeling that the decline of the nation and its assimilation to the larger United Kingdom had gone on for too long and at too high a price, symbolized by the terrible sacrifices on the battlefields of Europe. Scotland needed to change course, then. Amid the exhaustion of the people, their society and their economy, some necessary impetus might arise from creative spirits. In the event the Renaissance was first and foremost a literary and political movement, bringing a Scottish vernacular voice to the universal concerns of modernism. But it also had an artistic side.[58]

On a personal level, the man today reckoned the leader of the Renaissance, the poet Hugh MacDiarmid, venerated the teacher who had recognized his talents while still a schoolboy at Langholm in Dumfriesshire, F.G. Scott. They met again after the war, and Scott introduced MacDiarmid to the painter William McCance, a graduate of Glasgow School of Art who practised a bold post-impressionism. They shared a belief in their nation, and McCance persuaded MacDiarmid that this belief might be manifested in its art, too. It should no longer be art for a land of the mountain and the flood, but also embrace and align itself with modern movements in Europe – cubist, abstract, mechanistic and so on. Scottish art might then take its place in the vanguard, while in a progressive modern culture developing interests of its own.[59]

MacDiarmid was at this stage of his life a non-stop scribbler, while McCance would during much of his career depend for income on his work as a critic, so the pair of them were ready and eager for intellectual exchange or collaboration. Writing about McCance in 1925 in the *Scottish Educational Journal*, MacDiarmid said they both felt impressed with the 'necessity of coming to terms with the third factor, the Machine, and no longer confining ourselves to the overpast condition of affairs in which only two factors had to be reckoned with, Man and Nature'. The post-war Renaissance in Scotland would entail at once an 'alignment with ultramodern tendencies manifesting themselves internationally' and an 'accord with fundamental elements of distinctive Scottish psychology'. In an acid aside, he conceded that for the time being the cleft between these two aspects remained too wide: 'Let us no longer alienate our engineers from art. Let us advise our sentimentalists in art to migrate to spiritualism or let us equip an expedition for them to explore the possibilities of the Celtic Twilight... let them give up cumbersome paint and canvas and take to photographing fairies on an uninhabited island.'[60] Yet, while England and even France now had decadent cultures, Scotland was poised for renewal, which could indeed start from the huge part played in national life by heavy engineering, in anything from the Forth Bridge to shipbuilding on the Clyde. These feats of technology were the modern works of Scottish art. They promised a culture from which sentimentality was banned while art and science worked in harmony. McCance did not ramble on at MacDiarmid's length, but in essentials he agreed. He voiced similar propositions in an essay, 'The Idea in Art', published in 1930:

In my opinion Scotland is the great white hope of European art... When the Scot can purge himself of the illusion that art is reserved for the sentimentalist and realise that he, the Scot, has a natural gift for construction, combined with a racial aptitude for metaphysical thought and a deep emotional nature, then out of this combination can arise an art which will be pregnant with Idea and will have within it the seeds of greatness. Beside the awareness of this potentiality, however, the Scot must break through his narrow provincial barriers and gain a knowledge of what is actually taking place in the world.[61]

Fergusson at length also came to join this cultural constellation, but it took till the 1940s for him and MacDiarmid to collaborate on the journal *Scottish Art and Letters*. MacDiarmid also wrote a long essay, *Aesthetics in Scotland,* which owed a great deal to Fergusson (completed in 1950, it did not get published till 1981, once Alan Bold discovered it in the poet's papers after his death). Again, it showed both artists sharing some significant attitudes. In particular, they held the great ships of the Clyde to be products of skill in the dignity of co-operative labour, the modernist equivalent of a medieval cathedral as the collective artwork of anonymous craftsmen.[62]

The way things had stood by the First World War, the best Scotland could show in the way of modern painting was the work of the Glasgow Boys. But Fergusson felt forced to the conclusion that they finally failed the test of their times, fading out as a force in Scottish art because they never surmounted the academic conservatism ruling the roost at home. The task for a younger generation was not just to emulate the scene in Paris but also to inspire fresh artistic achievement in Scotland. A love of colour and its skilful manipulation remained with Fergusson for the rest of his life, as did the use of rhythmic line he absorbed from his wife Margaret Morris as a pioneer of modern dance. But he was something more than a Colourist, too. He came to share modernist concerns found right across Europe, especially the need to get on terms with the mechanistic civilization in which contemporary art had to function. He gave evidence of this in his *Damaged Destroyer* (1918), housed today at Kelvingrove, half industrial scene, half geometric abstraction. He later summed up his endeavour: 'The modern movement in art was an attempt to get down to truths, to fundamentals, and start afresh to create a free art, or an art freed from the academic imbecilities which at that time dominated the world.'[63]

Fergusson resumed his contacts with the European avant-garde once he returned to France after 1918. This was where he would spend most time for the next two decades, often clad in just a dookie on the Côte d'Azur. He said he 'decided to persist in being what I considered an artist, and a Scots artist, and the art atmosphere and the painting I was surrounded with in Scotland, in my opinion, were not Scots at all'. Scottish art now had tasks beyond the traditional landscapes and portraits: 'The new goal for the modern artist was to find ways of expressing the interior life.'[64] While pursuing this programme in France, Fergusson also returned home from time to time, if to a rather bemused public.

Today the two poles round which Fergusson's art revolved can be observed in the museum set aside for it in 1992 at Perth, in the county from which his family originally hailed. In the exquisite classical rotunda (1830) by Adam Anderson, first built for the city's waterworks, the collection is displayed on two floors. On the ground floor are works from Fergusson the modernizing Scottish painter, such as the female portraits – *Le Manteau Chinois, Hat with the Pink Scarf* and the like – restrained if falling far short of glum. There are landscapes too, tending towards abstraction though in a vivid way, which might have disconcerted the original viewers used to more sombre Highland scenes; here for the nation was a modest bounce into cultural modernity. But on the upper floor of the gallery at Perth we emerge into the sunlight of Provence, as it falls on the shades of pink and gold of female flesh stretched out amid exuberant vegetation. Fergusson had in fact been painting nudes since the turn of the century. Often on a large scale, they became, in a manner novel in Scottish art, almost his central subject matter. That might have been all very well for France but it would never do in Scotland, where at first he kept this impulse under wraps.[65]

But Fergusson was able to renew his modernizing mission at home after he returned at the outbreak of the Second World War. Himself a Leither by birth, he chose Glasgow as his place of retirement because of its tradition of heavy engineering, because it was a Celtic city and because it did not suffer from what he saw as the stultifying artistic tradition in Edinburgh, dominated by the academies. He wrote: 'It is not natural for them [Glaswegians] to be academic. What we would like to see is West Coast Glasgow art in the same class as the Queen Elizabeth [the liner launched on the Clyde in 1938].'[66]

Once back, Fergusson and his wife found a number of people with whom to make common cause. Repelled by the existing Glasgow Art Club because it would not admit women, he established the New Art Club in 1940 for discussion and exhibition. Out of it grew the New Scottish Group of artists, which held an annual show from 1943 to 1948 and again in the 1950s.[67] One of the group was William Crosbie, a surrealist somewhat tamed by the public art commissioned from him, his murals for the Empire Exhibition (1938) and for the police headquarters (1940). Having accepted the principle that an artist must engage with the realities of his culture at large, he worked with Margaret in designing theatrical sets for the Celtic Ballet she founded in 1947. She had the unsettling habit of leading her students out from her studio in Blythswood Square to dance barefoot in the gardens. This was all the same congenial to a Glasgow that in cultural terms defied the austerity of wartime and its aftermath, as it did in other spheres with the inauguration of the Cosmo Cinema in 1939, the Unity Theatre in 1941 and the Citizens' Theatre in 1943. The publisher Bill McLellan, nationalist and socialist, was an important ally of Glasgow's artists and poets: he brought out editions of the poetry of Hugh MacDiarmid and of Sorley MacLean, among others, while Crosbie designed his dust-jackets. Fergusson was in his element here. All the same, though he enjoyed some recognition, his personal circumstances did not match it: he sold seldom and never made enough to live off his art.

In 1943, McLellan also published Fergusson's book, *Modern Scottish Painting*. It revealed an author somewhat beleaguered but not letting this get him down. After all, no other Scottish painter of the twentieth century gathered and put on paper his thoughts, beliefs or commitments to art and politics (nationalist politics at that). Each chapter prompts variations on a central theme of painting and freedom – freedom from the tyranny of academic authority, artistic conventions and social priorities, freedom also from political pressures to conform in the British state. Fergusson's belief in Scottish independence runs right through these pages (not in its time a formula for a wide or appreciative readership). But for him the appeal lay in a link with artistic modernism, because both entailed renewal. To Fergusson's mind all this had to be articulated, as in his book, and not just practised: in no other way could conceptual progress start winning a public for modernism.[68]

Modern Scottish Painting appeared in the same year as Hugh MacDiarmid's autobiography, *Lucky Poet: A Self-Study in Literature and Political Ideas*, and Sorley Maclean's *Dàin do Eimhir*, which showed Gaelic poetry could be modernist too, even from within its own traditions. Taken together, these three books signal points of reference for a regenerate Scotland: Fergusson, MacDiarmid and MacLean might be seen together as artists whose shared vision of the nation has ever since nourished and inspired its cultural and political life. In furtherance of that project Fergusson's manifesto could be only a start, since there were few institutional or any other arrangements to rally Scotland's artists to a common cause. But for Glasgow in particular, it is perhaps not far-fetched to trace a path of development that fulfilled the new ideals he set, with painting as part of a modernist vision for Scottish culture, while also representing the people's dignity amid so much physical and social deprivation.[69]

These ideals did appeal to a younger generation in Glasgow,

among them Joan Eardley, who graduated from the School of Art in 1943. In her paintings and drawings she achieved sympathy without sentimentality, while depicting patience, endurance and even suffering. These gave an exceptional quality to her images of street children in the city and the nearby industrial towns, Greenock and Port Glasgow. In *Back Street Bookie* (1952), she seeks some deeper quality to a typical scene of life in the slums, though her human figures get somewhat lost in the formal arrangement of the picture. *Children, Port Glasgow* (1955) is more ambitious and successful. The colours of the ragged clothes – greys, browns and reds – together with their flat treatment and uneven outlines express the kids' impish vitality. It is reflected in the surroundings, so as to create out of the ensemble an urban habitat realistic in spirit if not in the actual image. In later pictures Eardley integrated other elements, including graffiti and collage, while adopting a freer technique enhanced by rich colour. These are pictures with a strong social inspiration, yet not idealist: they celebrate individuality in a setting where it might not be expected to flourish. The critic Cordelia Oliver observed that for Eardley 'a truly successful painting had to go deeper than a mere visual record, no matter how accurate... Her success lay in her ability to combine the acute, uncompromising painter's eye with a warm human sympathy and understanding.'[70]

Glasgow School of Art has remained Scotland's finest educational institution in its field, and one of the leaders in Europe. Much of the subsequent work in setting and maintaining its exemplary standards fell to Sandy Moffat, who was appointed to the staff in the 1970s and by 1998 had become head of painting. The best known of his own pictures is *Poet's Pub* (1980), which shows MacDiarmid, Maclean and half a dozen others engaged in their favourite activity apart from literary composition: drinking. Moffat was generous to rising generations of painters. He is himself a realist, but that did not stop him encouraging a range of dramatic and original innovations, especially by a group dubbed the New Glasgow Boys. Its novelty lay in its general challenge to the prevailing abstract and conceptualist trends in European art; it revived the figurative and narrative, without being bound by older traditions. The canvases often attained a large scale, borrowing from fantasy and myth to leaven the realities of contemporary life and thought. The most prominent of these painters were Steven Campbell, Ken Currie, Peter Howson and Adrian Wiszniewski.[71]

Steven Campbell forged his reputation during the early 1980s in New York, where he went immediately following his graduation from Glasgow. He had made a late start as an artist, after leaving school at sixteen to get his first job in the steelworks at Cambuslang. Only a decade later did he enter Glasgow School of Art, but he soon made up for lost time. It was a period there, during the late 1970s, of intense ideological and aesthetic debate, that made exceptional creative work possible. The energetic and hard-working Campbell took full advantage, producing a body of work that went well beyond the student norm. His degree show met, however, with a mixture of incredulity and hostility. Undaunted, he made the decision to leave for New York, where his career took off in sensational fashion. Having exhibited all over the United States and Europe, he surprised everybody by coming home to Glasgow in 1987. He said: 'I wanted to give myself more space coming back to Scotland... In New York it was all happening so fast. You could get yourself in an awful mess.' His return reconnected his native city with the international avant-garde. A flamboyant, even outlandish figure, Campbell looked as if he had arrived from the Paris or Vienna of the late nineteenth century. His paintings – crowded, colourful canvases – were spaces or theatres of the mind where the viewer would meet and experience bizarre utopias and dystopias.[72]

Peter Howson, who studied at the School of Art from 1975 to 1979, seeks to use the rhetoric of historical painting, problematic though this has become. Scotland after all had had few cultural links with the hotbed of this kind of art during the early twentieth century – the Soviet Union, in its efforts to idealize the proletariat. In Glasgow, it can be hard to separate the proletarian from the degraded, at least if the individual is also to be separated from the historical, as Howson wishes. He looks for inspiration in the streets of the city and its working-class masculinity. A striking example is *The Heroic Dosser* (1987), an ambiguous figure isolated and burdened, yet proud, strong and defiant. Still, there are places other than Scotland that bring out with greater force the human condition of steadfastness amid tragedy. Howson found as much when in 1992 he received a commission from the Imperial War Museum in London to be an official artist for the conflicts in the former Yugoslavia. In Bosnia-Herzegovina he produced some of his most shocking and controversial work, not flinching at the atrocities of a savage civil war – as in his paintings of *Plum Grove* (1994) with its grisly pastiche of a crucifixion, and *Croatian and Muslim* (1994) with its explicit images of rape; this the museum refused to accept for being too brutal.[73] Pain has been a prime force in Howson's life and work. He felt it during a traumatic childhood and responded to it in adulthood via the typical Glaswegian defensive mechanisms of drink and drugs. At last, in 2000, he found solace in conversion to Christianity. In subsequent work, spiritual change appears as the answer to the questions of existence for his rebellious, immoderate or eccentric subjects.

Ken Currie graduated from the School of Art in 1983. He is if anything even more political, again often in an intense, powerful and provocative manner. There is at the same time another side to him, drawing aesthetic inspiration from the European tradition of portraiture. Old Masters such as Velazquez, Goya and David fascinate Currie, and his own work has often recalled them. At his best he has been able to produce the haunting, luminous painting *Three Oncologists* (2002) and a searing nude self-portrait, *Unfamiliar Reflection* (2006). Just as important, he had while still a student

discovered the socially committed realist painting of Otto Dix
and George Grosz, who worked in Germany during the doomed
Weimar Republic, and of Diego Rivera, who developed the genre
of public murals depicting the everyday life of the Mexican people.
Currie's own paintings in this vein deal with matters of working-
class solidarity and self-improvement, but also bring out his
despair at contemporary conditions; Glasgow offers ample subject
matter. In 1987, he received a commission to paint a memorial
ceiling of eight panels at the People's Palace. It was a while since
much by way of historical painting had been produced in Glasgow,
least of all anything of a socialist interpretation. This was itself,
however, deeply problematic: moved by the revolutions in Eastern
Europe from 1989, Currie began to depict decaying and damaged
bodies as a response to what he felt was the universal sickness
of modern society.[74]

We must not imagine the New Glasgow Boys to be a uniform
group, however. In contrast to their habitual figurative grimness
stands the work of Adrian Wiszniewski, who trained at the School
of Art from 1979 to 1983. He soon shot to prominence with huge,
exuberant paintings at once redolent of fantasy or myth and
attuned to modern life or thought. With him we pass from the
dark and contorted suffering of Howson's or Currie's muscular
human images into a bright and colourful world of almost
Arcadian serenity. Here ideal youthful figures pose in surreal,
dream-like landscapes full of kaleidoscopic colours and symbolic
objects. Wiszniewski does not confine the harmony of his creative
optimism to painting. From the outset he had a versatile career,
taking a hand in everything from the design of parking garages to
multi-media events to writing novels. His best-known work is the
mixture of neon lighting and oil on canvas that forms *Gentleman's
Club* (2005) in the atrium of the Gallery of Modern Art. After
that he worked with the Scottish Philharmonic Orchestra in the
production of a musical narrative *The Girl, the Boy and the Hag*

(2007), as well as illustrating a book of the show. He brings the same creative energy to printmaking, sculpture, furniture and even wallpaper, while exploring new media as a central means of communication. He reminds us that, bleak as Glasgow might be at times, it is also a city where, in reaction, original spirits feel they must take wing.[75]

Indeed, in artistic terms Glasgow has defined itself it by transcending its harsher realities. As on the global scale one industrial revolution succeeds another, many cities fall into phases of decay. The best seek to recover. Some may do it by meretricious means, which has to some extent been true of Glasgow too. It has not treated its built environment well, and the buildings that remind us this was one of the finest Victorian cities are also the survivors of massive destruction. Glaswegians, once self-conscious about their slummy environment, now see how the remaining older buildings can still offer examples of elegance, construction and durability hard to find in their successors. It could well be argued that modernism has helped to liberate the city from its inferiority complexes. In its School of Art, Glasgow possesses one of the finest such institutions in the world, now more than a century old and today rising from the ashes of a disastrous fire of 2014. The city has less confidence about architecture, but its urban history and its openness to international contacts create future scope for renewal of the typical Glaswegian combination of swagger and style.

10

Imagination:
'An occupied country'

ON JULY 25, 1916, a young soldier from Glasgow, William Bryce, had a welcome break from the hardship and tedium of his life as a prisoner of war at the huge camp of Sennelager, near Paderborn in Westphalia. That day, he was summoned before two professors of English from Berlin, Alois Brandl and Wilhelm Doegen. Brandl was Germany's greatest expert on Shakespeare, Doegen a specialist in language, with a particular interest in phonetics. The German community of *Anglisten*, as their academic colleagues dubbed them, had felt excited by the arrival on their soil of so many prisoners (in the end 185,000 of them) from the British Isles. Most were captured in the early weeks of the First World War, as Kaiser Wilhelm II's armies broke through on the western front and advanced to the gates of Paris before being brought to a halt. Linguistic fieldwork was always an expensive business, but now the professors could exploit at no cost, for as long as the prisoners' detention lasted, a huge fund of evidence for their researches. Doegen came to Sennelager in pursuit of a personal project of recording – on newly invented phonological equipment – a particular biblical passage in as many dialects of the English language as possible (the results of which are today housed in the *Berliner Lautarchiv*, the Berlin

Sound Archive). The passage was the parable of the prodigal son,
Luke 5:11–32, and here is Bryce's rendition in his native dialect of
the first few verses:

> There was a man whae hed twa sons. The youngest o them
> said tae his faither, 'Gie me that pairt o yer guids that belangs
> to me.' So the faither gied him his share. No mony days
> efterwards, the young man gaithered aa his belangins together
> and went awa in'ae a faur country. There he wasted aa that he
> hed. When he hed spent aa thing, a great famine cam owre
> the country, and he began tae be in waant. Before lang he
> hed tae tak ony work he could get in'ae, and wes gled when
> he funn a man wi a place in that country. This man sent him
> in'ae the fields tae look efter the pigs. He had nae place tae
> sleep in. He saw ithers at their meals, but had naethin himsel
> tae eat. Mony a time he would hae been gled tae fill his belly
> wi the husks that he fed the pigs wi, but even sic food his
> maister begrudged him.

Bryce was twenty-five years old, a Protestant and a professional
soldier, according to the note on him in the German records:
'His mother tongue is Scots, views his learning of English as an
"additional language". Both parents from Glasgow.' But to my ear
his accent does not sound all that close to the Glaswegian of the
twenty-first century. It lacks the sing-song intonation that is often
supposed to have been introduced by Irish immigrants but that
had evidently not arrived by 1916, if we may judge from him. His
speech includes the infamous glottal stop, but it is infrequent: in
the passage quoted it affects only the consonant cluster of 'intae',
as I have marked it in my transcription. Of course we do not know
how far he was on his best linguistic behaviour, so to speak, in
performing for a pair of German professors. But altogether his
recitation would present only minor difficulties for a listener

accustomed to any other dialect of the English language – quite unlike, then, today's Weegie.[1]

Much of the history of this Glaswegian dialect has gone unrecorded. Its origins lie generally in the language of west central Scotland, which evolved inside the city as speakers of other dialects migrated there, as it developed its own slang and as standard English became the lingua franca for a trading community's contacts with the outside world. But the earliest known reference to Glaswegian dialect as such dates only from 1897, when the writer George MacDonald briefly referred to it in a letter to the Norwegian linguist, Johann Sturm.[2] The material in the *Berliner Lautarchiv* is therefore of immense value because it gives us not an attempt at written representation, but the actual sound of the dialect during a crucial stage.

The Glaswegian dialect was already looked down on as the language of the lowest classes, whose habits of speech matched their degraded social station inside a grim industrial system. The city's own children sat in classrooms being instructed in proper English, but it inspired few of them to adapt their way of speaking. While Glasgow has changed for the better in the twentieth century, its working class has still been diagnosed, on the evidence of teachers and employers, as suffering from linguistic insecurity. Young Glaswegians are said to become self-conscious and tongue-tied in the presence of figures of authority; even amid recent change towards greater linguistic egalitarianism, they can find it hard to get themselves taken seriously or treated with respect outside their own milieu. Whether this produces a sense of anxiety or of outrage depends on personality and occasion. It is a problem always likely when individuals need to operate beyond the community in which they normally live.[3]

The dialect has anyway continued to flourish at its own level and on its own terms. Some linguistic scientists believe Glasgow to be the source of the glottal stop today so common in urban British

English. Alongside it, the dialect has developed a peculiar quality of voice 'with phonetically slack articulation, jaw protrusion and harsh phonation'. It may be associated 'with the unwashed and the violent', but in fictional characters such as Rab C. Nesbitt it has been a positive advertisement for Glasgow.[4] A third aspect of this linguistic evolution is the much more frequent use of expletives, so that the grossest words have tended to lose their vigour and turn into mere adverbial intensifiers, leaving an originally milder term like 'wanker' to carry the full force of the user's anger or contempt. It is the complexity and punch of spoken Glaswegian that have today begun to rescue it from the disdain in which it was once held. As the posh Received Pronunciation of English loses its former prestige and supremacy in the British state, so the validity of other varieties has been asserted. In particular, humour is a help to broader acceptance of Glaswegian. The trend started with Stanley Baxter's 'Parliamo Glasgow' and continues through Billy Connolly to Kevin Bridges.

'Glaswegians do not speak English,' declared the sociologist Sean Damer in 1989.[5] If the extent of a language is defined by the degree to which users of different origins understand one another, then indeed Glaswegians do not speak English. They fully understand people from England or North America because of exposure to their dialects in radio, television or film. Yet those people often cannot understand Glaswegians, and when these appear on the small screen south of the border they may need to be dubbed. There are similar cases of Scots dialects, notably the Doric of Buchan. But that is a conservative dialect, which has resisted sound-changes carried through elsewhere in English and has retained a wide range of its historic vocabulary. Glaswegian is on the other hand a progressive dialect, an urban argot constantly inventing new words or expressions, and in pronunciation continuing its rapid advance from the kind of language spoken by William Bryce a century ago. For example, today kids consider it cool to say

'A fink' for 'I think', in place of the older Glaswegian 'A hink'. And they replace the trilled final Scots r by a gaping ah, which with a glottal stop results in 'bel'ah' (or 'bew'ah', since the l is often vocalized too) for 'belter', a term of approbation. These may once again be influences ultimately from England, transmitted through the broadcast media, though they still do not seem to have made Glaswegian any easier to understand for outsiders.

But once a language also generates a literature it can surely claim respect from other cultural communities. Over the last century this is in fact what Glaswegian has done. The origins of the development might be traced even further back. The Scottish novel first won international recognition with the works of Sir Walter Scott, a Borderer resident in Edinburgh. But he was only the most conspicuous and celebrated member of a school of novelists that had flourished from the middle of the eighteenth century. They appeared in different parts of the country too, though Glasgow and the west of Scotland were somewhat underrepresented. Still, the leading writer from the region, John Galt, is a rewarding one.[6]

Galt has a narrower focus than Scott in the material he chooses to write about – but for all that gives us, in thin disguise, real places and real changes in a real nation. It irked him to see how Edinburgh had won the epithet of Athens of the North, and he tried to create a fashion for calling Glasgow the Venice of the North; somehow this never caught on. A native of Irvine, his interest lay rather in the hinterland of the west of Scotland as it underwent the industrial revolution (in his time still in large part also a rural phenomenon). He grew up in Greenock, and finally retired there. Still, Glasgow itself – 'that opulent metropolis of the muslin manufacturers' – never ceased to astonish him.[7]

In Galt's fiction Glasgow still remained a rather distant presence, however. He did not go to live in the city till he was over forty, after several false starts to his career, with a spell in London and foreign travels thrown in. He had good political contacts and earned

money as a lobbyist for several causes, from the completion of the
Union Canal across the central belt of Scotland to compensation
for the United Empire Loyalists, many of them Scots, who had
defended Canada from American aggression in the war of 1812.
He also found the time to write his novels, and by 1826 had
published ten of them. The best were *Annals of the Parish* (1821),
The Ayrshire Legatees (1821), *The Provost* (1822) and *The Entail*
(1822). He depicted their various milieux realistically, including
the use by his characters of the local vernacular.[8]

If Glasgow does appear in its own guise in these novels, it rather
forms part of a general social and cultural background. The narrator
of *Annals of the Parish*, the Revd Micah Balwhidder, minister of a
village in Ayrshire, proudly tells us he mastered moral philosophy
at college in Glasgow during the 1750s (when Adam Smith was
teaching there) – though later he is worsted in debate by self-taught
young weavers who out of their meagre earnings subscribe to a
newspaper from London so as to follow the progress of the French
Revolution.[9] At the opening of *The Entail,* Glasgow comes more
vividly to life as the setting for accumulation of the wealth that
will be invested in land outside the city and later cause harrowing
conflicts. Yet this is still the Glasgow of the eighteenth century,
where a wealthy merchant vaunts himself on 'his carefulness, his
assiduity, his parsimony, his very honesty'.[10]

Here we approach one of the great mysteries of Scottish literature:
its failure to engage with the realities of industrial society as Dickens
did in his England, Balzac did in his France and Dostoyevsky did
in his Russia. Each of these countries underwent profound change,
thrusting on their novelists subject matter unknown to previous
generations. The novelists responded with literature of the highest
distinction. Scotland's classical novelists, led by John Galt in the
west together with Walter Scott and James Hogg in the east, had
actually preceded those European figures, and anticipated them in
presenting big themes – which in their artistic forms, of language

and content, remained unmistakably Scottish all the same. Just like the classical Scottish school of painting, however, this literature belonged to an age drawing to a close, 'the last purely Scotch age', as Henry Cockburn called it.[11] In the following period Scotland would be transformed internally and externally, in its own society and in its relations with the outside world. This momentous process deserved a literary expression of its own, and in similar advancing societies it found one. But in Scotland, while Scottishness did persist in literature, the concern with big themes faded away.

It may seem far-fetched to blame any linguistic problem, but Scotland did have one. Those other nations nurturing great authors – England, France, Russia – faced nothing of the kind. Their languages were just there as a natural medium for expression of all the huge challenges their modernizing societies needed to face, and the working out of those challenges in individual lives. In Scotland things took another turn. The poet Edwin Muir, a reluctant Glaswegian from the age of fourteen, would in the 1930s look back and lament that, for the Scots, modernity had brought about a fatal disjunction of heart and head.[12] The language in which they couched their most personal and intimate thoughts was not the same as the language in which they conducted systematic thinking or addressed the public. Even if the two languages turned out on analysis to be in reality similar, they still left a feeling that they ought somehow to be different: that English would never be the language in which a Scotsman or Scotswoman could best express love or fear or hope or despair, but that Scots was no longer the language in which they could depict great events, cast profound thoughts or win an intellectual argument.

One of Walter Scott's achievements was that he found at least a provisional solution to this linguistic problem, without which a national literature might no longer have been possible. If not a wholly satisfactory solution, it worked for him and for many other Scottish authors. During the eighteenth century they had written in English, with the exception of subversive poets such as Allan Ramsay and Robert Burns. By the end of the Enlightenment, Scottish prose had become, well, prosy. It needed enlivening for the genre Scott invented, the historical novel. The convention established by him, and almost universally followed since, was that while dialogue could go into Scots, narrative should go into English. It would prove a useful convention not only for historical novels but also for later realistic novels of the contemporary world, because in their everyday lives the Scottish people continued to speak one language to family, friends and workmates, another to strangers, to authority and, not least, to God. The deity might originally have revealed himself in Hebrew or in Greek, but to Scots he first did so in English. They had to make of that what they would.[13]

Yet it has been shown that, even as the domain of literary English expanded and literacy in it rose, a wealth of material in Scots continued to appear. It was the language Lowlanders actually spoke, and it needed only the right means to be transformed from a spoken tongue into written prose. As technological advance revolutionized communications, the printed word turned abundant and cheap. Once, about the only book to be found in every Scots household was the Bible, but now a huge range of other works became available; if there was no time to read books, the popular press could fill idle moments. By the end of the century there were more than 200 newspapers in Scotland, some also carrying articles in vernacular Scots. In this way a whole novel, William Alexander's *Johnny Gibb of Gushetneuk*, first appeared in instalments in the *Aberdeen Free Press*, before being published as a regular book in 1871. In Glasgow no newspaper seems to have attempted anything so ambitious, but material in Scots did appear in a satirical magazine, *The Bailie*, in a comic, *The Chiel*, in Alexander Petrie's *Glasgow Clincher* (in essence a vehicle for eccentric self-advertisement) and in the radical *Glasgow Weekly Mail*. Generally, however, it is local reference in the content rather than anything in the language itself that identifies the material as specifically Glaswegian.[14]

As for books in Scotland, it was no longer left to the learned alone to write and read them. Instead the option of cheap, popular editions heralded the literary era of the kailyard, named after the vernacular term for a cabbage-patch. It took shape in unchallenging stories about local, usually rustic matters. They featured a cast of predictable individuals playing out parodies of the Scottish character, from which their rather repugnant virtues emerged invariably affirmed. A number of the authors were Presbyterian ministers, notably the Revd John Watson writing under the pseudonym of Ian Maclaren, secure in a wealthy expatriate charge in Liverpool, whence he produced in 1894 a volume of which the very title is redolent of the kailyard school, *Beside the Bonnie Brier Bush*. This and its other products were, despite their innocent air, carefully packaged and then heavily promoted by William Robertson Nicholl, Gladstonian Liberal and former minister of the Free Church, latterly editor of the *British Weekly*. He viewed the kailyard as a force for 'tenderness, for purity, for a higher standard of life'.[15] No tension, then, no tragedy – and this in Scotland!

Still, perhaps the kailyard cannot be written off quite so easily.[16] We may note that a writer of quite different aspirations, Robert Louis Stevenson, was on good terms with a couple of its authors, J.M. Barrie and S.R. Crockett. After receiving a collection of the latter's stories on Samoa, Stevenson sent back saying what delight he felt at 'being *drowned* in Scotland, they have refreshed me like a visit home'.[17] If they had been false to the nation, he was at least gentleman enough not to say so. Without making any great claims for the literary abilities of money-spinning Presbyterian ministers, we might see in their works some dim reflection of certain problems of the time: at least, say, the growing challenge to religion, the decline of rural Scotland, the questioning of traditional authority, the gradual atrophy of self-regulating communities. Stevenson himself developed certain of the typical themes in his works. Behind both *Thrawn Janet* (1887) and *The Master of Ballantrae* (1889) lies a warped community of malicious gossips, or dour Calvinists turning into tormented zealots. In *Kidnapped* (1886) and *Catriona* (1893) we get quite a romantic picture of the Highlands, yet one undermined by the revelations of far from romantic double-dealing and cruelty.

While Stevenson was seeking to live out a tropical idyll on Samoa, a young Scotsman unknown to him, George Douglas Brown, had embarked on his studies at Balliol College, Oxford. Brown got there not on account of any social privilege: in fact he was the illegitimate son of a farmer from Ochiltree in Ayrshire and an Irish prostitute. He made it to Oxford because he was so clever, and afterwards he went to London to start on the chancy business of freelance journalism. In the midst of these time-consuming and often dispiriting labours he suddenly produced an extraordinary novel, *The House with the Green Shutters* (1901). It was the sort of *succès de scandale* that might have launched a literary career, except there was to be no career: Brown died a premature death the same year.[18]

Brown starts like any author of the kailyard with a small town where life seems safe and predictable, scarcely touched by modernity.[19] Here at Barbie (actually Ochiltree) there is a father, John Gourlay, proud and taciturn. There is a son, also John, insecure, neurotic and in the event unable to live up to the father's expectations. At home are a cowed wife and daughter who take refuge in novelettes or daydreaming. Outside they all become the object of spiteful comments and petty machinations from envious and idle villagers. Crisis arrives with a commercial competitor who proves hard for Gourlay to match. Instead he invests his hopes and his money in his son. Young John, however, is driven to drink by his inability to cope with life at the University of Glasgow. Tension mounts and in the end he accidentally kills his father. It is a melodramatic story, remarkable for having no pleasant characters at all. Even so it came across as the first truthful picture of Scottish provincial life since Galt's, and lit a fuse to the falsities of the kailyard. Indeed all the familiar conventions get destabilized, carted on to Brown's scene only to be upended. In place of make-believe we have savage parody, in place of hackneyed human relationships only grotesque and disturbing ones, in place of comforting social values others dealing destruction, in place of Christianity a lack of existential hope. There is nothing comforting here, only an utter lack of compromise.[20]

The book leaves us wanting to read more from the hand of a remarkable literary talent. Brown wrote to a friend from Balliol, the political scientist Ernest Barker, with a criticism of his own novel which is hard to fault: 'Well, I suppose you have read the Green Shutters by this time. 'Tis a brutal and bloody work; too sinister, I should think, for a man of your kindlier disposition. There is too much black for the white in it. Even so it is more complimentary to Scotland, I think, than the sentimental slop of Barrie, and Crockett, and Maclaren. It was antagonism to their method that made me embitter the blackness.'[21]

We can trace other connections from the kailyard to a successor literature that began to develop fresh variants on familiar themes. Brown's John Gourlay junior can, for example, be compared to the Eochan of George MacDougall Hay's *Gillespie* (1914), much more of a modern novel: both these youthful anti-heroes are alienated from family and community, uncertain of their identities and feeling their talents stifled under the limitations of their culture, society and country. Romantic history again yields to divided and hypocritical loyalties in Violet Jacob's *Flemington* (1911) and in some of the earlier fiction of John Buchan. The twentieth century that gave us, on television too, *Dr Finlay's Casebook* and *Para Handy* could hardly complain of the quality of Scottish culture it had inherited.[22]

What precisely was it, then, that had failed in the nation's literature? Perhaps for structural reasons, in the nature of the literary market rather than the quality of the literary product, Scotland was already being suffocated by the imposition of British norms. That body of fiction published in serial form in provincial newspapers did deal with realistic themes in Scottish life, especially urban life. But the very manner of the publication made this literature ephemeral, compared to the now-established British mechanisms for production of the novel.[23] At the same time, there can be no doubt about the genuine popularity of the kailyard. When Brown set out to destroy it, his originality lay in unsettling an unspoken convention between novelist and reader that time should stand still while representative Scots interacted in finally reassuring situations. Yet the greatest writers of Scottish fiction, Scott, Hogg, Galt and Stevenson, did not give us a static Scotland, or one limited by any pandering to their audience. Rather they took fictions that they knew would challenge their readers, so these might out of the encounter change their ideas about their country.[24] It was a high standard for successors to live up to, and the general state of Scottish culture did not always favour it – then or now.

Scotland never really began to find a full-throated literary voice again till after the First World War – perhaps in this branch of the national culture, too, a shock on such a vast and terrible scale was needed for that to happen.[25] Glasgow came more to the fore in two connected ways, in a kind of urban kailyard and then in a quest for proletarian authenticity.

It is true that Buchan, son of a minister of the Free Church of Scotland in Gorbals, was not given to the sentimental excesses of his rustic predecessors. There is always a spare and sinewy quality to his prose that makes his stories rattle along at a cracking pace: he never bores his readers. At the same time, the three novels he wrote with a background in Glasgow – *Huntingtower* (1922), *Castle Gay* (1930) and *The House of the Four Winds* (1935), all these involving Dickson McCunn and the Gorbals Diehards – show a degree of indulgence to the couthy qualities of the locals. McCunn appears as a reluctant hero, a retired grocer, down to earth and dogged, who in *Huntingtower* ventures forth from a settled existence to explore the big wide world. He is at once swept out of his petty bourgeois rut into adventures he had never dreamed of. To others' surprise this normal and modest man turns formidable and dangerous. He forges an alliance with the Gorbals Diehards, a group of six lads from the slums of Glasgow who have gone on a camping holiday and discovered something amiss at Huntingtower, so setting the adventure in motion. Wee Jaikie, the youngest, has won the respect of his older pals because he is so ferocious with his fists. He displays an ominous foible: when other boys weep it is a signal that they have lost the will to fight, but when Jaikie weeps, it means that he has only just begun to fight. There are further typical Scots characters in the broad spectrum of social classes and backgrounds that Buchan gives us. By the end of the story they have all bonded to fight for a common purpose, out of belief in right and wrong, and allegiance to Scotland. McCunn finally says to the Diehards:

> You're the grandest lot of wee laddies I ever heard tell of, and, forbye, you've saved my life. Now, I'm getting on in years, though you'll admit that I'm not that dead old, and I'm not a poor man, and I haven't chick or child to look after. None of you has ever had a proper chance or been right fed or educated or taken care of. I've just the one thing to say to you. From now on you're *my* bairns, every one of you. You're fine laddies, and I'm going to see that you turn into fine men.[26]

Here is a symbolic voice in praise of the sterling qualities Scots had always shown in adversity, not least during their terrible experiences of war. What would be the response? For those seeking an answer to that question there was a basic problem of inarticulacy in a dour popular culture that, if it rose above comforting fictions, might

only reach as far as the ranting Presbyterian sermon. Bourgeois
writers would need to exert themselves to give vent to any deeper
sentiment from below, and might not fully succeed.[27]

A previous chapter made reference to *No Mean City* (1935) by
the journalists H. Kingsley Long and Alexander McArthur (see
page 279), but that is perhaps a little too lurid for the present
discussion. The same year saw the publication of *The Shipbuilders*
by George Blake – also the work of a journalist, with the precision
of a good reporter. It extends its range over the conflicts of loyalties
that social class can impose, here in particular between two
characters, Leslie Pagan, former military officer and now director
of a failing shipyard, and one of his employees, Danny Shields,
who had also been his batman during the war. The relationship
does not always read well. The boss admires his workers, but an
overdrawn contrast between proletarian loyalty to city, nation,
class or craft and the capitalist's 'desertion, betrayal, surrender'
can fail to convince: in fact it verges on the sentimental. Later
Blake pleaded 'guilty to an insufficient knowledge of working-class
life and to the adoption of a middle-class attitude to the theme
of industrial conflict and despair'.[28] He had castigated the older
literary tradition, but here he almost transferred the kailyard to the
shipyard. The true virtues of the book lay in the author's love of
the sheer scale of Glasgow's industry and of the stirring history
behind it. Here he set precedents for the urban mythology
developed later in the century by Alasdair Gray, just as he set
them for William McIlvanney and James Kelman in his social
descriptions and in his criticism of Scotland's effete elites.

The couthy school of urban kailyard continues along its own path
down to the present, where there are still no end of books wallowing
in the sentimental side of life along the River Clyde, from *Ra Wee
Book a' Glesca Banter* (2012) to *Ten's a Crowd: The Heartwarming
Story of a Glasgow Family* (2015). This genre no doubt has a way to
go yet. At the opposite pole of literary ambition, the problem had

long ago emerged of finding the right standpoint and voice for proletarian authenticity. If bourgeois writers were to wander among the workers, they ran the risk of sounding patronizing. An ideal solution might be to discover a son of the people who nevertheless had the necessary skills to wend his way in a literary world not of his making. It was a demanding job description, which even after the Second World War met only a halting response. Edward Gaitens then appeared, a solitary youngster who found a patron in James Bridie, director of the Citizens' Theatre. Gaitens gave his admirers what they wanted in terms of scenes of the rough, tough life led by his characters in *The Dance of the Apprentices* (1948). They were also endowed with something Glaswegian writers often insist on in their depictions of the working class: the democratic intellect, to use the term first formulated by Walter Elliot, MP for Kelvingrove and later secretary of state for Scotland, when describing the national heritage in 1932.[29] It means that learning and art should not be confined to an elite but also be available and familiar to ordinary Scots who have a much harsher existence, all as the basis for an authentic national culture. In literature as in life it was a difficult ideal – and Gaitens dried up after a couple of books that were in essence collections of short stories.

It took till 1966 for a full-fledged proletarian novel of Glasgow to appear. Archie Hind's *The Dear Green Place* is a passionate account of a working-class man's desire to become a writer in defiance of all his personal and social problems. It is clearly in part autobiographical. Hind left school at the age of fourteen for a job in a factory, where his mates dubbed him Trotsky for the rigour of his communist convictions. There is a socialist-realist start to *The Dear Green Place*, an exact description and definition of the material facts that condition the background, which will be renewed from time to time as the plot unfolds, even in such an unlovely setting as a slaughterhouse. Hind's hero, Mat Craig, born into poverty like his creator, still manages to find personal space to read, think and dream of creating his own writer's world, something to give him 'a calm unaccountable feeling of pleasure'. Philosophic as the desire may be, the book is firmly rooted in a Glasgow warmly and vividly portrayed, from the prosperous suburbs – 'Rutherglen's wee roon red lums reek briskly' – to the dirty river that flows through and gives it life, flanked by factories and shipyards.[30] It is still quite a sombre urban picture overall, but Mat's family has begun to leave behind the violence and want of the past, which is contrasted with the hope evoked by the election of a Labour government in 1945: 'All his life, Mat had thought of domestic life, family life as a life of sordidness and squalor. Then all of a sudden it had become decent.'[31] *The Dear Green Place* won prizes but its author, though he had further writing projects, did not publish another complete novel. He is today less well known than the later writers he influenced – McIlvanney, Gray and Kelman.

The Scottish proletarian novel took another step forward with the work of Gordon Williams, who grew up in the most notorious of Paisley's sink estates, Ferguslie Park. Williams was the son of the scheme's policeman, in a family that kept a shelf of the Waverley novels in the front room, but the boy's passion for football forged a bond with his mates on the mean streets outside. The real difference between him and them lay in the fact that at the earliest chance he was heading out of Feegie whereas they were condemned to stay behind, here or somewhere similar. He found his passport in the writing of novels, the first of them *From Scenes Like These* (1968). It is a dismal story, though relieved by its humour, about a lad, Duncan Logan, much like a less talented Williams might have turned out: put upon in a dead-end labouring job, learning to smoke and drink too much, finishing up as a football hooligan. This is what Scotland has come to, as we are reminded by the reference to Robert Burns in the book's title: in his time, nobility could shine through the squalor but nowadays there is unrelieved degradation. Yet this was perhaps Williams just getting Paisley out of his system, and he afterwards showed little further interest in the place. He continued to write about Scots in exile in London or in America, but his energies were then diverted to the ghosting of real footballer's autobiographies and to film scripts.[32]

The genre of the Scottish proletarian novel was about to mature, however, in the masterpiece of William McIlvanney's *Docherty* (1975). It came out as his third book, the prelude to several more (though he was not a prolific author and had long periods of silence). His gratitude to his own working-class background formed their mainspring. On getting to the University of Glasgow he had found that none of the set texts in his course of English literature dealt with the life he knew back in his hometown of Kilmarnock – rich in character, incident and attitude. He set out to correct this imbalance. *Docherty*, at once gritty and poetic, was in his own words 'an attempt to democratize traditional culture, to give working-class life the vote in the literature of heroism.' His characters' language lies at the rough end of the west of Scotland's self-expression. This adds colour to bleak lives, but McIlvanney also had a deeper motive: 'I think if you disenfranchise people from their own speech you take a bit of their head away as well, you disenfranchise them from their own experience to some extent.'[33]

Like *The Dear Green Place*, *Docherty* drew on a period earlier than the time of writing: it starts in 1903 as the Irish Catholic immigrant minority starts to settle into Scottish society. A member of it, Tam Docherty, lives with his family in the fictional town of Graithnock (obviously Kilmarnock). The book has not a great deal of plot in the conventional sense, but instead shows a sense of time and place in which political, social and emotional adversity tests proletarian resilience to the utmost, this sustained by hard labour in hazardous conditions. We see the struggles worked out in the cases of Tam and his son Conn, a youngster clearly destined for greater things. They face hardships and challenges in different ways because they belong to two separate generations and draw on diverse personal resources, yet naturally they have much in common. They also admire each other – Conn perceives the essential dignity of his father's life amid so much degradation, while Tam eagerly waits to see his son get on in the world. But Conn's admiration is the greater: 'He's a wee man but he makes a big shadda.'[34] The book sealed McIlvanney's reputation as one of the finest writers of his generation.

Some of the admirers McIlvanney had won felt dismayed when he followed up with a crime novel. He used a tradition mainly developed in the United States and certain European countries to give Scotland a new and characteristic genre of its own. This next book, *Laidlaw* (1977), featured a thoughtful, troubled, obstinate cop confronted with Glasgow's underworld. The author's complexity refashioned this as a vehicle for dark emotions, demanding from him no less in the way of skills and imagination than any other kind of novel. It might have been made for Scotland, for Glasgow in particular: McIlvanney endowed the city with its fictional identity. All later Scottish crime writing – 'tartan noir' – comes out of *Laidlaw*.[35]

Laidlaw is an unusual cop, with his philosophic turn of mind. Doubt lies at the centre of his psychology: he keeps Kierkegaard, Camus and Unamuno in a locked drawer of his desk, 'like caches of alcohol'.[36] Of course, cases of murder are seldom open and shut; on the contrary, they tend to happen at the end of a chain of unpredictable tensions and apparently disconnected acts. Laidlaw's detective method is to plunge undaunted into these thickets of uncertainty. In Glasgow he becomes what he calls 'a traveller in the city', moving stealthily through its undergrowth, acting the man hard as any criminal hood, while despising his brother cops, not so much colleagues as rivals, for their unpleasant posturing and blinkered attitudes. They are also unworthy of the people of Glasgow, which McIlvanney describes as a place always talking to itself, where even the derelicts and failures realize and reveal themselves in conversation or even just in monologue. He delights in characters who may have mere walk-on parts that are only loosely, or not at all, related to the plot, yet who in appearance, movement and talk make their contribution to the novel's vitality.

Tartan noir let Glasgow redefine in suitably sublimated form its nature as a tough proletarian city, now with its dark places exposed for the pleasure and instruction of readers who might never have visited it, and who after getting through the book might not want to. They would all the same have been enriched. The crime novel had in the past been widely regarded as mere entertainment, but McIlvanney showed how much more could be mined from it. It deals with the darkest sides of human nature, with sudden, unexplained, sometimes inexplicable violence, and its air is laden with fear. In Glasgow's particular case, it penetrates hidden depths beneath a material culture that might offer its people little compared to other richer and more beautiful cities. Yet it is, for those living in it or taking the trouble to get to know it, rewarding despite or because of its inherent adversity.[37]

In an often tongue-tied proletarian milieu, a catalyst might be needed to realize cultural potential. One arrived in 1975 with Philip Hobsbaum, coming from an Anglo-Jewish background by way of the University of Cambridge, where the critic F.R. Leavis had taught him. Leavis's insistence on 'a social culture and an art of living' owed less to the academic Marxism of his day than to nostalgia for the traditional 'organic community'. This was probably what the no less morally earnest Hobsbaum came to find in Glasgow. He sought to act here as an animating force, something he had already done in academic posts elsewhere.[38]

It was a reasonable surmise on Hobsbaum's part that, with the linguistic and literary resources already apparent in Glasgow, it held in its hidden depths further talents overlooked by existing structures of literary production – structures built and controlled by a metropolitan elite in London. They were not totally exclusive but were, at least, likely to render the recognition of Glaswegian cultural potential less probable. Hobsbaum responded by setting up workshops in Maryhill, where people who felt a need to write or were trying to write could come for the purposes of practical criticism and mutual support. The Nobel laureate in literature, Seamus Heaney, who had earlier benefited from Hobsbaum's guidance at Queen's University Belfast, said he 'emanated energy, generosity, belief in the community, trust in the parochial, the inept, the unprinted'.[39] What above all marked the corresponding group in Glasgow was a liberated use of language and some agendas already going well beyond the current nationalist reawakening in Scotland at large. Among those enriched by Hobsbaum's confidence in them were Alasdair Gray, James Kelman, Tom Leonard, Aonghas MacNeacail and Jeff Torrington.[40] The whole exercise proved so successful that in 1995 it was formalized with the establishment at the University of Glasgow of an academic programme in creative writing directed by Philip Hobsbaum and the critic Willy Maley.

Gray took part in Hobsbaum's writing group from 1972 to 1974. He had already been working for a quarter of a century on his first novel, *Lanark*, which was to be published eventually in 1981. It immediately won recognition, in Glasgow and far beyond, as a literary achievement of a high order, though one not easy to approach with its combination of realism, fantasy and science fiction, all leavened in the final product by the clever use of typography and Gray's own illustrations. The critic Will Self called him 'a creative polymath with an integrated politico-philosophic vision' and 'a great writer, perhaps the greatest living in this archipelago today'; Gray called himself 'a fat, spectacled, balding, increasingly old Glasgow pedestrian'.[41]

A graduate of Glasgow School of Art, Gray had first earned his living, or at least some income, as a painter; his mural in his favourite restaurant, the Ubiquitous Chip, is still there to see, with another round the corner at the Subway station of Hillhead.

But early on he turned to literature too, and in 1977–9 was writer in residence at the University of Glasgow. In 2001 he became, with Kelman and Leonard, joint professor of its creative writing programme. Gray has also held forth on politics, in support of socialism and Scottish independence. He describes himself as a civic nationalist, stating in his short tract *Why Scots Should Rule Scotland* (1992): 'The title of this book may sound threatening to those who live in Scotland but were born and educated elsewhere, so I had better explain that by Scots I mean everyone in Scotland who is eligible to vote.' An essay composed in 2012 characterizes English people working in Scotland as either long-term 'settlers' or short-term 'colonists'; Gray – though mentioning the former with approval – found himself accused of being anti-English, and a critic of English immigration into Scotland. He disputed this.[42]

Lanark crystallized some ideas that have meanwhile become important to Glasgow, indeed to Scotland. Its most famous scene brings an egotistical student, McAlpin, into conversation with its hero or anti-hero, Duncan Thaw:

'Glasgow is a magnificent city,' said McAlpin. 'Why do we hardly ever notice that?'

'Because nobody imagines living here,' said Thaw... 'Think of Florence, Paris, London, New York. Nobody visiting them for the first time is a stranger because he's already visited them in paintings, novels, history books and films. But if a city hasn't been used by an artist, not even the inhabitants live there imaginatively.'

'What is Glasgow to most of us? A house, the place we work, a football park or a golf course, some pubs, connecting streets. That's all. No, I'm wrong, there's also the cinema and library. And when our imagination needs exercise we use these to visit London, Paris, Rome under the Caesars, the American West at the turn of the century, anywhere but here and now.

Imaginatively Glasgow exists as a music-hall song and a few
bad novels. That's all we've given to the world outside. It's all
we've given to ourselves.'[43]

Redemption remains uncertain: *Lanark* is if anything pessimistic
on the point. But if it does come it will do so through a process
of self-realization. In this sense, in the expression of abstract or
interior values, it is a postmodern novel, all the more so in its
combination of the mythical and the realist – its magic realism, as
the trope was then called.

At the most general level, *Lanark* endows Glasgow with the
imaginative life it has been lacking. It is all the same not a comforting
work. It notoriously has two narratives: the realistic story of Thaw,
an artist, and the fantastic story of Lanark (a renamed Thaw) in
the surreal city of Unthank, these narratives being set out in the
four different books of the novel. Thaw ('based on myself, he was
tougher and more honest') is a difficult, precocious child of poor,
frustrated parents in the East End. Amid the grim landscapes of
industrial Scotland, we follow his evacuation during the Second
World War, his education and his scholarship to the School of Art.
He is neither a brilliant student nor a successful human being. He
yearns to create epic works of art and to form loving relationships
with women, but he lacks the capacity or will for either. Over time
he descends into madness and at last drowns himself.[44]

We arrive at Unthank with a young man in a train who has no
memory of his past but keeps encountering things oddly familiar
to him. This holds true of Unthank itself, with its uncanny
likenesses to Glasgow, except there is no daylight and the citizens
are prone to vanish suddenly after contracting hideous diseases.
Lanark tries with little success to get on terms with them, but
begins to suffer himself from dragonhide, which turns his skin into
scales: an outward sign of inward repression. When in a second
book he returns to Unthank he finds it on the point of dissolution,

racked by political strife, economic meltdown, paranoia and avarice, in the face of which he is helpless. At the end he calmly awaits an apocalypse.[45]

On the one hand, then, we have a more or less conventionally naturalistic representation of the modern city, and on the other hand the city realized on a different, symbolic level, as a place tortured by spiritual desire yet condemned to emptiness. Within this structure, the stories of Thaw and Lanark interweave and reflect on each other. Over the whole work, there is never any question that the cities are the same city and the men the same man. And then the reader has to deal not only with the two central settings and characters but also with the author – for indeed, Gray himself is also here, juggling with his content and his readers, enjoying the authorial risks enhanced by his clear sight but belied by his sincerity of tone. He asks questions and plays games, speaking aloud from the page in accents at times exuberant, at times despairing, but always vivid. The story is a rich one then, but its interest lies less in its narrative development than in the voice and the standpoint it adopts. And there it rings true as the novel of a city of unrealized potential.[46]

If Gray still shows Glasgow's congenial face, Kelman is its hard man. He launched his authorial career with a book of short stories in 1973, the first fruits of his work in Hobsbaum's group.[47] Kelman, too, served a literary apprenticeship rather different from the British norm:

> My own background is as normal or abnormal as anyone else's. Born and bred in Govan and Drumchapel, inner city tenement to the housing scheme homeland on the outer reaches of the city. Four brothers, my mother a full-time parent, my father in the picture-frame-making and gilding trade, trying to operate a one-man business and I left school at 15 etc, etc... For one reason or another, by the age of 21–22 I decided to

write stories. The stories I wanted to write would derive from my own background, my own socio-cultural experience. I wanted to write as one of my own people, I wanted to write and remain a member of my own community.[48]

Compared to Gray, Kelman is more radical in his use of language, exploiting Glasgow's vernacular and reproducing its patterns of speech, with an unabashed use of expletives. Though abhorred by the more delicate judges of the Booker Prize, the swear words did not stop him winning it in 1994 with *How Late it Was, How Late*. There are actually none in the first paragraph of the book but by the second paragraph the swearing is in full swing:

He was wearing an auld pair of trainer shoes for fuck sake where had they come from he had never seen them afore man auld fucking trainer shoes. The laces werenay even tied! Where was his leathers? A new pair of leathers man he got them a fortnight ago and now here they were fucking missing man know what I'm saying, somebody must have blagged them, miserable bastards, what chance ye got. And then left him with these. Some fucking deal. Unless they thought he was dead; fair enough, ye could see that, some poor cunt scratching himself and thinking. Naybody's there, naybody's there, so why no just take them, the guy's dead take them, better that than them just sitting there going to waste, disintegrating christ sake why no just take them. Fucking bastard he should have checked properly.

Kelman has himself picked up on the debate about his use of offensive terms, arguing that the standard English of normal novels is for his purposes unrealistic. In an essay, 'The Importance of Glasgow in my Work', he compares his Scottish working-class characters with their counterparts in English novels, who with few exceptions come from a higher social level:

> Everybody from a Glaswegian or working class background, everybody in fact from any regional part of Britain – none of them knew how to talk! What larks! Every time they opened their mouth out came a stream of gobbledygook. Beautiful! their language a cross between semaphore and Morse code; apostrophes here and apostrophes there; a strange hotchpoth of bad phonetics and horrendous spelling – unlike the nice stalwart upperclass English Hero (occasionally Scottish but with no linguistic variation) whose words on the page were always absolutely splendidly proper and pure and pristinely accurate, whether in dialogue or without. And what grammar! Colons and semi-colons! Straight out of their mouths! An incredible mastery of language. Most interesting of all, for myself as a writer, the narrative belonged to them and them alone. They owned it.[49]

In form, too, Kelman is far from Gray's discursiveness. Instead he imposes on himself ferocious disciplines. For example, *How Late it Was, How Late* is the interior monologue of a man with no exterior visual stimulus because he has been suddenly blinded. In *Kieron Smith, Boy* (2008), Kelman uses for the main text itself, never taking refuge in gobbets of quotation, the developing linguistic abilities of a child. The author's prose may be pared down but, to an extent rare in literature, the content is the form, the necessary expression of what goes through a character's brain and tongue: the external facts of narrative, while not entirely lacking in interest, are at all times secondary to this central task.[50]

But ultimately the defining externalities are for Kelman our contemporary culture and politics: he is an activist intent on changing them, a task that entails a redefinition of the history behind them. In his introduction to *Born up a Close: Memoirs of a*

Brigton Boy (2006), Kelman summarizes his understanding of the
struggle that nations and classes face:

> In an occupied country indigenous history can only be radical.
> It is a class issue. The intellectual life of working class people
> is 'occupied'. In a colonized country intellectual occupation
> takes place throughout society. The closer to the ruling class
> we get the less difference there exists in language and culture,
> until finally we find that questions fundamental to society
> at its widest level are settled by members of the same closely
> knit circle, occasionally even the same family or 'bloodline'.
> And the outcome of that can be war, the slaughter of working
> class people.[51]

In 1990, when Glasgow was European City of Culture, Kelman
joined the oppositional group, Workers' City, in disparaging the
celebrations. Its name was chosen to draw the contrast of, say,
social reality on a housing scheme with the gentrification of that
part of central Glasgow now known as the Merchant City (a name
without historical precedent). This, the critics said, promoted the
'fallacy that Glasgow somehow exists because of... eighteenth-
century entrepreneurs and far-sighted politicians. [The merchants]
were men who trafficked in degradation, causing untold misery,
death and starvation to thousands.'[52] The campaign drew down
the wrath of Labour councillors and their hangers-on, objecting to
Kelman's disdain for the 'cultural workforce'. He remained ready
to lend his name to other such campaigns, in view of the fact that
'the parliamentary opposition parties are essential to the political
apparatus of this country which is designed to arrest justice'. In
the referendum of 2014, despite his personal reservations about
Scottish nationalism, he voiced his support for independence,
stating that 'any form of nationalism is dangerous, and should be
treated with caution. I cannot accept nationalism and I am not a

Scottish Nationalist. But once that is said, I favour a Yes or No decision on independence and I shall vote Yes to independence.'[53]

Yet more linguistically radical is the poet Tom Leonard. He also found with Hobsbaum's help an entry to a literary career – as a latecomer to university, which he reached through night classes, before editing the student magazine and taking his time to finish his degree. He works under the rubric that 'all livin language is sacred'.[54] In that he includes Glaswegian too, or rather above all. This is not just a literary but also a political stance in a society where social class determines an individual's pronunciation and vocabulary:

> helluva hard tay read theeze init
> stull
> if yi canny unnirston thim jiss clear aff then
> gawn
> get tay fuck ootma road

Leonard, true to the reality of this language, sees nothing wrong if it causes affront too, since obscene abuse is commonplace in Scots urban discourse. In this case, from his first published collection, *Six Glasgow Poems* (1969), that was indeed so: the printer refused to set up the type.

Like Kelman, Leonard imposes severe disciplines on himself, in his case linguistic. They have their demands and limitations, yet also offer the advantage of directness in a range of moods. The poet is as terse and as tough as the novelist, and funnier.[55] Leonard relies on the forms and rhythms of spoken Glaswegian, the tongue of the tenements, schemes and streets, to regulate his own usage. The reader may be first struck by his abandonment of the spelling conventions of standard English in favour of a personal phonetic system (which itself can sometimes add another layer of nuance). In the following poem, 'wayiz' means 'with us' and 'insane' means 'in saying'. It is the opening piece of *Six Glasgow Poems*, 'The Good Thief':

> heh jimmy
> yawright ih
> stull wayiz urryi
> ih
> heh jimmy
> ma right insane yirra pape
> ma right insane yirwanny us jimmy
> see it nyir eyes
> wanny uz
> heh
> heh jimmy
> lookslik wirgonny miss thi gemm
> gonny miss thi GEMM jimmy
> nearly three a cloke thinoo
> dork init
> good jobe theyve gote the lights

Even in these earlier poems Leonard captures not just the sound of the accent, but also the broken rhythm of everyday speech in its hesitations and false starts. They seem to be phonetic transcriptions printed without authorial comment, yet often there is more to them. They are in fact individualized: the speaker in 'Moral Philosophy' is a tangible presence:

> whiji mean whiji mean
> lissn
> noo lissnty mi toknty yi
> right
> h hawd oan
> whair wuzza

naw
aye
whitsiz name
him way thi
yi no yon
here
here yoo
yir no even lissnin
name a god
a doant no

'Moral Philosophy', beyond its absurdly incongruous title, and then its vividly immediate voice, resonates through the relationship of speaker to implied listener: urgent inarticulacy in the one, embarrassed indifference in the other. The relationship could stand for any in literature or society where dialogue is refused. Here we have a relationship of power, in other words, emerging in some complexity from a very lack of the poetic decoration we might otherwise expect to see relieving *vers libre*. The poems have been called 'a manifesto by example', which undermine complacency and in particular hit back at the educational system's intolerance of local expression and experience[56] – something typical of the range of daily oppressions the working class faces. While Leonard has not established this written language as a literary vehicle for anything beyond his own poetry, he has certainly helped to rescue the corresponding spoken language from the scorn and contempt it had long suffered.

Still, we must not imagine all Glaswegian literature to be a matter of sociological severity, stony psychology and swear words. By contrast, Jeff Torrington in *Swing Hammer Swing!* (1992) wrote a riotous urban picaresque novel, setting out at once to tickle his readers and pluck at their heart-strings. He previously worked in a car factory and had passed the age of fifty before he published this, his first book, after three decades of hard labour and seven drafts; by the time he completed the final one he had contracted Parkinson's disease, and could write no more novels. But the reader would scarcely be able to tell what adversity lay behind the book from its exuberant tone. The picaresque novel had not otherwise appeared in Scotland since the eighteenth century, and here it turned out to have been made for Glasgow. It was a milestone, or rather a turn into a colourful side-street from the flinty highway of tartan noir.[57]

This is another Glaswegian novel set in the recent past, in the form of a monologue from the mind and mouth of the hero, Tam Clay (though other voices are heard from time to time). It takes place during the 1960s in a Gorbals facing demolition, a setting that by the year of publication had vanished from the city in any physical sense. However unfamiliar it might be to a later generation of readers, its urban problems turn out to have changed little. The story follows Tam over a week on an odyssey of self-discovery. Christmas approaches and he is beset by problems: his pregnant wife lies in hospital expecting a premature baby; he awaits a housing transfer to desirable Castlemilk; he is out of work and his novel has so far found no publisher. If it is the season to be jolly, this hardly applies to him: getting drunk is the best he can do. It may be all his own fault, for he is rather direct and aggressive in manner, but his vulgar cheek and guts are what move the story along. And he is a master of language, his dialect peppered with droll puns, often combining lyrical verve with dark comedy, yet rising to philosophical issues as they come. Earnest critics made comparisons with the work of Kafka and Balzac (writers whom Torrington greatly admired), and saw here also the document of an 'end of an era'. Yet neither literary nor historical theory lie heavy on this work of wit and humour that is notable rather for its lack of affectation, at once readable and revelling in its own surreal jokes. Some critics complained of a lack of direction in the book, but Torrington retorted that 'plots are for cemeteries'.[58]

The novel of the west of Scotland continued during the last decades of the twentieth century to develop in unsuspected ways along lines of its own, little influenced by metropolitan literary fashion. But one thing it shared with the wider world was a decisive emergence of women writers. Though in society at large Glaswegian women are more liberated than they used to be, they hardly stand at the forefront of the modern feminist movement. It is not so much a matter of their own talents and abilities as of Glasgow's male chauvinism, which has proved hard to overcome however good the intentions of the city's more progressive sons. Easy to adopt as politically correct stances may be in public life, the everyday reality of the place – especially as we go down the social scale – preserves tougher traditions that live on in a battle of the sexes (still too often physical and not merely metaphorical). Under these conditions women writers have made, somewhat against the odds, outstanding contributions to the Glaswegian genre of the proletarian novel.[59]

Sometime in the late 1970s, Alasdair Gray and James Kelman went with their friend, the playwright Liz Lochhead, to a leisure centre at Alexandria, West Dunbartonshire. There they were to propagate the example of their own mentor Philip Hobsbaum by taking part in the work of a local writers' group. This time they met a middle-aged woman attending the class 'to get out of the house'. She had had a hard life that gave her two husbands and seven children, but she turned out to be the author of some of the darkest yet funniest stories of working-class life in Scotland. Her name was Agnes Owens, 'the most unfairly neglected of all living Scottish authors', according to Gray.[60]

Owens was not prolific and never received the recognition she deserved. In her tart vignettes, she told the stories mainly of poor people trapped in their predicament, based on the experience both of herself and of others like her. The tales are tragi-comedies: they may be at bottom depressing, but they are recounted with a saving wit. Owens' first collection, *Gentlemen of the* West, was published in 1984, and a year later she contributed eight pieces to *Lean Tales*, an anthology written together with Kelman and Gray. In 1994 she published *A Working Mother*, a harrowing novel of marriage to an alcoholic, and in 1998 *For The Love of Willie*, a tale of literary endeavour in a mental hospital. For those who knew about her, she was a tough, miniaturist chronicler of obscure corners of Scottish society. But few did know about her: Kelman commented that 'when she saw the squeak of a chance she grabbed it and produced those great stories we know. How much more could it have been?'[61]

The first novel by Anne Donovan, a graduate of the creative writing programme at the University of Glasgow, was *Buddha Da* in 2003. With it, the local dialect took a big step forward because she used it for narrative as well as for dialogue. The structure of the book rests on three characters: Jimmy McKenna, his wife Liz and their twelve-year-old daughter, Anne Marie, who take turns to tell the story. They not only talk among themselves and to others but also describe the development of the novel in their own words. Here the dialect assumes an unaccustomed structural role, at Donovan's hands most effectively too. At one point she almost launches into a discussion in Glaswegian of Kant's philosophy, after Liz has an affair with a graduate student; is that the language in which he is writing his thesis?[62]

Jimmy, the father of the family, works as a housepainter and decorator. He is a typical working-class male who likes drinking – he gets completely blootered in one scene – and football: he spends every Tuesday night down the pub with his mates in discussion of the beautiful game. Here is his daughter's description of him: 'He'd dae anythin for a laugh so he wid: went doon the shops wi a perra knickers on his heid, tellt the wifie next door we'd won the lottery and were flittin tae Barbados, but that wis daft stuff compared tae

whit he's went and done noo. He's turnt intae a Buddhist.'[63] Jimmy
has hit a mid-life crisis and, after the death of his father, realizes his
lifespan is limited. Tibetan lamas have arrived in Maryhill (perhaps
the book's least probable touch) and Jimmy goes to see what they
can do for him. He likes what he hears, gives up the booze, stops
eating meat, turns celibate and finally moves in with the lamas.
He is not a man with a huge interior life, but the enormity of
what he has done steadily dawns on him. The reader sees disaster
looming as Liz takes up with her student and gets pregnant, while
Anne Marie risks losing the chance to exploit her lovely singing
voice and to move, in the next generation, up from this milieu.
At last everything comes right: Jimmy returns to his family, ready
to forgive and accept it will soon have a new member lacking
his genes, while the lamas smile at this fresh example of human
perplexity. The ordinary life of Glasgow is vindicated: 'These folk
that talk about the happy medium have got it all wrang. Life has
its extremes, whether it's winnin the lottery or lossin yer family in
a car crash, but they're no the hard part. It's the rest of it.'[64]

Another new author of crime novels to spring from the
University of Glasgow's creative writing course is Louise Welsh. In
her first published work, *The Cutting Room* (2002), she moves away
from the working class towards the darker underworld that helps
to feed the roots of the city's bourgeoisie, such as it still is. Her
central character, Rilke, is an auctioneer processing and selling an
inventory of valuable contents in the house of an old man recently
dead. While sorting through an attic, he comes across a collection of
snuff pornography apparently documenting the violent death of a
mysterious young woman. Is it only simulated or are these horrible
pictures the record of a real event? Rilke's obsessive efforts to find
out lead him into a louche underworld of pornographers, rent
boys, drug dealers and transvestites. He is himself a homosexual,
an opportunistic one ready to indulge himself whenever he gets a
furtive chance. The physical setting of the narrative suits the rich

array of murky characters. The city here is dismal, decaying and frightening, its character lightened only by grim humour: 'You know, Glasgow imports more baseball bats than any city and there's not a single baseball team in town... Maybe all the drug dealers should get together and make up a squad.' There is in other words a refusal to romanticize the place in the way of its couthier authors: 'Glasgow likes to think it is a hard city but compared to London or New York, fucking Paris probably, we're a peaceful wee haven. Our career criminals are junkies and third-generation unemployed.' Paris is finally the place Rilke chooses – in the surprising company of his female boss – to escape to.[65]

With Denise Mina's *Garnethill Trilogy* (1998–2001) we revisit a Glasgow that seems scarcely to have changed from the bad old days, drinking and smoking furiously amid an urban milieu marked by foul and bloody serial crimes. At the centre of the trilogy is Maureen O'Donnell, who in the first novel has survived an abused childhood and a consequent range of psychological problems to establish a reasonably stable relationship – only for her boyfriend to get gruesomely murdered. It happens while she is sleeping off a heavy drinking session, and at first she is herself a prime suspect, along with her drug addict of a younger brother. It is all extremely Glaswegian in a somewhat old-fashioned sense, yet the novel is shot through with a new-fangled feminism, above all in the essential strength of Maureen's character: despite everything, she is at heart a nice and fair person but with the gumption to carry herself through the horrors she experiences. That comes out, for example, in her encounters with the rather dim, dull and feckless detectives who are on the case, a stark contrast with those hard men in earlier novels that chronicled the deeds of gritty Scots cops. Compared even to the tradition of tartan noir, the plot is marked by extreme violence. So in Glasgow, we learn, the women can be as tough as the men, perhaps even tougher.[66]

This book is written not in the conviction that the culture

of a nation, region or city gives us the best form of its history, just that it should be regarded as a necessary part of such history. Like its cousins – social history, economic history, political history, intellectual history and so on – cultural history makes an indispensable contribution to our view of the past. Alas, it is one, though not the only, kind of history that has been neglected by Scotland's historians, in an overwhelming majority empiricists and positivists who are given above all to statistical investigation and analysis. This certainly has its place among the various branches of the discipline, though it should not be a place excluding other branches or their characteristic methodology. But this is precisely what it has done, at least till recently, in Scottish history. There the pole position is occupied by social and economic history. Even political history has struggled to find a niche and is perhaps still not fully integrated with its fellows. Cultural history has been more or less completely ignored. Yet it is in cultural history (and to some extent political history) that Scotland has kept itself alive in the three centuries of a union with a more powerful neighbour, enjoying a strong culture of its own and in its metropolis having to hand numerous instruments of cultural hegemony. In intellectual terms, it has set the agendas for the social and cultural history of Scotland too, which show the strongest assimilation to British norms, while disregarding the political and cultural history of Scotland, which have retained some autonomy. Without that we would not be talking today about the renewal of national independence.

As Scotland's biggest city, Glasgow has taken a lead in this evolution, and within it has performed specific functions, notably as locus for the proletarian novel. Cities are multicultural places, but some turn out especially hospitable to a particular kind of cultural expression: painting in Amsterdam, music in Vienna, architecture in Rome, jazz in New Orleans, film in Los Angeles. So it is with the proletarian novel in Glasgow. This city produces other kinds of novels too, but here I have confined myself to what seems to me its most characteristic genre, and I have not attempted a comprehensive survey even of that, but taken only a representative sample.[67] Nor is Glasgow unique in this Scottish preference. Edinburgh produces proletarian novels too, as does Aberdeen, as does even Falkirk. Falkirk's own poet of the proletariat, Alan Bissett, has sought to situate this literature of the urban working class in the wider British culture dominated by the predilections of the bourgeoisie in the southeast of England, in their turn informed by the literary elite of London. Bissett asks why it is that the English novel is so often awarded the British cultural accolades while the Scottish novel gets hardly any of them; the prime example is the Booker Prize, which of Scots only Kelman has ever won in the half-century of its history.

One obvious part of the answer is that the English do not write, and have no taste for, proletarian novels. A flurry of them more than half a century ago, with Alan Sillitoe's *Saturday Night and Sunday Morning* (1958) or *The Loneliness of the Long-Distance Runner* (1959), and Stan Barstow's *A Kind of Loving* (1960), did not prove durable. Soon the English novel reverted to more comforting subject matter – what a practitioner and critic of it, Anthony Burgess, dubbed 'adultery in Weybridge'. This often seems poor stuff in relation to any international comparison, but is able to assert a British cultural hegemony because of the dominance of a metropolitan literary establishment that will never be shaken out of its complacency by the tastes of its bourgeois reading public. 'It's easy to suppose that judges prefer to see their own middle-class life reflected in fiction, and shun novels about the ravages of post-industrial life,' says Bissett.[68] Glasgow, and Scotland, belong to a different nation with a different experience and different interests, culturally autonomous if not yet politically independent.

ENVOI: 'Wider society'

JANUARY 31, 1919, saw the great riot break out in George Square, Glasgow, and it has formed part of the city's folklore ever since.[1] Violent clashes took place between the police and men demanding a cut in the long hours they had been putting in at their factories, workshops and shipyards to maximize the production of munitions for the First World War. The bosses proved stubborn despite the armistice two months before, and much of the labour force had now gone on strike. Thousands gathered in the square, with a Red Flag floating over them. They were there to support their leaders as they went into a meeting with the lord provost, Sir James Watson Stewart.

Stewart did not perhaps represent the sort of civic leader best fitted to deal with horny-handed sons of toil. An accountant by profession, he had earlier served as a councillor at Dumbarton before embarking on a second municipal career in Glasgow. During the first one, in 1904, he secured from the city an agreement not to extend its tramways westwards to his own burgh. He feared that if trams were to run on the Sabbath, the tranquil, leafy stretches of the lower Clyde would be invaded by day-trippers: 'It was explained that these districts were already seriously inconvenienced by people from Glasgow, that drinking and misconduct had been rampant, and if tramways were introduced that evil would be vastly increased.'[2]

At the City Chambers, Sir James faced the same sort of people, or at least their delegates, Manny Shinwell, chairman of Glasgow's trades council, and David Kirkwood, who was a shop steward in Beardmore's factory at Mile End. In the matter of working hours they had asked the lord provost to appeal for intervention by the British government, and were there now to receive the reply. The talks had not yet finished inside when the fighting erupted outside. The sources dispute what exactly sparked it off – one says that an unprovoked baton charge by the police was the cause, another that they only stepped in when the crush halted trams trying to travel through the square. The strikers pulled up iron palings to defend themselves against the truncheons, or seized bottles as ammunition from a passing lorry.[3]

With the commotion mounting, Shinwell and Kirkwood rushed out from their meeting to calm things down. But the police restrained them and, in a scuffle, knocked Kirkwood to the ground. Both men were arrested and charged with 'instigating and inciting large crowds of persons to form part of a riotous mob'. Meanwhile the sheriff of Lanarkshire, A.O.M. MacKenzie, who had been observing the fray from the opposite end of the square, came forward and tried to read the Riot Act. Strikers just tore his copy from his hands. Brawls spread into the surrounding streets as some sought to move off and resume the mass meeting on Glasgow Green. The police could scarcely maintain control but they did manage to apprehend a dozen of the ringleaders, who would later go on trial in Edinburgh.[4]

This apparent breakdown of public order in Glasgow provoked a sharp reaction from the government in London. The Scottish secretary, Robert Munro, described the disturbances as a 'Bolshevist uprising'. It fell to the secretary of state for war, Winston Churchill, to take decisive action of a kind he always relished. The same evening, about 10,000 soldiers with tanks, a howitzer and machine guns arrived in the city, in the largest military deployment Scotland had ever seen. The howitzer was positioned at the City Chambers while, on each side of the square in front, troops manned Lewis guns on top of the North British Hotel and the General Post Office. In Duke Street and Gallowgate the tanks stood ready, their engines running. Elsewhere in the city, patrols passed back and forth, while sentries mounted guard outside power stations and docks. These soldiers were English, since the government feared Scots regiments might go over to the workers, mimicking recent revolutionary scenes in St Petersburg and Berlin. The military occupation of Glasgow, for so we may dub it, went on for a week. The trouble had by then come to an end.[5]

After being laid out in 1781, George Square, now the biggest space in the centre of Glasgow, had replaced the Cross and the Green as the favoured venue for open-air assemblies of every kind. The City Chambers, opened on the eastern side in 1888, offered them a fresh focus. Otherwise, too, the architecture of the square was after a century losing its original classical harmony. The first terraces, built for residential purposes but meanwhile often converted into hotels or offices, steadily gave way to more massive buildings. In addition, a dozen statues had been put up in the central public garden as memorials to those public figures most admired by Glaswegians, from heroes of the whole nation such as Robert Burns and Sir Walter Scott to the city's own soldiers, scientists and civic dignitaries. The next addition to the statuary was to be the cenotaph guarded by lions, fierce of aspect yet benignly couchant. Unveiled in 1924, it reminded Glaswegians of the huge sacrifices they had made in the First World War, when 200,000 of them signed up to fight and 17,695 lost their lives.[6] At this spot, every year on Remembrance Sunday the city honoured those who had fallen (and still does). On VE Day in 1945, George Square was the focal point for spontaneous celebrations with the flags of all the Allied nations fluttering in the breeze and the whole space floodlit after dark, drawing the contrast with the blackouts – now a thing of the past. In two days of civic holiday, crowds thronged the space from morning till night – crowds mainly of women, since so many men were still away on active service – and rejoiced among the statues.

There are many cities where statues win public affection, and Glasgow is one of them. Yet the opening years of the twenty-first century have brought suggestions they should all be banished from George Square, or at least shifted to less prominent positions. The city council came to the conclusion they stood in the way of more profitable uses for this space right in the centre of town. It was open and accessible, lined by imposing structures and served by a range of public transport, yet mostly used by Glaswegians just to sit and stroll about (it is, of course, their collective property). Instead, it might be better exploited as a venue for private events generating a profit – the council would at length get away with charging more than £1,000 a day. Another sign of the council's new cost-accounting spirit came with its decision in 2011 to scrap celebrations of Hogmanay there because they no longer delivered value for money, leaving Edinburgh to monopolize, in the eyes of the world, the most Scottish of all holidays. By now Glaswegians at large were taking alarm. A campaign started to preserve the square in its traditional functions and to restore it to its earlier condition.[7]

This was because the city council had already embarked on a physical transformation of George Square. In 2006 it ordered the old lawns and flowerbeds to be ripped up and replaced with burnt red tarmac. A necessity had apparently arisen also to remove the statues for restoration, with the ominous suggestion that they 'may not return to the square', but instead be taken to 'an area of regeneration'. The council needed money after it voted £15 million for a 'makeover' to turn the square into 'a place fit for the twenty-first century'. But it had never told the people what exactly it had in mind, let alone asked their opinion. Not till 2013 did six shortlisted designs for the makeover go on public display, some providing for all the statues, others providing for only half of them, to stay put. The competition ran into controversy and in the end was abandoned: by coincidence, on the very day that the winner was announced. In the political practice of the city's Labour establishment, this lack of consultation had become normal. In consequence its own left hand did not now seem to know what its right hand was doing either.[8]

Besides, the council could never really stop Glaswegians using George Square for purposes of their own, as they always had done. During the twentieth century, outbursts of unionist patriotism alternated with manifestations of a different tenor. In the 1930s, marches of the jobless from the surrounding industrial towns had ended here: 'The unemployed dismissed and went home wearily to their bread and margarine,' wrote the journalist J.R. Allan in 1938. Radicalism revived as the century advanced. For a week in 1990, the square formed the scene for a hunger strike in protest at Margaret Thatcher's poll tax. Demonstrations took place against Tony Blair's war in Iraq on its outbreak in 2002. In November 2011, anti-capitalist protesters kept vigil in a camp on the square, as 'a means of gathering together as an open forum to discuss the problems we face in wider society and to explore how we get into a situation where it becomes progressive rather than destructive'.[9] This did not please municipal officials, who could see Armistice Day coming up, followed by Remembrance Sunday and, even more important, the switching on of the Christmas lights a week later. The council took legal action to get the protesters evicted. The same caution even greeted Thatcher's death in 2013: some Glaswegians wanted to hold a public celebration in the square, but the council urged them to stay away. And then finally, as we saw right at the beginning of this book, this was the scene of political hustings during the campaign for the Scottish referendum of 2014, mostly by supporters of Yes. Now nothing and nobody could stop them, or tried to, except the result on the night.

Within its constant dimensions, George Square has been emblematic also of constant change in the general urban history.[10] The space was originally laid out in the eighteenth century according to the classical taste of the merchant oligarchy. This continued to man civic government, but faced growing competition from a new class of industrialists with more eclectic preferences. They shaped the square as it appeared by the end of the nineteenth century with its monumental adornments, above all the City Chambers. From there the ruling class could impose its will on a proletariat that by and large calmly accepted the future envisaged for it from on high. A programme of ambitious if authoritarian reform aimed to create a model municipality – though, despite the time, energy and money poured into it, it never finally solved the human problems of the industrial revolution (which, indeed, persist today). It did help to give common values to the different classes of Victorian Glasgow, a city where the bosses rose out of the ranks of the workers and formed a social configuration different from anywhere else in Scotland. Glaswegians of every station in life felt united by a burning pride in their achievements. Yet these would be largely nullified by the economic consequences of the peace in 1918. Within a couple of decades, the high bourgeois hegemony had collapsed for good. The ensuing dictatorship of the proletariat had its own ideals and ambitions, which in their turn would prove not only hard to fulfil but also vulnerable to corruption. Their triumph was never complete, therefore: tower blocks erected just half a mile north of George Square still did not quite overshadow the inheritance of an earlier era, the battered but even yet handsome centre of the city.

While the history of Glasgow has been varied, then, there is a risk that some of this variety will be lost in its latest interpretations. Its basis lies in the written record, ever more copious as time goes on, and in many material survivals. But recent times have brought a certain reductive tendency, with special stress laid on the proletarian side of that history. Modern historians are aware how their long-dead Victorian colleagues, together with other cultural gurus, achieved an invention of Scotland, of a Scotia stern and wild, land of the mountain and the flood, with its tartans, bagpipes and haggis. It was alluring if scarcely accurate, but it exerted an influence on generations of Scots and of strangers who wanted to know about them. Much the same holds true of the invention of Glasgow under way today, of a city of industrial degradation and social militancy where revolution is postponed only by repression and betrayal.[11] It makes for potent myths, already to be found in the city's art and literature, more generally in its iconography. Again, it confirms certain ideas about Glasgow current in the outside world.

And perhaps none of it could exist without underlying grains of truth in the narrative. Certainly Glasgow inside its present municipal boundaries has become largely a proletarian city, with its old ruling elite consigned to oblivion and much of its present-day bourgeoisie preferring to live in suburbs where a council elected by the needy cannot tax them. The unfulfilled expectations of the working class have since 2014 at last led even to the rejection of the Labour Party, after eighty years of supremacy, because it had reached a dead end in its own by now stale and staid conceptions of socialism. The SNP set out to seize the ideological legacy for itself, and successively, in the referendum of 2014, in the British general election of 2015 and in the Scottish election of 2016, it has in purely electoral terms done so. In the local elections of 2017 it ousted the Labour Party, which with brief interruptions had ruled Glasgow since 1933, to become the biggest party in the City Chambers and to form a new administration. The SNP's ascendancy is, if anything, even more total than Labour's ever was, while a whiff of electoral impropriety here and there makes the similarity to the tainted *ancien régime* almost complete. Whether this might actually lead to something the people of Glasgow could call socialism is a question the new ruling party seems reluctant to answer.[12]

The victories of the working class remain limited in scale, then. Never enough to attain social equality even in the days of hope, they cannot now solve new problems as these arise to perpetuate old ones. Fulfilment used to be the story of Glasgow, but frustration has long replaced it. Even if we look away from the public life of the place into the more private spheres of art and literature, we may read desolation and despair. In fact politics, though scarcely qualifying as inspirational, seems by comparison one of the bright spots, offering for all the faults at least a chance of renewal. This urge for renewal remains clearly present among Glaswegians, if often diverted into mere hedonism. It is a matter of finding the right vehicle for this brave aspiration. Socialism in one city is scarcely possible, or even socialism in one nation, at any rate in a modern European nation. But for Glasgow and for Scotland a clear alternative destination, let alone the path to it, is slow to emerge.

The bright spot in a somewhat murky outlook is that history has here created not just a city in the sense of a locus for living and getting and spending. It has created a unique species of urban civilization, perennially productive and fruitful, conditioned by its own experiences yet capable of reaching out to the world. In that sense, and despite all its problems, Glasgow will continue to flourish.

NOTES

Chapter One

1. *Extracts from the Records of the Burgh of Glasgow* [hereinafter *ERBG*], I, *1573–1642* (Glasgow, 1876), 49.
2. D.E.R. Watt, *Ecclesia Scoticana* (Stuttgart, 1991), 60–3.
3. N.F. Shead, 'Origins of the Medieval Diocese of Glasgow', *Scottish Historical Review*, XLVIII (1969), 220–5.
4. G.W.S. Barrow, *King David I of Scotland* (Reading, 1975), 94.
5. As so often in Scotland, the exact origin is obscure. The convention survived till the administrative reorganization of 1975 and then became what it still remains, the Convention of Scottish Local Authorities.
6. *Records of the Convention of the Royal Burghs of Scotland, I, 1295–1597*, ed. J.D. Marwick (Edinburgh, 1867), 1–2.
7. T. Keith, 'The Origin of the Convention of the Royal Burghs of Scotland', *Scottish Historical Review*, X (1913), 384–402.
8. T.M. Devine, 'The Merchant Class of the Larger Scottish Towns in the Seventeenth and Early Eighteenth Centuries', in B. Dicks & G. Gordon (eds.), *Scottish Urban History* (Aberdeen, 1983), 92–III.

9. S.R. Epstein & M. Prak (eds.), *Guilds, Innovation and the European Economy 1400–1800* (Cambridge, 2008).

10. J.M. Reid, *History of the Merchants House of Glasgow* (Glasgow, 1967).

11. T.C. Smout, 'The Glasgow Merchant Community in the Seventeenth Century', *Scottish Historical Review*, XLVII (1968), 1961–2.

12. *ERBG, II, 1630–1662*, 38.

13. Glasgow City Archives, Maxwell Papers, T-PM 113/562, 572, 574.

14. *ERBG*, IV, 104.

15. *ERBG*, IV, 420.

16. J.J. McCusker, *Mercantilism and the Economic History of the Early Modern Atlantic World* (Cambridge, 2001).

17. *ERBG*, IV, 104, 138.

18. Ibid, 161, 173, 187, 413; J.W. Burns (ed.), *Miscellaneous Writings of John Spreul* (Glasgow, 1882), 46.

19. P.R. Rössner, *Scottish Trade in the Wake of the Union 1700–1760: The Rise of a Warehouse Economy* (Stuttgart, 2008); 'New Avenues of Trade: Structural Changes in the European Economy and Foreign Commerce as Reflected in the Changing Structure of Scotland's Commerce 1660–1760', *Journal of Scottish Historical Studies*, XXXI (2011).

20. A.M. Carstairs, 'Some Economic Aspects of the Union of Parliaments', *Scottish Journal of Political Economy*, II (1955), 58; J.H. Soltow, 'Scottish Traders in Virginia', *Economic History Review*, XII (1959–60), 90–6; H. Hamilton, *An Economic History of Scotland in the Eighteenth Century* (Oxford, 1963), 255; R.H. Campbell, *Scotland since 1707, the rise of an industrial society* (Oxford, 1965), 43.

21. D. Defoe, *Tour Thro' the Whole Island of Great Britain* (London, 1927), 743.

22. R.C. Nash, 'The English and Scottish Tobacco Trades in the Seventeenth and Eighteenth Centuries: Legal and Illegal Trade', *Economic History Review*, XXXV (1982), 364.

23. J.M. Price, 'The Rise of Glasgow in the Chesapeake Tobacco Trade', in P.L. Payne (ed.), *Studies in Scottish Business History* (London, 1967), 299–395; *Capital and Credit in British Overseas Trade: The View from the Chesapeake 1700–1776* (Cambridge MA, 1980), 24–9; J.M. Price, 'Glasgow, the Tobacco Trade and the Scottish Customs 1707–1730', *Scottish Historical Review*, LXIII (1984), 27.

24. Rössner, *Trade in the Wake of the Union*, 12–20.

25. T.C. Barker, 'Smuggling in the Eighteenth Century, the Evidence of the Scottish Tobacco Trade', *The Virginia Magazine of History and Biography*, LXII (1984), 393–7.

26. Price, 'Rise of Glasgow', 304.

27. J.M. Price, *France and the Chesapeake* (Ann Arbor, 1973), I, 604; 'Glasgow, Tobacco Trade and Scottish Customs', 1–36.

28. R.F. Dell, 'The Operational Record of the Clyde Tobacco Fleet 1747–1775', *Scottish Economic and Social History*, II (1982), 1.

29. Rössner, 'New Avenues', 14, 17, 25.

30. J. Gibson, *History of Glasgow*, (Glasgow, 1777), 106.

31. T.M. Devine, *The Tobacco Lords* (Edinburgh, 1975), 11, 56; 'The Colonial Trades and Industrial Investment in Scotland', *Economic History Review*, XXIX (1976), 3; A. Slaven, *The Development of the West of Scotland 1750–1960* (London, 1975), 20–1; B. Lenman, *An Economic History of Modern Scotland* (London, 1977), 91; *Integration, Enlightenment and Industrialization, Scotland 1746–1832* (London, 1981), 23–4, 42–7.

32. It is now the Gallery of Modern Art.

33. T.M. Devine, 'Glasgow Colonial Merchants and Land 1770–1815', in J. Ward & R.G. Wilson, *Land and Industry* (Newton Abbot, 1971); 'Glasgow Merchants and the Collapse of the Tobacco Trade', *Scottish Historical Review*, LII (1973), 50 *et seq.*; 'Sources of Capital for the Glasgow Tobacco Trade 1740–1780', *Business History*, XVI (1974), 113–26; *Tobacco Lords*, 18, 130, 157–8, 161, 171–3.

34. Gibson, *History,* 105.

35. J. Knox, *View of the British Empire* (Edinburgh, 1784), xliii.

36. D. Hamilton, *Scotland, the Caribbean and the Atlantic World* (Manchester, 2005), ch. 4.

37. J. Lindsay & Renwick, *History of Glasgow* (Glasgow, 1921), ch. 30.

38. Mitchell Library, GC f914.14353 STU.

39. Gibson, *History*, 246.

40. National Archives of Scotland, warrants of exchequer, E 8.40.

41. S. Nisbet, 'The Sugar Adventurers of Glasgow 1640–1740', *History Scotland*, IX, 2009, 28.

42. P.W.J. Riley, *King William and the Scottish Politicians,* 39–41.

43. W. Klooster & A.C. Solana, 'La República Holandesa y su posición en el contexto colonial americano después de 1713', *Anuario de Estudios Americanos,* LXXII (2015); W. Klooster, 'Inter-imperial Smuggling in the Americas 1600–1800', in B. Bailyn & P.L. Denault (eds.), *Soundings in Atlantic History 1500–1825* (Cambridge MA, 2009), 141–80; 'La relation complexe entre la guerre et la contrebande en l'Amérique atlantique', in B. Marnot & S. Marzagalli (eds.), *Guerre et économie dans le monde atlantique du XVIe au XXe siècle* (Pessac, 2006), 395–408.

44. E.H. Goveia, *Slave Society in the British Leeward Islands* (New Haven, 1965).

45. J.A. Rinn, 'Scots in Bondage', *History Today,* XXX (1980), 16–19.

46. *ERBG,* VI, 1739–1759, 102, 105; A. Cooke, 'An Elite Revisited: Glasgow West India Merchants 1783–1877', *Journal of Scottish Historical Studies*, XXXII (2012), 153.

47. S.M. Nisbet, 'Early Glasgow Sugar Plantations in the Caribbean', *Scottish Archaeological Journal*, XXXI (2009), 116.

48. S.G. Checkland, 'Two Scottish West Indian Liquidations after 1793', *Scottish Journal of Political Economy,* IV (1957), 136; D. Hamilton, 'Scottish Trading in the Caribbean: The Rise and Fall of Houston & Co', in N.C. Landsman (ed.), *Nation and*

Province in the First British Empire, Scotland and the Americas 1600–1800 (Lewisburg & London, 2001), 218.

49. *The Herald,* letters, Nov. 16, 2012.

50. T.M. Devine, *Recovering Scotland's Slavery Past* (Edinburgh, 2015), 231.

51. A.J. Cooke, *The Rise and Fall of the Scottish Cotton Industry 1778–1814* (Manchester, 2009), ch. 1.

52. J. Butt, 'The Scottish Cotton Industry during the Industrial Revolution 1780–1840', in L.M. Cullen & T.C. Smout, *Comparative Aspects of Scottish and Irish Economic and Social History 1600–1900* (Edinburgh, 1977), 120–1.

53. R.H. Campbell (ed.), *States of the Progress of Linen Manufacture in Scotland 1727–1754* (Edinburgh, 1973).

54. A. Liddell, *Memoir of David Dale* (Glasgow, 1854).

55. A.J. Durie, *Scottish Linen Industry* (Edinburgh, 1979), 90.

56. E.F. Heckscher, *Mercantilism* (London, 1935), II, 419.

57. Cooke, *Rise and Fall,* 100 *et seq.*

58. Parliamentary Papers 1835 XIII, *Report from the Select Committee on Handloom Weavers' Petitions,* iii-iv, xii.

59. Parliamentary Papers 1834 X, *Report from the Select Committee on Handloom Weavers' Petitions,* 41–60, 72–84.

60. C. Brogan, *James Finlay & Co, manufacturers and East India merchants 1750–1950* (Glasgow, 1951).

61. I. Donnachie & G. Hewitt, *Historic New Lanark, the Dale and Owen Industrial Community Since 1785* (Edinburgh, 1993).

62. R.A. Houston & I.D. Whyte, *Scottish Society 1500–1800* (Cambridge, 2005), 148–51.

63. D. Hancock, *Citizens of the World: London Merchants and the Integration of the British Atlantic Community 1745–1785* (Cambridge, 1995), ch. 5.

64. Ibid, ch. 10.

65. M. Duffill, 'The Africa Trade from the Ports of Scotland', *Slavery and Abolition,* XXIV (2004), 102–22.

66. C. Booth, *Zachary Macaulay* (London, 1934), 4–11.

67. Price, 'Rise of Glasgow', 305.

68. M.R.G. Fry, *The Scottish Empire* (Edinburgh, 2001), ch. 3.

69. Galatians 3.28.

70. D.B. Davis, *The Problem of Slavery in Western Culture* (Ithaca NY, 1968), 433–6; E. Spary, 'The "Nature" of Enlightenment', in W. Clark, J. Golinski & S. Schaffer (eds.), *The Sciences in Enlightened Europe* (Chicago, 1999), 281–2.

71. G. Carmichael, *S. Puffendorfii* [sic] *de officio hominis et civis, juxta legem naturalem ... supplementis et observationibus in academicae juventutis usum* (Glasgow, 1718), 100–1.

72. *Natural Rights on the Threshold of the Scottish Enlightenment: The writings of Gershom Carmichael,* ed. J. Moore (Indianapolis, 2002), ch. 16.

73. F. Hutcheson, *A System of Moral Philosophy* (London, 1755), I, 302–3.

74. Ibid, 293–301.

75. A. Smith, *Inquiry into the Nature and Causes of the Wealth of Nations* (London, 1776), bk. III, ch. 2, §9.

76. Ibid, I.10.

77. Ibid, I.11.

78. *Correspondence of Thomas Reid,* ed. P. Wood (Edinburgh, 2002), 209.

79. F. Ablondi, 'Millar on Slavery', *Journal of Scottish Philosophy*, VII (2009), 163–75.

80. *Caledonian Mercury,* February 9, 1792.

81. T.M. Devine, *Slavery Past, passim.*

82. *ERBG*, VIII, 397; F. Montgomery, 'Glasgow and the Movement for Corn Law Repeal', *History* (LXIV, 1979), 363–79.

83. Y. Kumagai, *Breaking into the Monopoly: Provincial Merchants and Manufacturers' Campaigns for Access to the Asian Markets 1790–1833* (Leiden, 2012), ch. 2.

84. D. Rutherford, *In the Shadow of Adam Smith: Founders of Scottish Economics 1700–1900* (Basingstoke, 2012), 3.

85. W. Smart, *Introduction to the Theory of Value* (London, 1891), 68.

86. Published as *The Return to Protection* (London, 1904).

87. I am grateful to Professor David Simpson for discussion of these Glaswegian economists.

Chapter Two

1. *Extracts from the Records of the City of Glasgow* (hereinafter *ERCG*), eds. J.D. Marwick & R. Renwick (Glasgow, 1876–1916), II, 234.

2. J. de Vries & A. van der Woude, *The First Modern Economy: Success, Failure and Perseverance of the Dutch Economy 1500–1815* (Cambridge, 1997).

3. Records of the Parliament of Scotland, 1661/1/344.

4. *ERCG*, I, 386.

5. G. Desbrisay, 'Authority and Discipline in Aberdeen 1659–1700', unpublished PhD thesis, University of Aberdeen (1989), 359–76.

6. *Charters and Other Documents Relating to the City of Glasgow, I*, ed. J.D. Marwick (Glasgow, 1897), ccclxxiii.

7. *ERCG*, II, 439.

8. *ERCG*, I, 385; II, 155–8, 200, 264; III, 121, 181; *Records of the Privy Council of Scotland*, 3rd series, VII, 597f.

9. G. Marshall, *Presbyteries and Profits: Calvinism and the Development of Capitalism in Scotland 1560–1707*, appendix, 'Manufacturing Enterprises in Scotland 1560–1707', 284–320.

10. D. McCrone, *Understanding Scotland: The Sociology of a Nation* (Edinburgh, 2001), 56.

11. Marshall, *Presbyteries and Profits*, appendix, nos. 36 & 87.

12. C. Gordon, *Memorial of Mr Cuthbert Gordon: Relative to the Discovery and Use of Cudbear* (London, 1785); R.A. Peel, 'Turkey Red Dyeing in Scotland: Its Heyday and Decline', *Journal of the Society of Dyers and Colourists*, LXVIII (1952), 496–505.

13. G. Macintosh, *Biographical Memoir of the Late Charles Macintosh of Campsie and Dunchattan* (Glasgow, 1847).

14. T. Hancock, *Personal Narrative of the Origin and Progress of the Caoutchouc or India-rubber Manufacture in England* [sic] (London, 1857).

15. R. Burns, *The Complete Poetical Works*, ed. J.A. Mackay (Darvel, 1993), 201.

16. J.R. Burns, *Industrial Archaeology of Glasgow* (Glasgow, 1974), 170.

17. B. Lenman, *Economic History of Modern Scotland* (London, 1977), 127. Lenman notes what he calls the 'lum-mania' of Scottish capitalists; the Port Dundas Townsend Chimney of 1859, at 454 feet even higher than Tennant's Stalk, was another example.

18. G. Dodd et al, *The Land We Live In* (London, 1847), II, 43.

19. R. Trotter (ed.), *Imperial Chemical Industries Ltd and its Founding Companies* (London, 1938), I, 20–3

20. N. Crathorne et al, *Tennant's Stalk* (London, 1973), 55–98.

21. S.G. Checkland, *The Mines of Tharsis* (London, 1967); W.G. Nash, *Rio Tinto Mine: Its History and Romance* (London, 1904); M. Rodríguez Bayona, *La investigación de la actividad metalúrgica durante el III milenio A.N.E. en el suroeste de la Península Ibérica* (Oxford, 2008).

22. J.E. Dolan, 'Alfred Nobel in Scotland', *Nobelprize.org*, Nobel Media AB 2014, www.nobelprize.org/alfred_nobel/biographical/articles/dolan

23. R. Trotter, *Imperial Chemical Industries*, 52–4; W.J. Reader, *Imperial Chemical Industries: A History* (Oxford, 1970), 24–5; J.M. Stopford, 'The Origins of British-based Multinational Manufacturing Enterprises', *Business History Review*, XLVIII (1974).

24. W. Knox, *Industrial Nation: Work, Culture and Society in Scotland, 1800 to the Present* (Edinburgh, 1999), 105.

25. B.F. Duckham, *History of the Scottish Coal Industry* (Newton Abbot, 1970).

26. P.L. Payne, 'The Decline of the Scottish Heavy Industries',

in R. Saville, *The Economic Development of Modern Scotland* (Edinburgh, 1985), 80.

27. *Royal Commission on Children's Employment* PP 1842 XVI, especially 449 *et seq.*

28. *Royal Commission on Labour*, PP 1893 XXXVII (1), 194.

29. *Report of the Commissioners Appointed to Inquire into the State of the Population in the Mining Districts*, PP 1844 XVI, 32.

30. Ibid, PP 1848 XXV, 236.

31. M.J.T. Lewis, *Early Wooden Railways* (London, 1970), 160–5; J. Lindsay, *The Canals of Scotland* (Newton Abbot, 1968), ch. 1.

32. C.K. Hyde, *Technological Change and the British Iron Industry 1700–1870* (Princeton, 1977), 151–5.

33. A. McGeorge, *The Bairds of Gartsherrie* (Glasgow, 1875).

34. *Royal Commission on the Employment of Children in Mines*, PP XVI 1842, pt. 2, 81.

35. J. Napier, *Life of Robert Napier of West Shandon* (Edinburgh, 1904), 101; D.D. Napier, *Life of David Napier: Engineer 1790–1869* (Glasgow, 1912), 93.

36. H. Bessemer, *An Autobiography* (London, 1901), 176–80.

37. H.A. Brassert, *Report to Lord Weir of Cathcart on the Manufacture of Iron and Steel by William Baird & Co Ltd, David Colville & Sons Ltd, Jas. Dunlop & Co Ltd, Steel Company of Scotland Ltd, Stewarts & Lloyds Ltd* (London, 1929).

38. G.G. Endres, *British Aircraft Manufacturers Since 1908* (London, 1995), 24.

39. P.L. Payne, *Colvilles and the Scottish Steel Industry* (Oxford, 1979).

40. R.H. Campbell, *The Rise and Fall of Scottish Industry 1707–1939*, (Edinburgh, 1980), 61 *et seq.*; J.R. Hume & M. Moss, *Clyde Shipbuilding* (London, 1975), 131–41.

41. H. Bell, *Observations on the Utility of Applying Steam Engines to Vessels* (Glasgow, 1813).

42. C.H. Wilson & W. Reader, *Men and Machines: A History of D. Napier & Son, Engineers Ltd, 1808–1958* (London, 1958).

43. F.E. Hyde, *Cunard and the North Atlantic 1840–1973: A History of Shipping and Financial Management* (London, 1975), 23.

44. J. MacLehose, *Memoirs and Portraits of One Hundred Glasgow Men* (Glasgow, 1906), 118; R.H. Thurston, *A History of the Growth of the Steam Engine* (London, 1883), 97; W.J.M. Rankine, *A Memoir of John Elder: Engineer and Shipbuilder* (Glasgow, 1883), 29–30.

45. C.M. Castle, *Legacy of Fame: Shipping and Shipbuilding on the Clyde* (Erskine, 1990), 59.

46. P.L. Robertson, 'Shipping and Shipbuilding: The Case of William Denny & Brothers', *Business History*, XVI (1974), 36–47.

47. M. Dominiczak, 'William Cullen and Joseph Black: Chemistry, Medicine and the Scottish Enlightenment', *Clinical Chemistry*, LVII (2011), 163 *et seq.*

48. C. Smith and M.N. Wise, *Energy and Empire: A Biographical Study of Lord Kelvin* (Cambridge, 1989).

49. W. Thomson, Lord Kelvin, *Mathematical and Physical Papers*, 6 vols. (Cambridge, 1882–1911).

50. S.P. Thompson, *The Life of William Thomson, Baron Kelvin of Largs* (New York, 1910).

51. *Report of the Royal Commission on Scientific Instruction and the Advancement of Science*, PP 1874 XXII, evidence, Q9512.

52. C.E. Montague, introduction to M. Bone, *The Western Front* (London, 1917), a collection of prints and drawings.

53. A. Cobbing, *The Japanese Discovery of Victorian Britain* (London, 1998), 187.

54. H.H. Peebles, 'A Study in Failure: J. & G. Thomson and Shipbuilding at Clydebank 1871–1890', *Scottish Historical Review*, LXIX (1990).

55. A. Carnegie, *A Rectorial Address delivered to the Students in the University of Aberdeen* (New York, 1912), 10.

56. B. Dunn, 'Success Themes in Scottish Family Enterprises', *Family Business Review*, VIII (1995), 17–28.

57. Mitchell Library, Glasgow, GC 920.04 BAI.

58. J.J. Jones, 'University Training for Commerce and Administration', *Proceedings of the Royal Philosophical Society of Glasgow,* XLIV (1913–14), 172.

59. R.A. Cage, *The Working Class in Glasgow 1750–1914* (London, 1987).

60. R. Duncan & A. MacIvor (eds.), *Militant Workers: Labour and Class Conflict on the Clyde 1900–1950* (Edinburgh, 1992).

61. I. MacLean, *The Legend of Red Clydeside* (Edinburgh, 1983).

62. N.K. Buxton, 'Economic Growth in Scotland Between the Wars', *Economic History Review,* XXXIII (1980), 538–55.

63. C.E.V. Leser & A.H. Silvey, 'Scottish Industries During the Inter-War Period', *Manchester School of Social and Economic Studies,* XVIII (1950).

64. W.J. Reader, *Architect of Air Power: The Life of the First Viscount Weir of Eastwood* (London, 1968).

65. J.M. Reid, *James Lithgow: Master of Work* (London, 1964).

66. T. Royle, *A Time of Tyrants: Scotland and the Second World War* (Edinburgh, 2012).

67. National Library of Scotland, Walter Elliot papers, Acc 6721/1/1.

68. K.J.W. Alexander & C.L. Jenkins, *Fairfields: A Study of Industrial Change* (London, 1970).

69. E. Lorenz, *Economic Decline in Britain: The Shipbuilding Industry 1890–1970* (Oxford, 1991), 96.

70. J. Reid, *Reflections of a Clyde-Built Man* (London, 1976).

71. The yard now has a website devoted to its history: www.fairfieldgovan.co.uk/heritage

72. R. Brown & C. Mason, 'The Evolution of Enterprise Policy in Scotland', in R.A. Blackburn & M.T. Schaper (eds.), *Government, SMEs and Entrepreneurship Development* (Farnham, 2012), ch. 2.

73. Ravenscraig also has a website, www.ravenscraig.co.uk

74. D. Sims & M. Wood, *Car Manufacturing at Linwood: The Regional Policy Issues* (Paisley, 1994).

75. T. Kelly & D. Keeble, 'IBM: The Corporate Chameleon', in M. de Smidt & E. Wever (eds.), *The Corporate Firm in a Changing World Economy* (London, 1990), 32–3.

Chapter Three

1. D. Stevenson, *The Scottish Revolution 1637–1644* (Newton Abbott, 1973), 88–101.

2. D. Stevenson (ed.), *The Government of Scotland under the Covenanters* (Edinburgh, 1982), xii–xiv.

3. *The Letters and Journals of Robert Baillie*, ed. D. Laing (Edinburgh, 1842), I, 42; *Diary of Sir Archibald Johnston*, ed. G.M. Paul (Edinburgh, 1911), I, 319–22.

4. Stevenson, *Scottish Revolution*, 102–15.

5. *Acts of the General Assembly of the Church of Scotland 1638–1842* (Edinburgh, 1843), 1–35.

6. *Baillie Letters and Journals*, 128.

7. *Registrum Episcopatus Glasguensis*, ed. C. Innes (Edinburgh, 1843).

8. J. Kirk, *Patterns of Reform* (Edinburgh, 2000), 358–61.

9. *Second Book of Discipline*, ed. J. Kirk (Edinburgh, 1980), 167, 216.

10. *The Autobiography and Diary of Mr James Melvill*, ed. R. Pitcairn (Edinburgh, 1842), 370.

11. Ibid, 48–56.

12. M. Todd, *The Culture of Protestantism in Early Modern Scotland* (New Haven & London, 2002), 402–12.

13. *Melvill Autobiography*, 611–4.

14. R. Fleming, *The Fulfilling of the Scripture* (np, 1669), 143.

15. J. Buckroyd, *Life of James Sharp, Archbishop of St Andrews, 1618–1679* (Edinburgh, 1987), 118.

16. M. Grant, *The Lion of the Covenant: The Story of Richard Cameron* (Darlington, 1997).

17. T. Harris, *Revolution: The Great Crisis of the British Monarchy* (London, 2006), 380–90.

18. W. Bell, *Dictionary and Digest of the Law of Scotland* (Edinburgh, 1861), 621.

19. J. Ramsay, *Scotland and Scotsmen in the Eighteenth Century,* ed. A. Allardyce (Edinburgh & London, 1888), I, 286.

20. J. Gillies, 'Some Account of the Life and Character of John MacLaurin', in *The Works of the Reverend John MacLaurin,* ed. W.H. Goold (Edinburgh, 1860), xv.

21. National Archives of Scotland, Records of the Commission of the General Assembly 1739–48, CH 1/3/24, ff. 439, 444; Records of the General Assembly 1746–9, CH 1/1/45, ff. 78, 79, 444.

22. *Correspondence of Robert Wodrow,* ed. T. M'Crie (Edinburgh, 1842), II, 676.

23. *Extracts from the Records of the Burgh of Edinburgh,* eds. J.D. Marwick et al, (1869–), IV, 48.

24. J. Robe, *Narratives of the Extraordinary Work of the Holy Spirit at Cambuslang* (Glasgow, 1790), 43–5.

25. 'John Erskine's Letterbook 1742–1745', ed. J. Yeager, *Miscellany of the Scottish History Society XIV* (Woodbridge, 2013), 235.

26. J. Wodrow, 'Account of the Author's Life and of his Lectures', prefixed to W. Leechman, *Sermons* (London, 1789), I, 18–19 [Leechman was the winner in the contest for the chair].

27. Anon, *Scotland and the Netherlands* (Edinburgh, 1987), 1–13.

28. A. Skoczylas, *Mr Simson's Knotty Case: Divinity, Due Process and Politics in Early Eighteenth-Century Scotland* (Montreal & London, 2001), 289–321.

29. P. Gay, *The Enlightenment: An Interpretation* (London, 1967), 278.

30. R.L. Emerson, *An Enlightened Duke: The Life of Archibald Campbell, Earl of Ilay, 3rd Duke of Argyll* (Kilkerran, 2013), 44–7.

31. A. Skoczylas, 'The Regulation of Academic Society in Early Eighteenth-century Scotland: The Tribulations of Two Divinity Professors', *Scottish Historical* Review, LXXXVIII (2004), 185.

32. Ibid, 195.

33. National Library of Scotland [hereinafter NLS], Fletcher of Saltoun Papers, MS 16582, f. 30.

34. H. Innes, *Scotland Alarmed by the Loud Cry of Threatened Judgments* (Glasgow, 1757), 24–5; letters of T. Reid, Nov. 14, 1765 & July 13, 1765, in *Philosophical Works*, ed. Sir W. Hamilton (Edinburgh, 1895), I, 40–1.

35. A.T.N. Muirhead, *Reformation, Dissent and Diversity: The Story of Scotland's Churches* (London, 2006), 80.

36. T. Brown, *Annals of the Disruption* (Edinburgh, 1876), 488.

37. S.J. Brown, *Thomas Chalmers and the Godly Commonwealth in Scotland* (Oxford, 1982), ch. 2.

38. 'Connexion between the Extension of the Church and the Extinction of Pauperism', *Edinburgh Review*, XXVIII, 1817, 24–5.

39. Royal Commission on Religious Worship and Education, Scotland, Parliamentary Papers 1854 XIX, lix.

40. Census of Attendance and Accommodation at Worship, PP XXXII 1852–3, accounts and papers.

41. A.B. Bruce, *With Open Face* (London, 1896).

42. M. Dods, *Revelation and Inspiration* (Glasgow, 1877), ch. 2.

43. Quoted in P. Hillis, 'Presbyterianism and Social Class in Mid-Nineteenth-Century Glasgow: A Study of Nine Churches', *Journal of Ecclesiastical History*, XXXII (1981), 54.

44. A.S Matheson, *The Church and Social Problems* (Edinburgh, 1893), 14.

45. Quoted in J.R. Fleming, *The Church in Scotland 1843–1874* (Edinburgh, 1927), 38.

46. D. Macleod, *Memoir of Norman Macleod* (Edinburgh, 1876).

47. A.M. Stewart, *Origins of the United Free Church of Scotland* (London, 1905).

48. J.W. Stevenson, *The Healing of the Nation* (Edinburgh, 1930).

49. S.J. Brown, '"Outside the Covenant": The Scottish Protestant

Churches and Irish Immigration 1922–1938', *Innes Review*, XLII (1991), 19–20.

50. A. Muir, *John White* (London, 1958), 239.

51. C. Prunier, *Anti-Catholic Strategies in Nineteenth-Century Scotland* (Frankfurt-am-Main & Oxford, 2004).

52. C. Brogan, *The Glasgow Story* (London, 1954), 183.

53. B. Collins, 'The Origins of Irish Immigration to Scotland in the Nineteenth and Twentieth Centuries', in T.M. Devine (ed.), *Irish Immigrants and Scottish Society in the Nineteenth and Twentieth Centuries* (Edinburgh, 1991), 1 *et seq.*

54. *Glasgow Evening Post*, July 23, 1831.

55. A.B. Campbell, *The Lanarkshire Miners: A Social History of their Trade Unions 1775–1874* (Edinburgh, 1970), 183, 317–8; J.E. Handley, *The Irish in Modern Scotland* (Cork, 1947), 117 *et seq.*; E. MacFarland, *Protestants First: Orangeism in Nineteenth-Century Scotland* (Edinburgh, 1990), 64, 153; W.S. Marshall, *The Billy Boys: A Concise History of Orangeism in Scotland* (Edinburgh, 1996), 34–7.

56. R.D. Lobban, 'The Irish Community in Greenock in the Nineteenth Century', *Irish Geography*, VI (1971), 279.

57. D. McRoberts, 'The Restoration of the Scottish Catholic Hierarchy in 1878', *Innes Review* (XXIX, 1978), 3–29.

58. A. Ross, 'The Development of the Scottish Catholic Community 1878–1978', *Innes Review* (XXIX, 1978), 30–56.

59. J. Scotland, 'The Centenary of the Education (Scotland) Act of 1872', *British Journal of Educational Studies* (XX, 1972), 121–36.

60. J.H. Treble, 'The Development of Roman Catholic Education in Scotland 1878–1978', *Innes Review* (XXIX, 1978), 111–39.

61. *Hansard*, House of Commons, June 26, 1918, vol. 107, col. 1088.

62. G. Blake, *The Shipbuilders* (Edinburgh, 1935), 69.

63. G. Walker, '"There's Not a Team Like the Glasgow Rangers": Football and Religious Identity in Scotland', in T. Gallagher & G. Walker (eds.), *Sermons and Battle Hymns: Protestant Popular Culture in Modern Scotland* (Edinburgh, 1990), 137–8.

64. I.S. Wood, *John Wheatley* (Manchester, 1990).

65. P. Dollan, 'Autobiography', Mitchell Library.

66. T.J. Fitzpatrick, *Catholic Secondary Education in South-west Scotland before 1972* (Aberdeen, 1986), 115, 152.

67. T. Gallagher, *Glasgow: The Uneasy Peace* (Manchester, 1987), 114–5, 173–4.

68. A. Massie, 'Vive l'Ecosse Libre'. *The Spectator*, June 5, 1982.

69. S. McGinty, *This Turbulent Priest* (London, 2003), 450.

70. 'Faith in the Flag: Scotland, Nationalism and Religion', *The Economist*, May 8, 2015.

71. C.G. Brown, *Religion and Society in Scotland since 1707* (Edinburgh, 1997), ch. 3.

Chapter Four

1. R. Emerson, *An Enlightened Duke: The Life of Archibald Campbell (1682–1761), Earl of Ilay, 3rd Duke of Argyll* (Kilkerran, 2013), 533.

2. NLS, Fletcher of Saltoun Papers, MS 17612, ff. 202–9.

3. F.A. Walker: *The Buildings of Scotland: Argyll and Bute* (London, 2000), 352.

4. M.R.G. Fry, *The Dundas Despotism* (Edinburgh, 1992), ch. 2.

5. Sir W. Fraser, *The Lennox* (Edinburgh, 1874), vol. I.

6. King James VI, *The Essayes of a Prentise in the Diuine Art of Poesie* (Edinburgh, 1584), 15.

7. K.M. Brown, *Noble Society in Scotland: Wealth, Family and Culture from the Reformation to the Revolution* (Edinburgh, 2000).

8. M.R.G. Fry, *A Higher World: Scotland 1707–1815* (Edinburgh, 2014), 264–6.

9. *The Cochrane Correspondence Regarding the Affairs of Glasgow 1745–6*, ed. J. Dennistoun (Glasgow, 1836), 100–1.

10. Sir J. Fergusson, *Argyll in the Forty-five* (London, 1951), 231.

11. *ERBG*, VIII, 12.

12. T.M. Devine, *The Tobacco Lords* (Edinburgh, 1975), 4.

13. J. Rae, *Life of Adam Smith* (London, 1895), VII.2; J. Strang, *Glasgow and its Clubs* (London, 1856), 36.

14. C.M. Peters, 'Glasgow's Tobacco Lords: An Examination of Wealth Creators in the Eighteenth Century', unpublished PhD thesis, University of Glasgow (1990), 281.

15. Ibid, 23.

16. Ibid, 449.

17. *Autobiography of Dr Alexander Carlyle of Inveresk*, ed. J.H. Burton (Edinburgh & London, 1860), 73.

18. *Charters and Documents Relating to the City of Glasgow*, ed. J.D. Marwick (Glasgow, 1894), II, 278–83.

19. M. Weber, *Die protestantische Ethik und der Geist des Kapitalismus* (Tübingen, 1905).

20. Peters, 'Tobacco Lords', 89.

21. Lloyds Bank Group Archives, Edinburgh, GB 1830 SHI, miscellaneous records.

22. Peters, 'Tobacco Lords', 157.

23. M.L. Robertson, 'Scottish Commerce and the American Revolution', *Economic History Review*, IX (1956), 123–31.

24. Library of Congress, George Washington Papers, series 4, general correspondence, no. 926, letter from R. Donald, June 6, 1793.

25. Glasgow Chamber of Commerce MSS, minutes, Mitchell Library, TD 76/1, 2.

26. Ibid, TD 76/1, 5.

27. Ibid, Colquhoun papers, 9, 14 & 21 June 1783; 4, 5 & 21 May 1785; 'Plan of a Public Agency in London for Commercial Affairs', October 1788.

28. E.F. Heckscher, *Mercantilism* (London, 1938), II, 419.

29. 'Petition from Glasgow Respecting the East India Company', *Hansard*, House of Commons, March 19, 1812, XXII, cols. 89–92.

30. D.G. Barrie, *Police in the Age of Improvement: Police Development and the Civic Tradition in Scotland* (Cullompton, 2008), 157 *et seq.*

31. M. Mackay, *Sermon Occasioned by the Lamented Death of the Late Kirkman Finlay* (Glasgow, 1842); Anon, *Glasgow Reminiscences, memoir of the late James Ewing* (Glasgow,1854); M. Higg, A. Riches, E. Williamson, *The Buildings of Scotland: Glasgow* (London, 1990), 178.

32. *ERBG*, 'Resolutions as to Reform', XI, 405.

33. W.H. Fraser, *Chartism in Scotland* (Pontypool, 2010), 132 *et seq.*

34. R.H. Trainor, 'The Elite', in W.H. Fraser & I. Maver (eds.), *Glasgow 1830–1912* (Manchester. 1996), 227–64.

35. John M'Ure, *The History of Glasgow* (Glasgow, 1830), 88.

36. R.D. McEwan, *Old Glasgow Weavers* (Glasgow, 1905), 95–6, 107–8.

37. W.H. Fraser, *Conflict and Class: Scottish Workers 1700–1838* (Edinburgh, 1988), 151–71.

38. A. Durie, *The Scottish Linen Industry in the Eighteenth Century* (Edinburgh, 1979), 80.

39. A. Cooke, *The Rise and Fall of the Scottish Cotton Industry* (Manchester, 2009), 165.

40. A.B. Richmond, *Narrative of the Condition of the Manufacturing Population* (London, 1824), 54.

41. W.M. Roach, 'Radical Reform Movements in Scotland from 1815 to 1822', unpublished PhD thesis, University of Glasgow, 1970, 188.

42. Fraser, *Conflict and Class*, 96.

43. P.B. Ellis & S. Mac A'Ghobhain, *The Scottish Insurrection of 1820* (London, 1970).

44. Home Office Papers, National Archives of Scotland, RH 2/4/110/417.

45. *Report of the Select Committee into Combinations of Workmen*, PP III 1837–8, 30–40, evidence of Angus Campbell.

46. A. Alison, *Some Account of My Life and Writings* (Edinburgh, 1883), I, 389.

47. G. Robertson, *General Description of the Shire of Renfrew* (1818), 57.

48. A. Dickson & W. Speirs, 'Changes in Class Structure in Paisley 1750–1845', *Scottish Historical Review*, LXIX (1980–1), 68–71; T. Clarke & T. Dickson, 'Social Concern and Social Control in Nineteenth-Century Scotland: Paisley 1841–1843', ibid, LXV (1986), 49–55.

49. W. Carlile, 'A Short Sketch of the Improved State of Paisley', *Scots Magazine*, July 1806, 17–18.

50. A.J. Reid, 'Employers' Strategies and Craft Production', in S. Tolliday & J. Zeitlin (eds.), *The Power to Manage: Employers and Industrial Relations in Comparative Historical Perspective*, (London & New York, 1991) 35–51.

51. Carlile, 'Short Sketch', 165.

52. *Report of the Select Committee on Handloom Weavers' Petitions*, PP 1834 X, Q166. The lord provosts meant by the witness were Henry Monteith 1814–16 and 1818–20, and Robert Dalglish 1830–2.

53. *Tait's Edinburgh Magazine*, supplementary no. for 1834, 788.

54. In 1883 a skilled tradesman on Clydeside might earn £200 a year, whereas an experienced clerk would be more likely to earn £80 a year. See H. Dyer, 'Technical Education, Glasgow and the West of Scotland', *Proceedings of the Philosophical Society of Glasgow*, XV (1883–4), 39.

55. R.D. Anderson, *Education and Opportunity in Victorian Scotland* (Edinburgh, 1989), 155.

56. See T.C. Smout, *A Century* [sic] *of the Scottish People 1830–1950* (London, 1986), 113–4, where he refuses to believe Scots workers earned good money, or T.M. Devine, *The Scottish Nation 1700–2000* (London, 1999), 264, who apparently thinks Scotland's industrial investment would have been better going into housing.

57. R.D. Baxter's analysis of *National Income of the United Kingdom*, published in 1867, identified the really rich in Scotland, with incomes of over £1,000 a year, as numbering 4,700, or a tiny

elite of one-third of 1 per cent of 'productive persons' in the country. But he also thought a further 276,300 individuals by his measure could be included in the middle and professional class. In all, this group made up nearly one-fifth of 'productive persons'.

58. L.W. McBride (ed.), *Reading Irish Histories: Texts, Contexts and Memory in Modern Ireland* (Dublin, 2003); N.C. Fleming & A. O'Day, *Ireland and Anglo-Irish Relations Since 1800* (Aldershot, 2008).

59. Queen Victoria, *Leaves from the Journal of our Lives in the Highlands* (Edinburgh, 1868), 11.

60. *Fraser's Magazine*, LXXVIII (1868), 333–4.

61. B. Aspinall, 'Glasgow Trams and American Politics 1894–1914', *Scottish Historical Review*, LVI (1977), 64–84.

62. H. McShane, *No Mean Fighter* (London, 1977), 74.

63. Quoted in D. Howell, *British Workers and the Independent Labour Party* (Manchester & New York, 1983), 320.

64. I. McLean, *The Legend of Red Clydeside* (Edinburgh, 1983).

65. T. Royle, *Flowers of the Forest: Scotland and the First World War* (Edinburgh, 2006).

66. A good example is Stewarts & Lloyds, for which see J. Boswell, *Business Policies in the Making: Three Steel Companies Compared* (London, 1983), especially 63–9.

67. A. Slaven, *The Development of the West of Scotland 1750–1950* (London, 1975), 163–182.

68. http://investglasgow.com/about-us/economy.

69. V. Cable, 'Glasgow: Area of Need', in G. Brown (ed.), *The Red Paper on Scotland* (Edinburgh, 1975), 236.

70. Office for National Statistics, regional labour bulletin, November 2015.

71. Cable, 'Glasgow', 233.

72. G. Donaldson, *Scotland, the Shaping of a Nation* (Newton Abbot, 1974), 117.

73. D. McCrone, 'We're A' Jock Tamson's Bairns: Social Class in Twentieth-Century Scotland', in T.D. Devine & R. Finlay (eds.), *Scotland in the Twentieth Century* (Edinburgh, 1996), 113.

74. G. Hassan, 'Tommy Sheridan and the Myth of Scotland's Compassionate Society', extract from introduction to G. Gall, *Tommy Sheridan: From Hero to Zero* (Cardiff, 2012), https://www.opendemocracy.net/ourkingdom/gerry-hassan.

Chapter Five

1. D. Macleod, *Memoir of Norman Macleod* (London, 1874), I, 4.

2. *Report for Inquiring into the Administration and Practical Operation of the Poor Laws in Scotland* PP 1844 XX, 642, Q11, 598.

3. Ibid, Q11, 602.

4. Ibid, Q11, 605.

5. S.J. Brown & M.R.G. Fry, *Scotland in the Age of the Disruption* (Edinburgh, 1993).

6. *Extracts from the Records of the Burgh of Edinburgh*, eds. J.D. Marwick et al, (1869–), IV, 48.

7. M.R.G. Fry, *A Higher World: Scotland 1707–1815* (Edinburgh, 2014), ch. 7; *A New Race of Men: Scotland 1815–1914* (Edinburgh, 2013), ch. 7.

8. R.A. Cage, *The Scottish Poor Law 1745–1845* (Edinburgh, 1981), ch. 1.

9. R. Mitchison, 'The Making of the Old Scottish Poor Law', *Past and Present*, LXIII (1974), 69–70.

10. Ibid, 60–2.

11. *Extracts from the Records of the Burgh of Glasgow*, II, 178–83.

12. Cage, *Poor Law,* iii.

13. Cage, *Poor Law,* 50.

14. Sir G. Nicholls, *A History of the Scottish Poor Law* (London, 1856), 32.

15. *Regulations of the Town's Hospital of Glasgow, With an Abstract of the First Year's Expenditure* (Glasgow, 1735).

16. R. Mitchison, *The Old Poor Law in Scotland 1574–1845* (Edinburgh, 2000), 103–9.

17. *Report for the Directors of the Town's Hospital of Glasgow on the Management of the City Poor* (Glasgow, 1818).

18. Nicholls, *Poor Law,* 32.

19. Mitchison, *Old Poor Law,* ch.7.

20. *Faculty Decisions,* Dec. 29, 1821.

21. J. Cleland, *Statistical Tables Relative to the City of Glasgow* (Glasgow, 1823), 56.

22. J. Cleland, *The Rise and Progress of the City of Glasgow* (Glasgow, 1819), 225.

23. Fry, *New Race,* 175–6.

24. S.J. Brown, *Thomas Chalmers and the Godly Commonwealth in Scotland* (Oxford, 1982), ch. 2.

25. T. Chalmers, *Works* (Edinburgh, 1851–4), XV, 149.

26. Brown, *Chalmers,* ch. 4.

27. M.T. Furgol, 'Thomas Chalmers' Poor Relief Theories and their Implementation in the Early Nineteenth Century', unpublished PhD thesis, University of Edinburgh (1987), ch. 7.

28. See M. Blaug, 'The Myth of the Old Poor Law and in the Making of the New', *Journal of Economic History,* XXIII, 1963, 151–84; M.E. Rose, *The English Poor Law 1780–1930* (Newton Abbot, 1971); L.H. Lees, *The Solidarities of Strangers: The English Poor Laws and the People 1770–1848* (Cambridge, 1998).

29. The novels of James Kelman give graphic insights into this world – not that I expect Kelman would have agreed with Chalmers.

30. M. Blaug, 'The Myth of the Old Poor Law and the Making of the New', *Journal of Economic History,* XXIII (1963), 151–84.

31. W.H. Fraser & I. Maver, *Glasgow, II, 1832–1912* (Manchester, 1966), 433.

32. A. Alison, *Some Account of my Life and Writings* (Edinburgh, 1883), I, 458.

33. W.P. Alison, *Observations on the Management of the Poor in Scotland* (Edinburgh, 1840), 123.

34. *The Scotsman*, Sept. 26, 1840.

35. E. Chadwick, *Report on the Sanitary Condition of the Labouring Population of Great Britain* (London, 1842), 99.

36. Ibid, 189.

37. Ibid, 176.

38. PP 1842 XXVIII, *Sanitary Condition of the Labouring Population: Local Reports for Scotland*, 165.

39. PP XXVIII 1842, 186–8, 190–1.

40. J.V. Pickstone, 'Dearth, Dirt and Fever Epidemics: Rewriting the History of British Public Health 1780–1850', in T. Ranger & P. Slack (eds.), *Epidemics and Ideas* (Cambridge, 1992), 125–48.

41. T.C. Smout, 'The Strange Intervention of Edward Twisleton: Paisley in Depression 1841–1843', in T.C. Smout (ed.), *The Search for Wealth and Stability* (London, 1979), 226–37.

42. D. Murray, *Reminiscences of Sixty Years in the History of Paisley* (Paisley, 1855).

43. P. Pusey, *The Poor in Scotland* (London, 1844), 70.

44. Public Record Office, Home Office Papers, July 4, 1842.

45. *Report from Her Majesty's Commissioners for Inquiring into the Poor Laws in Scotland*, PP 1844 XX, xiv.

46. NLS, Melville Papers, MS 642, f. 299.

47. R.P. Lamond, *The Scottish Poor Laws: Their History, Policy and Operation* (Glasgow, 1892), 56–7.

48. H. Hunter (ed.), *Thomas Chalmers: Problems of Poverty* (London, 1912), 370.

49. *Glasgow Herald*, August 7 & 8, 1868, September 15 & 16, 1869.

50. The two cases were *Thomson v Lindsay* and *M'William v Maxwell Adams, Session Cases 1849*, nos. 131 & 132.

51. J.H. Treble, *Urban Poverty in Britain* (London, 1979), ch. 4.

52. R. Stuart, *Views and Notices of Glasgow in Former Times* (Glasgow, 1848), 10.

53. Report by Dr H.D. Littlejohn and Dr J.B. Russell on Glasgow City Poorhouse, Sept. 20, 1897, Mitchell Library G362/5

54. PP 1878–9, XXX, *Annual Report of the Board of Supervision 1878–1879*, app. A, no. 4, 11.

55. *Report of the Royal Commission on the Poor Law and Relief of Distress*, PP XXXVII 1909, minutes, VI, 881.

56. Ibid, minutes, VI, 9.

57. *Report of the Royal Commission on the Poor Law*, majority report, vol. 1, 34.

58. M.A. Crowther, 'Poverty, Health and Welfare', in W.H. Fraser & R.J. Morris, *People and Society in Scotland, II, 1830–1914* (Edinburgh, 1990), 271.

59. R.H. Trainor, 'The Elite', in W.H. Fraser & I. Maver (eds.), *Glasgow, II, 1830–1912* (Manchester, 1996), 233–5.

60. J. Cleland, *The Annals of Glasgow* (Glasgow, 1829), 242.

61. O. Checkland, *Philanthropy in Victorian Scotland* (Edinburgh, 1980), 208.

62. W.H. Fraser, 'Competing with the Capital: The Case of Glasgow Versus Edinburgh', in L. Nilsson (ed.), *Capital Cities: Images and Realities in the Development of European Capital Cities* (Stockholm, 2000), 45–71.

63. W. Smart, *Economic Journal*, X (1900), 93–4.

64. Ibid, 216–32.

65. I. Levitt, *Government and Social Conditions in Scotland 1845–1919* (Edinburgh, 1988), 216–32.

66. R. Rodger, 'The Victorian Building Industry and the Housing of the Scottish Working Classes', in M. Doughty (ed.), *Building the Industrial City* (Leicester, 1986), 172–4.

67. Scottish Land Inquiry Committee, *Scottish Land* (London, 1914), 350–1.

68. R. Rodger, 'Urbanisation in Twentieth-Century Scotland', in

T.M. Devine & R.J. Findlay (eds.), *Scotland in the Twentieth Century* (Edinburgh, 1996), 122–52.

69. L. Paice, 'Overspill Policy and the Glasgow Slum Clearance Project in the Twentieth Century', *Reinvention* (I, 2008).

70. J. Butt, 'Working-Class Housing in Glasgow 1900–1939', in I. Macdougall (ed.), *Essays in Scottish Labour History* (Edinburgh, 1976).

71. Sir P. Abercrombie & R.H. Matthew, *The Clyde Valley Regional Plan* (Edinburgh, 1946), 3.

72. Glasgow Centre for Population and Health, *History, Politics and Vulnerability* (Glasgow, 2016), theme 3.

73. R. Bruce, *First Planning Report to the Highways and Planning Committee of the Corporation of the City of Glasgow* (Glasgow, 1946).

74. M. Glendinning & S. Muthesius, *Tower Block* (London & New Haven, 1996), 169–70, 224, 327.

75. A. Gibb, 'Policy and Politics in Scottish Housing since 1945', in R. Rodger (ed.), *Scottish Housing in the Twentieth Century* (Leicester, 1989), 155–83.

76. Centre for Environmental Studies, *Outer Estates in Britain: Easterhouse Case Study*, paper 24 (London, 1985).

77. *The Herald*, April 13, 1984.

78. A.P. Murie & Y.P. Wang, 'The Sale of Public Sector Housing in Scotland 1979–1981' (Heriot Watt University, Edinburgh College of Art, research paper no. 3, 1992), 11.

79. M. Cowen & C. Lindsey, 'City Centre Regeneration in an Urban Context: The Glasgow Experience in the 1980s' in J. Berry, S. McGreal & W. Deddis (eds.), *Urban Regeneration: Property Investment and Development* London, 1993).

80. M. Reid, 'Behind the Glasgow Effect', *Bulletin of the World Health Organization*, LXXXIX (2011), 701–76; P.D. Donnelly, 'Explaining the Glasgow Effect: Could Adverse Childhood Experiences Play a Role?', *Public Health*, CXXIV (2010), 498–9; A.J. Gavin et al,

'The Glasgow Effect: Useful Construct or Epidemiological Dead End?', *Public Health*, CXXV (2011), 561–2.

81. D. Walsh et al, '"It's Not Just Deprivation": Why Do Equally Deprived UK Cities Experience Different Health Outcomes?', *Public Health*, CXXIV (2010), 487–95.

82. I am grateful for this information to Dr Sin Chai. See also B. Jennett & G. Teasdale, 'Assessment of Coma and Impaired Consciousness, a Practical Scale', *The Lancet*, II (1974), 81–4.

83. S.D. Fraser & S. George, 'Perspectives on Differing Health Outcomes by City: Accounting for Glasgow's Excess Mortality', *Journal of Risk Management and Healthcare Policy*, VIII (2015), 99–110.

84. British Lung Foundation, *The Battle for Breath 2016*.

85. H. Burns, 'How Health is Created: A Hypothesis', in Glasgow Centre for Population Health, *Building a Healthier Future* (Glasgow, 2004), 15–17.

Chapter Six

1. P. Kinchin, *Miss Cranston: Patron of Charles Rennie Mackintosh* (Edinburgh, 1999).

2. *The Bailie*, October 2, 1889.

3. Quoted in Anon., *Charles Rennie Mackintosh* (Glasgow, 1987), 64.

4. N. Munro, *The Brave Days* (Edinburgh, 1931), 197.

5. *Letters of Edwin Lutyens to his Wife, Lady Emily*, eds. C. Percy & J. Ridley (London, 1985), 56.

6. W. Power, *Should Auld Acquaintance* (London, 1937), 186.

7. Munro, *Brave Days*, 198.

8. Power, *Auld Acquaintance*, 95–7; C. Brown & H. Whyte, *A Scottish Feast* (Glendaruel, 1996), 37.

9. N. Pevsner, 'George Walton, his life and work', *Journal of the Royal Institute of British Architects*, XLVI (1938–9), 538.

10. Kinchin, *Miss Cranston*, 94.

11. A. Crawford & W. Kaplan, *The Tearooms of Mackintosh* (New York, 1996).

12. J. Burkhauser, *Glasgow Girls: Women in Art and Design* (Edinburgh,1990), 132.

13. Ibid, 55–104.

14. R. McKenzie, *Glasgow School of Art in the Time of Charles Rennie Mackintosh* (Edinburgh, 2009).

15. Burkhauser, *Glasgow Girls*, 146–51.

16. D. Macmillan, *Scottish Art 1460–2000* (Edinburgh & London, 2000), ch. 14.

17. Burkhauser, *Glasgow Girls*, 163.

18. A. Strang (ed.), *Modern Scottish Women: Painters and Sculptors 1885–1965* (Edinburgh, 2015).

19. The catalogue was by W. Kaplan (Glasgow Museums, 1996).

20. J. Kinchin, 'Glasgow: The Dark Daughter of the North', in P. Greenhalgh (ed.), *Art Nouveau 1890–1914* (London, 2000), 311–15.

21. L. Euler, *The Glasgow Style: Artists in the Decorative Arts, Circa 1900* (Atglen PA, 2008).

22. R.K. Marshall, *The Days of Duchess Anne* (London, 1973).

23. NAS, Hamilton correspondence, C18154.

24. M.R.G. Fry, *The Union, England, Scotland and the Treaty of 1707* (Edinburgh, 2006), 303.

25. NAS, Hamilton correspondence, C18154.

26. E. Mure, *Some Remarks on the Change of Manners in My Own Time 1700–1790*, in W. Mure, *Caldwell Papers* (Glasgow, 1854), I, 262.

27. Ibid, I, 269–70.

28. J. Millar, *Observations Concerning the Distinction of Ranks in Society* (London, 1771), 183–4, 199–204; 'Of Justice and Generosity', in fourth edition of *An Historical View of the English Government* (London, 1803), 565 *et seq.*

29. Millar, *Observations*, 57, 63–5.

30. R.A. Houston, 'Women in the Economy and Society of Scotland', in R.A. Houston & I.D. Whyte (eds.), *Scottish Society 1500–1800* (Cambridge, 1989), 118–47.

31. S. Nenadic, 'The Victorian Middle Classes', in W.H. Fraser & I. Maver (eds.), *Glasgow, II, 1830–1912* (Manchester, 1996), 270–1;

32. W.P. Paterson & D. Watson, *Social Evils and Problems* (Edinburgh, 1918), 95–104.

33. C. Young, 'Middle-Class Culture, Law and Gender Identity: Married Women's Property Legislation in Scotland 1850–1920', in A. Kidd & D. Nicholls (eds.), *Gender, Civic Culture and Consumerism: Middle-Class Identity in Britain 1800–1940* (Manchester, 1999), 138–42.

34. T.C. Smout, 'Scottish Marriage: Regular and Irregular 1500–1940', in R.B. Outhwaite, *Marriage and Society: Studies in the Social History of Marriage* (London, 1981), 204–36.

35. G. Glasgow, *Glasgow's Guide to Investment Trust Companies* (London, 1935), table 7.4.

36. E.H. Clive, *The Law of Husband and Wife in Scotland* (Edinburgh, 1982), 261.

37. S. Nenadic, 'The Small Family Firm in Victorian Britain', *Business History,* XXXV (1993), 86–114.

38. C. Collet, 'The Social Status of Women Occupiers', *Journal of the Royal Statistical Society* (LXXI, 1908), pt. 3.

39. H. Corr, 'The Sexual Division of Labour in the Scottish Teaching Profession 1872–1914', in W.M. Humes & H.M Paterson (eds.), *Scottish Culture and Scottish Education* (Edinburgh, 1983), 137–50.

40. O. Checkland, *Philanthropy in Victorian Scotland* (Edinburgh, 1980), 227–8.

41. E. Gordon & G. Nair, 'The Economic Role of Middle-class Women in Victorian Glasgow', *Women's History Review* (IX, 2000), 791–814.

42. R.G. Wilson, *Disillusionment or New Opportunities?: The*

Changing Nature of Work in Offices, Glasgow 1880–1914 (Aldershot, 1998), 37.

43. M.A. Simpson, 'The West End of Glasgow 1830–1914', in M.A. Simpson & T.H. Lloyd, *Middle Class Housing in Britain* (Newton Abbot, 1977), 83; L. Davidoff, *Worlds Between: Historical Perspective on Gender and Class* (Oxford, 1995), 22.

44. E. Gordon & G. Nair, *Murder and Morality in Victorian Britain: The Story of Madeleine Smith* (Manchester, 2009).

45. PP 1824 V, *First Report from the Select Committee on Artisans and Machinery*, 525.

46. A. Clark, *The Struggle for the Breeches: Gender and the Making of the British Working Class* (London, 1995), 32.

47. PP 1843 LXI, *Accounts and Papers*, no. 27.

48. PP 1833 XX, *Factory Inquiry Commission: First Report on the Employment of Children in Factories*, 20.

49. Gordon & Gair, 'Economic Role', 807, table 6.

50. PP 1837–8 VIII, 167.

51. W.H. Fraser, 'The Working Class', in Fraser & Maver, *Glasgow*, 323–4.

52. T.C. Smout, 'Aspects of Sexual Behaviour in Scotland', in A.A. MacLaren (ed.), *Social Class in Scotland* (London, 1976), 59–60.

53. S. Macgill, *A Sermon Delivered at Glasgow... On the Opening of the Magdalene Asylum* (Glasgow, 1815).

54. L. Mahood, *The Magdalenes: Prostitution in the Nineteenth Century* (London, 1990), 130–4.

55. J.R. Kellett, *Railways and Victorian Cities* (London, 1979), 217–18.

56. 'Shadow', *Midnight Scenes and Social Photographs* (Glasgow, 1858), 49.

57. Ibid, 126.

58. *The Moral Statistics of Glasgow in 1863* (Glasgow, 1864), 152–5.

59. Ibid, 156–9.

60. M. Ramelson, *The Petticoat Rebellion* (London, 1967), 92.

61. S. Hamilton, 'The First Generation of University Women 1869–1930', in G. Donaldson (ed.), *Four Centuries: Edinburgh University Life 1583–1983* (Edinburgh, 1983); L.R. Moore, 'The Aberdeen Ladies Educational Association 1877–1883', *Northern Scotland*, III, 1977.

62. Glasgow Women's Studies Group, *Uncharted Lives: Extracts from Scottish Women's Experiences 1850–1932* (Glasgow, 1983), 78.

63. E. King, *The Scottish Women's Suffrage Movement* (Glasgow, 1982), 10 *et seq.*

64. R. Jenkins, *Asquith* (London, 1965), ch. 16.

65. W. Gallacher, *Revolt on the Clyde* (London, 1936), 52–8.

66. R. Whitfield, *The Extension of the Franchise 1832–1931* (London, 2001), 152–60.

67. J.J. Smyth, 'Resisting Labour: Unionists, Moderates and Liberals in Glasgow Between the Wars', *Historical Journal*, XLVI (2003), 375–401.

68. *Hansard*, November 18, 1969, col. 1176.

69. *The Guardian*, March 12, 2011.

70. D. Skelton, *Glasgow's Black Heart: A City's Life of Crime* (Edinburgh, 2009), ch. 14.

71. M. Baillie, 'The Women of Red Clydeside: Women Munitions Workers in the West of Scotland During the First World War', unpublished PhD thesis, McMaster University (2002), ch. 3.

72. 'Rolls Royce Strike, Hillington 1943', *New Propellor*, XXXVI (1943), Trade Union Congress Library Collections, London Metropolitan Collections.

73. D. McCrone, *Understanding Scotland: The Sociology of a Stateless Nation* (London, 1992), 82.

74. *The Herald*, July 20, 2012.

75. G.R. Wilson, 'Women's Work in Offices and the Preservation of Men's Breadwinning Jobs in Early Twentieth-Century Glasgow', *Women's History Review*, X (2001), 463–82.

Chapter Seven

1. *The Herald*, October 10, 1856.
2. G. Best, 'The Scottish Victorian City', *Victorian Studies*, XI (1968), 332 *et seq.*
3. C. Withers, 'The Demographic History of the City', in W.H. Fraser & I. Mavor (eds.), *Glasgow, II, 1830–1912* (Manchester, 1996), ch. 4.
4. A. Alison, *Some Account of my Life and Writings* (London, 1883), I, 344–6.
5. M.R.G. Fry, *Patronage and Principle: A Political History of Modern Scotland* (Aberdeen, 1987), 110.
6. S.G. Checkland, *The Upas Tree: Glasgow 1875–1975* (Glasgow, 1976), 29.
7. W. Smart, 'The Municipal Industries of Glasgow', *Proceedings of the Philosophical Society of Glasgow*, XXXVI (1894–5), 36.
8. J.S. Mill, *Considerations on Representative Government* (London, 1861).
9. *The Herald*, May 7, 1890.
10. J.B. Russell, *Life in One Room: Or Some Serious Considerations for the Citizens of Glasgow* (Glasgow, 1888), 14.
11. J.G. McKendrick, *Memoir of Sir James D. Marwick* (Glasgow, 1909).
12. *Biographical Sketches of the... Lord Provosts of Glasgow 1833–1883* (Glasgow, 1883), 6.
13. Anon, *Glasgow Reminiscences, memoir of the late James Ewing* (Glasgow, 1854).
14. *The Herald*, April 19, 1874.
15. *The Herald*, May 16, 1856.
16. E. Gallie, 'Archibald McLellan', *Scottish Art Review*, V (1954), 7–12.
17. A. Aird, *Glimpses of Old Glasgow* (Glasgow, 1899), 137–41.
18. D. Ross, *The Glasgow and South Western Railway: A History* (Catrine, 2014).

19. J. MacLehose, *Memoirs and Portraits of One Hundred Glasgow Men* (Glasgow, 1886), preface.

20. Anon, 'Notes of Personal Observations and Inquiries... on the City Improvements of Paris', Glasgow City Archives, D-TC 14.2.2/27/18.

21. R.L. Meek, D.D. Raphael & P.G. Stein (eds.), *Adam Smith: Glasgow Edition of the Works and Correspondence, V, Lectures on Jurisprudence* (Oxford, 1976), pt. 2, ch. 1.

22. Anon, 'Notes of Personal Observations, D-TC 14.2.2/27/3 (1866).

23. Ibid, D-TC 14.2.2/27/13.

24. J. Carrick, "Report to the Committee... with reference to the Properties belonging to the Trust", 1881, Glasgow City Archives MP 20.509, 1.

25. Ibid, Oct. 1, 1879, appendix 2, 255.

26. C.M. Allan, 'The Genesis of British Urban Redevelopment with Special Reference to Glasgow', *Economic History Review*, XVIII (1965), 602 *et seq.*

27. M. Glendinning, R. Macinnes & A. MacKechnie, *A History of Scottish Architecture* (Edinburgh, 1996), 273–4.

28. Register of Sasines for Glasgow (1873), 182; minutes of the city improvement trust, general committee, Dec. 27, 1870.

29. P. Reed, *Glasgow: The Forming of the City* (Edinburgh, 1993), 85–6.

30. W.W. Blackie, *John Blackie Senior* (London, 1933), 50.

31. M.M. Ramsay, 'Biographical Sketches of the Directors of the Clydesdale Bank', Clydesdale Bank archive, Glasgow, 88.

32. Glendinning, MacInnes & MacKechnie, *History of Scottish Architecture*, 248.

33. J. Bell & J. Paton, *Glasgow: Its Municipal Organization and Administration* (Glasgow, 1896), 224.

34. T. Bell, *Pioneering Days* (London, 1941), 86–96.

35. J. Butt, 'Working-class Housing in Glasgow', in S.D. Chapman (ed.), *The History of Working-Class Housing* (Newton Abbot, 1971), 57–92.

36. M. Bain et al, 'Why is Mortality Higher in Scotland Than in England and Wales?', *British Medical Journal*, XXVII (2005), 199–204.

37. University of Glasgow Archives, National Health Service Greater Glasgow and Clyde Archives, GB 812 HB 3–4, 6, 8, 10–11, 13–14, 17, 22–3, 25, 36, 42, 44–5, 47–8, 50, 65, 73, 79, 81, 90; HH 66–7. See also O. Checkland & M. Lamb, *Health Care as History: The Glasgow Case* (Aberdeen, 1982).

38. Mitchell Library, 920.04BAI

39. *Royal Commission on the Housing of the Industrial Population of Scotland, Rural and Urban*, PP 1917–18 Cmnd 8731, minutes of evidence, para. 794; *Reports from Assistant Commissioners on Handloom Weavers*, PP 1839 I, 93.

40. A. Gibb, *Glasgow: The Making of a City* (London, 1983), 142.

41. J.R. Russell, 'On the "Ticketed Houses" of Glasgow: With an Interrogation of the Facts for Guidance Towards the Amelioration of the Lives of the Inhabitants', *Proceedings of the Philosophical Society of Glasgow*, XX (1888–9), 1–24.

42. PP 1917–8 Cmnd 8731, para 806.

43. Limited liability was available to the Scottish banks under legislation of 1862 but they had not availed themselves of it, believing it would reduce public confidence in them: Checkland, *Scottish Banking*, 480; see also J. Carr, S. Glied & F. Mathewson, 'Unlimited Liability and Free Banking in Scotland', *Journal of Economic History* XLIX (1989), 975–6.

44. Checkland, *Scottish Banking*, 470–8.

45. Minutes of the city improvement trust, general committee, April 7, 1875, *The Herald*, November 10, 1879.

46. D.E. Keir, *House of Collins* (London, 1952), ch. 1.

47. Ibid, 128.

48. *The Lord Provosts of Glasgow from 1833 to 1902* (Glasgow, 1902), 326.

49. I. Maver, *Glasgow* (Edinburgh, 2000), 38, 100.

50. R. Anderson, *Description of the Ceremonial on the Occasion of Laying the Foundation Stone of the Municipal Buildings in George Square, Glasgow* (Glasgow, 1885), 59–60.

51. M. Higgs, A. Riches & M. Williamson, *The Buildings of Scotland: Glasgow* (London, 1990), 159–63.

52. M. Davies & A. Muir, *A Victorian Shipowner: A Portrait of Sir Charles Cayzer* (London, 1978), 160.

53. Fry, *Patronage and Principle*, 111.

54. I. Maver, 'The Comparative Experience of Municipal Employees and Services in Glasgow 1800–1950', in M. Dagenais, I. Maver & P.-Y. Saunier, *Municipal Services and Employees in the Modern City* (Aldershot, 2003), 191.

55. B. Aspinwall, 'Glasgow Trams and American Politics 1894–1914', *Scottish Historical Review*, LVI (1977), 64 *et seq.*

56. I owe this point to the late Colm Brogan.

57. I. Maclean & J. Wright, *Circles Under the Clyde: A History of the Glasgow Underground* (Harrow, 1997).

58. *The Herald*, September 28, 1923.

59. E. King, *The People's Palace and Glasgow Green* (Glasgow, 1985).

60. J. Kinghorn, *Glasgow's International Exhibition 1888* (Glasgow, 1988); K.D. Pelle, 'Glasgow 1901', in J.E. Findling (ed.), *Encyclopaedia of World's Fairs and Exhibitions* (Jefferson NC, 2008), 164–5.

61. British Telecom Archives, HIC 002/008/003.

62. J. Butt, 'Working-Class Housing in Glasgow 1851–1914', in S.D. Chapman (ed.), *The History of Working-Class Housing* (Newton Abbot, 1971), 79.

63. E. Gauldie, *Cruel Habitations: A History of Working-Class Housing* (London, 1974), 86.

64. A. Kay, *The Housing Problem in Glasgow* (Glasgow, 1902).

65. *The Herald*, July 11, 1900.

66. W. Smart, *The Housing Problem and the Municipality* (Glasgow, 1902), 19.

67. W. Smart, *Economic Journal*, X (1900), 93–4.

68. *The Herald*, May 27, 1890.

69. *The Times*, September 30, 1902.

70. *The Herald*, October 25, 1898.

71. *The Times*, October 6, 1902.

72. *Glasgow Echo*, March 24, 1894.

73. D.M. Stevenson, 'Preface', in *Municipal Glasgow: Its Evolution and Enterprises* (Glasgow, 1914).

74. Higgs, Riches & Williamson, *Buildings of Scotland: Glasgow* (1990), 63, 298, 407, 465, 470, 510, 525.

75. R. Martin (ed.), *Jahrbuch des Vermögens und Einkommens der Millionäre in den drei Hansastädten, Teil Hamburg* (Berlin, 1912), 13.

76. I. Maver, 'Local Party Politics and the Temperance Crusade: Glasgow 1890–1902', *Scottish Labour History Society Journal*, XXVI (1992), 58.

77. M.R.G. Fry, *A New Race of Men: Scotland 1815–1914* (Edinburgh, 2013), 163.

Chapter Eight

1. *Sydney Morning Herald*, February 21, 1893.

2. K.O. Morgan, *Keir Hardie: Radical and Socialist*, (London, 1975), 23–31.

3. Ibid, 7–9.

4. W. Adamson, *The Life of the Revd James Morison* (London, 1898), 238.

5. F. Reid, 'Keir Hardie's Conversion to Socialism', in A. Briggs & J. Saville (eds.), *Essays in Labour History 1886–1923* (London, 1972), 23; K.O. Morgan, 'The Merthyr of Keir Hardie', in G. Williams (ed.), *Merthyr Politics* (Cardiff, 1966), 67.

6. PP X 1873, *Select Committee on Coal*, Q4624.

7. *Ardrossan and Saltcoats Herald*, July 22, 1882.

8. National Records of Scotland, Rules of the Ayrshire Miners' Federation, FS 7/3.

9. D. Lowe, *Souvenirs of Scottish Labour* (Glasgow, 1919), 19.

10. J.G. Kellas, 'The Mid-Lanark By-Election (1888) and the Scottish Labour Party', *Parliamentary Affairs*, IV (1964), 325 *et seq.*

11. H. Pelling, *The Origins of the Labour Party* (London, 1984), 45.

12. M.R.G. Fry, *A New Race of Men: Scotland 1815–1914* (Edinburgh, 2013), ch. 12.

13. M. Crick, *History of the Social Democratic Federation* (Keele, 1994).

14. Lowe, *Souvenirs*, ch. 1; J. Paton, *Proletarian Pilgrimage* (London, 1935), 75 *et seq.*

15. J. McCaffrey, 'The Origins of Liberal Unionism in the West of Scotland', *Scottish Historical Review*, L (1971), 47–71.

16. D. Howell, *British Workers and the Independent Labour Party 1888–1906*, (Manchester, 1983), 34–6.

17. Glasgow Caledonian University Archives, GB 1847 2001/24.

18. Howell, *British Workers*, 150.

19. J.J. Smyth, *Labour in Glasgow 1896–1936* (East Linton, 2000), 41.

20. M. Cole & B. Drake, *Our Partnership* (London, 1948), 33.

21. W.E. Lawson, *People and Places: A Short History of the Scottish Co-operative Wholesale Society Ltd* (Edinburgh, 1968).

22. R. Dowse, *Left in the Centre: The Independent Labour Party 1893–1940* (London, 1996), 193.

23. Morgan, *Hardie*, 78 *et seq.*; F. Bealey & H. Pelling, *Labour and Politics 1900–1906* (London, 1958), 293; I.G.C. Hutchison, *A Political History of Scotland 1832–1924* (Edinburgh, 1986), 250 *et seq.*

24. Beeley & Pelling, *Labour and Politics*, 296.

25. I.S. Wood, 'John Wheatley, the Irish and the Labour Movement in Scotland', *Innes Review*, XXXI (1980), 71–85.

26. *The Call*, July 19, 1917.

27. R. McKibbin, *The Evolution of the Labour Party 1906–1914* (Oxford, 1974), 43; Hutchison, *Political History*, 243–65.

28. L. Thompson, *The Enthusiasts: A Biography of John and Katharine Bruce Glasier* (London, 1971), 52–3; Howell, *British Workers*, 133–43.

29. W.R. Scott & J. Cunnison, *The Industries of the Clyde Valley During the War* (Oxford, 1924), 138–61.

30. A. Clinton, *The Trade Union Rank and File: Trades Councils in Britain 1900–1940* (Manchester 1977), 31, 42–5, 76, 148, 170, 209.

31. I. MacLean, *The Legend of Red Clydeside* (Edinburgh, 1983).

32. T. Bell, *Pioneering Days* (London, 1941), 254.

33. J. Melling, 'Whatever Happened to Red Clydeside?', *International Review of Social History*, XXXV (1990), 3–32.

34. A. Marwick, 'The Independent Labour Party in the 1920s', *Bulletin of the Institute of Historical Research*, XXXV (1962), 11 *et seq.*; Howell, *British Workers*, 338–9.

35. S.R. Ball, 'Asquith's Decline and the General Election of 1918', *Scottish Historical Review*, LXI (1982), 44–61.

36. D. Tanner, *Political Change and the Labour Party 1900–1918* (Cambridge, 1990), 412–6.

37. NLS, Woodburn MSS, Acc 7656/4/3/ 'Recollections', 77.

38. R.K. Middlemas, *The Clydesiders* (London, 1965), 113.

39. E. Shinwell, *The Labour Story* (London, 1963), 124.

40. Middlemas, *Clydesiders*, 128–32.

41. Ibid, 160 *et seq.*; E. Shinwell, *I've Lived Through It All* (London, 1973), 66 *et seq.*; T. McNair, *James Maxton: The Beloved Rebel* (London, 1955), 153.

42. B. Pimlott, *Labour and the Left in the 1930s* (Cambridge, 1977), 100–1.

43. Middlemas, *Clydesiders*, 274 *et seq.*

44. G. Cohen, 'The Independent Labour Party: Disaffiliation, Revolution and Standing Orders', *History*, LXXXVI (2001), 200–21.

45. W.W. Knox & A. McKinlay, 'The Remaking of Scottish Labour in the 1930s', *Twentieth-Century British History*, VI (1995), 174–93.

46. I. Maver, *Glasgow* (Edinburgh, 2000), 237–49.

47. J.J. Smyth, 'Resisting Labour: Unionists, Liberals and Moderates in Glasgow between the Wars', *Historical Journal*, XLVI (2003), 392.

48. I.G.C. Hutchison, 'Unionism Between the Two World Wars', in C.M.M. Macdonald (ed.), *Unionist Scotland 1800–1997* (Edinburgh, 1998), 87–8.

49. Smyth, 'Resisting Labour', 393–9.

50. Smyth, *Labour in Glasgow*, 194.

51. M. Glendinning & S. Muthesius, *Tower Block* (New Haven, 1994), 220.

52. G. Hassan & E. Shaw, *The Strange Death of Labour Scotland* (Edinburgh, 2012), 34.

53. A. Gibb, 'Policy and Politics in Scottish Housing since 1945', in R. Rodger (ed.), *Scottish Housing in the Twentieth Century* (Leicester, 1989), 155–83.

54. Hassan & Shaw, *Strange Death*, 9.

55. G. Hassan, 'The Paradoxes of Scottish Labour: Devolution, Change and Conservatism', in G. Hassan & C. Warhurst (eds.), *Tomorrow's Scotland* (London, 2002), 128 *et seq.*

56. J. Allison, *Guilty by Suspicion: A Life and Labour* (Glendaruel, 1995), 54.

57. Hassan & Shaw, *Strange Death*, 256.

58. P. Jones, *From Virtue to Venality: Corruption in the City* (Manchester, 2013), 55.

59. J. Macdonald & N. Walker, *Halls of Infamy* (Glasgow, 2007), 7.

60. I. Maver, 'The Role and Influence of Glasgow's Municipal Managers 1890–1930', in R.J. Morris & R.H. Trainor, *Urban Governance: Britain and Beyond since 1750* (Aldershot, 2000), 69–85.

61. Macdonald, *Halls of Infamy*, 3.

62. U. Wannup, 'Regional Fulfilment: Planning into Administration in the Clyde Valley 1944–1984', *Planning Perspectives* (I, 1986), 207–29.

63. M. Burt, 'Ascertainment to Assessment: Developing a Role for

Social Workers in Local Authorities 1950–1975', unpublished paper, conference on Social Work, Health and the Home: New Directions in Historical Research, Glasgow Caledonian University, April 11, 2011.

64. P. Sillitoe, *Cloak without Dagger* (London, 1955).

65. A. Bartie, 'Moral Panics and Glasgow Gangs: Exploring "The New Wave of Glasgow Hooliganism" 1965–1970', *Contemporary British History*, XXIV (2010), 385–408.

66. G. Hassan, 'The People's Party, Still?', in G. Hassan (ed.), *The Scottish Labour Party* (Edinburgh, 2004), 7.

67. B. Garcia, 'Deconstructing the City of Culture: The Long-Term Cultural Legacies of Glasgow 1990', *Urban Studies*, XLII (2005), 1–28.

68. R. Finlay, *Modern Scotland 1914–2000* (London, 2004), ch. 9.

69. Macdonald, *Halls of Infamy*, 6.

70. Hassan, 'People's Party', 11.

71. J. McCormick & J. Saren, 'The Politics of Scottish Labour's Heartlands', in Hassan, *Scottish Labour Party*, 86–103.

72. www.apoliticalpodcast.com/27-steven-purcell

73. www.glasgow.gov.uk/index.aspx?articleid=17754

Chapter Nine

1. *The Herald*, December 16, 1909.

2. *International Studio*, XIII, March 1910.

3. Hence the section devoted to Glasgow in the Musée d'Orsay, Paris; there is no equivalent on London.

4. T. Mackay, *The Life of Sir John Fowler, Engineer* (London, 1900), 110.

5. J. Kinchin, 'Glasgow: The Dark Daughter of the North', in P. Greenhalgh (ed.), *Art Nouveau 1890–1914* (London, 2000), 311–15.

6. R.P. Robertson (ed.) *Charles Rennie Mackintosh: The Architectural Papers* (Glasgow, 1990), 222.

7. M. Glendinning, R. MacInnes & A. MacKechnie, *A History of Scottish Architecture: From the Renaissance to the Present Day* (Edinburgh, 2002), 276.

8. www.annanphotographs.co.uk/B14.

9. M. Higgs, A. Riches & E. Williamson, *The Buildings of Scotland: Glasgow* (London, 1990), 167.

10. Ibid, 57–62.

11. M. Moss, J.F. Munro & R.H. Trainor, *University, City and State: The University of Glasgow Since 1870* (Edinburgh, 2000), 33 *et seq.*

12. *The Herald*, November 10, 1868.

13. Moss et al, *University*, 39.

14. University of Glasgow, *The Curious Diversity: Glasgow University on Gilmorehill: The First Hundred Years* (Glasgow, 1970), 21.

15. Higgs, Riches & Williamson, *Buildings of Scotland: Glasgow*, 335.

16. University of Glasgow, *Curious Diversity*, 11.

17. Glendinning, MacInnes & MacKechnie, *History of Scottish Architecture*, 285.

18. D. Macgibbon & T. Ross, *The Ecclesiastical Architecture of Scotland* (Edinburgh 1897), III, 534–624.

19. G. Stamp (ed.), *The Light of Truth and Beauty: The Lectures of Alexander 'Greek' Thomson, Architect, 1817–1875* (Glasgow, 1999), 54.

20. Ibid, 78, 83.

21. G. Stamp, 'A View from the Bay Window', in S. McKinstry & G. Stamp (eds.), *'Greek' Thomson* (Edinburgh, 1994), 228.

22. R. McFadzean, *The Life and Work of Alexander Thomson* (London, 1979).

23. J. Summerson, 'On Discovering Greek Thomson', in McKinstry & Stamp, *'Greek' Thomson*, 3.

24. Ibid, G. Stamp, 'A View from the Bay Window', 224.

25. Higgs, Riches & Williamson, *Buildings of Scotland: Glasgow*, 545–60.

26. *The British Architect*, XIX (1888), 222; J. McKean, 'Thomson's City', in McKinstry & Stamp, *'Greek' Thomson*, 103–10.

27. Ibid, 238.

28. McFadzean, *Alexander Thomson*, 179.

29. R. Billcliffe, *Mackintosh Watercolours* (London, 1978), 9.

30. Burrell Collection, PR.1977.13.ar.

31. Higgs, Riches & Williamson, *Buildings of Scotland: Glasgow*, 344.

32. C.R. Mackintosh, 'Scotch Baronial Architecture', paper to Glasgow Architectural Association, 1891, Hunterian Museum Archive, MS F(c).

33. Higgs, Riches & Williamson, *Buildings of Scotland: Glasgow*, 213, 228–30.

34. See www.mackintoshchurch.com

35. H.J. Barnes & D.P. Bliss, *Glasgow School of Art and Charles Rennie Mackintosh* (Glasgow, 1988).

36. Obituary, *The Herald*, April 30, 1945.

37. J. Cairney, *The Quest for Charles Rennie Mackintosh* (Edinburgh, 2004), 251.

38. Higgs, Richards & Williamson, *Buildings of Scotland: Glasgow*, 83–5.

39. Ibid, 73–8.

40. Ibid, 510.

41. Ibid, 616.

42. F. Urban, 'Glasgow's Royal Concert Hall and the Invention of the Post-modern City', *Journal of Architecture*, XVIII (2013), 254–96.

43. www.architectureglasgow.co.uk/newcity.armadillo.html

44. T. Weaver (ed.), *David Chipperfield: Architectural Works* (Barcelona, 2003), 236.

45. www.glasgowarchitecture.co.uk/museum-of-transport-glasgow

46. E. Gordon, *The Royal Scottish Academy 1826–1976* (Edinburgh, 1976), ch. 1.

47. R. Billcliffe, *The Glasgow Boys* (London, 2008).

48. D. Macmillan, *Scottish Art*, (Edinburgh, 2000), ch. 14.

49. R. Marks, *Burrell: Portrait of a Collector* (Glasgow, 1988).

50. M. Bone, *Muirhead Bone 1876–1953* (London & New York, 1984).

51. E. Cumming & P. Long, *The Scottish Colourists 1900–1930* (Edinburgh, 2000).

52. Macmillan, *Scottish Art*, ch, 17.

53. J.D. Fergusson, *Modern Scottish Painting* (Glasgow, 1943), introduction.

54. J.C. Mackenzie, *The Scottish Colourists: Hunter* (London, 2012), 3.

55. F. Gilot, *Matisse et Picasso, une amitié* (Paris, 1991).

56. Fine Art Society, *The Scottish Colourists: Cadell, Hunter, Fergusson, Peploe* (London, 2000).

57. C.M.M. Macdonald, *Whaur Extremes Meet: Scotland's Twentieth Century* (Edinburgh, 2009), 301–4.

58. Macmillan, *Scottish Art*, ch. 19.

59. M. Gardiner, *Modern Scottish Culture* (Edinburgh, 2005), 173.

60. H. MacDiarmid, *Contemporary Scottish Studies* (Edinburgh, 1978), 58–9.

61. W. McCance, 'The Idea in Art', *The Modern Scot*, I (1930), 1–13.

62. H. MacDiarmid, *Aesthetics in Scotland*, ed. A. Bold (Edinburgh, 1984); Fergusson, *Modern Scottish Painting*, 21.

63. Ibid, 30.

64. Ibid, 22.

65. *The Fergusson Gallery* (Perth, 2005).

66. Fergusson, *Modern Scottish Painting*, 46.

67. D. Farr, *New Scottish Painting* (Edinburgh, 1968), 6.

68. Macmillan, *Scottish Art*, 350–1.

69. M.P. McCulloch (ed.), *Modernism and Nationalism: Literature and Society in Scotland 1918–1939* (Glasgow, 2004), 52–3.

70. C. Oliver, *Joan Eardley RSA* (Edinburgh, 1988), 48.

71. A. Moffat & A. Riach, *Arts of Resistance: Poets, Painters and Landscapes of Modern Scotland* (Edinburgh, 2008).

72. A. Godfrey, *Steven Campbell* (London, 1987).

73. 'War Artists: Witness in Paint', *The Economist*, May 20, 1999.

74. T. Normand, *Ken Currie: Details of a Journey* (Aldershot, 2002).
75. A. Kidson, *Adrian Wiszniewski* (Bristol, 2014).

Chapter Ten

NB: In these notes, I generally make reference to works of literature by number of chapter, rather than number of page, given that many have appeared in more than one edition and sometimes in numerous editions.

1. *Berliner Lautarchiv*, C1315/1/444. The transcription is mine.
2. C. Macafee, *Traditional Dialect in the Modern World: A Glasgow Case Study* (Frankfurt am Main, 1994), 29.
3. Ibid, 56.
4. J. Stuart-Smith, 'Glottals Past and Present: A Study of T-Glottalling in Glaswegian', *Leeds Studies in English* (XXX, 1998), 182–201; 'Glasgow: Accent and Voice Quality', in G. Docherty & P. Foulkes (eds.), *Urban Voice: Accent Studies in the British Isles* (London, 1999), 211.
5. S. Damer, *From Moorepark to Wine Alley: The Rise and Fall of a Glasgow Housing Scheme* (Edinburgh, 1999), x.
6. C. Craig, *The Modern Scottish Novel: Narrative and the National Imagination* (Edinburgh, 1999).
7. J. Galt, *Literary Life and Miscellanies* (Edinburgh, 1834), 114.
8. H. Cockburn, *Memorials of His Time* (Edinburgh, 1856), 241.
9. J. MacQueen, 'John Galt and the Analysis of Social History', in A.S. Bell (ed.), *Scott Bicentenary Essays* (Edinburgh, 1972), 172–86.
10. Ch. iv.
11. Cockburn, *Memorials*, 52.
12. E. Muir, *Scott and Scotland* (London, 1936), 110.
13. G. Tulloch, *The Language of Sir Walter Scott* (London, 1980), ch. 8.
14. W. Donaldson, *The Language of the People: Scots Prose from the Victorian Revival* (Aberdeen, 1989), 1–8.

15. *British Weekly*, XII, Jan. 1897.

16. Donaldson, *Language of the People*, 9–16.

17. B.A. Booth & E. Mehew (eds.), *Letters of Robert Louis Stevenson* (London & New Haven, 1994–5), VII, 352.

18. C. Lennox, *George Douglas Brown: A Memoir* (London, 1903).

19. I. Campbell, *Kailyard* (Edinburgh, 1981), 12–16.

20. Ibid, 86–101.

21. Quoted, ibid, 7–8.

22. C. Harvie, *No Gods and Precious Few Heroes: Twentieth-Century Scotland* (Edinburgh, 1998), 136–8.

23. W. Donaldson, *Popular Literature in Victorian Scotland: Language, Fiction and the Press* (Aberdeen, 1986).

24. Campbell, *Kailyard*, 92, 113.

25. A. Petrie, 'Scottish Culture and the First World War 1914–1939', unpublished PhD thesis, University of Dundee, 2006.

26. Ch. 16.

27. I. Hayward, *Working-Class Fiction: From Chartism to Trainspotting* (London, 1997), 1–3.

28. G. Blake, *Annals of Scotland 1895–1955* (London, 1956), 37–8.

29. W. Elliot, 'The Scottish Heritage in Politics', in John Murray, Duke of Atholl et al, *A Scotsman's Heritage* (London, 1932), 64.

30. A. Hind, *The Dear Green Place* (London, 1966), ch. 1.

31. Ibid, ch. 6.

32. D.J. Taylor, 'Gordon Who?', *The Guardian*, October 22, 2003.

33. W. McIlvanney, 'Stands Scotland Where It Did?' *Radical Scotland* (XXX, 1987), 25.

34. W. McIlvanney, *Docherty* (London, 1975), ch. 10.

35. L. Wanner, *Tartan Noir: The Definitive Guide to Scottish Crime Fiction* (Glasgow, 2015).

36. W. McIlvanney, *Laidlaw* (London, 1977), ch. 2.

37. A. Massie, 'Scotland's Master of Crime Is Also Its Camus', *The Telegraph*, May 25, 2013.

38. P. Reilly, obituary, *The Herald*, July 4, 2005.

39. H. Clark, *The Ulster Renaissance: Poetry in Belfast 1962–1972* (Oxford, 2006), 60.

40. The poet Liz Lochhead is often said to have been a member of the group, but denies this is so.

41. P. Moores (ed.), *Alasdair Gray: Critical Appreciations and a Bibliography* (2001), 4, 122; A. Gray, *The Ends of our Tethers* (Edinburgh, 2005), dustjacket (recto).

42. *The Herald*, December 18, 2012.

43. A. Gray, *Lanark: A Life in Four Books* (Edinburgh, 1981), ch. 22.

44. Book 1, 121–204.

45. Book 3, 3–97.

46. R. Crawford & T. Nairn, *The Arts of Alasdair Gray* (Edinburgh, 1991).

47. P. Kravitz, *The Picador Book of Contemporary Scottish Fiction* (London, 1997), xiii–xv.

48. J. Kelman, 'The Importance of Glasgow in my Work', in *Some Recent Attacks: Essays Cultural and Political* (Stirling, 1992), 78–84.

49. Quoted in S. Dodson, 'The Mystery of the Missing Scots', *Litro Magazine*, March 9, 2013.

50. J. Wood, 'Away Thinking about Things', *New Yorker*, August 25, 2014.

51. J. Kelman (ed.), *Born up a Close: Memoirs of a Brigton Boy, Hugh Savage 1918–1966* (Glendaruel, 2006), introduction.

52. J. Kelman, 'Foreword', *Some Recent Attacks*, 1–4.

53. *The Scotsman*, April 3, 2012.

54. T. Leonard, *Ghostie Men* (Newcastle-upon-Tyne, 1980), 14.

55. P. Batchelor, 'Outside the Narrative', *The Guardian*, October 3, 2009.

56. R. Watson, *The Literature of Scotland: The Twentieth Century* (Basingstoke, 2007).

57. J. Loose, 'Glasgow über alles', *London Review of Books*, July 8, 1993.

58. J. Torrington, *Swing Hammer Swing!* (London, 1992), 161.
59. See the website of the Glasgow Women's Library, www.womenslibrary.org.uk
60. She died in 2014.
61. J. Kelman, appreciation, *The Herald*, October 27, 2014.
62. Interview, *Barcelona Review* (XXXVII, 2003).
63. A. Donovan, *Buddha Da* (Edinburgh, 2003), 1.
64. Ibid, 165.
65. L. Welsh, *The Cutting Room* (Edinburgh, 2011), 112, 164.
66. M. Ellis, 'Face to Face, Denise Mina', *The Herald*, December 13, 2010.
67. Notably and regrettably, I have left out Alan Spence, but only because he had, so far as I know, no connection with the circle round Philip Hobsbaum which I have chosen as the best illustration of my thesis in this chapter. See also P. Booth & R. Boyle, 'See Glasgow, See Culture', in F. Bianchini & M. Parkinson (eds.), *Cultural Policy and Urban Regeneration: The West European Experience* (Manchester, 1993), 21–47.
68. *The Guardian*, July 27, 2012.

Envoi

1. For an assessment, see D. Howell, *A Lost Left: Three Studies in Socialism and Nationalism* (Manchester, 1986), 195 *et seq.*
2. *Milngavie & Bearsden Herald*, November 10, 1922.
3. D. Kirkwood, *My Life of Revolt* (London, 1935), 104–6; E. Shinwell, *I've Lived Through It All* (London, 1973), 118.
4. *The Scotsman*, April 15, 1919.
5. War Cabinet papers, January 31, 1919, CAB 23/9.
6. *The Herald*, August 4, 2013.
7. *Evening Times*, August 20, 2013.
8. *The Guardian*, January 27, 2013.

9. *The Firm*, October 31, 2011.

10. M. Higgs, A. Riches & E. Williamson, *The Buildings of Scotland: Glasgow* (London, 1990), 175–8.

11. Launched by James D. Young, a man from central Scotland who yet loved to be in what he regarded as a revolutionary city, it comes down today to figures such as Professor Arthur McIvor of the University of Strathclyde.

12. G. Hassan & E. Shaw, *The Strange Death of Labour in Scotland* (Edinburgh, 2012).

LIST OF ILLUSTRATIONS

1. C5179, Crane loading a locomotive on to a ship, Broomielaw, c.1910. Reproduced by kind permission of Glasgow City Archives
2. C1697, Shipbuilding: group of apprentices in Fairfields Submarine Engine Department, Govan Rd, 1915. Reproduced by kind permission of Glasgow City Archives
3. John Slezer, 'The Prospect of ye Town of Glasgow from ye North East' from *Theatrum Scotiae* by John Slezer. Reproduced by permission of the National Library of Scotland
4. C59, Mr McDowall, weaver, with 'Wee Maggie', Calton, 1916. Reproduced by kind permission of Glasgow City Archives
5. 'The Blacksmith' by Stephen Adam (1848–1910) © CSG CIC Glasgow Museums and Libraries Collections
6. C2531, Open court with a privy midden (Annan), 267 High St, 1897. Reproduced by kind permission of Glasgow City Archives.
7. C1540, Boy at ashbin, 59 Crown St, Gorbals, c.1910. Reproduced by kind permission of Glasgow City Archives
8. C8691, Corporation housing with children, c.1925. Reproduced by kind permission of Glasgow City Archives
9. Kate Cranston (Catherine Cranston) by James Craig Annan, 1890s © National Portrait Gallery, London
10. Interior View of Glasgow City Chambers Building © Steve Vidler / Alamy Stock Photo

11. Interior Kelvingrove Museum Art Gallery Glasgow Scotland © Relaximages / Alamy Stock Photo

12. A rare view into the past of the 1950s in Glasgow of one of the corporation trams, number 332 on Argyle Street © Simon Webster / Alamy Stock Photo

13. Keir Hardie speaking at a peace rally in Trafalgar Square, 2nd August, 1914 © Heritage Image Partnership Ltd / Alamy Stock Photo

14. Red Flag in George Square, 1919 © Glasgow and Herald Times

15. Zaha Hadid, Riverside Museum © Lynne Sutherland / Alamy Stock Photo

Index